P9-AQS-844

AL CAPONE'S BEER WARS

AL CAPONE'S BEER WARS

A COMPLETE HISTORY OF ORGANIZED CRIME IN CHICAGO DURING PROHIBITION

JOHN J. BINDER

59 John Glenn Drive
Amherst, New York 14228

Published 2017 by Prometheus Books

Cover design by Jacqueline Nasso Cooke
Cover images courtesy of the Federal Bureau of Investigation (Al Capone)
and © Pictorial Press/Alamy Stock Photo (dumping bootleg liquor)
Cover design © Prometheus Books

Author owns all images throughout the book except where otherwise noted.

Inquiries should be addressed to
Prometheus Books
59 John Glenn Drive
Amherst, New York 14228
VOICE: 716–691–0133
FAX: 716–691–0137
WWW.PROMETHEUSBOOKS.COM

21 20 19 18 17 5 4 3 2 1

Library of Congress Cataloging-in-Publication Data Pending

Printed in the United States of America

To John Landesco, who started it all.
And to Merton Miller, Martin Middlebrook, and John Keegan,
a trio of extraordinary scholars, for valuable guidance and inspiration.

CONTENTS

ACKNOWLEDGMENTS

I am grateful to many fine historians and numerous friends for many things. I have learned much about the Chicago Heights and south suburban gangsters from my long-time comrade-in-research Matt Luzi. Matt has also been a great sounding board for ideas, and he read the entire manuscript and provided comments. Mars Eghigian, another coauthor and friend, was ever ready to discuss Chicago's underworld and to share anything that he himself uncovered. Chapter 7, which is based on our joint research, owes much to him and also to Jeff Thurston. Jeff is a tireless investigator of the Windy City's long criminal history, especially its gangland murders. In his own research he has found many nuggets of valuable information and has produced numerous insights, which he has gladly passed on. Furthermore, he, like Mars Eghigian, has always been available to hear new ideas and to critically comment on them.

Mario Gomes, whose only shortcoming is that he lives in Canada, read the entire manuscript and has been an extremely energetic participant in discussions with me about the Prohibition Era over the past twenty-plus years. He also shared with me copies of many useful documents he has uncovered. His excellent website *My Al Capone Museum* is the gold standard when it comes to careful historical research on the Internet. Another Canadian, Rose Keefe, is the poet laureate of the North Side gang. She has been a great source of information on Dean O'Banion and his gang. Bob Marzewski, who lives near Chicago, read various parts of this book in its early stages and helped me explore a number of topics from different angles. Bill Balsamo provided a variety of information over the years on New York's underworld and the early careers of Al Capone and John Torrio.

I have had quite a few spirited dialogues with Mark Levell since 1991, when I joined the Merry Gangsters Literary Society (MGLS) in Chicago. He is a treasure trove of information and a master of the literature on Al Capone and Prohibition. I am also forever grateful to the late Nate Kaplan, who was one of the founders and the chief architect of the MGLS. He relaxed the rules so that I could join the group, which greatly accelerated my interest in the subject. Nate later encouraged me to serve as its president, and he vigorously supported me during my years in that office.

Bob Schoenberg and Larry Bergreen kindly shared with me various materials they used in their biographies of Al Capone, and Bob, in particular, has greatly influenced my research in this area. Retired investigators and police officers Art Bilek, Bob Fuesel, Wayne Johnson, and Chuck Schauer have been excellent sources of information on police work, weaponry, and organized crime. So were the retired members of the Chicago Police Department's Intelligence Unit who allowed me to attend their monthly meetings. Mari Huff was another stalwart of the Merry Gangsters who left no stone unturned—not even a tombstone!—when digging into the city's gangster history. She provided me with valuable information on many major hoodlums. Another old friend, the very knowledgeable Jeanette Callaway, most graciously searched the Chicago Crime Commission's files for specific information and checked several important facts. Rio Burke, John O'Brien, and Bill Roemer, who are now departed, were very helpful in explaining intricacies of Chicago's underworld to me. I miss all three of them.

A number of the aforementioned individuals have written their own books and articles on the subject. Collectively this "feisty group of local tommy gun historians," as William Brashler once described the MGLS and which also applies to its adjunct members, has contributed a great deal, through very careful research, to our understanding of the Prohibition Era in Chicago, the bootleggers, the other racketeers, and the Beer Wars.

Separately, Bill Brashler and the late Ed Baumann, both very talented authors, gave me excellent advice about writing and publishing. I have also benefitted from Alex Hortis's knowledge of the publishing world and his contacts in it. Most recently, Deirdre Bair and Diane Capone took time out from writing their own books to read the entire manuscript and to comment on it. Deirdre also counseled me on writing and publishing. I owe a further debt to Scott Mendel for his diligent work as my agent, and to my editor, Steven L. Mitchell, and the other wonderful people at Prometheus Books for their help in bringing this book to publication. Mark Eckstein helped greatly by preparing the maps that appear here.

Valuable assistance was provided by the special collections departments at the University of Chicago and the University of Illinois at Chicago libraries and the staff of the Chicago History Museum's research center, especially by Lesley Martin. Furthermore, I am grateful to various individuals, some of whom knew the bootleggers quite well, who provided me with information or photos, including several people who do not want attribution.

This book began as a joint project with Professor Arthur Lurigio of Loyola University in Chicago. Unfortunately, his teaching, administrative, and research commitments made it much too difficult for him to be actively involved as things progressed. Nonetheless, I am grateful to him for his generous assistance. Finally, a large thank you goes to my family. Over the last twenty-five years they have indulged my research into Chicago's nefarious past and the collection of photos related to it. I am sure they wondered at times what, if anything, would come from all those hours of digging and collecting. This book is, among other things, what came of it.

I can be reached by e-mail at wsidejack@yahoo.com.

December 2016
River Forest, Illinois

PREFACE

"Facts are stubborn things; and whatever may be our wishes, our inclinations, or the dictates of our passion, they cannot alter the state of facts and evidence."

—John Adams

Since the 1920s much has been written about gangland in Chicago during Prohibition. In fact so much has appeared in print that the reader can be forgiven if he or she believes that it has all been done already. However, a careful examination of the literature shows that a complete history of the subject has yet to be written.

The recent histories of the Chicago Outfit had little to say about Prohibition. For example, Gus Russo devotes just forty-six pages to the almost one hundred years from 1837 to 1932.[1] Similarly, in terms of bootlegging, Robert Lombardo covers the Prohibition Era in roughly twenty pages.[2] Neither volume contains any major, new research on the bootleggers and their era.

Broader books on Chicago's underworld are also incomplete accounts of the Dry Era. John Landesco's highly commendable study, which is the first academic research done on organized crime (in Chicago or anywhere else), only extends to the middle of 1928.[3] This is probably because he was under *extreme* time pressure to complete his work for publication in 1929 as part of the Illinois Crime Survey.[4] In the process, Landesco discusses most of organized crime in Chicago from 1905 to 1928, although he does not mention narcotics trafficking, labor racketeering (outside of its use of bombing as a tool), or policy gambling. He also tends to survey a variety of specific events, as opposed to chronicling the broader evolution of each racket.

Other works that appeared before the repeal of Prohibition focus on the most sensational, and therefore the most violent, incidents during the Dry Era in Chicago.[5] These include the drive-by shooting at the Hawthorne Hotel in Cicero, the St. Valentine's Day Massacre, and the murders of Dean O'Banion, Earl "Hymie" Weiss, the Genna brothers, William McSwiggin, "Diamond Joe" Esposito, and Jake Lingle. The famous booklet *X Marks the Spot* by Hal Andrews is also incident-driven, although it provides a somewhat broader look at the world of bootlegging.[6]

Herbert Asbury and Virgil Peterson cover the history of organized crime in Chicago beginning in the 1800s. However, each volume devotes only about sixty pages to the Prohibition Era—in fact, Asbury barely mentions 1931—and the focus is heavily on the Capone gang and, once again, on the most interesting violence.[7] Although Kenneth Allsop's work is entirely devoted to Chicago's bootleggers; on that subject his book does not go beyond 1930.[8] These authors also retell the Dry Era stories that receive so much attention from earlier writers without bringing anything new to the table.

The Capone biographies, not surprisingly, deal largely with Alphonse Capone and his gang.[9] In terms of the gang wars, they are primarily interested in Capone's mob, its allies, and its most important enemies, and they go little beyond the St. Valentine's Day Massacre.[10] These books are also rooted in the tradition of telling the story primarily by recounting the most interesting murders. Mars Eghigian's masterful biography of Capone's successor Francesco Nitto (aka Frank Nitti) contains much information on organized crime during the time period in question. Yet the focus on its intended subject, Frank Nitti, does not allow it to cover all aspects of Chicago's underworld.[11]

The emphasis on major gang killings and attempted murders, which runs through most of the literature on the underworld in Chicago and elsewhere, regardless of the era, is likely because these events are fascinating in their own right. Admittedly they often contribute to the larger view because the deaths of gang leaders frequently affected the outcomes in gang wars in major ways, although the murders of reporters and politicians played no part in that. But this focus shifts attention away from the important issues of how the various gangs during Prohibition arose, expanded and contracted, and sometimes fell. It also misrepresents the violence in various ways. For example, many of the most famous events are spectacular because the Thompson submachine gun was used in them, giving the impression that this weapon was far and away the most common tool in the gangland arsenal. However, a careful examination of gangland killings indicates that it was, in fact, used quite infrequently during the Dry Era—even in Chicago where it was introduced into the underworld. And this emphasis on violence shifts attention away from what the gangs were really doing—running illegal businesses to enrich the members.

In sum, in what has been written to date many of the major bootlegging gangs are barely discussed or are not mentioned at all, and parts of the gang wars receive little or no attention. Also, there is no accurate map showing the areas controlled by the bootlegging mobs in Chicago at a given point in time much less multiple maps that illustrate changes in the landscape over time. Therefore, there is no full history of Prohibition Era organized crime in and around Chicago. Similarly, the story of how the Torrio-Capone gang, which was one of a dozen bootlegging mobs in Chicago at the start of the time period, with an often minor presence in other rackets, came to control virtually all of the city's underworld in 1934 has not yet been told.

Furthermore, there has not been a full treatment of the evolution of prostitution, gambling, labor racketeering, business racketeering, and narcotics trafficking—what organized crime consisted of before Prohibition and what it returned to afterward. There has not even been a complete discussion of the business aspects of bootlegging in the books to date. Frankly, the essence of organized crime in the Dry Era is missing in much of what has been written.

This book hopes to remedy the situation by providing a complete history of Chicago's underworld during Prohibition. It covers not only the bootlegging and the fighting between the bootlegging gangs, but also the other important rackets that existed before and during the Dry Era. To that end, it begins with a discussion of organized crime before 1920 and examines the evolution of those activities over time. In terms of the bootlegging gangs and the gang wars, while it covers the details as necessary it concentrates more heavily on the broader picture. It also examines the effects of law enforcement and politics on the underworld, especially how the authorities and various citizens' groups fought organized crime, a topic that has not received the attention it deserves. In the process this book refutes a number of myths and misconceptions about the gangs, the gang wars, and the rackets in Chicago.

I have used a variety of resources to tell the story. First and foremost are the major Chicago newspapers, which even at this late date have still not been fully examined. The crime reporters in Chicago were experts in their field and were generally very well informed about what was going on in the underworld—partly because some of them had one foot in that world. They also had important contacts in the upperworld, especially with the police. Various inaccuracies that have arisen over the years can often be corrected based on newspaper articles alone.

There are also a number of official records that are important in this history, such as material in the files of the Chicago Crime Commission (CCC), Chicago Police Department (CPD) crime statistics, reports, and ballistic tests done in conjunction with the department, as well as investigations into prostitution and gambling conducted by private agencies such as the Juvenile Protective Association (JPA) and the Committee of Fifteen. A variety of genealogical records, including birth and death certificates, have also been examined to better understand who the criminals, and the victims, really were.

Finally, over the years I have been contacted by scores of relatives of Chicago organized crime figures. Usually they were seeking information about the careers of their gangster kin, because when they were growing up not a single word was said about it in their home. However, in several cases they and other informed individuals had interesting details, and more, which they were willing to share. I have used that material when it was credible, either because it was well documented or it was supported by other facts.

Chapter 1

BEFORE PROHIBITION

I have been welcomed to many friendly doors,
By beauties, too—why do I keep in mind
Your greeting, Minnie, to your festal floors
Above so many hospitable and kind?

The dullness, darkness of Chicago nights
Drove youth to seek the brilliance of your house,
Where there were music, dancing and delights
And girls in silk with snood upon their brows.

Girls who have lived through much of false and true
Of this world's folly, in and out of luck;
And who had found reality and knew
How much it is, how little it is to f—.[1]

—Edgar Lee Masters, "Minnie Everleigh,"
unpublished poem, 1941

The story of the Chicago Outfit, which dominated organized crime in the Chicago area at the end of Prohibition and reached far beyond Illinois, begins with James "Big Jim" Colosimo. Born Vincenzo Colosimo in 1878 in the town of Colosimi, which is located in the hardscrabble region of Calabria in the toe of the Italian boot, he came to Chicago in 1891.[2] Perhaps Colosimo planned to earn a tidy sum and return to Italy to live a life of relative comfort; perhaps he hoped to prosper and stay in the United States. Regardless of his intentions, even in his wildest dreams Colosimo would never have imagined that the criminal enterprise he started—which John Torrio and Al Capone later ran—would eventually become the most successful of the Cosa Nostra crime families.

Fig. 1.1. "Big Jim" Colosimo.

Chicago in the late 1800s was Colosimo's green pasture. It was still very much a wide-open, frontier town.[3] The Great Lakes region was a sparsely populated wilderness until the opening of the Erie Canal in 1825, which greatly reduced the costs of shipping between the Upper Midwest and the East Coast. People from the Northeast and Europe flowed to the shores of Lake Erie, Lake Huron, and Lake Michigan, and, in return, produce flowed from there and the adjoining areas via the lakes, canals, and later railroads to the Atlantic coast.[4] Chicago was unusually well situated to take part in that trade, whatever the method of transportation, and its location served the city well again during Prohibition.

From before the Civil War until the early 1900s, the region encompassing the Great Lakes was known as the West rather than the Midwest. Long after 1900 the predecessor of the Big Ten Conference in college athletics was still called the Western Conference. The region was western rather than eastern in character as well; growing and advancing, rather than staid and settled. Its values were those of the frontier and the individual, with an emphasis on self-reliance, including in the handling of disagreements, and an acceptance in some quarters of the use of force to settle disputes. The majority of Chicago's immigrants came from continental Europe. Many brought with them a belief, based on the semifeudal nature of the world in which they had been raised, that the system was there to be exploited by individuals for their personal gain as opposed to the idea that individuals worked for the common good. After all, for years many of them and their families had been dominated by the nobility in their homeland.

Unlike Boston, New York, and Philadelphia on the Eastern Seaboard, or even Pittsburgh, Cincinnati, and St. Louis, river towns that were all established and thrived much earlier, these ideas pervaded Chicago. For years this mindset created a tolerance in the city and the surrounding areas of activities that were strongly frowned upon elsewhere, as evidenced by the long and continuing history of political chicanery in Illinois. These characteristics made Chicago a fertile ground for organized crime, with the city's motto, "I Will," which indicates an "anything is possible" attitude, often meaning "anything goes."

Organized crime in Chicago began long before Colosimo's arrival and therefore well before Prohibition. The first Frenchman to step out of a canoe and permanently reside in Chicago, Pierre Moreau, brought liquor with him and immediately violated the ordinance against selling alcohol to Native Americans in France's colonies.[5] Gambling and prostitution were certainly well established in the city by at least the mid-1830s.[6] However, before James Colosimo became an underworld powerhouse, organized crime was small in scale and highly specialized.

For example, one group of individuals dealt almost exclusively in gambling. From 1876 to the mid-1890s, illegal betting in Chicago was controlled by Michael Cassius (aka Mike) McDonald.[7] He syndicated gambling and was therefore the man "who had to be paid by anyone engaging in the gambling business."[8] During the McDonald era, illegal betting centered on table games such as faro and roulette. As the leader of the saloon keepers and the "sporting elements," McDonald was a major power in Chicago politics. He closely advised several mayors who were Democrats, causing one newspaper to ask, "Is Carter Harrison or Mike McDonald Mayor of Chicago?"[9] Due to his clear understanding of the links between organized crime and politics, McDonald is generally regarded as the first powerful figure in the Chicago underworld. He retired around 1894 after a wave of reform challenged the gambling establishments.

Various stories about Mike McDonald, such as the following, illustrate his (dis)regard for the law. "We're raising a little money, Mike," a man who came into his gambling den said, taking up a collection. "We'd like to put you down for two dollars."[10]

Fig. 1.2. Mike McDonald (left) in his later years with his carriage driver.

"What's it for?" asked McDonald.

"Well, we're burying a policeman."

"Fine!" said Mike. "Here's 10 dollars. Bury five of 'em!"

A second story demonstrates McDonald's political connections and acumen. After he bribed the necessary public officials, the American Stone and Brick Preserving Company (a McDonald front) was awarded a contract to apply a secret "preserving fluid" to the County Court House. When the job was finished in December 1886, the county was presented with a bill for $128,250.[11] The preserving fluid was a thoroughly useless mixture of chalk and water.

The arrests for gambling and separately for prostitution (referred to in what follows as vice) in Chicago per annum from 1875 to 1973, along with the city's population (measured in thousands), are reported in the first panel of the table in Fig. 1.3. The arrest data are from the CPD's *Annual Reports.*[12] The number of arrests per capita, referred to as the Gambling and Vice Indexes, are standardized to equal one hundred in 1920. The numerator of each index equals the number of offenses committed multiplied by the percentage of offenses that led to an arrest. Therefore, if the number of offenses per capita was constant, the index would indicate how the enforcement of the relevant laws, due to mayoral policy and public pressure, changed over time.[13] The second panel of the table reports the average values of the indexes for each mayor during his consecutive years in office.

Fig. 1.3
Gambling and Vice Arrests in Chicago (1875–1973)

Year	Population	Vice Arrests	Gambling Arrests	Vice Index	Gambling Index	Mayor
1875	400	2216	544	349	44	Colvin (D)
1876	408	2145	526	331	42	Heath (R)
1877	420	1827	332	274	26	Heath (R)
1878	437	1662	439	239	33	Heath (R)
1879	465	1601	217	217	15	Harrison Sr.(D)
1880	503	2611	372	327	24	Harrison Sr.(D)
1881	530	2659	378	316	23	Harrison Sr.(D)
1882	561	2027	284	227	16	Harrison Sr.(D)
1883	590	2116	344	226	19	Harrison Sr.(D)
1884	630	2194	341	219	18	Harrison Sr.(D)
1885	700	1956	783	176	36	Harrison Sr.(D)
1886	826	2825	694	215	27	Harrison Sr.(D)
1887	850	2494	1306	185	50	Roche (R)
1888	876	2438	1275	175	47	Roche (R)
1889	900	3234	1235	226	45	Cregier (D)
1890	1099	3899	1567	223	46	Cregier (D)
1891	1215	4181	1954	216	52	Washburne (R)
1892	1295	5208	2993	253	75	Washburne (R)
1893	1315	4525	1259	216	31	Harrison Sr.(D)
1894	1400	2817	1122	127	26	Hopkins (D)
1895	1425	3299	2105	146	48	Swift (R)
1896	1440	6130	2849	268	64	Swift (R)
1897	1535	2523	904	103	19	Harrison Jr.(D)
1898	1641	2804	1298	107	26	Harrison Jr.(D)
1899	1652	2821	943	107	19	Harrison Jr.(D)
1900	1699	2049	1606	76	31	Harrison Jr.(D)
1901	1701	2229	1685	82	32	Harrison Jr.(D)
1902	1703	1727	2259	64	43	Harrison Jr.(D)
1903	1709	1507	2761	55	53	Harrison Jr.(D)

Year	Population	Vice Arrests	Gambling Arrests	Vice Index	Gambling Index	Mayor
1904	1714	1031	5399	38	102	Harrison Jr.(D)
1905	1740	1723	5875	62	110	Dunne (D)
1906	1802	5059	7774	177	140	Dunne (D)
1907	1875	1790	2084	60	36	Busse (R)
1908	1924	2565	2237	84	38	Busse (R)
1909	2074	3435	2130	104	33	Busse (R)
1910	2185	3203	1651	92	25	Busse (R)
1911	2199	3331	2947	95	44	Harrison Jr.(D)
1912	2210	5048	4433	144	65	Harrison Jr.(D)
1913	2265	7016	5390	195	77	Harrison Jr.(D)
1914	2369	10106	3566	268	49	Harrison Jr.(D)
1915	2448	10239	3074	263	41	Thompson (R)
1916	2492	5904	3365	149	44	Thompson (R)
1917	2492	9731	5745	246	75	Thompson (R)
1918	2546	5405	4421	134	56	Thompson (R)
1919	2600	3724	6466	90	81	Thompson (R)
1920	2702	4295	8312	100	100	Thompson (R)
1921	2821	6520	6054	145	70	Thompson (R)
1922	2902	6533	3420	142	38	Thompson (R)
1923	3011	12453	6057	260	65	Dever (D)
1924	3156	19966	7722	398	80	Dever (D)
1925	3263	22645	5755	437	57	Dever (D)
1926	3297	26526	4674	506	46	Dever (D)
1927	3402	19400	2752	359	26	Thompson (R)
1928	3397	24398	5587	452	53	Thompson (R)
1929	3373	38627	13944	720	134	Thompson (R)
1930	3376	30216	11395	563	110	Thompson (R)
1931	3342	19610	11120	369	108	Cermak (D)
1932	3237	15836	7628	308	77	Cermak (D)
1933	3200	13165	3764	259	38	Kelly (D)
1934	3180	10059	1243	199	13	Kelly (D)
1935	3200	8064	2989	159	30	Kelly (D)
1936	3200	5334	3120	105	32	Kelly (D)
1937	3250	5019	5897	97	59	Kelly (D)
1938	3300	4403	4989	84	49	Kelly (D)
1939	3350	5783	6710	109	65	Kelly (D)
1940	3397	5121	3607	95	35	Kelly (D)
1941	3456	4472	4772	81	45	Kelly (D)
1942	3466	3162	6571	57	62	Kelly (D)
1943	3327	2180	6861	41	67	Kelly (D)
1944	3350	2422	7814	45	76	Kelly (D)
1945	3390	2202	5061	41	49	Kelly (D)
1946	3416	1942	4220	36	40	Kelly (D)
1947	3476	1911	5283	35	49	Kennelly (D)
1948	3528	1146	9889	20	91	Kennelly (D)

Year	Population	Vice Arrests	Gambling Arrests	Vice Index	Gambling Index	Mayor
1949	3567	1894	8649	33	79	Kennelly (D)
1950	3606	1481	5253	26	47	Kennelly (D)
1951	3619	2571	7602	45	68	Kennelly (D)
1952	3615	3787	7653	66	69	Kennelly (D)
1953	3611	2294	7327	40	66	Kennelly (D)
1954	3605	1992	7459	35	67	Kennelly (D)
1955	3598	1883	7373	33	67	Daley (D)
1956	3590	2608	7722	46	70	Daley (D)
1957	3581	3642	9008	64	82	Daley (D)
1958	3571	3502	10088	62	92	Daley (D)
1959	3560	NA	NA	NA	NA	Daley (D)
1960	3547	NA	NA	NA	NA	Daley (D)
1961	3534	NA	NA	NA	NA	Daley (D)
1962	3519	NA	NA	NA	NA	Daley (D)
1963	3503	NA	NA	NA	NA	Daley (D)
1964	3486	7510	10989	136	102	Daley (D)
1965	3468	7390	10581	134	99	Daley (D)
1966	3449	4162	9238	76	87	Daley (D)
1967	3429	5117	7571	94	72	Daley (D)
1968	3408	4068	7949	75	76	Daley (D)
1969	3386	3860	7870	72	76	Daley (D)
1970	3363	4254	7669	80	74	Daley (D)
1971	3340	3822	8500	72	83	Daley (D)
1972	3330	5269	7444	100	73	Daley (D)
1973	3320	7167	7082	136	69	Daley (D)
Average				166	57	

Average Index Values for Each Mayor (1875–1973)

Years	Mayor	Party	Vice Index	Gambling Index
1875	Colvin	D	349	44
1876–1878	Heath	R	281	33
1879–1886	Harrison, Sr.	D	240	22
1887–1888	Roche	R	180	49
1889–1890	Cregier	D	225	45
1891–1892	Washburne	R	235	64
1893	Harrison Sr.	D	216	31
1894	Hopkins	D	127	26
1895–1896	Swift	R	207	56
1897–1904	Harrison Jr.	D	79	41
1905–1906	Dunne	D	119	125
1907–1910	Busse	R	85	33
1911–1914	Harrison Jr.	D	176	59

1915–1922	Thompson	R	159	63
1923–1926	Dever	D	400	62
1927–1930	Thompson	R	524	81
1931–1932	Cermak	D	338	92
1933–1946	Kelly	D	101	47
1947–1954	Kennelly	D	37	67
1955–1973	Daley	D	84	80

NA = not available
Population is measured in thousands.
The symbols (D) and (R) denote Democratic and Republican mayors, respectively.

Gambling arrests per capita in Chicago were relatively low before the turn of the century. The Gambling Index was greater than the long-term average of fifty-seven in only two of those years. Clearly, early Chicagoans were fairly tolerant of games of chance; otherwise their mayors would have cracked down on them as hard as the later ones did. Some of the mayors before 1900, such as Hempstead Washburne and George Swift, did work to suppress illegal betting, while Mike McDonald's ally Mayor Carter Harrison Sr. had quite a bit of difficulty "finding it" inside the city limits. In fact, the Gambling Index was at a historical low during Harrison's initial eight years in office (see the second panel of the table in Fig. 1.3), with an average value of twenty-two. For example, only 217 gambling arrests were made in 1879 when the city's population was nearly half a million. Enforcement during this time period was generally more lax when the mayor was a Democrat instead of a Republican. For example, from 1875 to 1899, the average value of the index was forty-nine when a Republican was the mayor, but only twenty-seven when a Democrat was in office.

The reform movement of the early 1890s dissipated, and in 1897 Carter Harrison Jr. returned Chicago to the "wide open town" policy. During the younger Harrison's first period as mayor, the Gambling Index had an average value of forty-one. By this point in time, the emphasis of illegal betting had shifted somewhat away from table games and more heavily toward bookmaking on horse racing, with the bets taken in gambling dens (handbooks) operating throughout the city and in pool rooms. Customers of the handbooks included "lawyers, doctors, writers, waiters, chauffeurs, and business men" as well as, it was admitted, "pimps and thieves and thugs."[14]

Fig. 1.4. Mayor Carter Harrison Jr. and his wife.

At the time, four separate groups dominated gambling in the city. The South Side faction was led by James O'Leary, son of the Mrs. O'Leary whose cow was falsely blamed for the Great Chicago Fire of 1871. O'Leary worked out of a stockade on S. Halsted, which one newspaper article describes—with some exaggeration—as "fireproof, bombproof, burglarproof, and policeproof."[15] Although the walls were solid and the doors were made of steel and oak, it was in fact raided by the police many times. The downtown (Loop) area was controlled by a group led by John O'Malley, Patrick O'Malley, Tom McGinnis, and First Ward aldermen Michael "Hinky Dink" Kenna and John "Bathhouse" Coughlin. On the North Side, Mont Tennes and his brothers William and Edward were in charge, while on the West Side a group allied with Tennes, which included Alderman Johnny Rogers, held sway.[16]

The political situation changed in the early 1900s when Edward Dunne became mayor. A Democrat but also a reformer, he waged a vigorous campaign against organized crime, including gambling. Dunne's policy deviated from the prevailing practice of the Republicans advocating "good government" and the "closed town." In 1906, during Mayor Dunne's last year in office the total revenue of the gamblers in Chicago was $15 million, with between $12 and $13 million coming from horse racing and the rest from other types of wagering.[17] Republican Fred Busse, who succeeded Dunne, was essentially the first mayor from his party—but not the last—to let the town run wide open.[18] Although gambling was rampant at the time, with Chicago

Fig. 1.5. Mayor Edward Dunne.

regarded as the pinnacle of handbook betting in the country, enforcement declined dramatically in the city from 1906 to 1910 as the Gambling Index dropped from 140 to 25.

The various gambling factions coexisted fairly peacefully until Mont Tennes obtained a Chicago monopoly in 1905 on the horse racing results supplied by the Payne News Service of Cincinnati and charged his rivals a monopoly price for the service—namely, half of the profits from their race track betting.[19] No gambling house making book on horse races could operate without the instantaneous results from tracks around the country that this service provided. On the one hand, winning bettors wanted to be paid quickly, and the house wanted to move on to the next race. On the other hand, bookies who had delayed information could be taken to the cleaners by bettors who knew the results before they did. Tennes was allied at the time with John O'Malley, McGinnis, and Loop gambler John Condon against a group led by O'Leary.

Tennes's rivals responded with violence in June 1907, and from that point through October 1909 thirty-three gambling-related bombings occurred.[20] Mont Tennes was attacked at the onset of the hostilities while walking with his wife, and his properties, including his home, were bombed four different times. John Rogers's saloon at Madison and May was bombed twice, as was John O'Malley's, and Condon's home was hit as well. In retaliation, O'Leary's Halsted Street headquarters was damaged by explosions on three occasions.

When the dust finally settled, Tennes had essentially won a complete victory over his enemies that gave him local control of the racing news. He soon reached a higher level of power and dominance by founding his own General News Bureau, driving the Payne service out of business as his agency gained a national monopoly in the provision of racing results. Tennes sold the news bureau in the late 1920s to Moses Annenberg, Jack Lynch, and others.[21]

In 1911, Carter Harrison Jr., supported by the gambling interests, returned to office. Because Harrison favored the open town, little changed after he replaced the gambling friendly Busse. In fact, gamblers from various parts of the United States flocked to Chicago after the election.[22] The city was soon divided into three large zones, each controlled by a czar who dispensed gambling and vice privileges.[23] Those who wanted to operate on the South Side, between Madison Street and Sixty-Third Street, had to first get permission from "Hinky Dink" Kenna. He was the linchpin in the system, given his close ties to the younger Mayor Harrison, which explains why he owned so many gambling operations directly. Politician Barney Grogan controlled the West Side while "Hot Stove" Jimmy Quinn, a former protégé of Tennes, controlled the North Side. Quinn and his relatives also ran the gambling at the Riverview amusement park on the North Side.[24]

Frank Solon and politician Tom Carey, who presided over the area south of Thirty-Ninth Street, aided Kenna. North Side alderman Herman Bauler and Herman Lutzenkirken had the Rogers Park area and the remainder of the far North and Northwest Sides. They worked under Quinn while politician Manny Abrahams controlled the Maxwell Street district. The protection money the gamblers paid so they could operate unmolested flowed through these men to the police and other politicians, with plainclothes police officers who were the "personal men" of the lieutenants and other higher-ups doing the actual collecting.[25]

An inquiry led by federal judge Kennesaw Mountain Landis in 1916 revealed that the group of twelve to fifteen handbooks in Chicago directly owned by Tennes handled from six to seven thousand dollars in bets per day and turned a net profit of approximately $54,000 per year. In addition, profits to Tennes and his partners from the General News Bureau amounted to nearly $270,000 per year; further net income, albeit not reported or estimated, was generated by casino gambling.[26] Although no precise figure for the citywide profits from all types of gambling was ever calculated for 1911, an admittedly rough estimate for Chicago is $4.1 million.[27]

The lottery game known as policy was active in Chicago decades before Prohibition. Contrary to assertions that it was invented or introduced by "Patsy" King or "Policy Sam" Young in the 1890s, policy games were running in Chicago long before 1890.[28] For example, one old-time Chicagoan remembered the game operating in Morton's policy shop, across from the old *Chicago Tribune* building, in the era of Abraham Lincoln and Stephen Douglas, while an article states that the game was active before the Great Fire.[29] It was also thriving in the Windy City, and across the country, during the 1870s.[30] Policy was certainly being played in New York City in the 1850s, and it is mentioned by newspapers there before 1820. Therefore, neither King nor Young brought the game to the city, although Young might have been the first to operate in the African American community, which later became its stronghold.

In the modern form of the game, numbers from one to seventy-eight were placed in a drum. A bettor, playing a "gig," bet on three

Fig. 1.6. Policy betting slips.

numbers, such as 1-10-50. The policy company, commonly referred to as a "wheel," usually held a morning and an afternoon drawing, giving the player who bet that day two chances to win. Twelve numbers were pulled from the drum in each drawing. If the three numbers bet were among the twelve pulled in that drawing, the wheel paid the winner one hundred times the amount bet.

The actual probability of winning with one drawing (rather than two) is 1 in 345.8, as opposed to the astronomical estimates that have frequently been claimed. For example, several writers assert that the odds against winning in one drawing are 76,076 to 1![31] In fact, it is rather surprising that these extreme overestimates persisted for so many years because as early as 1886 the correct calculation appeared in a newspaper article.[32] Based on the true odds, the expected payoff in a game with two drawings is about fifty-eight cents for every dollar bet. In other words, the house's expected take (defined as what it made after paying off winning bets but before its other expenses, which in policy gambling were quite large) was roughly forty-two cents of each dollar bet. Of course, this calculation assumes that the drawing was not rigged. In fact, most observers claim that the policy games were scrupulously clean.[33]

During the 1870s, policy shops were found in all parts of the city, although they were located most heavily on the South Side. The players tended to be of low income, but as one observer remarked, "Side by side may be found the city official of high life, the dusky African, the heathen Chinee [sic], the Hebrew, the German, the Polander, the Swede, and occasionally Irish and Italian, and of these nationalities women and boys are found playing also."[34] The legal status of the game remained unclear for a long period of time, causing it to be heavily raided during some years and largely ignored by the police in other years. By 1890, after considerable police interference, the number of policy betting places had declined from several hundred just a few years earlier to about thirty.[35]

Policy gambling continued to ebb and flow until Carter Harrison Jr. was elected mayor in 1897. A Presbyterian minister and reformer in the Jefferson Park neighborhood on the North Side stated that a person active in the game "contributed $20,000 for the election of the present Mayor and that neither the District Attorney, nor the courts nor the Judges dare touch him."[36] The change was dramatic. In 1901, nine separate policy wheels (games) were running in Chicago, with bets taken by a total of 4,175 offices (policy shops) and human runners spread throughout the city. The runners visited the customers to save them the trouble of going to an office to bet.

The acknowledged regent of the game at the time was "Patsy" King, who ran the Frankfort and Kentucky wheel (the biggest in the city), the Red and Green wheel (with drawings done in Canada), and the Interstate and Springfield wheel, and headed the policy syndicate that controlled the game in Chicago.[37] First Ward aldermen Michael Kenna and "Bathhouse" John Coughlin, along with Democratic county committeeman Tom McNally and other individuals, ran three (or one-third of the existing) wheels. The nine wheels in operation handled an estimated $10 million in bets annually, with profits purportedly in excess of $3 million. The Frankfort and Kentucky had its main office within five hundred feet of police headquarters, even though Chief Kipley publicly claimed that no gambling was occurring in Chicago at the time.[38]

Although the police were inactive in fighting policy around the turn of the century, in the early 1900s African American ministers, such as Reverend R. C. Ransom, campaigned vigorously against what they perceived as an evil in their communities. The gamblers responded by bombing Reverend Ransom's church at Dearborn and Thirty-Eighth Street on the South Side in 1903.[39] However, the anti-policy movement ultimately prevailed when the Illinois legislature passed a bill in 1905 that attacked both sides of the game by penalizing the gamblers and their employees as well as the players. In 1907, only two policy wheels were in operation, with roughly three hundred shops and runners servicing them.[40]

The crackdown on policy explains the great increase in gambling arrests in Chicago from 1902 (2,259) to 1904 (5,399). External pressures, as opposed to a change in philosophy, forced Carter Harrison Jr. to send in the police. This is evidenced by the fact that vice remained unhindered during this period. The new law against policy also likely accounted for many of the gambling arrests in 1906 and 1907. Over the next few years, policy faded into the background, although it never completely disappeared.

During the five years before Prohibition, a syndicate oversaw gambling in the South Side black enclave. Centered in the Second Ward, just south of the First, the political ruler of that area, Alderman Oscar De Priest, provided the necessary "clout" for the group, which was headed by policy heavyweight Henry "Teenan" Jones.[41] Jones was the collector for the syndicate and was most likely also the person reported to have a private telephone line into the office of Captain Stephen Healy, the commander of the Stanton Avenue police district. Dan Jackson eventually held great power in the Second Ward and the neighboring area and replaced De Priest as the political leader of the African American gambling syndicate.[42]

Active gambling, other than policy, also occurred in Chicago's small African American community near Twenty-Second and Michigan by at least the 1890s. The first gambling kingpin was St. Louis transplant John V. "Mushmouth" Johnson, who was described as the

Fig. 1.7. South Side alderman Oscar De Priest.

"Negro political boss" of the First Ward under Kenna and Coughlin.[43] In 1890, he opened a place on State Street and subsequently became involved in policy in the late 1890s. Upon Johnson's death in 1907, his rival Robert Motts, a brother-in-law of Dan Jackson, succeeded him as the city's most prominent African American gambler. Motts followed Chicago's expanding African American population into the Second Ward and was a political power there until his death in 1911. Jackson and Henry "Teenan" Jones were also active in the "Black Belt" before World War I. Jones operated gambling houses located in the predominantly white Hyde Park neighborhood, which offered the usual casino games to an African American clientele.

A second criminal group was involved with labor unions. The methods used by the labor racketeers were fairly straightforward. They would organize a union or "muscle in" on an existing one in order to control the supply of labor in a particular area. Through the use of violence they monopolized the field by stopping non-union members from working and dissuading employers from hiring non-union labor (especially during strikes), which admittedly allowed them to raise their members' wages. The racketeers' rewards came from controlling the union's funds, which enabled them to appropriate some of those monies, and from extorting further money from employers or contractors by threatening to strike. Labor racketeering seems to have been the least important, in terms of net revenues, of the three main provinces of organized crime in Chicago before Prohibition.

Although many individuals preying on Chicago's heavily unionized workforce from 1890 to 1920 controlled one or no more than a handful of unions, others aspired to much broader influence over organized labor.[44] Martin B. "Skinny" Madden was Chicago's pioneer labor racketeer. He came to the city from Kansas City, Missouri, in 1895 and began as a steamfitter's helper and quickly rose to the position of business agent for the Junior Steamfitters' Association.[45] Madden's power was based on the sluggers he employed to attack non-union workers as well as union reformers opposed to his methods. In the former case, early in his career Madden employed several dozen toughs who attacked replacement workers at locations under strike. His goons would single out one or two of the men and beat them so severely that they were unable to work the next day, sending a clear and powerful message to the other strike breakers.[46] The use of guns by hired labor "muscle" came into practice circa 1905, when Madden disrupted the elections of the Chicago Federation of Labor (CFL), which he controlled through surrogates he had voted into office.

As president of the Associated Building Trades (ABT), a consortium of unions involved in areas related to construction, "Skinny" Madden was the boss of more than fifty thousand workers. Madden controlled this body starting in 1902, and shortly thereafter he assumed the office of president for life. He extorted money from contractors and building owners by offering to settle strikes for a fee and by fining them for nebulous infractions, such as when he held up construction of the Chicago and Northwestern railroad terminal in 1910 in an attempt to garner a $50,000 payment.[47] He also preyed on the organization's members by forcing them to renew their work permits at a cost of a dollar per week. Madden's power was broken when the better elements in the labor movement revolted against his methods. By early 1910, a number of unions, including the carpenters, lathers, electrical workers, and painters, left the ABT to join the CFL-backed Building Trades Council, effectively destroying the former group.[48]

Maurice "Mossy" Enright was born in Ireland in 1883 and immigrated to the United States the following year.[49] A product of the area behind the Union Stockyards, he burst into the newspapers in March 1911 when he was charged with the murder of rival labor slugger Vincent Altman, who was a "Skinny" Madden adherent.[50] Enright escaped hanging for that offense by the vote of one juror. At the time, Enright commanded a band of gunmen who prowled the streets, in his limousine known as the "gray pirate car," for the Building Trades Council. A month later, Enright killed his recently dismissed associate William "Dutch" Gentleman.[51] Enright rose to lead the Garbage Handlers' Union and was involved in others, including the Street Cleaners' Union.

Enright's crew included hardened criminals from the Back of the Yards, such as his brother Tommy, his brother-in-law Sonny Dunn, James Ragen (who would graduate to other rackets), "Big Tim" Murphy, the psychopathic Gene Geary, and the fearsome Walter Stevens. Murphy, who was later a mail robber and state legislator,

Fig. 1.8. "Big Tim" Murphy and his wife (at the left).

was a silver-tongued battler who started out as a newsboy and then caught the attention of local politicians.[52] With the help of Enright, he became the business agent for the Street Cleaners' Union. Geary was involved in several labor-related killings. He was eventually found to be legally insane, which likely surprised no one, and died in the psychiatric ward of the Illinois state penitentiary at Menard.[53]

The term *gunman* was reportedly coined to describe Walter Stevens, whose police record extended back to the 1890s and included more than two hundred arrests.[54] By 1922, he was reputed to have been involved in sixteen murders.[55] One Chicago newspaper called him, "A man of temperate and violent habit—temperate where [his habits] might hurt him, violent when they would hurt the other fellow."[56] Little restrained Enright's goons. For example, one of his men struck Mother Superior Xavier of the Franciscan convent in Hammond, Indiana, while inside the Criminal Court Building in Chicago.[57] She was trying to protect a young girl in her charge who was a witness against another of Enright's confederates.

Labor racketeer Cornelius "Con" Shea was born in Massachusetts and was reported to have been involved in bombings, a standard labor tactic used to convince unwilling employers to meet union demands, when he was only sixteen years of age.[58] Between the unions, the gamblers, and others who struck at their foes through property damage, bombings were a common occurrence in Chicago prior to 1920 and continued for years thereafter.

Shea was elected president of the International Brotherhood of Teamsters (IBT), which belonged to the American Federation of Labor, in 1903. He came to Chicago shortly thereafter and formed an alliance with "Skinny" Madden.[59] Shea's dictum was that "[A broken nose] is an occupational hazard of the profession of union organization."[60]

A 105-day strike that Shea led during the summer of 1905 cost the IBT and Chicago businesses more than $9 million combined. It also cost twenty-one men their lives and injured 416 others, and, in the process, it split the teamsters in the Chicago area into two factions. The locals run by John Sheridan and Michael Galvin refused to join in the strike because of Shea's extreme methods. These "Outlaw" or Chicago Teamsters, who after the strike were outside the IBT, operated (in terms of Sheridan's organization) north of Seventy-Ninth Street in Chicago and west of about Pulaski (known as Crawford at the time) Avenue. The Chicago (Outlaw) Teamsters also covered suburban Cook County (under Galvin), extending to the southern suburb of Chicago Heights.[61] Most of the violence in 1905 resulted from this division between the IBT and the Chicago Teamsters, which set the stage for transportation-related union difficulties for many subsequent years in the Windy City.

Fig. 1.9. Cornelius "Con" Shea.

Shea's professional and

private lives soon turned dramatically downward. He lost the presidency of the Teamsters at the 1907 annual convention, and in 1908 he abandoned his wife and family. The next year he stabbed his mistress twenty-seven times in a drunken rage and was sentenced to several years in a New York prison. Upon his release, he returned to Chicago and was active in Big Tim Murphy's rackets as well as in petty crime before 1920.[62]

Michael J. "Umbrella Mike" Boyle, another Madden protégé, reigned over the Electrical Workers' Union. In wet or dry weather, Boyle, the czar of union shakedowns in Chicago, stood in a saloon at the appointed hour, his umbrella hanging by its handle from the edge of the bar. Electrical contractors and others eager to avoid labor trouble dropped bundles of currency into the umbrella. Boyle's labor improprieties frequently brought him trouble with the law, but just as frequently obliging politicians came to his rescue. For example, in 1923, after fixing the jury in Illinois governor Len Small's trial for earlier misuse of state funds, Boyle was sentenced to six months in jail for contempt of court. Small pardoned him before Boyle had served even two months of his sentence.[63]

A third group of racketeers was involved in vice, with male and female operators running brothels in select areas of the city. Although prostitution was illegal in the state of Illinois, as it was in most of the rest of the country, for many years the respectable elements in Chicago (and in many cities) tolerated the world's oldest profession as long as it was geographically segregated into so-called red-light districts. The stated reasoning was that it was a necessary evil—that society was better protected if men were able to find pleasure from willing, professional companions. Specifically, a detailed

Fig. 1.10. "Umbrella Mike" Boyle.

report by the Hartford Vice Commission argued that permitting limited, segregated vice 1) decreased solicitation on the public streets, 2) kept the brothels out of the residential neighborhoods, 3) minimized the corruption of youth, 4) kept men from forcing their attentions on women, 5) minimized police corruption, 6) decreased crimes of other types, and 7) minimized disease.[64] Although at least one of these assertions (the fifth) clearly contradicts the facts, this report illustrated the claims by officialdom at the time.

Prostitution was thriving in Chicago well before the Civil War, and it produced a number of interesting characters in the years preceding 1890. The first of the famous vice lords was the physically unimposing Roger Plant Sr., who was barely five feet tall.[65] In contrast, one newspaper unflatteringly described his massive wife Anna Maria as his "elephantine consort."[66] Born in Worcestershire, England, in the middle of the 1830s, the pair, along with the diminutive Gus Anderson, ran the Under the Willow resort at Wells and Monroe, which housed roughly forty women in the 1860s.[67] A contemporary newspaper describes it as a "notorious den of infamy."[68] By 1880 the Plants were long gone from Chicago. They operated a saloon—and a brothel as well, given the number of young women who lived there according to the US Census that year—in St. Louis.[69] Missouri death records indicate that Roger Plant Sr. died in Los Angeles, where he owned considerable property, in 1894.[70] Not to be outdone, his son Roger Plant Jr. returned to Chicago in the early 1880s. He owned a saloon on S. Clark Street, where he was charged with assault, running a disreputable house, and selling liquor at times without a license.[71]

The madam known as Carrie Watson was born Caroline Victoria Watson in Canada—probably in Hamilton, Ontario, where she lived with her parents in 1861, twenty years after her birth.[72] This enterprising young woman reportedly decided that prostitution with lucrative pay was more desirable than the mundane jobs with menial wages at which her middle-class friends toiled. She took up the trade in Chicago and first appeared in the city directory in 1867 in a location on N. Wells where she operated a bordello.[73] By 1870 she was the proprietor of a house on S. Clark that housed six prostitutes and soon became one of the city's finest brothels. According to the US Census, ten years later eleven other women were living there with her, some of whom, given their ages, were surely servants. Based on the 1900 US Census, Carrie Watson was still going strong at that location at the turn of the century.

If ever there was a prostitute with a heart of gold, a character who is beloved by Hollywood movies but rarely found in the real world, it was Carrie Watson. Although she amassed at least one fortune, if not several, at the time of her death the money was largely gone due to her charitable work.[74] William R. Payne, an attorney intimately familiar with her financial affairs, stated that she had "almost a passion for doing charitable deeds."[75] According to Payne, "It was her custom to pick up friendless children from the streets, to clothe them, and to send them down to the Kankakee farm [she owned] to live and to go to school at her expense for years. Her charities in other directions were just as numerous, and perhaps even more munificent."[76] When one of her brothers died, she brought his children to the farm in Kankakee and made sure they had all the comforts and advantages of life.[77]

Of greater interest, because it dovetails with Watson's own seeming attitude that working as a prostitute should be voluntary, is an incident that does not involve young children. Carrie Watson once delivered a seventeen-year-old repentant prostitute to a shelter designed to help rescue such women. She paid for her stay there until the girl's father could come from California to take her back to a normal life. It was all done as anonymously as possible.[78]

In the late 1860s it was estimated that 2,000 harlots worked in Chicago. This was at least partly due to the large number of women widowed by the war who turned to prostitution because they were bereft of financial support. There were roughly 225 brothels at the time, plus a number of assignation houses, where men brought women for immoral purposes, and rooms attached to saloons that served the same purpose.[79] In 1882, 6,600 prostitutes and 1,000 bordellos operated in Chicago, generating revenues of $4 million per annum.[80] By 1895, the Windy City boasted 10,000 harlots and 2,000 houses of ill-fame.[81] However, this increase is not extraordinarily large because the city's population nearly tripled in those thirteen years. One observer estimates that in 1906 there were as many harlots as in 1895, and that they produced $20 million a year in revenue.[82] About 350 large bordellos, referred to as "parlor houses," contained 4,000 women and brought in $8 million a year in revenue. Two thousand women working in small flats received $4 million a year, and the remaining $8 million was generated by women inside 292 shady hotels. Clearly, even before 1910, parlor houses, the traditional brothels, did not handle the bulk of the city's sex trade.

The first district in Chicago called "the Levee" was located just south of the Loop around State Street, between Harrison and Taylor, and consisted of low-end whorehouses. The section known as Little Cheyenne was only slightly west of there, on Clark Street between Van Buren and Twelfth Streets (now Roosevelt Road). One block east of Clark Street was Custom House Place, centered on the street by the same name (now called Federal Street) and bounded by Harrison to the north and Twelfth to the south. In 1882 the area between Clark, State, Van Buren, and Twelfth, which encompassed all three of these districts and was dubbed "the Black Hole" by the writer using the name "Americus," contained five hundred brothels and three thousand fallen women—almost half of the total for the entire city.[83] Political pressure led to the closure of these sin strips in 1903 because the municipality was embarrassed by very visible vice so near to the expanding central business district.[84]

Brothels first appeared around Twenty-Second Street during the 1880s, and the bordellos driven from Custom House Place and the adjoining areas near the downtown soon reopened there. After 1903 prostitution south of the Loop was concentrated near Dearborn and Twenty-Second Street. On some streets, such as State and Wabash, the houses of ill repute extended south to Thirty-First or Thirty-Fifth Street.[85] This newly sanctioned haven of vice was the largest in the city and was also called the Levee. In its heyday, the new Levee housed bordellos ranging from the world-famous Everleigh Club and other high-class resorts to places that were so debauched they probably made a majority of Chicago's hardened prostitutes shudder.[86] A number of brothels near Twenty-Second Street, along with other nearby buildings, were connected by underground passages and tunnels, giving the inhabitants multiple escape routes during police raids.[87]

Vic Shaw was the queen of the Levee in the years just before 1900 and ran the fanciest bordello in Chicago at the time. She was born

Emma Elizabeth Fitzgerald in Nova Scotia, Canada, and initially worked as a burlesque dancer on West Madison Street.[88] By her own, most probably fictional, account, she eloped with Ebie Shaw, the son of a millionaire, while performing at the Chicago Opera House and thereafter took his last name as well as his nickname for her, Vic, as a first name.[89] She was in fact married to one of the Levee's most important pimps, Roy Jones (whose real name was Royal Ludwig), at least once during her life and died as Emma Elizabeth Ludwig in 1951. Vic Shaw spent forty years in vice on the city's South Side, most prominently on Dearborn, Armour, and Prairie. In the late 1930s, when she was almost seventy years old, Shaw still ran a flat on S. Dearborn. Illustrating the closeness between the purveyors of vice and the First Ward politicians, "Bathhouse" John Coughlin gave Madam Shaw a photo of the

Fig. 1.11. Vic Shaw. (Image from the Vic Shaw family album, Lawrence Gutter Collection of Chicagoana, Special Collections, Richard J. Daley Library, University of Illinois at Chicago.)

Fig. 1.12. Gladys Martin was Vic Shaw's second most popular girl. (Image from the Vic Shaw family album, Lawrence Gutter Collection of Chicagoana, Special Collections, Richard J. Daley Library, University of Illinois at Chicago.)

White House, which was inscribed, "Where we will celebrate in 1900, Compliments, John J. Coughlin" on the back.[90]

The Everleigh sisters, Ada and Minna, were born Ada and Minna Simms in Virginia in 1864 and 1866, respectively.[91] During their lives, they frequently reinvented their personal histories. For example, in the 1900 US Census the sisters are listed as living on S. Dearborn with the surname Glenhigh, while in the 1920 US Census, and in their 1909 passport applications, they used the surname Lester. On the latter documents Ada (who sometimes went by Aida as well as Ray) claimed to be the widow of Arthur Lester, who was born in Charlottesville, Virginia, in 1870, and Minna stated that she was never married. However, a thorough examination of the US Census and other genealogical records has not unearthed any Arthur Lester who matches this description.

Ada stood five foot six inches tall and had gray eyes and light brown hair. Minna was an inch taller with hazel eyes and dark brown hair.[92] After a successful stint operating a brothel in Omaha, Nebraska, they chose Chicago as the next location for their enterprise.[93] In February 1900 they opened a highly upscale bordello in the Levee.[94] Initially,

Fig. 1.13. Ada Everleigh.

Fig. 1.14. Minna Everleigh.

the Everleigh sisters had at least four women working for them. Their professional names included Phoebe Holington, Ruth Efonnes, and Lonna Sefton.[95] From this modest beginning, if such a term can be applied to a brothel, the Everleigh Club grew to twenty-four women in 1910. Those who worked there in 1910 possessed melodic aliases, such as Iva Pink Carroll, Mable Devo, and Madora Marat.[96]

When Prince Henry of Prussia, the brother of Germany's Kaiser Wilhelm, toured the United States in 1902, there were many things that he could have seen and done during his twenty-hour stop in the Windy City. He was expected to meet with several of Chicago's "captains of industry."[97] An editorial in the *Chicago Tribune* suggested that he visit "the most distinctive things we have," including the Union Stockyards because they dealt with the "grossest necessities of life."[98] Mrs. Carter Harrison, the prince's hostess at a ball given in his honor, stated, "We shall endeavor to welcome him in the good old Chicago way."[99] Prince Henry seemed to have gotten the message only too well because he set aside a block of time so that he could enjoy the Everleigh Club after leaving a formal ball in his honor at the Auditorium Hotel at about 12:30 a.m. on March 4. His visit to the club was reportedly a memorable one, where during a special performance the Everleigh courtesans pranced around in fawn costume—at least initially—for His Highness and his entourage.[100]

The Everleigh harlots earned between $100 and $500 per week.[101] On the other side of the ledger, the sisters acknowledged paying $8,000 a year in rent with operating expenses of $225 per day. If the expenses included all the costs of operation other than rent and taking $300 per week as an estimate of what the average girl made (and therefore the house also retained from what the customer was charged), at the club's height the sisters' profit was more than $275,000 per year.

The club was closed in October 1911 by the direct order of Mayor Carter Harrison Jr., who became incensed when a pamphlet extolling its "virtues" was shown to him.[102] The mayor stated, "It is a disgrace to Chicago that such a place should be one of its most widely known features."[103] The brochure that fell into his hands was actually quite subdued.[104] It contained photos of the exterior and interior of the club itself but not of the women who worked there, and it included only two paragraphs of text:

> While not an extremely imposing edifice without, [the club] is a most sumptuous place within. . . . [It] has long been famed for its luxurious furnishings, famous paintings and statuary, and its elaborate and artistic decorations. "The New Annex," [next door], formally opened November 1, 1902, has added prestige to the club, and won admiration and praise from all visitors. With double front entrances, the twin buildings' [sic] within are so connected as to seem as one. Steam heat throughout, with electric fans in summer: one never feels the winter's chill or summer's heat in this luxurious resort. Fortunate indeed, with all the conforts [sic] of life surrounding them, are members of the Everleigh Club.
>
> This booklet will convey but a faint idea of the magnificence of the club and its appointments.

The Everleighs retired with a considerable fortune—and held almost $200,000 in IOUs from the club's customers that were never paid—when they moved to New York City to escape notoriety.[105] In 1914, the sisters sold their remaining properties in Chicago, as well as apparently two resorts in Indianapolis and one in Cleveland.[106] Many of their girls at the house in Chicago went to work at the brothel next door run by Ed Weiss's wife Aimee Leslie, herself a former Everleigh courtesan.[107] Minna Everleigh died in New York in 1948, followed by Ada in 1960. They are buried as Minna Lester Simms and Aida Lester Simms in Alexandria, Virginia.[108]

The splendor of the Everleigh Club and the glamor surrounding its women, including the claim that several of them married wealthy clients, greatly misrepresents life in the Levee. Zella Patton's story, which is based on genealogical research and a newspaper article written by reformer Kate Adams, is far more typical of prostitution in Chicago during that era.[109] Born in Chicago in April 1890 to Victor and Lina Patton, Zella was a free spirit who refused to be restrained. When her marriage to John Taylor More, a surveyor for a mining company in Colorado, ended in divorce in September 1911, she gravitated to Denver's underworld before descending into the depths of Chicago's Levee.

In 1912, she went from the Morals Court to Coulter House, which was designed to help wayward girls. Kate Adams, who was the secretary (proprietress) of the institution, was greatly impressed by her exuberance and enthusiasm. On one occasion, before the board of directors came to the house for a meeting, Zella playfully told Miss Adams, "I will now assume an expression of advanced reformation." Yet leaving "the life" was difficult for her. After Zella got back on the straight and narrow, she went to Springfield, Illinois, and became addicted to drugs. Despite being treated and "cured" three times for her addiction and attempting to climb the steep hill of reformation a fourth time, she took her own life in Chicago on August 16, 1916. She is buried as Zella Patton in Oakwoods Cemetery on the city's South Side.

Sex was clearly Chicago's biggest business, in terms of organized crime, in the period before Prohibition. The Vice Commission of Chicago, a blue ribbon committee appointed by the mayor and the city council to investigate conditions, estimated that $15.7 million of profits was generated by prostitution and related liquor sales in Chicago in 1910.[110] This figure does not include blackmail of the customers by the cadets (pimps) who oversaw the women, which one writer claimed was a common occurrence, or theft from the men while they were engaged with the women.[111]

Consistent with the authorities turning a blind eye toward segregated red-light districts, prostitution at the time was heavily concentrated in a few areas. In 1911, approximately 47 percent of the vice establishments in the city were in the Levee near Twenty-Second Street and in the adjoining Douglas area on the South Side, with 23 percent on the near West Side, in the vicinity of Madison and Ashland, 8 percent in the Loop, and 9 percent in two districts just north and west of downtown, which are part of today's North Loop and the Rush Street areas.[112] There was also at the time a small vice district in the South Chicago neighborhood, which was located along the lake between about Seventy-Ninth Street and Ninety-Fifth Street.

In every year before 1894, the Vice Index was greater than the historical average value of 166. This is consistent with officials' continual efforts before the demise of the Levee to keep prostitution out of most parts of Chicago, at the urging of the city's better elements, and to close down those who operated without permission, at the urging of the syndicates controlling vice in the segregated areas. Before 1897 selective but consistent vice enforcement cut across political lines because the average value when a Republican was mayor (232) was almost the same as when a Democrat was mayor (236).

Interestingly, given the later attack on organized prostitution spawned by public pressure, the Vice Index, and therefore enforcement, declined noticeably after Carter Harrison Jr. was elected in 1897. The index had an average value of seventy-nine during his first eight years in office. Conversely, the reform-minded Mayor Dunne cracked down on prostitution, just as he did on gambling. Nonetheless, the laxity returned during Fred Busse's term. When Dunne was the mayor, the average value of the Vice Index was 119, but this number dropped to eighty-five under Busse.

Chicago's vice commission report provided a variety of compelling data on the city's prostitutes and the life they chose. In 1910, an estimated five thousand women—both prostitutes and madams—were in the city. The prostitutes evenly divided the money they received from customers with the keeper of the house. A survey of twenty-nine harlots working in the better parlor houses in the city indicates that their ages ranged from twenty-one to thirty-two, with an average age of 24.1 years, and that they had entered "the life" at 19.5 years old on average.[113] Before turning to prostitution, they had almost all worked in what might be termed menial occupations, often as salesgirls, domestics, or waitresses, in which they earned on average $5.10 per week.

This very select group of twenty-nine women in the world's oldest profession earned between $50 and $400 a week. Not surprisingly, fourteen of the women gave economic reasons for choosing this career, such as that they wanted to escape their low-paying jobs, or that they desired the nice things that a higher income would allow them. Twelve of the women reported that they had what were considered moral failings in that era, such as they had been seduced by men they knew, or they had been corrupted by excessive alcohol use. The results for streetwalkers or prostitutes in saloons, dance halls, and lower-end whorehouses are fairly similar, except that they earned considerably less than the high-end women and in a few cases were much older. Many of the prostitutes, as well as their cadets, were addicted to cocaine or morphine.[114]

Information about the lower end of the profession, including the details of brothel operations, comes from the records seized during a police raid on a one-dollar house.[115] The place's busiest days of the week were Saturday and Sunday, the latter always ranking second. This was surely attributable to customer availability, with Sunday—and also Saturday in some professions—a day off for almost all working men. In addition, men working six days a week liked to enjoy themselves on Saturday night. For this low-end bordello the most detailed data are available for the week from March 7 to March 13, 1908. In that seven-day period approximately nineteen women worked each day. The prostitutes serviced 13.88 customers per day on average and almost certainly made at least $25 a week. At the extreme, a harlot in this house entertained forty men on Saturday, March 7, 1908. However, this performance is by no means a record. A madam in a small West Side bordello, who worked alongside her lone girl, had sexual encounters with sixty men in one night in 1907.[116]

A careful survey of brothels in the Levee can be performed based on information in the 1910 US Census.[117] The census taker for enumeration district 162 in Chicago, which was bounded by Nineteenth Street, State Street, Twenty-Second Street, and Armour Avenue (later called Federal Street), was quite graphic in his reporting. The madams were listed as "resort keeper," and their business or industry was described as "ill repute." Each woman who lived and worked at such a location as a prostitute was called an "inmate." If we add to the totals for this district the number of women working on the west side of the street on two blocks of S. Armour, virtually all the visible bordellos of the Levee are included.[118] Fig. 1.15 is based on a detailed map constructed by Courtney Vaccaro.[119] It shows that in 1910 the vast majority of the Levee brothels were located inside an L-shaped area comprising eight city blocks. Saloons, with vice of a different kind, were sprinkled throughout the area, mostly at the intersections.

In 1910, the district was home to ninety-eight separate brothels, with a total of 655 prostitutes and madams. In other words, approximately 40 percent of the people living in that area were directly involved in the sale of sexual favors, although this does not include the adjunctive staff of porters, maids, cooks, seamstresses, and others who were also employed in those houses as well as the employees of

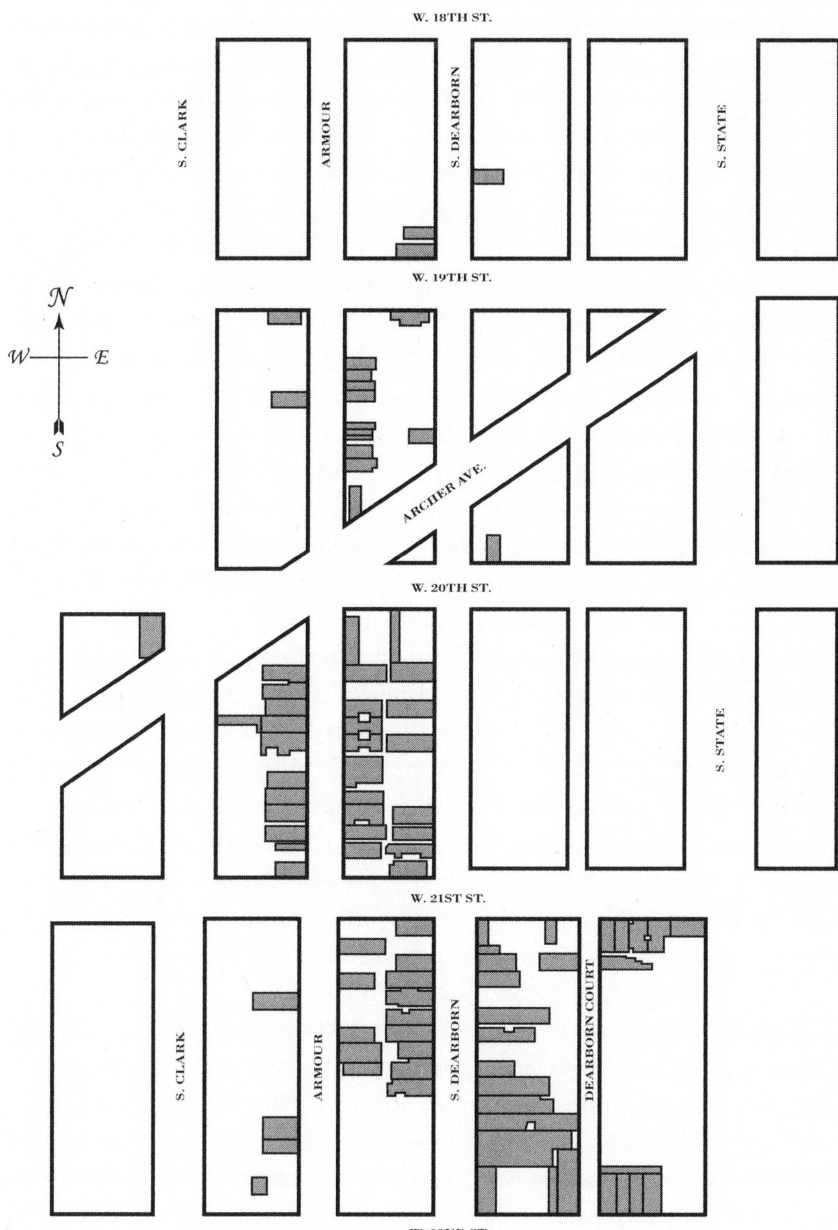

Fig. 1.15. Chicago Levee in 1910. (Image based on Vaccaro 2013.)

saloons and other businesses dependent on the nearby brothels. A number of the saloon residents might have been prostitutes. Some houses of ill repute contained one woman, while at the other extreme there were brothels with two dozen women. The woman shown as the resort keeper might not have been the owner in every case but instead the senior person actually living at that site.

In the Levee, the great majority of the prostitutes before 1920 were white, with a small number of African Americans and a smattering of women from other ethnic groups.[120] Based on the 1910 US Census, the Levee housed twenty-three African American prostitutes and madams in four racially segregated whorehouses. The largest of these was "Black Mag" Douglas's place on Armour, which contained eleven women. There were also five Japanese women in a house on Armour, but otherwise the inmates were all Caucasians.[121] Of the 655 sex workers, about 20 percent (128) were foreign born. The largest number (forty-four) came from France, and there were additionally seven French-Canadians, which was greatly disproportionate to the small French immigrant population in the Chicagoland area at the time.[122]

These numbers reflect the tastes of the clientele for French women and the types of services they tended to provide, with oral sex at the time viewed as a type of perversion that was referred to as "French," given its origins.[123] Italy was a distant second in foreign birth, with fifteen women working in the Levee. Ireland (four women) and Germany (ten women) were greatly underrepresented in the vice trade at the time, compared to immigration from those countries to the Chicago area. This is probably indicative of the morals as well as the economic status of these ethnic groups.

The Everleigh Club's twenty-four courtesans were all native born. This was most likely due to the sisters' requirement that their girls carry an informed conversation in English with the establishment's upper-class clientele about various topics. Fourteen were from the Midwest, three from the East, two from California, and five from the South (perhaps reflecting the sisters' own antecedents). In 1910 these women ranged from twenty to twenty-eight years old, with an average age of 23.29 years. In comparison, the nineteen women who worked for Vic Shaw at S. Dearborn were, on average, 25.42 years old. Fifteen of them came from the United States or Canada. The so-called House of All Nations on S. Armour was anything but the United Nations of prostitution. According to the 1910 US Census, three of the sixteen "inmates" in this supposedly diverse brothel were from France, one was from Germany, and the remaining twelve were American-born women whose parents were American-born.

The Vice Commission's exposé produced no legislative action by Chicago's City Council. Instead, the reaction to open prostitution over the next two decades came from individual elected officials, as circumstances dictated, and from citizens' groups. In the latter category, the Committee of Fifteen and the Juvenile Protective Association (JPA)—both privately funded organizations—were at the forefront of the war on vice in Chicago for many years.

As was the case in other large cities in the United States, organized crime in Chicago around the turn of the century, especially gambling and labor racketeering, was heavily the province of Irish and Jewish immigrants (and their offspring) because they predated the Italians in terms of significant immigration to America. Even in 1920, only 4.8 percent of Chicago's population listed themselves in the census as Italian in nationality, still behind the Irish at 5.4 percent.[124] During Prohibition, ethnic succession occurred, and organized crime around the country was soon dominated by Italians.[125]

Returning to "Big Jim" Colosimo, who laid the foundation for John Torrio and Alphonse Capone in Chicago's underworld, in his youth he was involved in several trades before finding employment as a street sweeper in the First Ward.[126] However, being a mere broom pusher belied his ambitions. Colosimo formed the "white wings"—so called because of their white uniforms—into a club that became a union controlled by Big Tim Murphy and later by Mike Carrozzo. This beginning led Colosimo into politics, with a position as a precinct captain in the organization of Aldermen Coughlin and Kenna and a promotion to street and alley inspector.

Interestingly, Colosimo seems to have been on the right side of the law before about 1902. For example, he lodged a complaint against saloonkeeper and later major Levee operator Andy Craig for throwing garbage into the alley behind his establishment.[127] He also cooperated with police when his banker brother-in-law fled Chicago after swindling investors in 1900.[128]

By marrying Victoria Moresco, who owned two brothels in 1902, "Big Jim" Colosimo became active in prostitution. From this foundation, he built an empire centered on vice. His first properties in the Levee included the Victoria (named by Colosimo after his wife) at Archer and Armour Avenues and the Saratoga at Dearborn and Twenty-Second Street, which was next to the Everleigh Club. In turn, Coughlin and Kenna appointed him as their bagman for vice in the First Ward—the "outside man" who knew all the operators and saved them the trouble and embarrassment of personally collecting protection money from the various illicit sexual activities within their purview.[129]

The First Ward payoffs were substantial because the district was full of brothels, gambling houses, and illegal saloons as well as perpetrators of every criminal act imaginable. The routine—at least during the period when Colosimo was the conduit for the vice payoffs in the Levee—consisted of the owners of the various establishments meeting him at his headquarters on the appointed days with the money, which ranged from $10 to $200 per week depending on the type of concern.[130] Colosimo and the graft collectors in the Levee kept a share of the money, and the police and the aldermen also received a cut.[131] The aldermen also dictated the purchase of whiskey, provisions, groceries, insurance, and clothing by Levee establishments as well as the use of taxis.

Fig. 1.16. Colosimo's first wife, Victoria, in her younger days.

In 1911, Minna Everleigh claimed that the Twenty-Second Street Levee as a whole had paid over $15 million to the politicians for protection since its inception.[132] This is consistent with the estimate by another source that the Levee's political tribute was nearly $2 million annually in the period just before its closure.[133] Protection cost the Everleigh sisters alone more than $100,000 during their years of operation.[134] In their case, the money was especially well spent because their club—the most famous house of ill repute in the country, if not the world—was conspicuously absent from a police department list of brothels dated August 16, 1910. Operators of illegal enterprises in the Levee who did not pay were summarily raided by the police. Police officers not only made arrests on those occasions, but—as a lesson to the guilty parties and an example to others—destroyed the offenders' places of business using axes.[135]

To augment their weekly collections, Coughlin and Kenna's First Ward Club threw a ball each year during the Christmas season at the Chicago Coliseum. The First Ward Ball was described by one reform report as the "annual underworld orgy given by Alderman Michael Kenna and Alderman John Coughlin . . . for the purposes of retaining control of prostitutes and criminals of the First Ward Levee for political purposes and for political funds."[136] The ball was estimated to have netted the aldermen at least $25,000 per annum.

Fig. 1.17. Chicago's Coliseum.

Colosimo did not ascend from being a simple crib operator to the king of the Levee in one step, but instead continually improved his services and reputation.[137] For example, gambling (casino games and slot machines) was added to prostitution in order to keep the customers content and engaged.[138] This upgrading culminated in the 1910 opening of Colosimo's decidedly hoity-toity café on S. Wabash. An ad for Colosimo's referred to it as "The Finest Italian Restaurant in Chicago," stating,

> Table D'Hote Dinner 6 to 9 P. M. $1.25
>
> A la carte service at all times. Public dancing. Refined cabaret. 1,000,000 yards of spaghetti always on hand. Our operatic trio will render selections during dinner hours.[139]

It attracted clientele ranging from millionaires and opera singers to whorehouse madams and politicians and was known nationwide. One editorial describes its ambiguous nature as "[a] night club frequented by bon vivants of high and low society, who would spend a merry time there, relishing both the fresh meat from the kitchen, and the highly-seasoned variety from the . . . gutter."[140]

Colosimo was a large, broad-shouldered, dark, handsome man with black hair and a mustache. He was loud and gregarious, a back-slapping, fun-loving individual who probably was an enthusiastic consumer of the food, drink, women, and gambling that his enterprises provided. Unlike many successful American gangsters, who lived quietly in a style far below their incomes, Colosimo sought the many comforts attendant with wealth. He bought a fine house for his father, his wife, and himself, complete with servants and chauffeured autos. At the peak of his power, he wore diamonds set in numerous rings and other jewelry, adorned various parts of his dress with them, and he even carried loose cut stones as playthings in a bag on his person.[141]

As Colosimo's empire grew, so did his gang. By the mid-1910s, he commanded Chicago's largest and most successful group of racketeers. This multi-ethnic lot included Italians such as John Torrio, Joey D'Andrea, Roxy Vanilli, and Joe Adducci aka Adduci; as well as Jews like "Jew Kid" Grabiner and probably the Guzik brothers;

Irishmen ("Chicken Harry" Cullet and W. E. Frazier, alias Mac Fitzpatrick); and others, such as Billy Leathers and Mike "the Greek" Potson (or Potzin), who began his criminal career in prostitution and eventually managed Colosimo's café.[142] The Colosimo mob was the lineal ancestor of the Torrio-Capone gang and the later Chicago Outfit. It was also the first gang to resemble modern Chicago organized crime in structure, with ethnically broad membership, diversified criminal activities that were spread throughout the city and the county, as well as close connections with politicians who provided blanket protection, including at the extreme the hoodlums' takeover of the political machinery in some suburbs.

Colosimo's chief lieutenant was John Torrio, who earlier was a leader of the James Street gang and then a high-ranking member of the notorious Five Points gang in New York City. Torrio arrived in Chicago no later than 1909, as opposed to what has been stated elsewhere.[143]

For example, a newspaper article in 1907 notes that "Eastern sporting man" John Torrio was looking to wager $1,000 on an important boxing match scheduled to take place in the Chicago suburb of Dolton.[144] Two years later he was listed as the manager of the Saratoga and was indicted for white slavery, a charge that was dropped because the primary witness refused to testify against him.[145] Later newspaper articles describe him—with his name sometimes spelled Turio—as the manager of brothels on Armour, Dearborn, and/or of the Victoria.

Fig. 1.18. John Torrio.

According to the standard accounts, when Colosimo was bothered by extortionists John Torrio interceded—with fatal results for the extortionists. The details related of this incident were uncovered only recently. On the night of November 22, 1911, Felice Danello, his brother Stefano, and Pasquale Damico met a hail of bullets in the Rock Island Railroad underpass at Archer Avenue near Clark Street. Chicago police captain Patrick Harding described the trio as the "most desperate gang of Black Handers that ever infested the city."[146] Felice Danello and Damico died at the scene while Stefano Danello clung to life until December 19. Stefano Danello summoned Colosimo to his hospital bedside right after the shooting, but whatever recriminations were on his mind went unsaid because when police officers entered the room with Colosimo, Danello refused to speak.[147]

If not in 1911, then certainly by 1914, Torrio—who some sources claim was a relative of Mrs. Colosimo, although there is no evidence to support this—was Colosimo's right-hand man.[148] Although Colosimo increasingly delegated authority to Torrio, his management style can accurately be described as "hands-on." Such as when he punched *Chicago Tribune* reporter Morrow Krum after he found Krum investigating prostitution in Burnham.[149]

Pressure for reform, spurred by the publication of the Vice Commission of Chicago's official report as well as various books exposing the evils associated with the sexual trafficking in women, led to the closing of the Levee—at least temporarily—in late 1912.[150] After the closure, official tolerance of prostitution waxed and waned, depending largely on who was the mayor and to a lesser extent the Cook County state's attorney. For example in 1914, when Maclay Hoyne was the state's attorney, the Levee soon reopened at least temporarily. Three major rings led by Colosimo, Julius and Charlie Maibaum, and the Marshall brothers controlled much of the activity there, as opposed to the eight major players who ran things a few years earlier.[151]

However, after 1912 vice in Chicago was never the same again because segregated red-light districts were simply too visible a target for reformers. For example, the Committee of Fifteen took credit for closing 518 disorderly houses and driving well over a thousand prostitutes from Chicago in the twelve-month period through July 1914.[152] Although activity on the near South Side and in the Douglas neighborhood continued, the Levee was no longer the undisputed center of prostitution. Its further decline was hastened by an incident in the summer of 1914 that directly involved Colosimo's gang.

When plainclothes CPD officers from the recently formed Morals Squad made an arrest on Twenty-Second Street on July 16, 1914, they were accosted by a group of hoodlums from the district. Regular police detectives soon arrived, and in the confusion shots were fired, killing Detective Sergeant Stanley Birns of the Morals Squad. John Torrio, Roxie Vanilli, and other Colosimo spear carriers were at the scene that night, and Torrio helped Vanilli into an automobile after he was wounded during the gunfire. One of Colosimo's men almost certainly fired at the police.[153] Mayor Carter Harrison Jr. and State's Attorney Maclay Hoyne were both outraged by this public incident and moved strongly against the Levee. Harrison transferred the vice-friendly captain of the Twenty-Second Street police station, Michael Ryan, to the western outskirts of the city and replaced him with the vigorous and honest Max Nootbaar, who immediately cracked down on prostitution.

During Carter Harrison Jr.'s last term in office, the Vice Index jumped from 95 in 1911 to 144 in 1912, 195 in 1913, and 268 in 1914 due to the first and second closings of the Levee district. In response to this clampdown on vice, organized prostitution moved more heavily into other parts of the city, which the segregated red-light districts were intended to prevent. For example, in 1911, commercialized vice appeared in only nine of seventy neighborhoods in Chicago; however, nine years later, such evidence was found in twenty of the seventy areas. In 1920, only 10 percent of the brothels in the city were in the Levee, with another 20 percent in the nearby Douglas, Oakland, and Grand Boulevard neighborhoods, indicating that a good deal of the Levee's trade had moved south.[154] Activity in two of the old vice districts, the Near West and Near North Sides, which contained 24 percent and 20 percent, respectively, of Chicago's bordellos in 1920, even exceeded that in the Levee. Clearly vice in the Near North and Near West Side districts had greatly expanded since 1911 as the South Side Levee contracted.

The form of prostitution also changed in response to legal assaults. Smaller, more clandestine bordellos, which moved frequently, as well as operations using rented apartments, flats, and hotel rooms, heavily replaced the parlor houses that had earlier operated openly. Dance halls and cabarets—basically saloons and establishments that sold liquor and provided entertainment that resembled the later nightclub—emerged during the period after 1912 as major venues for prostitution, with prostitutes or cabaret entertainers arranging liaisons with male customers in less obvious ways than in the sanctioned vice districts.[155] Purveyors from the Levee were at the helm of moving vice into the cabarets.[156] One report in February 1916 states,

> Thus we see the cabaret evil in sections of the city is the illegitimate heir to the old vice rule. People who prospered when practically licensed prostitution was permitted in Chicago, now find remuneration and familiar employment in some of the cabarets. Old foes appear with new faces. Instead of the old segregated [L]evee district, there is vice in all of the "Loop" hotels and in many of the cabarets and dance halls.[157]

Heading into the 1920s, prostitution had shifted noticeably toward unorganized crime.[158] The bulk of the activity was no longer in the open nor was it tightly located in a few areas. Hence, the major operators and politicians had greater difficulty excluding independent purveyors from the business. Although organized crime was active in vice for decades after 1910, freelancers of various types who operated apart from the standard bordellos became much more important in the period immediately before Prohibition.

Taking advantage of the mobility the automobile afforded its customers, organized vice also moved beyond the city limits to brothels and roadhouses on the major arteries leading from Chicago. This reduced prostitution for a time within the city by approximately 60 percent, but it did so largely by shifting it elsewhere.[159] Colosimo and Torrio were at the forefront of the spread of organized vice into the suburbs, pushing south into Burnham, South Chicago, Chicago Heights, Posen, Burr Oak, and Blue Island as well as to towns just inside Indiana.[160] On the one hand, this diaspora allowed the Colosimo-Torrio brothels to operate virtually without police interference because they were able to gain great influence in the suburbs. It also introduced political competition, breaking the monopoly that the police and politicians in Chicago had on the provision of protection (when they did allow the bordellos to operate).

Burnham was a thoroughly disreputable place. Its "boy mayor," Johnny Patton, was a confederate of Colosimo and Torrio, and it became the first mob-controlled suburb in the Chicago area. Noting the town's proximity to both Chicago (where the saloons closed at 1:00 a.m.) and the Indiana steel mills (which ran three shifts a day), Patton allowed the Burnham taverns to operate around the clock.[161] Gambling and vice soon followed. The town's flagrant lawlessness was demonstrated in 1914 when Chicago policemen pursuing armed robbers were driven from a saloon there by a hail of bullets after the patrons at the bar drew their guns and opened fire. Chicago police captain Morgan Collins referred to it as "an outlaw region" and "a menace to . . . Chicago."[162]

This small town was home to thirty-five brothels in 1918, and virtually all the prominent places on the vice strip along Gostlin (also called Howard) Avenue were run by major players from the old Levee in Chicago.[163] At the time, Burnham boasted more prostitutes per capita than any similar location in the world; in fact, one strike by the authorities in 1919 netted more than two hundred soiled doves.[164] Naturally, the women there, enjoying very broad immunity from law enforcement, were especially brazen. At the Speedway Inn, an inmate named Margaret said to an operative of the Committee of Fifteen, while feeling his private parts, "Come on, Honey, let's f—."[165] About two weeks later at the same location, a girl known as Madge told one investigator, "Come on, Baby, let's go to my room and jazz [have intercourse]."[166] In each case, the price quoted was two dollars.

Organized crime in Chicago in general received a major boost when Republican William Hale Thompson was elected mayor in 1915. Thompson was a blue blood from the upper-crust section of the Second Ward just south of the Loop who fancied himself a cowboy. Although he entered politics on a lark, "Big Bill" Thompson was absorbed by it almost immediately. He developed close ties to the aldermen in the First Ward and to Republican political mastermind William Lorimer. A nimble and flexible campaigner, Thompson promised everyone everything. In the process, he built a Republican political machine that won the mayoralty by impressive vote margins and, for a time, dominated politics in Cook County as well as across the state.

Fig. 1.19. Johnny Patton.

Although he sometimes engaged in juvenile antics, Thompson was politically astute as well as corrupt. During his first two terms as mayor, his supporters fed at whatever troughs he controlled and certainly kicked part of what they got back to the mayor, causing scandals in City Hall, the police department, and the public schools. Prostitution was tolerated (to the extent that political pressures allowed), and various police chiefs, who were personally selected by the mayor, largely ignored gambling.[167] For example, the average value of

Fig. 1.20. "Big Bill" Thompson throws out the first ball at Wrigley Field.

the Gambling Index from 1915 to 1922 was sixty-three, roughly equal to the average during Carter Harrison Jr.'s last term in office. The second attack on the Levee continued during Thompson's first years in office, as public outrage overwhelmed the mayor's preferences, but vice enforcement dropped off noticeably after 1917. Much of the graft fell into Thompson's pocket because he dispensed protection directly from his office. For example, Colosimo was still the bagman for the First Ward vice, but he now paid the mayor's office rather than the ward's aldermen.[168]

The staunchly anti-Thompson *Chicago Tribune,* which was typically a Republican Party cornerstone, summarizes his career as mayor after he was defeated for reelection in 1931 with these words:

> For Chicago, Thompson has meant filth, corruption, obscenity, idiocy and bankruptcy. He has given the city an international reputation for moronic buffoonery, barbaric crime, triumphant hoodlumism, unchecked graft and a dejected citizenship. He nearly ruined the property and completely destroyed the pride of the city. He made Chicago a byword for the collapse of the American civilization. In his attempt to continue this he excelled himself as a liar and defamer of character. He's out.
>
> He is not only out, but he is dishonored. He is permanently deserted by his friends. He is permanently marked by the evidence of his character and conduct. His health is impaired by his ways of life and he leaves office and goes from the city the most discredited man who ever held place in it.[169]

These strong sentiments are not confined to the *Chicago Tribune.* Editorials in *twenty-two* other major American newspapers refer to Thompson as an "international clown" who "made himself typical of the worst in American politics" and "made Chicago almost a synonym for rampant crime and corruption."[170] In terms of a summary judgment, while many big-city mayors turned a blind eye toward Prohibition violations during the 1920s or gambling and vice at various times, few ran their cities as wide open, before or during Prohibition, did as much financial damage to them, or participated as closely in the workings of the underworld (as is discussed in chapter 4) as

Thompson did in Chicago. The fact that almost two dozen newspapers outside of Chicago damned him when he was turned out of office is quite telling.

As time went on, James Colosimo, despite his successes in the underworld, became increasingly involved in the upperworld, with Torrio handling more and more of the activities related to gangland. If Colosimo had only seen the potential in large-scale bootlegging, it might have been a long time before the average Chicagoan became very familiar with John Torrio or Al Capone. However, success seemed to have unspoiled Colosimo. Perhaps his new love, singer Dale Winter (who was the star attraction at his café), and the upscale clientele with whom he socialized made him think that he could distance himself from the criminal world. At any rate, Colosimo seemed quite interested in respectability and was largely uninterested in the millions of dollars the alcohol racket could provide.

However, the underworld reached up for Colosimo on May 11, 1920. Shortly after he returned from his honeymoon, having divorced Victoria Moresco and subsequently married Dale Winter in less than two months, Colosimo drove to his Wabash Avenue café for a 4:00 p.m. appointment with a man he did not know.[171] About fifteen minutes after arriving, he was fatally shot in the vestibule near the front entrance. The police theorized that the killer hid in a cloak room near the front door and emerged as Colosimo walked by. He fired two shots as the victim turned toward him. One struck Colosimo behind the right ear and entered his brain, dropping him to the floor where he lay in a pool of his own blood, his own weapon undrawn. The other bullet missed its target and shattered the glass door of the nearby telephone booth.

Fig. 1.21. Dale Winter, Colosimo's second wife.

It was a classic gangland execution, quick and neat with no witnesses and carried out in the victim's inner sanctum where he felt secure, and therefore he would not have been overly cautious. The gunman was almost certainly Brooklyn gang leader Frankie Yale (whose last name was actually Ioele), who was working on a contract from John Torrio. Yale closely fit the description of a man who had been hanging around the restaurant for two days: twenty-five to thirty years old, five foot six inches to five foot eight inches, fat-faced with a dark complexion and wearing a black derby, a black overcoat, patent leather shoes, and a white standup collar.

According to New York organized crime historian William Balsamo, Yale was quite a madman.[172] Not content with the easy money that came from labor racketeering on the Brooklyn docks and bootlegging, Yale did contract killings for as much as $10,000, a subject that will be discussed again in a later chapter. No hints of conflicts with other gangs were apparent at the time, and no evidence suggests any reprisals by Torrio, who quietly took Colosimo's place, indicating that his own associates had decided that Colosimo had "gotten soft" and had to go.[173]

Fig. 1.22. Frankie Yale (circa 1915).

Colosimo's wealth was estimated at half a million dollars, but it proved difficult to trace with only $80,000 in assets officially found.[174] However, gangster fortunes are nearly impossible to estimate, much less find. First, observers often confuse the personal wealth of the individual with the assets of the gang. Just as the CEO of IBM does not own the assets of the corporation but instead manages them in return for a salary and bonuses, the gang leader generally does not own the assets of the gang. Therefore, while Colosimo owned his famous café and likely some specific properties outright, whatever was part of the gang's activities would have completely reverted to his gangster successors unless he had personally bankrolled it. Second, being clandestine individuals by nature, gangsters are very adept at hiding wealth. Thus, whatever was officially recognized and turned over to his father as his heir, when the estate was settled, would most likely have been a mere pittance in relation to what he had secreted away.

"Big Jim" Colosimo's funeral was the first—but certainly not the last—of Chicago's lavish Prohibition Era gangster burials. Like his life, it was a mixture of the upper and lower worlds. His pallbearers, actual and honorary, included an opera singer, three judges, eight aldermen, a congressman, and several ward bosses and other political figures as well as John Torrio, Mike Potson, Mike Merlo, "Diamond Joe" Esposito, the Republican committeeman of the Nineteenth Ward who had strong connections to its Italian gangsters, and Levee dive keepers Jake Adler, Ike Bloom, and Andy Craig.[175] In fact, Merlo was a partner in Colosimo's restaurant.[176]

Ike Bloom gave the underworld synopsis of Colosimo's life:

> There wasn't a piker's hair in Big Jim's head. Whatever game he played he shot straight. He wasn't greedy. There could be dozens of others getting theirs. The more the merrier as far as he was concerned. He had what a lot of us haven't got—class. He brought the society swells and the millionaires into the red light district. It helped everybody, and a lot of places kept alive on Colosimo's overflow. Big Jim never bilked a pal or turned down a good guy and he always kept his mouth shut.[177]

Chapter 2

BOOTLEGGING

"[Organized crime's] sole purpose is to make money."

—David C. Williams, director of the Office of Special Investigations

"A group of people. . . . They conspire and they go into deals. . . . To make money."

—Joey "the Clown" Lombardo, when asked to define the Chicago Outfit

Alcohol has long been part of American life.[1] On the frontier, it was treated as almost a staple, beginning in the Colonial period. One of the first major challenges the new federal government faced after the Revolutionary War was related to alcohol. Starting in 1791, Western Pennsylvania farmers protested vigorously against a federal tax on whiskey, and government troops had to be called out to quell the Whiskey Rebellion. Immigration from Europe in the 1800s and the early 1900s fueled the demand for alcohol among the population of the United States, with the Germans, Irish, Poles, Czechs, and Italians (to name some of the most prominent immigrant groups) viewing beer, whiskey, and wine as essential parts of their lives.

Chicago, in particular, was a hard-drinking town. Its German citizens (primarily) rioted in 1855 when the city sextupled the fee for saloon licenses and tried to enforce the law against saloons being open on Sunday.[2] The city's entire police force was needed, plus 150 special deputies, to handle the Lager Beer Riot, which escalated into a full-scale gun battle along the Chicago River. In 1906 there were 7,300 licensed saloons and probably another thousand blind pigs (unlicensed bars) in the city.[3] At the time the average Chicagoan drank three and one-half times as much beer as the average American. Chicagoans' consumption of hard liquor was almost three times as much as the national average.

The roots of Prohibition were set in the Temperance Movement, which also began during the Colonial period. A prominent early opponent of alcohol was Dr. Benjamin Rush, surgeon general of the Continental Army, patriot, father of modern psychiatry, and signer of the Declaration of Independence.[4] Various temperance societies, whose members pledged abstinence, sprang up around the country during the 1800s. They preached the evils of alcohol and issued pamphlets containing sermons and songs that opposed the consumption of liquor. Their message was, of course, not entirely unfounded. Women and children often suffered the most from the effects of liquor because husbands who were too fond of drink spent a large share of the family income in saloons and sometimes abused their wives and children after returning from a night of drinking.

Not surprisingly, women were at the forefront of the Temperance Movement, and local groups used a variety of methods, including prayer, moral suasion, monetary inducements, and outright violence, to close the saloons during the 1800s.[5] Although the early anti-liquor crusaders were boisterous, they achieved little real success. Like the Abolitionists long before the Civil War, for years the temperance advocates were little more than a fringe group.

These efforts were rejuvenated by the founding of the Woman's Christian Temperance Union (WCTU) in 1874, which was headquartered first in Chicago and then in the neighboring suburb of Evanston. Led by the idealistic Frances Willard, the WCTU's goal was a constitutional prohibition of alcohol. The WCTU and the later-formed Anti-Saloon League organized on the local level and had some success persuading individual counties and states to vote themselves dry. By 1917, thirteen states prohibited the manufacture and sale of alcohol, although the statutes were not always enforced.[6] In fact, in many dry states and counties a bustling illegal market in alcohol, which was an omen of things to come, simply replaced the previously legal trade.

As with the Abolitionists, it took a war to help the Prohibitionists achieve their goal. While the country's young men fought in Western Europe during World War I, the battle over liquor was joined in the US Congress. When the United States was fighting Germany, all things German—including German American brewers such as Pabst, Schlitz, Miller, Stroh, Ruppert, and Busch—became suspect. Wartime prohibition was passed as an emergency measure in 1917, the logic being that the inputs used to manufacture beer, wine, and strong drink could be used to make food instead. At the same time, the "Drys," as the anti-liquor forces were known, pushed the Eighteenth Amendment to the Constitution, calling for national Prohibition through Congress in late 1917. It was ratified by the necessary number of states on January 16, 1919. Tellingly, the citizens of Chicago voted against a local ordinance closing the saloons in 1919 by a margin of almost three to one.[7]

The law, like many other statutes, lacked teeth unless there was a mechanism to enforce it. That mechanism was the Volstead Act, named after the Minnesota congressman who proposed it, which placed penalties on the manufacture, sale, or possession of intoxicating liquor (but not the consumption per se) and assigned enforcement duties to the Department of Justice and the Bureau of Internal Revenue. Of course, there were exemptions, such as near beer (containing less than one half of one percent alcohol), sacramental wines, and medicinal liquors prescribed by a physician. On January 17, 1920, the first day that the Volstead Act was in effect, the attempt at true national Prohibition began.

Prohibition was the single most important event in the history of organized crime in the United States. The new law dramatically changed the provision of alcoholic beverages in the country and who profited from that business. As many of the pre-Prohibition vendors complied with the statute, gangland filled the void, greatly enriching the gangsters as well as their fellow travelers—corrupt politicians and members of law enforcement. The retail prices for alcoholic beverages rose dramatically, due to the greater costs of production, including bribes to officialdom and the possibility of incarceration or worse, and the monopoly position of the gangsters in the market. For example, before Prohibition Chicago saloons paid from $3.50 to $7 for a barrel of average-quality beer. During most of the Dry Era, the price of beer in Chicago was $55 per barrel for a product that generally was not as good as what had been served previously.[8]

The saloons were already in place. Hence, the gangsters, once they settled into business operations, started out as distributors, monopolizing the sale of the product in specific areas to maximize their profitability. Of course, to maintain that position, it was necessary to secure a steady supply of the product. The gangsters quickly went into the beer brewing business.

At the other end of the spectrum, pre-Volstead Chicago was the world manufacturing center of legally made pure alcohol.[9] Such production continued to an extent post-Volstead, because alcohol was a basic ingredient in a number of common products, such as perfume and pharmaceuticals. Much of the legally sanctioned output was, however, diverted for drinking purposes after 1919, and a massive illegal industry sprang up alongside it. Pure alcohol was used to create low-quality substitutes for hard liquors, such as whiskey and scotch, which are usually aged before consumption by adding water and some flavoring and coloring.[10] It could also be added to near beer, in a process called "needling," to raise its alcohol content back to the level of the real, illegal thing.[11]

Fig. 2.1. Frank J. Parker (center), "the airplane bootlegger."

Of course, genuine liquor products, other than beer, still came into the country illegally. For example, Canadian whiskey found its way directly to Chicago by truck, car, and even plane.[12] It also came on land by way of Detroit and later via New Orleans.[13] Frank J. Parker, known as "the airplane bootlegger," flew whiskey into Chicago from Canada. He was the owner of the largest distillery in Montreal and reportedly used five airplanes in this business, which gave him a net worth of $5 million in 1930.[14]

Similarly, scotch destined for

the Windy City generally entered the country via New York, Florida, New Orleans, and other locations on the East Coast, and most of the products from the Caribbean came in through Miami and New Orleans.[15] In fact, Al Capone's purchase of a winter home in Miami in 1928 appears to have been at least partly business-related because he no longer trusted his old New York friend Frankie Yale regarding the importation of liquor.[16] Often the original product was cut with water and pure alcohol to produce more but lower-quality booze for ordinary consumption. However, not everyone was happy with cheap substitutes, and for a price discerning patrons obtained the real thing at a quality establishment near them. Or they had it delivered directly to their homes in fashionable areas such as the Gold Coast on Chicago's North Side or in the posh neighborhoods on the South Side.

Not surprisingly, the licensed sales of sacramental wine, which was especially heavily used in Judaism, skyrocketed after the Volstead Act was signed. There was quite a stir in 1923 when it was revealed that legally permitted withdrawals of wine from controlled stocks for Chicago exceeded those for New York City by 50 percent, even though the latter had a much larger Jewish population.[17] Later a five-man ring, which included Capone liquor liaison Nate Goldberg, Brooklynite Maurice Kaminski, and a California vineyard owner, bought wine permits from rabbis in New York and used them to purchase the California wine. It was delivered by ship to New York and then sent via the Baltimore and Ohio railroad to Chicago as well as on to other cities including Milwaukee, Minneapolis, and St. Louis. During a seven-month period this group sold 400,000 gallons of religiously sanctioned wine in Chicago for four dollars per gallon.[18]

Although the main focus of Chicago's bootlegging gangs was the production and sale of beer, wine, pure alcohol, and hard liquor, they were almost all involved in gambling to one extent or another, often including slot machines and sometimes handbooks or casinos with the usual array of table games. But this was a sideline for most of the liquor mobs. By the mid-1920s, a few of them were active in labor racketeering in fairly minor ways. Most of the bootlegging groups, especially the non-Italians, shied away from prostitution, partly for religious reasons and because it was not tolerated by the citizens in some of the areas where they operated. For example, George E. Q.

Johnson, the US attorney for Northern Illinois, stated that North Side gang leader Earl "Hymie" Weiss "would have nothing to do with prostitution and scorned the Capone crowd for that reason—because they were engaged in prostitution, particularly Ralph Capone."[19] Obviously, Colosimo's old gang was the major exception in the early 1920s to this revulsion by the bootlegging gangs against the sex trade.

Because the sole goal of organized crime is to enrich the members, it is instructive to look at the money it generated during Prohibition. Estimates of the total revenues of organized crime within the city limits of Chicago are available for a few of the years during Prohibition or can be extrapolated from profit figures. The overall profits of organized crime-related activities in 1927 are estimated as $75 million—$30 million from beer and alcohol, $25 million from gambling, and $20 million from vice and other rackets.[20] If profits were 15 percent of revenue for each of the major rackets, then organized crime in Chicago generated $500 million in revenue in total in 1927, with $200 million coming from beer and alcohol, $167 million from gambling, and $133 million from other activities.[21] In 1930, the *Chicago Daily News* estimates that revenues in Chicago from all facets of organized crime were $326 million, with $183 million coming from bootlegging, $65 million from gambling, $52 million from vice, and $26 million from labor racketeering and other activities.[22] In the bootlegging category, $103 million came from beer sales, $56 million from hard liquor, and $23 million from essentially pure alcohol. By the late 1920s, gambling had passed vice in importance, but bootlegging was an even larger illegal business.[23]

The decrease in profits from 1927 to 1930 was due partly to the negative effects of the Great Depression. Also, there was a truce between the Capone mob and the North Side gang during most of 1927, but they were fighting again in 1930 with a detrimental effect on underworld business. Furthermore, the St. Valentine's Day Massacre caused a citywide clampdown on gang activities, which lasted several years and is reflected in the numbers for 1930. The total dollar figures did not all belong to the bootlegging groups; many of the gamblers were independents, and much of the vice trade was not controlled by the liquor mobs. However, it can be taken as an upper estimate of the total revenue of the bootlegging gangs.

Chicago was clearly an important element, if not the center, of bootlegging in the United States during the Prohibition Era. James O'Donnell Bennett estimates the illegal sales of alcoholic beverages for the entire country as $3.6 billion in 1926, making the $200 million figure for Chicago the following year 5.6 percent of the total for the nation.[24] However, the city's population was only 2.5 percent of the country's total in 1920 and 2.8 percent in 1930. More importantly, Chicago was a mass producer of pure alcohol and alcoholic beverages. Consistent with this prominence, Prohibition enforcers designated the near western suburb of Cicero as the "wettest spot in the United States," meaning that it was the area with the worst violations of the Volstead Act.[25] The Calumet region, which extends from the South Side of Chicago to the northwest corner of Indiana and includes southern suburbs such as Chicago Heights, was the second-wettest place in the country.[26]

Figures for individual gang revenues or profits during Prohibition are scarce and generally pertain only to the Capone mob. For example,

Fig. 2.2. Twenty-Second Street in Cicero.

the Capone gang's total revenue was estimated at $90 million in 1925; in 1927 the figure is $105 million, with $60 million coming from beer, liquor, and alcohol; $25 million from gambling and cafés; $10 million from labor and related rackets; and $10 million from vice.[27] In 1931, the Capone mob grossed $70 million from bootlegging alone, with reportedly $20 million from beer sales and $50 million from hard liquor sales and the manufacture of pure alcohol. These numbers clearly demonstrate the importance of illegal alcohol distilling in the Chicago area in general and to the Capone gang in particular.[28] In tandem, the numbers for 1927 show that the Capone organization was almost certainly the biggest of the gangs when it came to bootlegging in Chicago, controlling some 30 percent of the revenue. It had a much smaller share of the market at the time—only about 15 percent—in gambling and vice/racketeering. But the Capone gang surely surpassed all the other bootlegging gangs in the latter areas, because the other rumrunners tended to be highly specialized.

The bribes paid to police, Prohibition agents, and politicians, which were necessary for the gangs to operate because the sale of alcoholic beverages was highly visible, were a major expense. Lawman Pat Roche described the situation as follows: "A one-legged Prohibition agent riding a bicycle could dry up the Loop in half a day provided he were [sic] honest."[29] The US attorney for Northern Illinois, Edwin A. Olson, estimated in 1926 that graft in Cook County was $30 million a year.[30] The widespread corruption related to bootlegging was amply illustrated when Chief Charles Fitzmorris, a crony of Mayor Thompson, admitted that, "Reports and rumors reaching me indicate that 50 percent of the men on the Chicago police force are involved seriously in the illegal sale or transportation of liquor."[31] As the *Chicago Tribune* notes in an editorial at the time, "A man in police uniform has a good many opportunities to operate as a bootlegger, with his uniform as protection. The opportunities are not so good as those of an internal revenue or prohibition enforcement agent, but they are fairly good."[32] A few years later, Olson claimed similarly that at least half of Chicago's police officers were taking bribes from bootleggers.[33]

They were also paid in kind. According to Reverend Elmer Williams, who in 1923 was an officer of the Illinois Anti-Saloon League, "There is one saloon on the [N]orth [S]ide where a flivver squad of

Fig. 2.3. Beer is dumped at the Warren Avenue police station.

the police department drives up each morning and obtains its supply of liquor for the day. From this same place recently a police officer wearing gold braid [of very high rank] was carried out, too intoxicated to walk on his own feet."[34]

Some police officers, such as Detective Sergeant Edward "Hard-Boiled Eddie" Smale, were not content with receiving a small percentage of the deal in order to look the other way. A confidante of prominent Levee characters such as Ed Weiss and Vic Shaw, Smale, in 1917, ran a string of illegal card games and handbooks while simultaneously heading the police department's South Side gambling detail.[35] In late 1920 his squad stopped a truck transporting one hundred cases of whiskey. This was part of a much larger cache, brought in by vice king Mike Heitler, James O'Leary, the McGovern brothers, and several others. A $1,000 bribe had already been paid by the importers to a different group of policemen who intercepted the total shipment when it first arrived in Chicago. Nonetheless, the insatiable Smale allegedly took not only all one hundred cases, but

Fig. 2.4. "Hard-Boiled Eddie" Smale inscribed this photo to Madam Vic Shaw and her girls. An arrow points suggestively to the tip of his nightstick. (Image from the Vic Shaw family album, Lawrence Gutter Collection of Chicagoana, Special Collections, Richard J. Daley Library, University of Illinois at Chicago.)

also the money and jewelry of the men he captured conveying it.[36] In 1921 Smale and a different group of Chicago policemen seized 215 cases of whiskey while pretending to be federal officers. After the man in charge refused to pay $12,000 to smooth things over, they kept the liquor for themselves.[37] Eddie Smale was eventually convicted of fixing a jury and sent to the federal penitentiary at Leavenworth.

On the other side of the coin, many Chicago police officers were honest, including some of the police captains and a large percentage of the men in the detective bureau. For years, the latter were the elite, front-line troops in the war on crime, at least before there were specialized groups that focused on organized crime, such as the Intelligence Unit. Fearless and equally proficient with their fists or any type of gun, the CPD's detectives put a large number of bandits, stickup men, and occasionally some bootleggers in the cemetery. When things got out of hand in terms of violence related to organized crime in a particular part of town, the usual response was to send in hand-picked squads of detectives with more or less *carte blanche.* The police would also crack down by closing all the speakeasies, vice joints, and gambling places in a part (or sometimes all) of the city for a period of time when the public was outraged by lawlessness. In extreme cases, an incorruptible captain would be put in a specific police district with orders to keep everything closed indefinitely. This hit the gangsters where it hurt them the most—in their pocketbooks.

Of course, the bootleggers, given their political clout, regularly had difficult police officers sent to the far corners of the city. For example, when Frankie Lake was stopped with a .45-caliber automatic in his possession, he told the arresting detectives, "You fellows better lay off of me if you know what's good for you. Some of you'll be back in the sticks if you're not careful."[38]

Prohibition agents suffered from the same problems as the local police. As a result, some of them were not only corrupt, but in fact became bootleggers after serving a short apprenticeship with the federal government. This was also true of various Chicago police officers. To their discredit, many Prohibition agents, while unable to locate the operations of major bootleggers, were extremely heavy-handed when enforcing the law against more or less average citizens who were suspected of making and selling some liquor. One reform group estimated at the start of 1932 that since the beginning of Prohibition the number of dry agents and officers killed plus the number of civilians killed by them totaled 1,500. Few lawmen were felled by members of professional bootlegging gangs or by non-gangsters, indicating that the dead were largely ordinary citizens.[39] US senator Edward Edwards claimed, after doing a considerable amount of research, that many of the victims had been shot in the back by trigger-happy Prohibition agents.[40]

On the one hand, as with the Chicago police, there were sterling examples of incorruptible Prohibition agents in Chicago. Brice Armstrong delighted in hamstringing the gang led by Terry Druggan and Frankie Lake, as well as other bootleggers, during his roughly ten-year career in Chicago. He was responsible for closing 93 percent of the breweries still operating in the city during 1923—at the same time he refused $25,000 in bribes.[41] Like other troublesome members of law enforcement, Armstrong was transferred elsewhere at least once. His home was bombed on another occasion, although he, his wife, and his niece escaped injury.[42]

On the other hand, George "Hard-Boiled" Golding conducted a campaign of terror as soon as he arrived in Chicago in March 1928. Golding's team of twenty undercover Prohibition agents clashed with the local police, were reprimanded by the courts, and shot two innocent bystanders during raids, in one case with a "dum-dum" bullet designed to deform on impact to inflict maximum damage to the victim.[43] He and his men were sent far away in August of the same year. In this instance, the pressure to get them out of the city came from the newspapers and outraged citizens instead of the hoodlums. Golding was replaced as chief of the unit by Alexander Jamie, whose young brother-in-law, Eliot Ness, later led the famous unit of Prohibition agents known as "the Untouchables."

During the Dry Era segment of his first two terms as mayor, William Hale Thompson, as was his standard practice, directly collected the protection money from the major bootlegging gangs.[44] From 1923 to 1927, when reformer William Dever was mayor, by necessity a new system arose in which the payoffs from the underworld went directly to the police captain in the districts that were not squeaky clean. The bagman, or "satchel," who collected for the captain was generally a police officer, usually a detective who worked in plainclothes. But in some rare cases the captain actually used someone from outside the police department or even had the money delivered directly to his office.[45] During Dever's mayoralty the protection money moved on from there to Homer Galpin, the chairman of the Cook County Republican Party, who was the political overseer of the system post-Thompson.[46] In surrounding Cook County, the sheriff was paid to look the other way in the unincorporated areas, as were the police in many of the individual suburbs. In fact, for years the position of Cook County sheriff was viewed openly and unabashedly as an opportunity for the office holder to become rich; however the taint that accompanied it almost always ended his political career.

The policies and corruption of the Thompson administration extended beyond the city, because the Republican political juggernaut he built in conjunction with Illinois governor Len Small and Cook County state's attorney Robert Crowe controlled major offices in the county as well as the state government during much of Prohibition. The workings of the Small-Thompson-Crowe machine caused a virtual breakdown of law and order in Cook County and made it a perfect breeding ground for all types of crime. Professor E. W. Burgess of the University of Chicago labeled it an "unholy alliance between organized crime and politics," with major gangsters virtually immune from punishment.[47] Describing Chicago's underworld situation overall, the Juvenile Protective Association (JPA) called it "the filthiest in any big city in the country."[48]

In this unholy alliance, to use Professor Burgess's label, gangland funneled money and gave election support to its political allies. For example, Al Capone reportedly raised $200,000 for Mayor Thompson's election campaign in 1927.[49] Similarly, the head of the Chicago Crime Commission (CCC) charged that Capone gave Thompson $260,000 in campaign funds for the 1931 primary and general elections.[50] Neither Thompson nor Capone denied these allegations, and tellingly they did not sue the *Chicago Daily News*, the *Chicago Tribune*, or the CCC for libel. Capone and some of his most prominent associates, along with apparently John Torrio, are clearly visible in a photograph

Fig. 2.5. William Hale Thompson (#1) at Wedron, Illinois, in 1930. The crowd includes Al Capone (#2), most probably John Torrio (#3), Claude Maddox (#4), and John Russo (#5), along with other hoodlums (notice the pearl gray fedoras, a Capone gang trademark, worn by several of the men on the roof).

of the attendees at "William Hale Thompson Day," a political event staged by the mayor in Wedron, Illinois (near LaSalle-Peru, some ninety miles south of Chicago), on an unusually warm December 9 in 1930.[51] More violently, gangland exerted tremendous efforts in trying to elect the Thompson slate of candidates in the famous Pineapple Primary in 1928, which is discussed further in chapter 5.[52]

In return, the CPD was largely ineffective in fighting organized crime when Thompson was Chicago's mayor. The Employers' Association of Chicago charged that gangster weapons seized in raids were resold by the police. Displaying a magazine from a submachine gun, the group's president stated, "Unfortunately we have been unable to get one of the guns itself. The resale value out of the back door of a police station seems to be more than we can offer."[53] As ordinary crime escalated, the Chicago police responded by simply not recording offenses, grossly understating the reported statistics. For example, the police department's annual report for 1926 claimed that there were 1,206 burglaries, 5,645 larcenies, and 1,427 robberies in the city as opposed to 14,110 burglaries, 12,900 larcenies, and 7,191 robberies reported by the CCC.[54] Meanwhile, CPD chief Michael Hughes made the utterly absurd claim that crime was down "625 percent."[55]

The State's Attorney's Office was equally riddled with problems during Crowe's tenure. In 1926, 12,543 felonies were committed in Cook County, of which a mere 4,982 cases went to trial. Only 2,449 of these crimes (19.53 percent of the offenses committed) resulted in the accused being found guilty of a felony. In 1,377 of the 4,982 cases tried, the charge was reduced to a misdemeanor, and the guilty parties received at worst minor punishment.[56] In many other instances, the charges were simply dropped or stricken from the record. The landmark *Illinois Crime Survey* places the blame for this abysmal record on "incompetent and indifferent assistant state's attorneys" who were nothing more than political appointees during Crowe's years in office.[57]

The felony convictions that did result were largely negated by Governor Len Small's system of freely granting the offenders paroles and pardons. Summing up the situation, one newspaper refers to Len Small as "the worst governor the state ever had. We believe he is the worst governor any state ever had."[58] For example, his parole board returned 950 dangerous offenders to Cook County alone within a period of less than two years, which was "undoubtedly one of the causes of Cook County's appalling crime record."[59] This mass prison exodus included Walter Stevens, James "Fur" Sammons, "Spike" O'Donnell, William "Three-Fingered Jack" White, Frank McErlane, and Ralph Sheldon, who were among the most dangerous criminals in Chicago (if not the entire country).

Fig. 2.6. Governor Len Small.

Illinois state representative Lee Browne was particularly interested in Stevens's release.

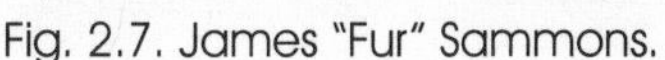

Fig. 2.7. James "Fur" Sammons.

He persuaded the head of the parole board, Major M. A. Messlein, to not only give the matter Messlein's full attention but to also concern himself with whether Walter Stevens had comfortable shoes while in the penitentiary at Joliet![60] In what was surely not a coincidence, Stevens, in his wife's name, owned $5,000 of stock in Messlein's engineering firm Major Engineering.[61] George "Bugs" Moran was paroled before Stevens, to the custody of Major Messlein himself, after allegedly buying $300 of stock in the major's firm.[62]

Despite the various expenses involved, the gangsters and their ilk still made out like bandits, as the estimate of $75 million in profits during 1927 indicates. As in legitimate businesses, inside the bootlegging gangs the reward system depended on what one brought to the party. There were plenty of mouths to feed, and the profits did not all go to the boss. Low-level gunmen with no business acumen or administrative ability, as necessary as they were during the violence of the Prohibition Era, were plentiful and therefore not especially well paid. James O'Donnell Bennett estimates that they earned approximately $100 per week in straight salary.[63] Upper-level members, who

Fig. 2.8. Al Capone dining with his wife (left), his mother (right), and his brother Umberto (standing with the tray).

worked in a supervisory role with control of specific activities, received a percentage of the profits from the operations they oversaw. This percentage was higher if they themselves bankrolled the business as opposed to it being financed with the gang's money. These big shots of gangland reportedly earned between $2,000 and $5,000 per week.[64]

Organized crime in Chicago certainly generated an abundance of wealth for the leaders of the bootlegging gangs. In Guy Murchie's opinion, at its height Al Capone's personal income exceeded $1 million annually.[65] By his own estimate, Capone frittered away $7.5 million, much of it by betting on horses and shooting dice, between the time he came to Chicago and 1929, which is consistent with an income of this magnitude and also Capone's later financial condition.[66] Similarly, Hymie Weiss was reported to have been worth almost $2 million when he died in 1926, a somewhat lesser value than Capone's wealth at the time, and Vincent Drucci was said to have had assets over $1 million in 1926, while Joe Saltis accumulated $3 million by the end of Prohibition.[67] Weiss and Drucci did not show off their wealth, while Saltis, like Capone, flaunted his by purchasing an estate in the vicinity of Hayward, Wisconsin, complete with a golf course and a fox farm. Once he employed the majority of its inhabitants and was able to control the ballot box, he had the town renamed Saltisville.

Chapter 3

THE GANGSTERS

"The Volstead act gave the brainy gangster his big opportunity. There were millions in it and force was the first requirement."

—*Chicago Tribune,* May 18, 1933

"It [the Prohibition law] looked like a good opening for a lot of smart young men."

—Al Capone

The bootlegging gangs in Chicago drew their members largely from the neighborhoods they operated in, which gave many of them a distinct ethnic flavor. For example, those in the large West Side and South Side Irish belts were heavily Irish. Dean O'Banion's North Side gang partly reflected the ethnic mix of the area it controlled, giving it a more cosmopolitan makeup. While there were many Irish members, there were Poles, Germans, and several Italians as well, and quite a few Jews originally from the Near West Side. In fact, only one of the North Side gang's four leaders was Irish. The Saltis-McErlane gang mirrored the Back of the Yards area on the South Side, with Poles and Bohemians in abundance along with several Irishmen and a smattering of other groups. The gangs in the large Italian districts on the near west, near northwest, and the lower north sides were predominantly of that ethnicity.

The Torrio-Capone gang, although it was heavily populated with Italians, was an ethnic smorgasbord, continuing the recruiting policies instituted by "Big Jim" Colosimo. It also seems to have drawn the most heavily from outside of Chicago, which was at least partly due to the strong connections that Torrio and Capone had, given their origins, with New York City gangland. Robert Lombardo, based on Guy Murchie's list of Capone gangsters, estimates that 41 percent of the group's members were Italian.[1] There are, however, several problems with Murchie's enumeration and therefore with this figure. First, several individuals appear there more than once. Second, various mobsters' non-Italian aliases are shown rather than their true names. For example, Frank Diamond was born Frank Maritote, Jimmy Emery was actually Vincenzo Ammirati, and Charlie Carr's real name was Carl Torraco. Third, a number of gangsters on the Murchie list were never with Capone, or were his allies at one time but never joined his gang, such as the six Genna brothers and the South Side O'Donnells. In other cases the hoodlums joined Capone later, when their gangs were folded into his, but were not originally with the Torrio-Capone gang at the start of Prohibition.

To obtain an estimate of the ethnic makeup of the Torrio-Capone bunch at the beginning of the Dry Era, these errors are corrected, and anyone who was involved in organized crime before joining this group is excluded. This revised list contains 101 individuals, and fifty-eight of them were, after further research, clearly of Italian origin. Therefore, it appears that almost 60 percent of the Torrio-Capone gangsters were Italian at the start of the Dry Era.

In Chicago, the bootleggers were mostly new faces to organized crime, as the major players in gambling, vice, and labor racketeering largely stayed in their own backyards. The violators of the Prohibition law came primarily from the ranks of ordinary crime before 1920. They generally started out while still young boys as members of local street gangs before working as thieves, robbers, and labor and/or election sluggers.[2] Also, bootlegging was primarily a young man's game, as innovation often is. As a result, many of the city's prominent bootleggers were born around the turn of the century and did not reach the age of thirty until the 1920s (if they ever did).

Quite a few of them, such as Dean O'Banion, Walter Stevens, "Spike" O'Donnell and his siblings, "Mossy" Enright, the McErlane brothers, and various members of the Colosimo gang, served as hired goons for the *Chicago Tribune*, the *Chicago American*, and other daily newspapers as they fought to increase sales in the newspaper Circulation War that began in 1900 and ended in about 1913.[3] Overall, the Circulation War resulted in more than two dozen deaths. The *Chicago Tribune*'s publisher, Colonel Robert R. McCormick, claimed that twenty-seven were killed, although, given his self-interest, this figure is likely downward-biased.[4] Based on a more neutral source, Jackie Cooney puts the figure at forty.[5] Separately, a number of the Prohibition Era hoodlums received training in violence courtesy of Uncle Sam during World War I, as evidenced by their war records and by their later funerals, where full military honors were provided by the Veterans of Foreign Wars' posts they belonged to.

Consistent with the illegal and semi-military nature of the underworld, the loyalty of gang members to the group's leader was an important asset. This was achieved by recruiting people who the leader or top members had worked with previously or who were known individuals, either because they came from the same area as the leader or because they were otherwise vouched for. This is confirmed by Lou Corsino's detailed examination of the various ties that connected the gangsters in Chicago Heights to each other.[6] However, the strongest bonds of loyalty were usually created, as they had been for thousands of years, by kinship through birth or by marriage. Therefore, many of the bootlegging gangs were family affairs, with numerous brothers, brothers-in-law, or other relatives prominently placed around the leader.

Although exact or even approximate data on the number of members in each gang are not readily available, several estimates can be culled from published sources. For example, Guy Murchie reports that in late 1923 the Torrio-Capone gang had seven hundred members overall.[7] One contemporary source states that Al Capone, near the end of his reign, had five hundred "gorillas" in his gang.[8] Similarly, James Doherty estimates that Capone had five hundred gunmen in his employ "at the height of his power," which would have been in 1931.[9] Richard Enright, writing in 1931, has the same figure.[10] As a rough comparison, the North Side gang had two hundred tough men, who were extremely proficient in violence, working for the Republican candidates in the November 1924 election.[11] However, the Capone gang increased noticeably in size over time through mergers and acquisitions, so a reasonable estimate of the number of gunmen in the Torrio-Capone outfit in late 1924, when the North Siders had two hundred such men, is somewhere between three hundred and four hundred.

Most gangs had a leader whose word was law. In that sense they were very autocratic organizations.[12] For example, when describing the Chicago Outfit, which got its work rules from the Capone gang, veteran IRS organized crime investigator Robert Fuesel said, "They make the US Army look like a democracy."[13] Because the gang leader could not be everywhere and do everything himself, he delegated authority to his various subordinates. The most important of these was his chief lieutenant, who in the modern parlance would be referred to as the underboss.[14] The gangs were organized by function, with sub-lieutenants overseeing the major activities, such as gambling, beer, liquor, and vice (if they dealt in prostitution). Reporting to them were the men who ran the individual gambling places, brothels, breweries, or distilleries. There was also a man in charge of payoffs, who worked closely with the sub-lieutenants to make sure that officialdom was taken care of and that those in power looked the other way. Other individuals or groups were delegated specific tasks. For example, in late 1931 the Capone mob, now including former subsidiary gangs, had separate men in charge of brewery construction, alcohol production, and beer production and sales, and there was an enforcement group that included the likes of Jack McGurn, Claude Maddox, Tony Capezio, and Sam Hunt.[15]

In terms of leadership style, when there was trouble, most of the top men in the non-Italian-dominated gangs led from the front, meaning they generally took care of it themselves. Certainly this was the case in the North Side gang, as Dean O'Banion, Earl "Hymie" Weiss, Vincent Drucci, and George Moran regularly did their own dirty work. Similarly, Joe Saltis and Frank McErlane were at the forefront of the violence that went on for years around the Union Stockyards on the South Side. Saltis was suspected by the CPD in twenty gangland killings from 1925 to early 1929, and if someone had trouble with whatever gang Frank McErlane belonged to, given the twists and turns in the underworld over time, McErlane came for him personally—and God help him if he did.[16] On the other hand, Chicago

Prohibition Era gang leaders such as John Torrio and, except in a few cases, Al Capone delegated the killing to subordinates, which is typical of latter-day Cosa Nostra crime families in America where the higher-ups are far removed from the violence.

The rules of the Italian-based gangs also differed from those dominated by other ethnicities. When someone joined the Torrio-Capone gang, barring some exceptions, he joined for life. In most of the other gangs, members came and went without any difficulties. For example, O'Banion's driver and bodyguard Jerome McMahon, at the behest of his fiancée, gave up a life of crime for more mundane but law-abiding employment.[17] Similarly, North Side gangster Maxie Eisen retired and went on an extended world tour after making a fortune.[18] In the same way, Valley Gang leader Frank Lake absented himself from his companions after amassing considerable wealth. In several cases, hoodlums moved from one gang to another, often without any real animosity. This was partly due to connections/alliances between some of the bootlegging mobs. Of course, it did not apply in every case, as defectors from the North Side to the Capone gang discovered, and it certainly was not true for the Torrio-Capone organization.

During the Dry Era, the Italian-dominated bootlegging gangs were more focused, if not more professional, than their counterparts. As ordered by their leaders, the members worked on the important business at hand, such as bootlegging or gambling, as opposed to the freelance robberies other mobsters regularly committed. These differences likely stem from the fact that the roots of the Torrio-Capone mob, and possibly also the Genna brothers' gang, were grounded in organized crime before 1920 as opposed to theft and robbery and other ordinary crime.

Before we delve into the conflicts between them, a survey of the major bootlegging gangs in Chicago in the early years of Prohibition is in order. The gangs that came on the scene later are covered in the following chapters as part of the broader evolution of Chicago's underworld. Because there has not been a complete discussion of Chicago's bootlegging gangs, no accurate map delineating the areas controlled by them during Prohibition has appeared in the books published to date. Fig. 3.1 shows the locations of the major bootlegging mobs as of January 1, 1924, in terms of the police districts in the

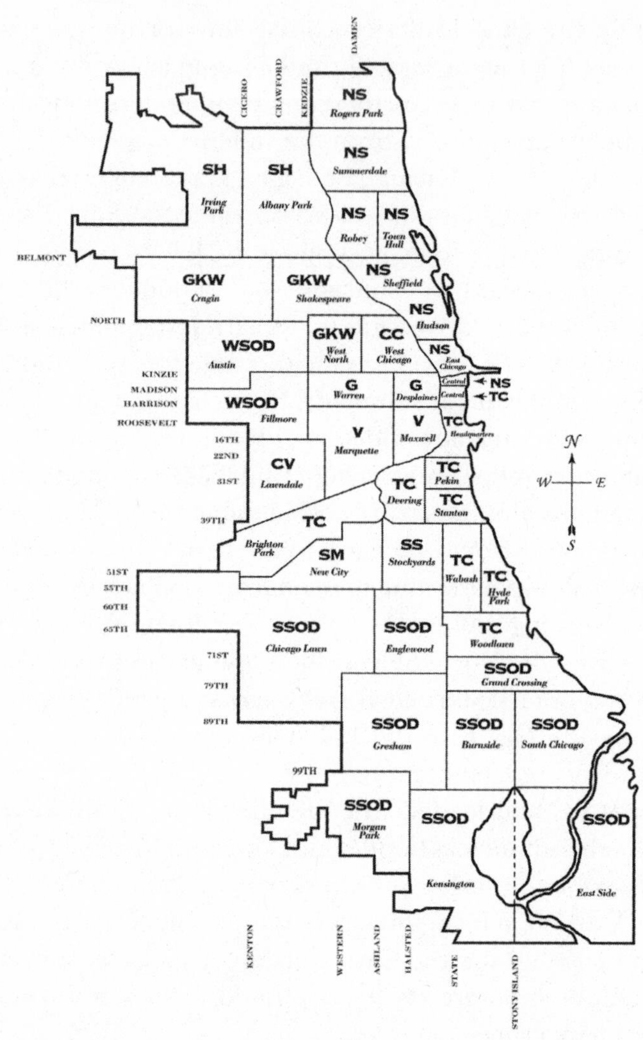

Fig. 3.1. Map of the major bootlegging gangs in Chicago. January 1, 1924.

Legend:
CC = Circus Café
CV = Cook-Vogel
G = Genna
GKW = Guilfoyle-Kolb-Winge
NS = North Side
SH = Schultz-Horan
SSOD = South Side O'Donnells
SS = Sheldon-Stanton
SM = Saltis-McErlane
TC = Torrio-Capone
V = Valley (Druggan-Lake)
WSOD = West Side O'Donnells

city in 1932, which were largely unchanged for much of the Prohibition Era.[19] It is based on a very accurate map for 1932 created by reporter Hal Andrews, less detailed maps of bootlegging in Chicago, a verbal description by a Chicago police officer of where the gangs were located, and a variety of information about the bootlegging mobs and how they rose, expanded, and also declined over time.[20]

THE NORTH SIDE (O'BANION–WEISS–MORAN) GANG

Starting in the northeast portion of the city, the gang Dean (who is sometimes incorrectly called Dion) O'Banion led until his death, followed by Hymie Weiss and later George Moran (often referred to as the North Side gang), controlled the area north of Madison Avenue, east of the Chicago River's north (and partly south) branches and extending on the north to the city limits. Through their allies they were also active in the northern suburbs. In the city, their domain included seven police districts and part of another (the Central district), which also gave the gang a section of downtown Chicago between Madison Street and the Chicago River (as it ran east toward Lake Michigan). According to Rose Keefe, Dean Charles O'Banion was born in Maroa, Illinois, near the city of Decatur, on July 8, 1892.[21] He was brought to Chicago in 1901 by his widower father. They settled in an Irish district on the Near North Side, just south of Chicago Avenue in the vicinity of Holy Name Cathedral. In a childhood accident, Dean O'Banion broke his left leg in two places, leaving it one inch shorter than the right and causing him to limp noticeably for the rest of his life.

Fig. 3.2. Dean O'Banion.

His physical impediment did

not, however, impede his criminality. On October 5, 1909, O'Banion was sentenced to nine months in Chicago's House of Corrections for burglarizing a post office.[22] An official record from 1917 shows that he was a bartender at the Liberty Inn run by John and William McGovern at Clark and Erie Streets just north of the Chicago River, a notorious dive where he had apparently worked for years.[23] O'Banion entered the big leagues of ordinary crime when he started working with Charles "the Ox" Reiser. Reiser and his men were known as the most expert safecrackers in the Midwest.[24] Some of O'Banion's most formidable henchmen during Prohibition were also members of the Reiser gang.

As a bootlegging gang leader, O'Banion was a fearsome adversary. However, he was not the sharpest of underworld kingpins or the most diplomatic. James O'Donnell Bennett paints him as a "mix of ferocity, childishness, and mawkishness" that was quite easily ignited.[25] Hal Andrews characterizes the gang leader as flamboyant and always looking for trouble.[26] At the time of his death, one newspaper describes O'Banion and the contradictions in his personality as follows:

> Generous to a fault, but also cruel. Loyal to his friends; unforgiving toward his enemies. Champion of some of the weak; hated and feared by many of the vicious. O'Banion had little personal use for a lot of money, but he constantly risked his life for it. O'Banion never was known to take a drink of beer or whiskey. Liquor was a commodity and not a beverage.[27]

For example, O'Banion was said to have been responsible for at least twenty-five murders.[28] Yet he refused to fire a guard on his booze shipments when some of his men complained that the guard was a homosexual, telling them to find another job if they didn't like it.[29] As discussed in the next chapter, his uncontrollable behavior played a major part in the evolution of gangland in Chicago during Prohibition.

O'Banion's chief lieutenant in 1924 was Hymie Weiss. Vincent Drucci, George "Bugs" Moran, Louis Alterie, Dan McCarthy, Samuel Jules "Nails" Morton, Maxie Eisen, and Frank Foster were other impor-

Fig. 3.3. Earl "Hymie" Weiss (standing at left) with his girlfriend Josephine Simard (seated at the far right). (Courtesy of Mario Gomes, MYALCAPONEMUSEUM.COM.)

Fig. 3.4. Vincent "the Schemer" Drucci.

tant members. Weiss, who was born Henry Earl Wojciechowski before his mother anglicized the last name, was a close friend of O'Banion. Weiss had also worked with Reiser earlier, before O'Banion brought him into bootlegging, and he was as shrewd as he was dangerous, which is saying quite a lot of someone reputed to be the only man whom Capone feared. On one occasion, he shot his brother Fred in the chest; another time he threatened to kill his first cousin after the latter knocked him down with his fists during an argument.[30]

Vincent Drucci, a veteran of World War I, was known as "the Schemer" because he was "clever in the cultivation of influential alliances."[31] Baptized as Lodovico D'Ambrosio, which translates from the Latin that Catholic priests still used at the time to "Louis D'Ambrosio," Drucci possessed a fiery temper and was another long-time friend of O'Banion. Early in his criminal career, he was arrested numerous times for looting the coin boxes of public telephones. Later he was indicted for larceny and robbery, due to auto theft, bank robbery, and a hijacking, and for carrying a concealed weapon.[32]

The gangster known as George "Bugs" Moran was born in St. Paul, Minnesota, in 1891 with, given his *nom de guerre*, the unusual name of Adelard Cunin.[33] His parents were of French extraction. Initially, Moran committed petty crimes in Chicago and McLean County, Illinois, including stealing a horse and buggy. On the same day that he was released from the county jail for this offense, he was caught burglarizing a saloon in Bloomington, Illinois. Police officers found him with a bottle of whiskey in each hand.[34] Moran soon returned to Chicago and joined the Reiser gang. In 1921, following a stint in the state prison, he became part of the North Side bootlegging mob. The nickname "Bugs" was an allusion to Moran's continual, off-center behavior.

Louis Alterie was christened Leland Varain in California and was sometimes referred to as "Diamond Jack." Alterie was quite the mad hatter, even in the O'Banion gang, and was given to crazy statements and crazier actions, traits that seem to have run in his family. He had a ranch near Denver, Colorado, which the North Siders and their broader circle frequently visited.[35] His brother wounded him in the back with a blast from a shot gun during a quarrel there in June 1927.[36] On another occasion in Colorado, a drunken Alterie shot two

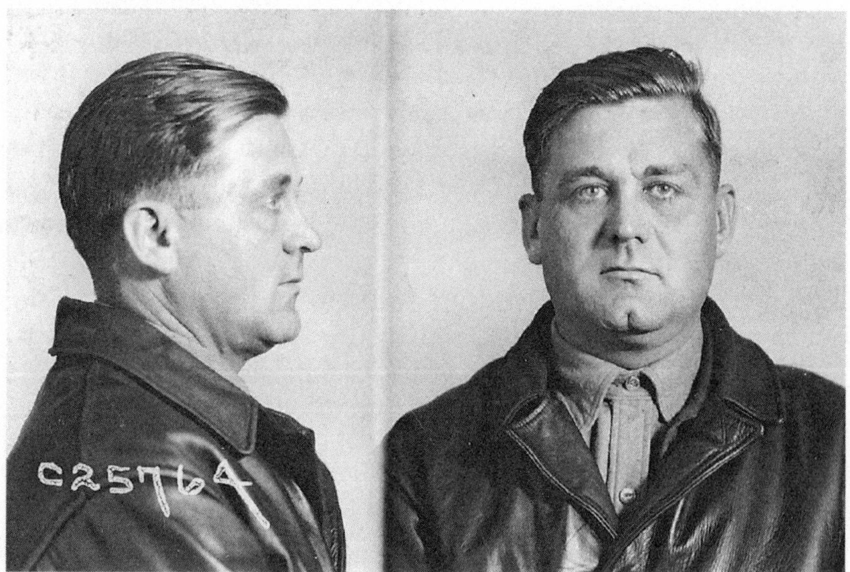

Fig. 3.5. George "Bugs" Moran.

men and pistol-whipped a third.[37]

Dan McCarthy, known as "Dapper Dan," ran the Plumbers' Union. In his youth, he shot a policeman who arrested him for evading the draft. In 1922, he was tried for the murder of two other CPD officers, and he killed Steve Kelliher, president of the Chicago Theater Janitors' Union, the following year.[38] The latter killing cleared the way for Louis Alterie and O'Banion ally "Con" Shea to control that organization.

If not for Samuel Jules "Nails" Morton, the North Siders might have been nothing more than a band of pirates who hijacked liquor sporadically and simply resold it. Born in New York City in 1893, Morton lived in the Maxwell Street district in Chicago as a young man and boxed as "Kid Nails," which made him famous in the city's West Side Jewish community.[39] Volunteering for military service before the draft was imposed, Morton landed in France with the 132nd Infantry Regiment and went "over the top" three times. On the third trench raid, he was wounded in the arm by a bullet, in the leg by a shell, and was the only man out of eight who returned to the American lines. His bravery won him the French Croix de Guerre and ultimately a lieutenant's commission.

After first organizing the bootlegging racket in the Maxwell Street area in the early days of Prohibition, Morton joined with O'Banion.[40] He taught the wild Irishman the finer points of organized crime, including how to run a bootlegging empire.[41] Although we will never know for certain, it is possible that Morton, if he had not been killed in a horse riding accident on north Clark Street in May 1923, would have been a calming influence on O'Banion throughout the Dry Era.

Fig. 3.6. Samuel Jules "Nails" Morton.

Max David "Maxie" Eisen was

a friend of Morton from the Near West Side who, along with several other Twentieth Ward Jewish gangsters, joined the North Side gang. There is considerable confusion regarding Eisen, because there were actually two prominent Maxie Eisens in organized crime in Chicago during this era. The Chicago Crime Commission (CCC) refers to Morton's friend as Maxie Eisen #2.[42] As mentioned, he left the O'Banion gang a wealthy man in the mid-1920s, but he lost much of his fortune after returning to Chicago due to the Great Depression. He is buried in the Morton family plot in the Jewish Waldheim cemetery in Forest Park, Illinois. The other Max Eisen, labeled Maxie Eisen #1 by the CCC, was a business racketeer who ran various "associations" in the Jewish community. He is discussed in greater detail below.[43] Another Maxwell Street protégé of Morton who went with him to the North Side was Frank Frost (aka Frank Foster). Frost was born in Bucharest, Romania, in 1899, to a Jewish couple who immigrated to the United States in 1903.[44]

Fig. 3.7. Max David Eisen (aka Maxie Eisen #2). (Courtesy of Craig Eisen Collection.)

THE SCHULTZ-HORAN GANG

Moving counterclockwise on the map, the Schultz-Horan gang operated in the northwest corner of the city from the north branch Chicago River on the east, to Belmont Avenue on the south, and to the city limits on the north and west. Although this was a large area in square miles, it was smaller in population than the map implies because much of it was still open space during the 1920s. Albert

Schultz, whose surname was originally Schuetz, was of German extraction and owned a saloon on W. Montrose Avenue near Lincoln Avenue. Schultz had close ties to the Belle Plaine Athletic Club, which played its home baseball games at Welles Park across the street from his establishment.[45] His gangland partner, John Horan, operated the Terminal Café at Kimball and Lawrence and was the brother of Eleventh Ward alderman Dennis Horan. Jack Callahan apparently became Horan's top aide after Schultz's death in 1922. Thomas McCarthy also belonged to the gang.[46]

THE GUILFOYLE-KOLB-WINGE (GKW) GANG

South of the Schultz-Horan gang, bootlegging and gambling in the Cragin, Shakespeare, and West North Avenue police districts were controlled by the Guilfoyle-Kolb-Winge (GKW) gang. This gang also had the beer concessions in near northern suburbs such as Niles Center (later renamed Skokie) and Morton Grove, working with the North Siders.[47] Its members ran a brisk beer business, selling their own product as well as handling $1 million a year worth of beer that came from the Gilt Edge brewery in Lawrence, Massachusetts, on the Boston and Maine railroad and was off-loaded in Morton Grove.[48] At one time there was a spirited rivalry between them and "soft drink" merchants Louis and Max Sommerfeld (sometimes spelled Summerfield) for domination of the hard liquor business in that area in the city.

The rather corpulent Matt Kolb, who was born Mathias Kalb in 1891, was one of the leaders of the GKW gang. He was an old-timer in the beer racket on the city's Northwest Side, and he later owned extensive gambling interests in the northern part of the county. Marty Guilfoyle had a cigar store before Prohibition, which was really a gambling emporium, on S. Wabash in the Levee district, where he shot and killed labor slugger Peter Gentleman in September 1919.[49] Guilfoyle was active in gambling as well as bootlegging and ran a string of North Side betting places. He also operated slot machines in the same, if not a much larger, part of the city during the early 1920s.

Al Winge, who was known as Chicago's toughest cop, rose to the rank of lieutenant in the detective bureau in the early 1920s. At least

Fig. 3.8. Matt Kolb.
(Courtesy of David Brown.)

that was his official job. Initially Winge moonlighted as a bootlegger in partnership with Kolb and Guilfoyle. He was indicted in 1925 for his part in the gang's importation of beer from Massachusetts. But in the corrupt metropolis called Chicago, that offense earned him a mere thirty-day suspension from the police force.[50] He was permanently relieved of his duties only after he was caught delivering beer to a saloon in Cicero some six months later.[51]

Matt Kolb's brothers Ted and Al, who was known as "Bunk" and was once a police detective, also

Fig. 3.9. Al Winge (standing with the straw hat).

belonged to the GKW gang. Other major figures in the organization included Joey Fisher, who was the sales manager in alcohol; Jimmy Barry; Sam "Red" Thompson; and Leonard Boltz. Boltz did quite well monetarily as a bootlegger and later worked as a "labor counselor," which indicates his importance as a labor racketeer. The GKWs were closely linked with the Touhy gang, which arose later in the northwest suburbs, and also with the North Side gang, as evidenced by Al Winge's detective squad openly cabareting with prominent North Side members in early 1926 and Kolb's connections to them.[52]

THE WEST SIDE O'DONNELL GANG

The West Side O'Donnell gang did the bootlegging in the Austin and Fillmore police districts, as well as in the northern part of Cicero and most likely in the near western suburb of Forest Park.[53] It was for many years an important liquor and gambling emporium, and its saloons, which were centered along Madison Street just west of Harlem Avenue, also served the neighboring towns of Oak Park, River Forest, Maywood, Berwyn, and Riverside. These five villages were dry by local ordinance at one time or another and were generally squeaky clean, which forced their residents to get the forbidden fruits from elsewhere.

This bunch of O'Donnells was led by William (known as "Klondike"), Bernard (aka "Barney"), and Myles (sometimes spelled Miles) O'Donnell, whose parents John and Anna came to America from Ireland in 1885. The family lived in the Valley district on Chicago's Near West Side in 1920, and the brothers started out with the Valley Gang before branching out on their own.[54] However, the O'Donnells maintained close ties with the Valley bunch throughout Prohibition. "Klondike" O'Donnell, who served in the army from September 22, 1917, until April 10, 1919, was the leader of the gang. He was called "Klondike"—or more simply "Klon" by his intimates—because of the large amounts of liquor he brought in from Canada by truck.[55] Myles was the youngest of the three and ran the Pony Inn on Roosevelt in Cicero.[56] Although his police record began in 1921, he was labeled as "Immune" by knowledgeable observers because he was

Fig. 3.10. "Klondike" O'Donnell is standing next to his wife, Ray, in a gag photo.

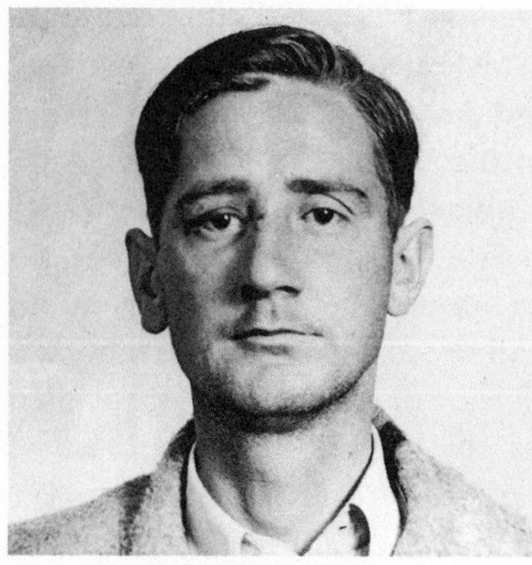

Fig. 3.11. Myles O'Donnell.

never arrested or penalized for a major crime. However, Myles was tubercular and did not live to see the end of Prohibition. Bernard O'Donnell, ever present but never overly important, was the third of the brothers in this mob.

This group was made up heavily of Irish Americans. The O'Donnell brothers' other prominent gang mates included James Doherty (often spelled Dougherty), who ran a saloon on W. Roosevelt with Myles O'Donnell and was one of their top men; Tom "Red" Duffy; and Edward "Shaggers" Hanley, a former police officer who was the driver and bodyguard for Myles. One of their more notable escapades involved siphoning whiskey with hoses from barrels stored at the Morand brothers' bonded government warehouse on S. May Street in Chicago in March 1927. "Klondike" O'Donnell, George Davis (aka James Driscoll), John Barry, and James "Fur" Sammons were sent to federal prison for that offense.[57]

Regarding the West Side O'Donnells, John Barry, aka "West Side Jack" Barry, was a bootlegger and a labor racketeer of some note who grew up on the Near West Side. "Fur" Sammons, whose real name was

James Sammon, was one of Chicago's most dangerous and demented characters, during the Dry Era or otherwise. He was first sent to prison in 1900 for his part in the rape of an eleven-year-old girl.[58] Only three months after his parole in 1903, he shot and killed South Side saloonkeeper Patrick Barrett during a robbery and was eventually sentenced to life imprisonment. Obliging Illinois governor Len Small commuted that to a fifty-year sentence in 1923, allowing Sammons to be paroled a year later.

Sammons was less than five feet three inches tall, but he compensated for his lack of height by becoming an expert with a submachine gun. His later boss Al Capone made sure that Sammons was accompanied by bodyguards when he went out on a gangland hit.[59] The goal was not to protect Sammons; instead, Capone was trying to shield the public from the man, because he liked to shoot at pedestrians with his submachine gun as a form of target practice when he was driving around Chicago.

THE CIRCUS GANG

The Circus (or Circus Café) Gang controlled the West Chicago Avenue police district. It included the traditional southern Italian neighborhood along Grand Avenue that in 1920 ran from the river to roughly Western Avenue. The gang's headquarters was the Circus Café, located initially near Ashland Avenue and W. North Avenue and later, more famously, about two blocks west of there. The café itself was owned by Tony "Tough Tony" Capezio, Claude "Screwy" Maddox (whose real name was John Edward Moore), and Raymond McGinnis (aka Johnny Shocker, Ray Shocker, and Ray Schulte). Capezio and Maddox were the acknowledged leaders of the gang.[60]

Maddox was born in 1901 in St. Louis, Missouri. He served in the army during World War I and reached the rank of sergeant in Company E of the Eighteenth Infantry Regiment. After the war he served jail terms for petty larceny in St. Louis in 1919 and 1920 while he was a member of the notorious Egan's Rats gang.[61] Based on the US Census for 1920, Maddox left the Gateway City sometime after January 3, 1920. He was certainly in Chicago by 1922 at the latest,

Fig. 3.12. John Moore aka Claude Maddox.

Fig. 3.13. "Tough Tony" Capezio (left).

since he was arrested by the city's police four times that year.[62] Additionally, he and Anthony Kissane were involved in a battle with rival bootleggers in November 1924, and Maddox was a suspect in the 1925 slaying in Chicago of police officer Patrick McGovern, who was safeguarding a deposit from the Pantheon theater to a bank.[63] His criminal portfolio included further arrests for burglary, vagrancy, carrying concealed weapons, disorderly conduct, auto theft, and assault with a deadly weapon.

Tony Capezio was born in 1901 and lived in the Grand Avenue neighborhood in the early 1920s. Between 1920 and 1928 he was charged with vagrancy, disorderly conduct, motor vehicle violations, assault, robbery, and violation of the Volstead Act.[64] Raymond McGinnis was a two-gun man from St. Louis, meaning that he carried two guns at all times. The usual method was to have them in shoulder holsters under each arm, but some gunmen favored holsters elsewhere or even coat pockets. He had ties to noted St. Louis desperado, robber, and killer Fred "Killer" Burke.

By far the most famous alumnus of the Circus Gang was Antonino Leonardo Accardo, the young son of an Italian shoemaker who was born in 1906 on Grand Avenue near Ashland Avenue in Chicago.[65] Accardo's maiden offense was a motor vehicle violation in 1922. It was followed by ten arrests for disorderly conduct from 1923 to 1928.[66] According to one account, Accardo's nickname "Joe Batters" stemmed from when he was a young man around Grand Avenue on Chicago's Near West Side. Regardless of whether it was given to him by Al Capone (as is usually claimed) or some time earlier, he clearly reveled in it, telling the census taker in 1930 that his name was Joseph Batters.[67] Other notable Circus Gang members included Tony Capezio's brother Dominick; John Borcia (aka Borcy), who was later a prominent gambler in Los Angeles; and Jimmy "the Swede" Johnson. Johnson came from St. Louis and served time in the Illinois state penitentiary at Pontiac where he met Louis Campagna, who was his introduction into organized crime in Chicago. Johnson was Claude Maddox's roommate in Chicago for several years and occasionally used the last name Moran.[68]

The Circus gangsters were rivals of the North Side gang and therefore allies of the Torrio-Capone forces in the later gang wars.

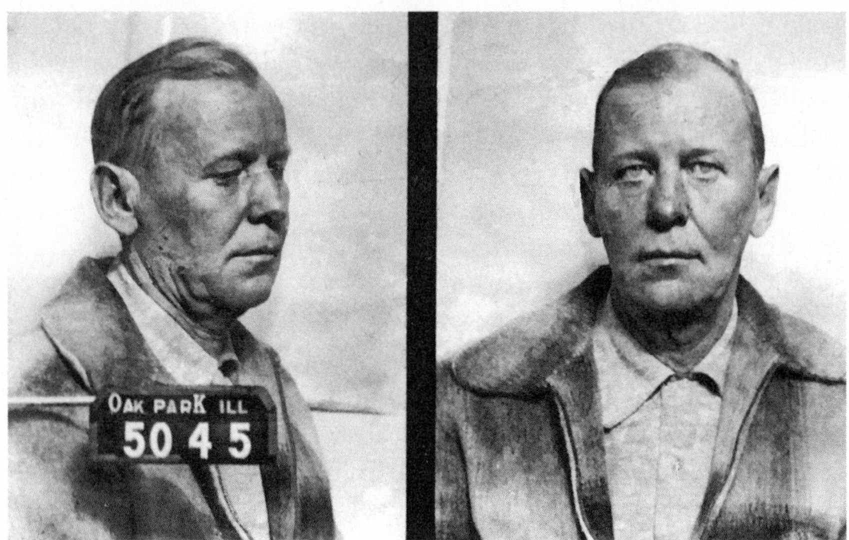

Fig. 3.14. Jimmy "the Swede" Johnson. (Image from Chicago History Museum, ICHi-092808.)

According to "John Smith" who knew Maddox personally, North Sider George "Bugs" Moran told him very undiplomatically during a meeting that his gang was going to work with the North Siders; the only question was whether Maddox would be dead or alive.[69] The independent and extremely ferocious Maddox, who was otherwise predisposed to work with his mostly non-Italian gangland neighbors on the other side of the Chicago River, responded by going with Al Capone instead, giving the latter an important beachhead on the Northwest Side.

THE GENNA GANG

The area from approximately the Chicago River on the east to Kinzie Street on the north, Kedzie Avenue on the west, and Roosevelt Road on the south was the home of the six Genna brothers and their gang. They were the children of Tony Genna and Maria Lucari and came from Marsala, Sicily.[70] According to one account, James (born as Vincenzo) Genna was the overall leader.[71] Angelo, the youngest of the six, was the hard case among the brothers. He was active, along with other Genna gangsters, on the side of aldermanic candidate Anthony D'Andrea in the Nineteenth Ward political wars in the early 1920s that led to thirty deaths.[72] Michele aka Mike Genna was known as "the Devil" and was the disreputable one of the bunch. The brothers kept him subordinated with low-level tasks related to violence, while Tony (born Antonino), the polished aristocrat of the family, remained aloof from the dirty work. Salvatore, known as "Sam," handled the gang's political connections, and Pete ran a saloon. The Gennas had a cozy relationship with the police officers in the Maxwell Street district who enforced the law, more or less, in the southern tip of their domain. The police regularly lined up in front of the Genna headquarters, a warehouse on W. Taylor Street near Morgan Street, for their payoff money. In return, they sometimes escorted Genna alcohol shipments to the far corners of the city so that they were not interfered with by either side of the law.[73]

Fig. 3.15. James Genna.

Fig. 3.16. Pete Genna.

The brothers began their bootlegging careers by peddling a little wine along Taylor Street, the main thoroughfare in the heavily Italian enclave they soon controlled, at the start of the Dry Era. They

Fig. 3.17. Angelo Genna.

quickly went on to much broader endeavors, setting up a massive (in aggregate) cottage industry in alcohol distilling through the Unione Siciliana, an organization that will be discussed shortly. Attorney Henry Spingola, whose sister Lucille later married Angelo Genna, developed the idea of paying ordinary citizens, mostly Italian immigrants, to operate stills in their homes for the Unione.[74] The Unione's alky-cooking operations went well beyond Chicago's Near West Side. They extended into various parts of the city and into the Chicago suburbs, as well as Gary, Indiana. The ingredients were supplied to them, and the alcohol was picked up by the bootleggers on a weekly basis. In return, the still tender received a nice salary for a small amount of work.

The economics of distilling are interesting. In terms of pure alcohol, a one-thousand-gallon still, if allowed to operate for thirty days before the gangsters and the local police arranged for it to be raided to placate higher authorities, produced thirty thousand gallons of alcohol. The alcohol generated $150,000 of revenue, against the $25,000 cost of the equipment, $25,000 for operating expenses and the legal representation provided for the alky cookers when they were arrested, plus the $50,000 bribe paid so the still could operate for a month without being raided.[75] The Genna brothers benefitted handsomely from this business, although much of the production in the Unione's network was on a much smaller scale than the one-thousand-gallon still just discussed. The Gennas' gross revenues from pure alcohol were estimated at $4.2 million and their profits at $1.8 million per year.[76] The six brothers had an estimated combined wealth in 1924 of $5 million.

The Unione Siciliana, whose Illinois chapter was incorporated on

September 17, 1895, was originally a fraternal and benevolent organization active in several cities.[77] Its leaders were linked to organized crime long before 1920, as indicated by a banquet photo taken in Colosimo's café in 1914, where Mike Merlo is sitting in a prominent position among the Colosimo gangsters.[78] The Genna gang had close ties to the Unione's Chicago head in the early 1920s, the aforementioned Anthony D'Andrea, and his successor, Mike Merlo.[79] In fact, Angelo Genna followed Merlo as the head of the Chicago branch after his death in 1924.[80] Similarly, Al Capone and his underling Carmen Vacco were close to Merlo and oversaw his funeral arrangements in 1924.[81]

The Unione's reputation was so unsavory that it officially elected retired judge Bernard Barasa president in 1921 to try and clean up the group's image. The organization's name was even changed to the Italo-American National Union in 1925. However, the *Chicago Tribune* in 1928 summarily dismissed Barasa as merely the "titular head" of the group, while over time a host of gangland characters were the real leaders.[82] Barasa was, in fact, far from irreproachable. Beyond his figurehead position with the Unione, he was a political crony of William "Big Bill" Thompson.[83] After several of the rechristened Unione's actual leaders were killed during Prohibition, the charade ended when former Capone bodyguard Phil D'Andrea took over the organization in 1934 and brought prominent Chicago mobsters such as Tony Accardo, Charlie Fischetti, Paul Ricca, John Capone, and Nick Circella in as members.[84]

John Scalisi (whose surname is usually spelled Scalise) and Albert Anselmi, the so-called "Murder Twins," were two of the Gennas' top killers. Anselmi first arrived in the United States in 1913 and returned again in November 1924 after going back to Italy for a time.[85] He came from the Gennas' hometown of Marsala. John Scalise emigrated from Italy to St. Louis before relocating to Chicago, and he ran a restaurant on S. Halsted. Another of the gang's gunmen was Orazio Tropea, known as "the Scourge." Tropea was dreaded by the Italian community for the extreme methods he used to collect the defense fund for the Murder Twins after they killed Chicago police detectives Harold Olson and Charles Walsh and wounded Michael Conway in one of the city's most flagrant gangland murders in June

Fig. 3.18. Albert Anselmi (left) and John Scalise (center).

1925. The well-dressed and very dangerous Salvatore Amatuna, nicknamed "Samoots," was a high-ranking member of the gang and ran the Unione Siciliana for a brief time.[86] As these names indicate, the Genna gang was primarily composed of Italian immigrants and Italian Americans.

THE COOK–VOGEL GANG

South of the West Side O'Donnell's bailiwick, the Lawndale district was controlled in 1924 by a gang under Ernie "Butch" Cook and George "Dutch" Vogel, who had a beer storage facility across the street from the police station.[87] Both men were products of the Valley Gang. In fact, Vogel killed a Chicago police detective in Valley Gang leader Paddy Ryan's saloon on S. Halsted in February 1919.[88] In his younger days, Vogel was a pickpocket, burglar, and robber whose police record dated back to 1901.[89] He was called "Immunity Vogel" by the newspapers due to his ability to avoid punishment, and in 1920 he ran a saloon in the vicinity of Douglas Park on the city's Near West Side. George Vogel should not be confused with 1920s Cicero racketeer Edward Vogel, known as "Big Eddie" Vogel. Eddie Vogel was Bohemian while George Vogel was of German—often referred to in the United States as "Dutch"—extraction. "Butch" Cook was a prominent saloonkeeper who was also active in labor racketeering.[90] Frank "Porky" Dillon (who reportedly had some bootlegging interests farther south around Marquette Park), Daniel Hartnett, and Frank Reda were other members of this gang.

THE VALLEY GANG

The neighborhood known as the Valley, bounded roughly by Fourteenth Street on the north, Canal Street on the east, Sixteenth Street on the south, and Racine on the west, was a few blocks south of the Genna headquarters. It was just south of the Maxwell Street entry port for Eastern European Jewish immigrants to Chicago. Once heavily Irish, it was home to the Valley Gang, a rough-and-tumble crew of robbers and thieves in the days before Prohibition who were an outgrowth of the Henry Street gang that had plagued the neighborhood in the 1890s.

"Ammunition Eddie" Wheed led the gang in the years before 1920. He confessed to police that he was behind twenty or more robberies in the twelve months before the payroll holdup at the Winslow Brothers Iron Works in which he killed two messengers with a shotgun.[91] Wheed was hanged in February 1918 for his part in those murders. Paddy "the Bear" Ryan, so called because of his fighting style, succeeded Wheed as the gang's leader until he was killed in his saloon in June 1920 by a fellow gang member.[92]

Ryan was followed by Terry Druggan, whose real name was Drugan, as head of the gang.[93] Born in 1897, Druggan was three-quarters Irish. His closest aide, and for years his inseparable companion, was Frankie Lake. Lake was born in 1893 and was three-quarters

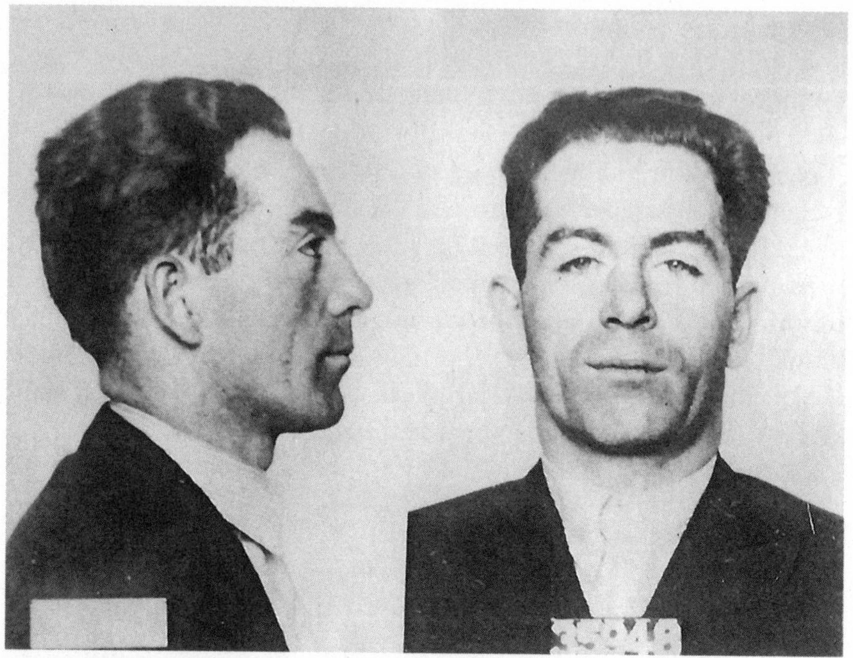

Fig. 3.19. Terry Druggan.

Fig. 3.20. Frank Lake.

German and one-quarter Irish. He worked as a Chicago fireman before Prohibition, and his father was a city ward superintendent. One source describes Druggan as an impetuous leader who frequently made the headlines, while the very calm and deliberate Lake got the important things done in the background.[94]

From their headquarters in the Little Bohemia café on S. Loomis, the Valley (or Druggan-Lake) Gang controlled most of the Maxwell and Marquette police districts. The Valley produced a number of Chicago's important bootleggers, including, beyond those already mentioned, John Touhy of the northwest suburban Touhy gang and "Red" Bolton. Due to their close ties to other gangs, Druggan and Lake had easy access to Lake County, Illinois, where they wholesaled beer to a local mobster. They were also active at one time in the adjoining counties of DuPage and McHenry. But before they worked with the Valley Gang, the McHenry County authorities had to learn how to create an unholy alliance. Fortunately for them, Hymie Weiss and Dan McCarthy were available to instruct Sheriff Lester Eddinger and other officials during the months they spent in the McHenry County jail on a bootlegging conviction.[95]

Shrewdly, Druggan and Lake quickly bought a major interest in five breweries from the Stenson family: the Stege on S. Ashland, the Standard on S. Campbell, the Gambrinus (later called the Illinois Beverage Company) on W. Fillmore, the Hoffman on W. Monroe, and the Pfeiffer Products Company on N. Leavitt.[96] The other owners of the Standard included several aldermen and state legislators from both political parties, and even a congressman.[97] The Standard had an impressive output of five thousand barrels of beer per day, or, if run seven days a week, roughly 1.8 million barrels a year. Based on the purchase prices of the other four breweries, their combined beer output rivaled that of the Standard and gave the gang a brewing capacity of over 3.5 million barrels a year.[98] For a time, they ran their breweries in high gear, supplying their own customers as well as wholesaling to their allies, such as the Torrio-Capone gang and most likely selling beer to the Gennas because several of their breweries were in Genna territory.

When the retail price (to the saloon) was fifty-five dollars a barrel, Druggan and Lake sold their beer wholesale to other gangs at thirty dollars per barrel. Their costs, which most likely were just the direct costs of production, were two dollars per barrel.[99] The graft paid to officialdom was estimated at around $7.50 per barrel.[100] While there were a variety of other costs involved, such as salaries of gang members as well as compensation for likely time in jail and the other hazards involved in the gangster life, the profits per barrel appear to have been very large, which is consistent with the fortunes amassed by top gangsters. The federal government estimated the Druggan-Lake gross revenues through January 1926 from brewing beer at $15 million, earning them about $2 million a year in profit.[101]

Fig. 3.21. William Druggan (right).

Fig. 3.22. George Druggan.

Sadly for the bootleggers, this foamy Nirvana inside the city limits could not last forever. In April 1924, Reverend Elmer Williams, now with the Better Government Association (BGA), reported that only seven old-time breweries were still running in Chicago, as opposed to sixty-five operating before Prohibition and fourteen running in 1923, and he named three of the Druggan-Lake properties among them.[102] In return for his crusading efforts, the bootlegging elements bombed the reverend's house on N. Winchester on April 28, 1924, blowing out the front of the structure.[103] It was bombed again in January 1925.

However, Reverend Williams's work was not in vain. A federal judge issued injunctions closing the gang's breweries, the last one for the Hoffman in August 1924. At that time, Druggan and Lake had already been sentenced to a year in jail for Prohibition-related violations at their other properties. For example, when dry agent Brice Armstrong inspected the Standard, he found beer flowing from the brewery through pipes to a garage across the street, where it was put in barrels and then moved by truck.[104] By November

1924 a radical change had occurred. Only five pre-Prohibition breweries were operating inside the city, and all of them were making near beer.[105] The bootleggers who were not needling near beer with alcohol were forced to import the real thing from Wisconsin and other locations outside Chicago or to run smaller, clandestine breweries in garages and other buildings in the city.[106]

Terry Druggan's brothers George and William also belonged to the Valley Gang, as did their uncle on their mother's side, Robert "Unk" Long. Outside the family, there was a larger cast of characters: gunman Danny Vallo; Grover Dullard, who was Terry Druggan's driver and bodyguard at one time; Henry Sullivan, who served Frankie Lake in a similar capacity; and Martin O'Leary. On one occasion, George Druggan provided some painful, yet comic, relief to gangland. When he was shot in the back by a rifle in December 1927, he told police that it was a self-inflicted wound that happened accidentally when he was on his way to go hunting![107]

THE TWENTIETH WARD GANG

Just north of the Valley, between roughly Roosevelt Road and Maxwell Street, was the Maxwell Street neighborhood. It was completely inside the Druggan-Lake territory, which caused friction at times. At the start of Prohibition, this district was controlled by the Twentieth Ward gang, a collection of largely Jewish hoods who were initially led by Hirschie Miller and "Nails" Morton. This group doubled as sluggers for the political heavyweight in the ward, Morris Eller.[108] Hirschie Miller, a one-time boxer who was known as the toughest man on the West Side, ran the Hirschie Miller Benevolent and Athletic Club before 1920. On August 23, 1920, he shot and killed two off-duty Chicago police detectives he and Morton had quarreled with, reportedly over a liquor deal.[109] Three of his brothers, Davy, a boxing referee, Max, and Al, were active participants in gangland, including conducting some gambling in the Lawndale neighborhood. Another brother, Harry, was a Chicago police officer who was also fond of breaking the law.[110] Boxer William "Sailor" Friedman, Dave Edelman, Sammy "the Greener" Jacobson, Johnny Armando,

Jules Portugese, Sammy Kaplan, and Nate Goldberg were actively involved in this group at one time or another.[111]

THE SHELDON–STANTON GANG

Moving farther south, the Sheldon-Stanton gang controlled the Stockyards police district. Although this gang was originally one unit with the Saltis-McErlane mob, because they split in late 1925 the two are discussed separately in this chapter. Ralph Sheldon, who was born in October 1901, was their leader after the breakup. Of Irish lineage, he was a railroad switchman, at least according to what he told the census taker in 1920. In reality, Sheldon was arrested numerous times before 1921 for robbery and burglary before graduating to bigger and more violent crimes.

Many of the gang's members were Irish Americans who lived in the heavily Irish South Side area they controlled. Danny Stanton, the son of a private watchman, was born in September 1896 and was cited for valor in World War I.[112] Early in his career, he worked as a slugger for the Checker cab company during its struggles with the rival Yellow cab concern. A description of Stanton's criminal escapades

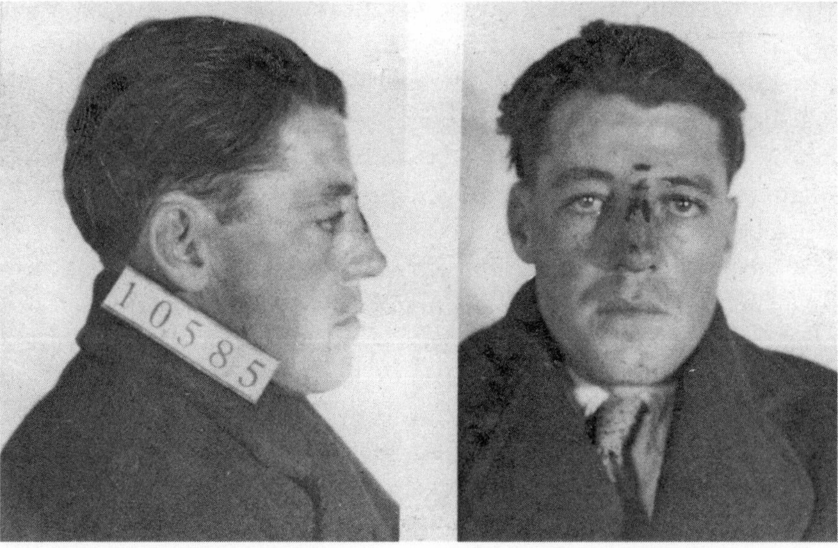

Fig. 3.23. Ralph Sheldon.

in the files of the *Chicago Tribune* states that he "has been arrested so many times since he first broke into print . . . that it's hard to count them up."[113] Later in his career, his future mother-in-law charged Stanton with abducting her daughter, who was married to another man at the time, and holding her prisoner.[114]

Fig. 3.24. Danny Stanton.

Stanley Sheldon, Ralph's brother, was prominent in the organization's ranks until he was shot and killed by a police officer during election-related violence in 1925.[115] Other gang members of note were Edgar "Hiker" Smith, who was Stanton's roommate in 1920 and later served as his bodyguard; Danny McFall, a municipal court bailiff and sometimes political candidate; Herbert "Red" Golden, Sheldon's partner in a saloon; and the appropriately nicknamed Joe "Bullets" Newton.

The Sheldon-Stanton gang drew heavily from the Ragen's Colts, a notorious social-athletic club of the era, of which Stanton had been an officer at one time.[116] The Colts were named after Frank Ragen, who earlier was the star pitcher on their baseball team. In 1916 they had almost two thousand members, and, according to Ragen, at the group's height the figure grew to three thousand.[117] The organization had two distinctly opposite sides. On one end, a number of its members became successful, law-abiding citizens and achieved notoriety as civic leaders and athletes. A fiercely patriotic bunch, 462 of the Colts were in military uniform in April 1918.[118]

However, there was also a wild, violent side to the Colts that gave them a criminality that few social-athletic clubs of the day equaled. One reporter describes them as "for nearly 20 years . . . the best of the [S]outh [S]ide schools of crime."[119] Another article refers to their clubhouse on S. Halsted as "long a hangout for Chicago's toughest gangsters."[120] Surrounding neighborhoods, which rightly saw them as a threat, formed their own clubs in defense against them.

The Colts' dances were as depraved as the earlier First Ward balls. As one observer stated in 1915, "No Roman saturnalia could have been wilder than that dance. We thought we had improved conditions a little, but a glimpse at the revel of the 'Ragen Colts' showed how mistaken we were. The old costumes—baby doll, French doll, boy's attire, pajamas—all made their appearance again."[121] The club's New Year's ball at the Coliseum in 1918 was little better than an orgy. According to a report by the Juvenile Protective Association (JPA), it was "[t]he vilest dance ever attended by our officers." The observer noted that "startling indecencies, gross misconduct, wholesale intoxication, and general violation of city ordinances were found on a greatly enlarged scale."[122]

There was also a racist element to the Colts, which was likely related to the expanding African American community to the east of their neighborhood. For example, on March 7, 1926, Sheldon-Stanton gangster Hugh "Stubby" McGovern and David "Yiddles" Miller lured a black man, James Thompson, to the rear of the Colts' clubhouse with the promise of free drinks. After forcing him to commit indecent acts, they stabbed and fatally shot Thompson.[123] According to the police, this was not an isolated incident.[124] Furthermore, the Colts figured prominently in Chicago's 1919 race riot when the Near South Side exploded after a young African American boy was stoned to death for swimming near a "white's only" beach.[125]

THE De COURSEY GANG

At or near the south end of the Sheldon-Stanton sphere of control and apparently on very good terms with Ralph Sheldon, the De Coursey gang produced beer and alcohol, which it distributed to several other states.[126] The leaders were David, Thomas, and John De Coursey (whose original family name was DeCourcey). David De Coursey began his criminal career as an armed robber and later owned a saloon near Forty-Second and Wentworth.[127] His brother Thomas appears to have been a newspaper slugger some years earlier. He helped sell 1,750 cases of bonded whiskey stolen from the Sibley warehouse in 1924.[128] Victor and Joseph Armanda, Joe Brandenberg, Miles Smith, Ed Crosby, and Frank Ostrowski were members of the De Coursey gang.

THE SALTIS–McERLANE GANG

West of Halsted Street, the New City police district was controlled by Joe (often ethnically erroneously referred to as "Polack Joe") Saltis and his top aide Frank McErlane. New City contained about three hundred saloons, and it was one of the best beer districts in Chicago. As Saltis said about his operations inside Chicago to police captain John Stege, "My district extends from Thirty-Ninth to Fifty-[F]ifth sts., and from the city limits to Loomis st. And I'll kill any [expletive] who cut in on my business."[129] The Saltis-McErlane gang also operated in the suburbs of Evergreen Park and Oak Lawn and in the area west of there, using the Nineteenth Hole at Roberts Road and Ninety-Fifth Street as a headquarters, which gave them a good-sized piece of the southwestern suburbs.[130]

Fig. 3.25. Joe Saltis. (Courtesy of J. Mark Weber, Chicago.)

Joe Saltis was born in Budapest, Hungary, on September 8, 1894 and came to the United States when he was twelve years old.[131] His father was an officer in the Austro-Hungarian army, and the original spelling of the last name was Soltis. Saltis worked in the stockyards when he was young and later as a mechanic at the Continental Bolt and Iron Company. He also boxed at one time. Unlike most of his gangland contemporaries, Saltis was an expert marksman. The Winchester company paid him to test and use their guns in competitions, and he preferred a lever-action Winchester rifle when game hunting. His only known arrest before Prohibition was for burglary in 1911.[132]

Saltis's partner in crime, was Frank McErlane, who one watchdog agency referred to as "the most cruel, dangerous, and vicious type of criminal."[133] He was also labeled quite correctly as "the most vicious killer in the country."[134] While most other mobsters killed because they felt it was necessary, McErlane likely enjoyed it. According to the 1900 US Census, his father kept a saloon on Eggleston on the South Side, which might explain his fondness for drink. During his criminal career Frank McErlane was arrested on charges of vagrancy, disorderly conduct, murder, carrying concealed weapons, conspiracy, reckless driving, fornication, being a fugitive, larceny (including stealing a horse and separately an auto), robbery, accessory to murder, aiding a prisoner to escape, and kidnapping. In 1913 McErlane was an associate of auto bandit Teddy Webb and later belonged to a gang led by Lloyd Bopp, both of whom were extremely desperate men. Webb killed Chicago police detective Peter Hart in 1913, and Bopp, accompanied by McErlane, killed Oak

Fig. 3.26. Frank McErlane.

Park policeman Herman Mallow and wounded another officer on June 14, 1916.[135]

Joe Pollak was an old-time hard liquor dealer who handled that end of the bootlegging in the Saltis area as an independent partner.[136] Pete Kusanski, known as "Three-Fingered Pete," had two fingers shot from his hand by the police in 1920. He was the number three man in the Saltis-McErlane mob until he did away with the rest of himself on October 23, 1926, when he tripped and the nitroglycerine he was carrying in his coat pocket exploded.[137] In his place, John "Dingbat" O'Berta, who was of Polish extraction—according to the 1920 US Census his real name was Obyrtacz—rose to prominence in the gang. An active gunman with Saltis in the mid-1920s, he was just below Saltis and McErlane in the hierarchy, and by 1928 he was also the Republican committeeman of the Thirteenth Ward. Saltis's brothers Steve and John were involved in the gang to one extent or another, as was McErlane's brother Vincent, who was repeatedly arrested for larceny, robbery, burglary, and auto theft before 1920.[138] Saltis and McErlane could also call on hard men such as Frank "Lefty" Koncil (aka Koncel), who played baseball at one time; George Darrow, who

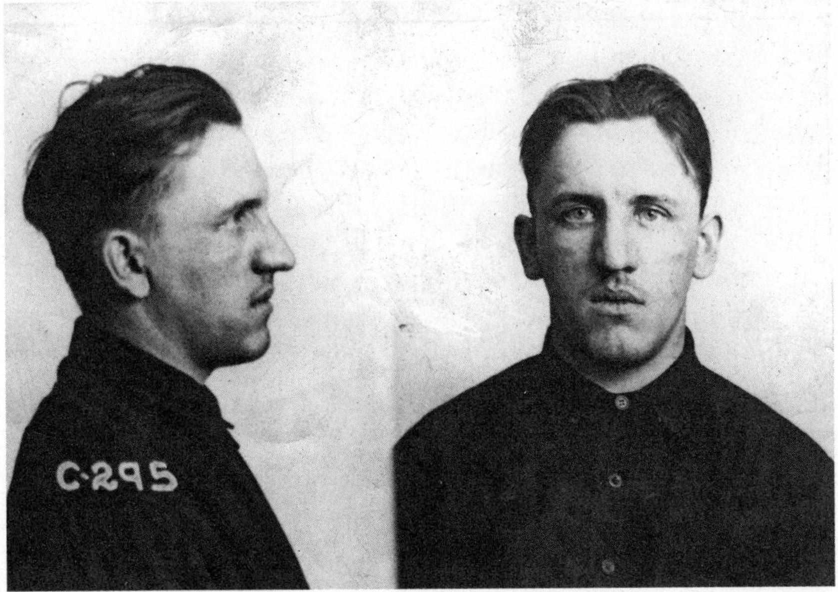

Fig. 3.27. Vincent McErlane.

was the torturer in their outfit; Patrick "Paddy" Sullivan, a former Chicago police officer who was Saltis's bodyguard; and killers of the caliber of Willie Niemoth, Nick Kramer, and "Big Earl" Herbert whenever they were needed.

THE SOUTH SIDE O'DONNELL GANG

The South Side O'Donnells, led by James Edward "Spike" O'Donnell, were by far the largest band of brothers in Prohibition Era gangdom and the most misunderstood of the bootlegging gangs in Chicago. According to the usual accounts, Spike went to prison at the beginning of the Dry Era and was not released until 1923.[139] It is claimed that in the interim his brothers were not a force in bootlegging; only when Spike O'Donnell returned to Chicago did they assemble a gang that tried to break into the existing order.

In reality, nothing could be further from the truth. Spike O'Donnell was sent to the state penitentiary in Joliet in February 1919 for the robbery of the Stockmen's Trust and Savings bank in December 1917. But he was released on a writ in June 1919, and he did not go back to prison until December 13, 1922. Due to his vast political influence, he was paroled on June 30, 1923.[140] Not only was O'Donnell around Chicago for essentially the first three years of Prohibition, but his gang was of major importance before 1923 as well as for almost the next decade, which also conflicts with what has been written previously.

For example, his brother Charles O'Donnell brought 350 cases of beer into Chicago on a boat in 1919.[141] In 1920, Spike O'Donnell was running beer from a Joliet brewery to the city, and in 1922, he was called a "beer agent."[142] Steve O'Donnell was caught bringing beer into Chicago in 1923 while Spike was in prison.[143] Regarding the situation at that time, one newspaper states,

> They [the South Side O'Donnells] were in the beer business seriously. Even while he was doing his bit in "stir," "Spike" O'Donnell gave the closest attention to the business with Steve and Walter and Tommy O'Donnell, his brothers, acting as his agents.[144]

Fig. 3.28. James Edward "Spike" O'Donnell.

Of equal importance, at the time of his parole Spike was known as the "head of a beer running syndicate" and his gang had "a virtual monopoly of the beer business on the [S]outhwest [S]ide, under police protection."[145] Therefore, the O'Donnell brothers clearly were quite active in the field of bootlegging before 1923, which is consistent with them having a thriving gang that operated, at minimum, on a large part of the South Side.

Determining the territory controlled by the South Side O'Donnell gang is somewhat

Fig. 3.29. Steve O'Donnell (with the cigar).

more difficult. The consensus opinion of the contemporary sources, exemplified by two maps that show the situation around 1930, is that the Torrio-Capone gang did not have the bootlegging rights on the far South Side.[146] Similarly, the police officer who wrote using the pseudonym "John Law" in 1930 has the Capone gang operating only as far south as the Sixth Ward, which did not extend beyond Sixty-Seventh Street.[147] Also, in the newspaper accounts of Eliot Ness's raids no Capone brewery or distillery was located south of Sixty-Seventh Street nor is one mentioned in the 1931 indictment of Al Capone and his associates for bootlegging. Furthermore, in 1931, well after Frank McErlane joined forces with the South Side O'Donnells, McErlane, Spike O'Donnell, and a number of their gang mates lived in the Gresham police district or in the South Shore neighborhood. If this was Capone territory, it would not have been a safe place for them to hang their hats when they were fighting Capone's allies.

Significantly, Hal Andrews states that Frank McErlane, when he led his own gang from 1931 to 1932, was in control of most of the far South Side.[148] Andrews notes further that this area was in the hands of the Spike O'Donnell mob when McErlane, after leaving the Saltis gang, was his chief lieutenant from 1929 to early 1931. When the O'Donnell-McErlane gang split up in 1931, McErlane took the bulk of their territory—roughly the area south of Seventy-First street on the east side of State Street and south of Ninety-Ninth street on the west side of State Street—with him while the newly formed Downs-McGeoghegan-Quinlan (DMQ) gang grabbed one police district and the South Side O'Donnells retained two others.[149]

If Torrio and Capone did not have the far South Side in the years just after 1920, and there are no reports of it having been taken from them (or from Joe Saltis or Danny Stanton), then how did O'Donnell and McErlane get it? Either Spike O'Donnell's group controlled it previously or McErlane brought it with him when he left the Saltis gang in 1929. No evidence suggests that the Saltis gang had this territory at one time or that McErlane took it peacefully from Saltis when they parted company.[150] In fact, by Saltis's own admission his bailiwick in the city in 1927 was only the New City police district. Also, if Frank McErlane had brought this much into a partnership with Spike O'Donnell, surely he would have been the boss and O'Donnell would have been the subordinate in their joint gang as opposed to the other way around.

Consistent with this conclusion, Joseph Bucher, when asked where he delivered O'Donnell beer in 1923, answered, "On the South and West Sides. Sure, they drink it all over."[151] Also, a truckload of champagne belonging to the O'Donnells was intercepted in 1924 at Sixtieth and State Streets, which is at the junction of the Englewood and Woodlawn police districts.[152] Furthermore, as discussed in chapter 6, in 1933 Joe Saltis controlled the Southeast Side of Chicago, which he would have inherited from Frank McErlane as a result of their renewed partnership in 1932. These facts reinforce the conclusion that this area was never in the hands of Capone and Torrio. Therefore, the most likely scenario is that the South Side O'Donnells operated primarily south of Fifty-Fifth Street, in the area west of State Street, and south of about Seventy-First Street on the east side of State Street at the beginning of Prohibition. Like the far Northwest Side, much of this neck of the woods was not densely populated during the 1920s, and some of these areas were also uppercrust neighborhoods that had been dry earlier or did not tolerate lawlessness. In consequence, the bootlegging districts on the far South Side were not nearly as profitable as many others in the city. Spike O'Donnell's gang also controlled the suburb of Summit, near Sixty-Third Street and Harlem Avenue.

Spike O'Donnell was born in Chicago on November 29, 1889, to Patrick and Anna O'Donnell, who were both Irish.[153] He started out as an election and labor slugger and was arrested for various robberies and burglaries before 1920.[154] O'Donnell also operated a saloon on W. Forty-Seventh Street in 1918, and he may have boxed at one time.[155] Of his many brothers the seven oldest, Charles, Tommy, Percy, Steve, Walter, John, and Ray, were all part of the action. The only exception was Leo, who was likely too young to be involved because he was born in December 1911. Conspicuous in the O'Donnell ranks were Spike's brother-in-law, William Barcal, his bodyguard, Joe Cainski, and top gunman James "Daffy" Quigley.

THE TORRIO–CAPONE GANG

A large section of the South Side near the lake, beginning at Madison Street and extending to about Seventy-First Street, along with the Deering and Brighton Park police districts just below the south branch of the Chicago River and its extension, was in the hands of Colosimo's old gang at the start of 1924. It controlled a total of eight police districts, plus much of the Loop, which was the best bootlegging province in the city given the multitude of hotels, bars, and nightclubs there that served locals and tourists. Importantly, the gang's control of Deering and Brighton Park gave it easy access to western suburbs such as Cicero.

Led by John Torrio, this group is initially called the Torrio-Capone gang. After Capone replaced Torrio in 1925, it is referred to as the Capone gang. Torrio was in several ways the antithesis of Colosimo. Quiet and well spoken, he reportedly did not partake of any of the pleasures his business offered. Instead, Torrio spent his evenings at home reading and listening to music with his wife.[156] It is accurate to describe him as a vegetarian who just happened to manage the best steakhouse in the city. However, when it came to business, Torrio was all business. He understood that the objective was to enrich himself and the gang; everything else was secondary. His watchword was, "We don't want any trouble," and he went to great lengths to avoid it, unlike some of the hotheads who led other bootlegging mobs.[157]

Although Torrio did not have a college education, he was a sage business strategist. He is credited with calling Chicago's various bootlegging gangs together in June 1920 during the early days of Prohibition.[158] Torrio proposed a cartel agreement dividing up the city along geographical lines, based on the sections each gang already controlled. Each group was granted a monopoly in its own area, and it was to stay in that area. The separate gangs could, if they desired, buy the beer they sold to the speakeasies in their areas from Torrio or other cartel members. The agreement was a smart move that anticipated various potential problems before they happened. But it was far from perfect.

Alphonse Capone was born in Brooklyn to law-abiding Italian

immigrant parents on January 17, 1899. He and several of his brothers started out as members of a local street gang before advancing into the ranks of organized crime as young men. According to the most reliable accounts, Capone came to Chicago in 1919.[159] By his own admission in 1926, he had been in Cook County, Illinois, for about seven years.[160] Certainly his arrest in New York City in 1919 for disorderly conduct indicates that he was most probably still there during at least part of that year.[161] Frankie Yale, his boss in Brooklyn, convinced Capone to leave town before rival gangster "Wild Bill" Lovett killed him in retaliation for his attacks on Lovett's men. According to statements he made in 1932, Capone worked for seven years in a box company and then became the manager of a "dance hall in New York City. Six months later he resigned to accept a similar position at Chicago."[162] This evidence strongly contradicts the claim that he worked for a construction company in Baltimore for two years before coming to Chicago.[163]

When he arrived in the Windy City, Capone started at the bottom. Various Levee old-timers remembered him working as a roper/doorman/bouncer at the Four Deuces on S. Wabash.[164] Obviously, this version of the events differs greatly from the claim that John Torrio arranged for Capone to join him as a partner.[165] If Torrio, who was permanently based in Chicago by 1909 at the latest, knew Capone before he left New York, Capone would have been a small boy in knee pants, someone who would hardly have made an important impression on a much older gang leader.[166] Therefore, the accounts by Robert Schoenberg and William Balsamo and John Balsamo of how Al Capone came to Chicago are much more plausible than what appears in print elsewhere.[167]

Capone's level of formal education is unclear. If what a booking officer at the Cook County Jail recorded is correct, he had some high school education.[168] However, Capone told a psychiatrist at the federal penitentiary in Atlanta during an interview that he left school during the sixth grade at fourteen years of age.[169] While Capone's score of ninety-five on the Binet IQ test was not overly impressive, in reality he not only possessed a great deal of common sense but was also intelligent. The *Sioux City Journal* admits as much in 1931 when it says in an editorial, "He has wonderful powers of organization. He is a good executive. He is a dominant personality. All these traits, highly developed, are employed in the wrong direction, against society, but not because of feeblemindedness."[170] Capone would have been incapable of running an illegal, multimillion-dollar business otherwise. And this is consistent with his rapid rise from the bottom level of the Colosimo organization to the position of John Torrio's underboss by about 1923.

The details of Al Capone's first three or four years in Chicago are somewhat minimal, with little mention of him in the press. He was convicted in 1921, under the alias Al Brown, for operating slot machines and a house of ill repute in two locations in Burnham, one of which was the notorious Speedway Inn.[171] By 1922, he was back at the Four Deuces as the manager.[172] In 1924, Capone was most certainly Torrio's number two man; he would almost certainly not have had the income to make wagers on horse races that won him $500,000 in a few weeks if he was of lesser stature.[173]

The Torrio-Capone gang included a broad range of characters, many of whom were not part of the pre-Volstead Colosimo crime machine. At the muscle end of the spectrum, Jack Heinan, who was born John Heinen, was the toughest of the bunch. He fought nine times professionally between 1908 and 1921 and once worked as the sparring partner of heavyweight champion Jess Willard.[174] Heinan was active in bootlegging. Robert Lawrence "Big Bob" McCullough was, according to his testimony before the Kefauver Commission, a native Chicagoan and was arrested for burglary twice circa 1909.[175] He was recruited by Al Capone in about 1921 to work at the Roamer Inn at 115th and Western, just outside of Chicago, before becoming a brewery lookout and guard. From there, he graduated to serving as a Capone bodyguard and gunman.

Born in Italy on September 22, 1892, by the mid-1920s Frank Maritote (aka Frank Romano or Frank Diamond) was arrested for receiving stolen property, larceny, murder, keeping a gambling house, and burglary. In 1923, he was working as an armed guard on liquor shipments, and within a few years, he was one of Capone's bodyguards.[176] The Fischetti brothers, Charlie and Rocco, are believed to have been distant cousins of Capone.[177] They came to Chicago from Brooklyn in 1922 or 1923 and lived for a time in an apartment building, which likely housed a brothel as well, on Wabash Avenue near the Levee with Al and Ralph Capone.[178] Early in their careers, they served as bodyguards and killers in the Torrio-Capone organization.

Fig. 3.30. Frank Maritote working in his ice cream business.

Dennis Cooney, Nick Juffra, Ralph Capone, Jake Guzik, and Frank Nitti were in the managerial ranks of the gang. Cooney was born in the Valley district on February 24, most likely in 1878.[179] He and his twin brother John were frequently arrested by the police, but for the longest time were not convicted because they were impossible to tell apart.[180] Ultimately they were seen committing a crime together, neatly solving the identification problem for the authorities. Dennis Cooney was arrested in 1907 for causing the

Fig. 3.31. Charlie Fischetti.

Fig. 3.32. From left to right: "Klondike" O'Donnell, Jack White, Murray Humphreys, Marcus Looney, and Rocco Fischetti.

delinquency of a child, and by 1918 he was running a hotel and saloon (which was also a brothel) near Twenty-Second and State with William Marshall, one of the Marshall brothers who were Levee heavyweights before 1915.[181] In the early 1920s, Cooney was the gang's whoremaster, controlling all vice on the Near South Side while personally owning and operating the Frolics Café and the Rex hotel.[182]

Nick Juffra was born Nick Guiffra in Italy on May 13, 1896.[183] His earliest known arrest was in 1919 for pandering when he kept a nineteen-year-old woman in bondage in Burnham. Juffra was soon heavily involved with breweries and beer distribution, including setting up the World Motor Service Company, which acquired trucks for the gang, two of which were purchased by young Al Capone in 1921 under the alias Al Brown.[184] Juffra was arrested for bootlegging twenty-four times from the beginning of the Dry Era to June 1924, making him the leading violator in Chicagoland at the time of the Volstead Act.[185]

Ralph Capone was born in Naples, Italy, in 1894 and immigrated to the United States in 1895.[186] By his own account, he left New York in 1922, although his first arrest in Chicago occurred in 1921.[187] Ralph

Capone prospered in Chicago gangland by hanging on to his younger brother Al's coattails, working closely with him in setting up the gang's operations in and around Cicero and then managing various aspects of them. As Al Capone rose, so did his brother Ralph, which explains Ralph's later prominence in the gang. This process was repeated in reverse a few years later after Al Capone went to prison.

Jacob Guzik, who was more commonly known as Jake, although he preferred to be called Jack, was born in Russia in 1886 and came to the United States the following year.[188] A dour little man who was not prone to violence, Guzik had a calculator inside his head that made him invaluable to Torrio and Capone. He worked in the front offices of the organization, using his formidable brain to direct various business activities. Guzik most likely cut his teeth in the gambling profession after two years of high school education, while working in his father Max's cigar stores on the Near West Side and in the Levee district from 1902 to 1914.

From there Guzik entered the world of prostitution, as his frequent bouts with venereal disease attest to, first in the Levee and then in Burnham at the Speedway Inn, most certainly under the tutelage of his older brother Harry.[189] Harry Guzik got his start in vice in Custom House Place before moving with that crowd to the Twenty-Second Street Levee around 1903. The elder Guzik brother was attached for a time to Levee powerhouse Roy Jones, managing some of his properties before venturing out on his own on the South Side and in the south suburbs. Jake Guzik also committed bigamy when he eloped to Crown Point, Indiana, in August 1909 with Victoria Ullman even though he had married Rose Lipschultz there some thirty months earlier.[190]

Francesco Nitto, who was more commonly known as Frank Nitti, was born in Angri, just south of Naples, Italy, on January 27, 1886.[191] He is often claimed to have been a Capone cousin. If so, he was a second or more distant cousin. Possibly he was just a countryman, meaning an individual from the same region or town as the Capone brothers or their ancestors, whom the family was close to and whom they described to others with the loose Italian term "cousin."[192] Regardless of the exact relationship, Nitti lived only a few doors from the Capone family in Brooklyn at one time and belonged to the same youth gang as Al and several of his brothers.[193]

Fig. 3.33. Frank Nitti in court.

According to his World War I draft card, Nitti was in Chicago by 1918 at the latest, although there is evidence that he may have arrived as early as 1913. At the time of the Great War, he worked as a grocery broker who traveled to New York on business, which likely kept him in touch with family and old friends. On the side, Nitti was acquainted with a saloonkeeper and an imaginative criminal named Alex Louis Greenberg who was his entrée into fencing stolen goods and the liquor business.[194]

It would have been natural for the Capones to look Nitti up when they came to Chicago and likewise for him to later join the Torrio-Capone ranks on the Capones' recommendation, assuming that he was not involved with Colosimo and Torrio before Prohibition. Or perhaps Greenberg put Nitti in touch with his old Brooklyn neighbors after they arrived in Chicago and with John Torrio as well. In any case, Nitti, given his position with the Torrio-Capone outfit in 1925, was clearly in the gang by the early 1920s. He was a headquarters man, who worked at the Metropole hotel and the organization's other front offices where his skills in business, both legal and illegal, were put to good use. Nitti was never directly linked by the newspapers to gangland violence, as the nickname later given to him by the press, "The Enforcer," implies. There were scores of lower ranking and more able men who Nitti sent out when it was necessary to enforce edicts from the boss. The other label the reporters used frequently for Nitti, calling him the gang's treasurer, was much more appropriate during most of Prohibition.[195]

Building partly on Colosimo's vice activities outside the city, Torrio expanded further in the suburbs, primarily west of Chicago. Cicero, a hotbed of gambling long before the arrival of Torrio in that suburb, was rich with handbooks, slot machines, punchboards, chuck luck, poker, monte, faro, craps, and roulette.[196] A large number of gambling places were within two blocks of the massive Hawthorne Works plant at Cicero Avenue and Twenty-Second Street owned by the Western Electric Company. The local residents had the "gambling spirit," with some employees at the Hawthorne plant spending part of their lunch hour at the tables. Even the schoolchildren in Cicero regularly pumped coins into the slot machines.[197]

After reaching a forced accommodation with slot machine kingpin Eddie Vogel and town officials, the Torrio-Capone gang began selling beer and cooking alky in Cicero in the autumn of 1923 and moved into the existing gambling operations. In conjunction with Jimmy Mondi, Frankie Pope, and Al Lambert, they operated the Ship, the Subway, and Lauterbach's, where some nights the gambling was as fast and heavy as at any place in the country, as well as the Hawthorne Smoke Shop.[198] Parts of Cicero were soon peppered with illegal stills. Twenty large capacity distilleries were uncovered during just one series of raids there in early 1926.[199] Because prostitution was not tolerated in Cicero at the time, the Torrio-Capone bordellos were placed in nearby suburbs such as Stickney, Lyons, and, slightly later, Forest View. In the mid-1920s, Cicero generated $3 million a year for the Torrio-Capone gang.

Fig. 3.34. Eddie Vogel.

Torrio and Capone operated whenever possible on the Burnham model by winning control of the political apparatus in a town and thereby gaining a stranglehold on the entire entity. Their major suburban coup was the complete takeover of Cicero. The local Republicans were facing a stiff challenge from the Democrats in the April 1924 election and turned to the Torrio-Capone mob for assistance. On Torrio's behalf, Capone directed a multi-gang force—including muscle borrowed from the North Siders in exchange for a cut of the action in Cicero—that slugged and intimidated voters and election officials. In the process, Capone lost his brother Salvatore, aka Frank, who was killed by Chicago police detectives deputized to halt the violence, but a Republican victory was the end result. The Cicero politicians quickly learned that they had made a deal with the devil when the hoodlums completely took over the town. Capone and his henchmen even publicly slugged town officials who displeased them on at least two occasions and a policeman on another.[200]

In neighboring Stickney, they committed massive election fraud to install their candidates, led by village president Anton Rench. Reformer Edward Kabella stated that "gunmen and bandits control our government in Stickney."[201] In revenge, Kabella was severely beaten when he was elected village president in 1929. The events in tiny Forest View, which was south and west of Stickney, were similar. Pretending to be legitimate businessmen, Al and Ralph Capone set up the Stockade and Maple Villa. The residents of these two brothels accounted for forty-seven of the fifty-five registered voters in Forest View in 1926, giving the Capones control of the ballot box. Chicago police captain John Stege described the town as "devoted to vice, gambling, and the manufacture of beer."[202] It soon became unofficially known as "Caponeville" in the newspapers. Similarly, Torrio gangster Charles Special, who at one time managed the Roamer Inn, was the mayor at various times of a nearby village that was named Specialville in his honor.[203]

Torrio also monopolized vice in tiny Lyons, which was just west of Stickney and Forest View and was, therefore, well located to serve Cicero as well as other locales such as Riverside and Brookfield. A suburb of only two thousand inhabitants, Lyons housed twenty-three saloons in 1913 where gambling and vice could be found.[204] Abe Markowitz, who got his start in prostitution on Chicago's Near West Side, was the local crime czar, but Torrio was the real power in the town.[205] His brother-in-law, Thomas Jacobs, ran one of the roadhouses, and

Torrio personally threatened a brothel keeper with bombing and, if necessary, death, unless he sold out to the syndicate that controlled local vice.[206]

The move into the western suburbs in the 1920s was spurred by events in Chicago. Reform temporarily raised its head in 1923 when Mayor Thompson, immersed in scandal and facing a stiff challenge in the Republican primary, declined to run for reelection.[207] Consistent with the changed mood of voters, Democrat William Dever won the general election. Of Irish extraction, Dever was a decent, upstanding man who championed good government. He had served as an alderman for eight years before winning a judgeship in 1910.[208] As the mayor, he reformed the police department in various ways and, although he was personally opposed to Prohibition, instructed the chief to enforce all laws, whether they were popular or not. Dever's statements included, "I'll put an end to every vice dump and gambling den in the city of Chicago if I have the power to do it" and "It is my intention to close every saloon or soft drink parlor in the city where law violations are found."[209] Organized crime was initially hopeful that the reform was a charade when Dever appointed Morgan Collins as the city's police chief, because he had been the captain of the wide-open Chicago Avenue district on the Near North Side. But Chief Collins, in order to keep his new job, followed the mayor's instructions to the letter, hitting hard at the bootlegging, gambling, and vice that thrived under his predecessor.

Fig. 3.35. Mayor Dever (right) with Al Jolson.

By setting up further operations just west of the city, the Torrio-Capone forces gave the West Side of Chicago a simple alternative to the places Dever closed, while residents of the South Side also had the old option of going to the southern and southwestern suburbs. Consequently, they were not hurt nearly as much as most other gangs by the crackdown while they also further diversified into areas beyond bootlegging. To avoid the heat in Chicago, the gang moved its headquarters to the Hawthorne Hotel on Twenty-Second Street in Cicero, which was owned and operated jointly with the North Siders.[210]

By the mid-1920s, Torrio had largely reinvented the old Colosimo gang. He changed its core activity from vice to bootlegging, without any catastrophic response by the authorities, and greatly expanded into gambling. Torrio also forged important links with other gangs and astutely extended the group's suburban operations. It added up to millions of additional dollars per annum. Even "Big Jim" Colosimo would probably have applauded what his former subordinate had achieved in a few short years.

Among the suburbs, Chicago Heights deserves special attention due to its prominent lawlessness during Prohibition—it was a hotbed of alky cooking, gambling, and vice—and its later importance (after the Dry Era) in the Chicago Outfit. Originally a planned industrial town backed by Chicago businessmen including brewer Charles Wacker, by 1920 it was home to a large population of Italian immigrants who were drawn by the jobs available in its factories.[211] At the start of Prohibition, the dominant gang there was led by Anthony Sanfilippo, Jim Lamberta, Phil Piazza, and Joe Martino. Sanfilippo owned a drugstore and served for several years as a Chicago Heights alderman. Lamberta was his chief lieutenant and operated a nightclub, as did Piazza, while Martino had a poolroom. This group was heavily Sicilian in membership and tied to the Unione Siciliana as well as the Torrio-Capone gang, as evidenced by the fact that three delegations of Heights racketeers attended Frank Capone's wake in 1924.[212] An ocean of illegal alcohol flowed from the area around Chicago Heights. For example, a federal indictment in 1929 charged that seventy-five stills in Chicago Heights, Harvey, Calumet City, and Steger produced three million gallons of alcohol from January 1, 1925, to March 1, 1929.[213] This was most likely sold initially, at least partly, to the Torrio-Capone gang.

In Chicago Heights, a separate but important Sicilian gang was led by the Costello brothers, Charles, Joe, Nick, Sam, and Tony, whose surname, before they anglicized it, was originally Castelli.

They operated Costello Brothers Confectioners, a wholesale candy business, and then established a large network of stills. The Zeranti brothers, Curley, George, and Pete, were at the helm of another prominent gang of Sicilians. The non-Sicilian bootlegging group in the Heights was led by relative newcomers Domenico (Dominic) Roberto, born on January 15, 1896, in Sambiase, Italy, near Cosenza in the province of Calabria, and Jimmy Emery, who was born Vincenzo Ammirati in Cosenza on November 2, 1892. Their chief

Fig. 3.36. Dominic Roberto. (From the collection of Matthew J. Luzi.)

Fig. 3.37. Jimmy Emery at the wheel of his Hudson in 1921.

Fig. 3.38. Frank LaPorte with his wife Margaret.

lieutenant was Roberto's slightly younger first cousin Francesco Liparota, better known as Frank LaPorte, who was also from Sambiase. Although they were supposedly house painters, Roberto and Emery were active in the rackets at the very beginning of the 1920s and owned a nightclub, among other things. The Roberto-Emery group and the other, smaller factions bought their political protection from the ruling Sanfilippo mob.

The situation in Chicago Heights was fairly stable until the evening of April 19, 1924, when Sanfilippo was shot four times in the back of the head as he drove his automobile in the company of two men. His death cleared the way for Phil Piazza, who was almost certainly behind the killing, to become the boss in the Heights.[214] Piazza soon distanced himself from the Torrio-Capone forces while maintaining his connections with the Unione, partly through Giuseppe "the Cavalier" Nerone. Nerone was a Piazza relative who established himself in Chicago Heights after leaving the Genna gang in Chicago.

The outlying areas were also an important source of beer for the Chicago gangs in the early days of Prohibition. As already alluded to, for a time beer flowed from at least two breweries in Joliet, the Porter Products Company and Citizens' Products Company, to Chicago up the Joliet Road. Joseph Stenson, a younger son of the Stenson family that was prominent in pre-Volstead brewing in Chicago, is reported to have had an interest in both of them, in partnership with the McFarland brothers.[215] Lawrence "Butch" Crowley and Richard J. Burrill did a brisk trade from the Elgin Ice and Beverage Company and another brewery they owned in the central Illinois town of

Pekin. Crowley, the son of a dog catcher in Joliet, reportedly made $1.5 million as a bootlegger by 1924.[216] The Pure Products Company in the suburb of West Hammond, which was renamed Calumet City in 1924, was owned directly by Torrio and resulted in his first violation of the Volstead Act. The Malt Maid Products Company (formerly known as the Manhattan brewery) and the Sieben brewery in Chicago, which he owned jointly with O'Banion, along with the Pure Products Company and some operations in Chicago Heights supplied much of the beer at Torrio's command.[217]

Before turning to the Beer Wars, it is useful to survey vice, gambling, and labor racketeering in Chicago during the early 1920s and to also discuss the relatively new field of business racketeering. In 1923, Big Bill Thompson was squeezing the city's vice lords for millions of dollars a year in graft, after reaching accommodations with the West and Near North Side districts.[218] With only five of 6,222 Chicago policemen assigned to the suppression of vice, it was running rampant in the city, accompanied by venereal disease. Conditions in Chicago were "worse than in any other large city in the United States," with an estimated 500 places of ill repute staffed by 2,500 women generating a profit of $13.5 million per annum.[219] In terms of prostitution, this was almost a return to the state of affairs in the early 1910s.

Visible parlor houses remained in the minority.[220] Instead, much of the trade was conducted in assignation houses, hotels, rented rooms, cabarets, saloons, and through street corner solicitation. In many cabarets, women encouraged men to buy them drinks and received from the place's owner a percentage of the money the men spent, and some saloons on the South Side were essentially open houses of prostitution.

In late 1922, investigators for the JPA found six women in negligees turning three-dollar tricks at the Rex Hotel on W. Twenty-Second Street and some fifteen women, clad in transparent chemises and mostly between eighteen and twenty-one years old, working upstairs at the Four Deuces managed by Al Capone at S. Wabash.[221] The general situation in terms of vice enforcement was illustrated when an undercover man for the Committee of Fifteen visited an assignation house on N. Winchester in the Ravenswood neighborhood (just across the street from Reverend Elmer Williams's home) on April 24, 1922. The proprietor, Peggy Holmes, told him that although she had nothing to fear from the Chicago police, she had to be careful because the Committee of Fifteen was watching her![222]

At the end of Thompson's second term as mayor, a syndicate (cartel) ran more than twenty-five houses of prostitution largely on the Near South Side and the West Side of Chicago.[223] These were lower-end, three-dollar parlor houses, and the syndicate's goal was to monopolize this part of the business. The group's edge was that it could guarantee to the working girls and the customers that, except for the occasional show raid, its places would not be bothered by the law. When one investigator expressed false concern about getting arrested to draw a girl at the Rex Hotel out, she told him, "Don't be a fool. Danny [Dennis] Cooney owns this place and they never raid anything that belongs to him."[224]

The syndicate paid off the relevant aldermen as well as the police. In turn, the member houses turned over half their profits to it.[225] The JPA stated further that, when raids did occur, "a former member of the state's attorney's office takes care of their [the syndicate's] interests. This man whose name was quoted as *Attorney Hoyne* [italics added] is reputed to have sufficient political affiliations to bring about immediate release with small fines."[226] Duke Cooney and a man named Barnes were the syndicate overseers on the South Side.[227]

Starting at the turn of the century and continuing, barring some intermissions, until nearly the end of the Capone era, Austrian born Mike "de Pike" Heitler was a power in prostitution on the Near West Side.[228] He served as a collector of bribes in the Desplaines police district for Police Inspector McCann circa 1910 and opened up the Carpenter Street vice district in July 1911 after being driven out of Curtis Street.[229] Heitler was an adherent of Torrio, and his web spread well beyond the city, with interstate connections in Pittsburgh, Milwaukee, St. Louis, Indianapolis, and Gary, Indiana, ultimately leading to his July 2, 1916, conviction for violating the Mann Act.

By about 1920, Jack Zuta had established himself in the vice trade just west of Ashland Avenue in the Warren Avenue police district with operations on W. Madison, in four nearby saloons, and in the Home, Newport, Florence, and Harvard hotels.[230] When he tried to move into the Desplaines police district, he came into conflict with Heitler and Torrio.[231] Each side sent sluggers into its rival's places to shoot, beat, and rob the occupants. However, in early 1923 Zuta had supplanted Heitler in the area. Zuta and Ollie Mullenbach, who was a long-time friend of Torrio, were the syndicate leaders in that neck of the woods at the time.[232]

Fig. 3.39. Mike "de Pike" Heitler.

The situation changed dramatically when William Dever became mayor. By December 1923, constant police raids had driven two-dollar houses to raise their prices to three dollars and former three-dollar houses to now charge five dollars per customer.[233] Many of the most flagrant saloons were shut down, and streetwalkers were greatly curtailed, pushing the prostitutes back again into clandestine locations in residential areas. Consistent with these policies, the Vice Index had an average value of four hundred during Dever's term of office, more than double the average during the preceding eight-year Thompson regime.

Geographically, a relative resurgence of bordellos had occurred on the Near South Side by the mid-1920s, with the Levee, Douglas, Oakland, and Grand Boulevard neighborhoods accounting for 61 percent of Chicago's total in 1924. This development came at the expense of the Near West and Near North Sides, which housed only 12 percent and 8 percent, respectively, of the city's brothels.[234] Prostitution was also prominent in the Uptown and Lake View areas on the North Side adjoining Lake Michigan, which contained 10 percent of the houses of ill repute in 1924 compared to only 5 percent in 1920. The growth of the South Side vice was at least partly due to a great increase in the number of African American prostitutes in the city, which began around 1920.[235]

A number of old-timers were still active in gambling during the early 1920s. For example, until his death in 1925 James O'Leary was thriving at his place on S. Halsted Street. So was Mont Tennes, who finally sold his gambling houses to his partner Jack Lynch in 1924 but retained his share of the wire service.[236] In the mid-1920s, hundreds of independently owned gambling places still existed around Chicago, as had been the case for years. However, several prominent syndicates had a sizeable part of the business.[237]

John Torrio and Al Capone, working with the Guzik brothers and old-time gambler Jimmy Mondi, operated in the Loop, on the Near South Side, and in Cicero and other suburbs. Marty Guilfoyle had multiple holdings on the Near Northwest Side, in the area where he and his partners controlled the bootlegging. "North Side Frankie" Pope had a number of places in the Loop and on the Near North Side. William Johnson, Billy Skidmore, and Julius "Lovin' Putty" Anixter ran a string of joints located primarily in the Lawndale neighborhood and a few miles north of there, in the vicinity of Irving Park Road and Cicero Avenue. Anixter was also a power in the payoff system that funneled graft from the gamblers to the police, as was Skidmore.[238] The latter was "Patsy" King's gambling partner at one time in handbooks as well as a power in the Democratic Party on the West Side.[239] For years Skidmore collected the protection money from gamblers on the West and South Sides, including the policy operators, a group he belonged to before 1910.[240] Jack Zuta also had important gambling interests, most likely in conjunction with Anixter.[241] A syndicate in the Taylor Street area and in Chicago's Greek Town near Halsted and Madison was run by "Dago Lawrence" Mangano and "West Side Frankie" Pope. Jack Lynch's vast holdings appear to have been scattered around the city.

The Dever administration attacked gambling as vigorously as it did vice and bootlegging. Raids were conducted in the Near South Side Second and Third Wards, in the latter area for the first time in years, and on the West Side as the mayor counteracted police captains who were being paid off.[242] The Chicago police also closed two hundred Loop handbooks in one year.[243] It was, of course, impossible to stamp out illegal betting in Chicago completely, because if one place was closed, the same gamblers usually reopened at a nearby location, known as a "relay joint," which they had already purchased for just such a purpose.[244] However, "[d]uring these years, in the main, the gambling was suburban with the chieftainship in the hands of the Capone syndicate."[245] In 1923 a syndicate headed by Blue Island gambler James Hackett and the son of an unnamed major politician controlled all gambling in the county outside of Chicago.[246]

Although Reverend Elmer Williams of the Better Government Association (BGA) raided outlying spots such as the White House on Irving Park and River Road, the Villa Venice at Milwaukee Avenue and the Des Plaines River, and the Bridge Inn (later called the Morton House) at Dempster and Ferris in Morton Grove, suburban enforcement was otherwise minimal.[247]This explains why the Gambling Index was on average almost the same during the Dever years as in the prior eight years; although enforcement went up, the amount of gambling in the city went down as the proprietors pulled up stakes and moved to the suburbs. Prostitution could not have done the same as easily, because such a move would have required in many cases closing up a broader business such as a saloon or cabaret, and unorganized vice would not have been tolerated in towns controlled by a syndicate.

Policy visibly resurfaced in 1915 after a long lull when "Policy Sam" Young opened up again on South State Street.[248] A few years later the *Chicago Defender*, the leading newspaper in the African American community, reports that slips from the drawings were lying everywhere in the Black Belt just as they had been in the "old days."[249] In June 1923, three of the traditional wheels, the Frankfort and Kentucky, the Interstate and Springfield (run by Dan Jackson), and the Black and White, had the lion's share of the market, with about a dozen smaller wheels running alongside them on the South Side.[250] At that time Dan Jackson tried to gain control of the policy racket, apparently unsuccessfully even though he was allied with Sam Young.[251] In the years just before 1925, Julius Benvenuti was the only white man operating a policy wheel in Chicago. He ran it, in partnership with Sam Young, out of his saloon on S. La Salle Street.[252]

The *Chicago Defender*, which during its long life frequently attacked policy gambling and the so-called "policy kings" who ran the games, told the players, "You are not only an accessory to the act of robbery, but you are a blamed fool to the extent that you are paying for the privilege of being your own damphool [sic] victim."[253] Looked at carefully, the well-known charitable contributions of various policy kings to "the Race" (as the *Defender* referred to African Americans) and the reinvestment of their private wealth in their own community were less admirable than they might appear.[254] Visibly putting money back into the surrounding area created good will, which was well worth the expenditure. Clearly, doing a good deed for a church or a community organization influenced the local residents to conclude that the individual was an "all right guy" and to not report his activities to the authorities. Also, if the African American policy lords were heavily discriminated against due to their race, then their investment opportunities were in fact limited outside their own community, and reinvesting in businesses/institutions on Chicago's South Side was necessary, as opposed to benevolent, behavior.

The years from 1920 to 1925 were violent ones in the labor union arena in Chicago, resulting in a number of major killings. When "Mossy" Enright's man Hugh Lynch was replaced in 1919 by Mike Carrozzo as head of the street sweepers, through the machinations of "Big Tim" Murphy, Enright responded by blocking Murphy's efforts to organize the gas workers. Murphy, Carrozzo, and several others with ties to Colosimo retaliated by attacking Enright, while his very lethal bodyguard Walter Stevens was elsewhere, on February 3, 1920.[255] As he pulled his car to the curb in front of his magnificent home on W. Garfield, Enright was struck by eleven slugs fired from a sawed-off shotgun, and he died almost instantly. In November of that same year, William "Slick Bill" Tynan, who was with the Enright unions, was killed by Joseph Carville, a henchman of Murphy, in a saloon at Thirty-First Street and Lock.[256]

On May 17, 1920, John Kikulski, president of the Amalgamated Meat Cutters and Butchers' Workers Union, was attacked near his home on N. Central Park Avenue. One assailant beat him with a pool cue, while another fired two shots into him, one of which pierced several vital organs. He died four days later. Kikulski, who had been active in organizing workers at the Union Stockyards and had recently been charged with misuse of funds, was feuding at the time with John Johnstone of the Stockyards' Labor Council. Spike O'Donnell was sought by police for questioning in the shooting. Similarly, Antonio Abinanti, an official of the Tracklayers' Union, was slain in June 1922, followed by Martin De Vries of the Bakery Wagon Drivers' Union in November 1923, and Samuel Bills, a business agent of the Ice Cream Drivers' Union, in April 1924. In the Bills slaying, labor slugger Robert Devere was also killed and six bystanders were wounded.[257]

Various acts of labor violence during this time period were associated with the two branches of the Teamsters Union. When Edward Coleman, president of the Chicago Teamsters, was shot to death in his downtown office on April 22, 1920, police suspected that it was the outgrowth of difficulties inside the outlaw union. Coleman had been feuding with James "Lefty" Lynch, head of the Coal Teamsters, for about six years and more recently with Lynch's allies Mickey Norris and John Haley.[258]

The Chicago Teamsters and the International Brotherhood of Teamsters (IBT) locked horns in January 1924 when the Commission Drivers' Union switched from the latter to the former, a move that greatly decreased the Chicago membership of the IBT. Related to these issues, Patrick "Paddy" Berrell, president of the local 705 of the IBT, was shot in the leg at Halsted and Randolph on January 6, 1924. On February 3, 1924, a group of gunmen invaded a dance hosted by the Chicago Teamsters in a hall at Van Buren and Ashland. When the shooting was over, one man was dead and twelve people were wounded.[259] Although numerous attendees identified Valley Gang member Anthony Kissane as one of the men doing the shooting, he was acquitted when a dozen witnesses disappeared before his trial.

Some of the worst violence was related to the building trades. The unions took offense when non-union tradesmen did work at Chicago's two Major League Baseball parks in 1923. In what amounted to a warning, their members appeared on opening day with signs that read "Unfair to organized labor, Sox and Cubs Park." Shortly thereafter, several thousand dollars of plumbing was vandalized at Wrigley Field, and a bomb was hurled at Comiskey Park.[260] A much more serious crime occurred in the early-morning hours of May 10, 1922, when two police officers, Lieutenant Terrence Lyons and Patrolman Thomas Clark, were killed, and Officer Albert Moeller was wounded in two separate incidents as a crew of labor bombers attacked various businesses.[261] The officers were shot as they confronted the suspected bombers. Fred "Frenchy" Mader, president of the Building Trades Council, Murphy (the real power in the council), Con Shea, "Dapper Dan" McCarthy, and several others were indicted for the killing of Lyons.[262] John Miller, the driver of the car of gunmen, and Charles Duschowski, who Miller named as one of the slayers, were ultimately convicted of the murder while the others went free.

The modern form of business racketeering was in its infancy in Chicago in the early 1920s, although the newspaper Circulation War could be described as a primitive version of racketeering; however, it did not culminate in a monopoly in the market. In a business racket, firms in the industry were formed into an association (cartel) in order to raise prices and profits. Violence and other methods of persuasion were necessary to achieve this end, because some existing firms refused to join or because new firms entered the industry outside the association, in both cases charging less than the cartel price.

There were two types of business rackets, the Collusive Agreement and the Simon Pure racket.[263] The successful Collusive Agreement generally had several important elements. Often the firms involved organized the group and/or were willing participants because they greatly profited from it. There was also a racketeer whose reputation and musclemen put fear into dissidents for a fee, politicians who were paid to tolerate the arrangement, and usually a union or unions that helped maintain group discipline in return for part of the profits. The grandfather of them all in the Chicago area, the Master Cleaners and Dyers Association, was a full-fledged racket by 1919 at the latest and illustrates how this type of association worked.[264]

During the 1920s, Chicago housed about ten thousand small tailor shops that took in clothing for cleaning and dyeing from their customers.[265] The garments were then sent by wagon to large (master) cleaning and dyeing plants to have the actual work done before coming back to the customers by the same route. Employees of the plants belonged to the Cleaners, Dyers, and Pressers' Union, while the wagon drivers were members of the Laundry and Dye House Chauffeurs, Drivers, and Helpers' Union, led by John G. Clay.

An advisory board, drawn from the members of the association, ran the entire cartel, with the assistance of these two unions. The board set prices and told each tailor shop which plant would clean the garments it received. Any plant that did not follow the association rules to the letter would see its workers go on strike and the drivers would refuse to deliver clothing to it. A tailor shop that ran afoul of the association found that the drivers refused to take garments from it to a plant. If union intervention was insufficient to bring the recalcitrant into line, the goons entered the picture. The plant or tailor shop would be bombed, the owner or his employees would be slugged, and/or exploding suits would be sent to be cleaned at offending plants while the clothing dropped off at offending tailor shops was vandalized.

The Simon Pure racket was a one-dimensional effort in which a racketeer and his henchmen formed an association and forced the businesses to join and pay various fees. Maxie Eisen #1 was the premier example of this form of organization and led at various times the Retail Fish Dealers' Association, the Wholesale Fish Dealers' Association, the Poultry Dealers' Association, the Hebrew Master Bakers of the Northwest Side, and the Hebrew Master Butchers' Association.[266] His czardom of the Fulton Street Fish Market, through the wholesalers' association, helped him dominate the retail dealers as well, because if they stepped out of line, he could stop them from obtaining fish. Some Simon Pure rackets expanded into collusive ones. For example, someone who controlled the retailers of a product could use this as leverage to organize the manufacturers in cooperation with the relevant unions.

Such was the underworld in Chicago in early 1924, before the bootlegging gangs went to war in a major way, and the bootleggers moved heavily into other areas of organized crime.

Chapter 4

TORRIO, CAPONE, AND THE BEER WARS: 1922–1927

Sad and sudden was his call,
So dearly loved by one and all;
His memory is as sweet today,
As in the hour he went away.

—poem dedicated to Earl J. "Hymie" Weiss
by his mother, sister, and brothers,
from the In Memoriam column of the
Chicago Tribune, October 11, 1929

John Torrio's master plan for bootlegging in Chicago faced two well-known problems that are inherent in all cartels. One issue was that those outside the agreement, seeing the profits earned by the cartel members, naturally wanted to enter the business. This was relatively simple to deal with for two reasons. First, because the sanctioned bootlegging gangs were paying the authorities to operate, it would also have been easy for the hoodlums to learn about interlopers from them. If necessary, the local police could have been used as an enforcement device against the independents—as what happened both before and after Prohibition in other areas of organized crime. After all, too much competition would have killed the golden goose, of which officialdom received a large slice.

Second, the cartel was illegal, because both bootlegging and, under the Sherman Antitrust Act, cartels themselves were illegal, making the agreement unenforceable in the courts. Therefore, the gangsters used alternative methods that were much more lethal than lawsuits to keep outsiders out. This was very effective because the independents tended to be small and easily outgunned. As is discussed in chapter 7, the victims in many of the bootlegging-related killings in Cook County during Prohibition were independents who had the nerve and/or lack of sense to cross the established gangs.

The other major problem with the collusive agreement was that some members were inclined to cheat on it and the offended members, especially in a cartel of gangsters, were inclined to not take it lightly. A gang was obviously not in favor of anyone else selling in its territory. But its profits would have increased if it sold into another gang's area as well. This created an incentive to break the deal if a gang leader thought that the resulting violence justified the benefits. The major flaw in Torrio's master plan was, as is discussed further below, that (despite claims to the contrary) it lacked a well thought out enforcement device to punish member gangs who violated its terms.

Admittedly, it is unreasonable to expect Torrio to have been intimately familiar with, at least initially, organizations such as the US railroad cartels before 1890 and the sophisticated methods they used to detect and punish, and therefore minimize, cheating in order to hold their agreements together. These included opening each firm's accounting books to other cartel members and levying fines on those caught cheating. It is also not appropriate to blame the breakdown of the cartel entirely on Torrio, given how unstable some of the other gang leaders were. However, the violence that erupted, in what senior Chicago police officers called the "Beer Wars," tore apart the underworld and made the gangland map of the city in January 1932 much different than what it was at the start of 1924.

Obviously, a great deal has been written about certain aspects of Chicago's Beer Wars.[1] This chapter and the two that follow focus heavily on the broader picture of who was fighting whom, as well as when and why, and what resulted from it. This is ultimately the story of the ascendancy of the Torrio-Capone gang and the eventual creation of the Chicago Outfit after the turbulent Prohibition Era. The extended details about some of the more famous shootings and killings during this time period are found in other books on the subject.

The discussion of the Beer Wars that follows is based on the Chicago Crime Commission's (CCC) enumeration of gangland killings in the Chicago area during this time period, which is analyzed in greater detail in chapter 7, as well as newspaper accounts of underworld violence and the standard works on the city's Prohibition Era. The identification of the killers in the various slayings is based primarily on a detailed letter written by Cook County coroner Herman Bundesen and secondarily on contemporary reports in the newspapers.[2] Working with the CPD, Bundesen supplied ballistics expert Major Calvin Goddard with information on one hundred gangland victims from late 1923 to January 1929 and the names of the people the CPD suspected in each killing. In many cases Goddard also received the slugs removed from the victims' bodies and separately weapons taken from various suspects when they were arrested. Bundesen also listed the type of bullet(s) removed from each body. The Bundesen letter, because it contains information from the CPD, and because in some cases Goddard matched the bullets from the dead to specific weapons, is generally the most reliable source of information on who killed whom during the Beer Wars.

Although it was not part of a broader conflict, the first bootlegging gang battle with fatalities occurred at the end of August 1922 near the village of Elk Grove, which is northwest of Chicago. Schultz-Horan gangsters were returning to the city from Elgin with a three-truck cargo of beer when they were intercepted by hijackers from the Valley Gang. Witnesses reported that at least fifty shots were fired by the approximately twenty men involved in the melee. When the smoke cleared, Albert Schultz was dead, John Horan and Edward McEvoy, a sergeant in the CPD who was in the Schultz-Horan contingent, were wounded, and it was believed, but not confirmed, that at least one Valley gangster was killed and another was wounded.[3]

The first Prohibition gang war in Chicago, referred to as one of the Back of the Yards Wars, was between the South Side O'Donnells and the Saltis-Sheldon gang in the area south of the Union Stockyards. The Back of the Yards Wars were a multipart, revolving conflict that ebbed and flowed for some ten years on the South Side of Chicago. As noted in the previous chapter, the South Side O'Donnells were firmly established on the broader South Side in the early days of Prohibition, as opposed to being a group of upstarts who came on the scene in 1923. Therefore, it is unimaginable that a strategist of Torrio's caliber would not have at least approached them about joining the cartel when he formed the organization. Logically, this leaves two possibilities; either these O'Donnells were initially part of the agreement, or they were asked to join but refused.

Spike O'Donnell and his brethren were, however, buying beer in 1923 from Malt Maid Products, which was owned by Torrio and Dean O'Banion.[4] Thus, contradicting the usual accounts, which asserted that the South Side O'Donnells were outside the cartel and bucking it, it is virtually certain that they were in the cartel, at least initially, because cartel beer would have only been available to the members.[5] Therefore, the fighting on the South Side in 1923 was due to difficulties within the cartel.

While the O'Donnells have usually been blamed for starting the trouble by invading the Saltis-Sheldon territory in September 1923, the problems, in a more minor way, began quite a bit earlier. O'Donnell gangster George Meegan was wounded in a South Side saloon in June 1922 during a "bootleggers' quarrel," which speaks of intergang violence.[6] Similarly, Michael Corbitt (or Corbett) was shot in February 1923 near Lemont in a "gun battle between rival gangs of beer runners," which may be what the *Chicago Examiner* reported as the Saltis gang stealing a truck load of beer from the O'Donnells on the road from Joliet to Chicago.[7] It appears from these episodes that the Saltis-Sheldon gang was most likely responsible for the earliest violence related to the Southwest Side.

The details of what happened next are less than perfectly clear. Based on the evidence, the most likely conclusion is that the Saltis-Sheldon gang first invaded the O'Donnell areas by underselling them on beer, which again shows that the O'Donnells were well established in their own right. For example, the *Chicago Daily News* states in an article in September 1923 that Walter Stevens, now a Saltis-Sheldon beer runner, "*[s]ome months ago* [italics added] . . . started cutting into O'Donnell territory" with the aid of Danny McFall and "Red" Golden.[8] This was probably while Spike O'Donnell was in the penitentiary at Joliet. Sometime later, Stevens and Spike shot at each other, although neither was wounded, when they accidentally met in a bar. Similarly, Joe Saltis admitted to a Chicago police captain that he undersold the South Side O'Donnells, and three other newspaper accounts named his gang as the instigators in the trouble, the first major difficulty behind the stockyards.[9] In response, Captain Thomas Wolfe of the New City police district personally visited saloons, at least in the southern end of his bailiwick, in June 1923 and leaned on them to buy O'Donnell beer.[10] This was an officially sanctioned O'Donnell counterattack on the Saltis-Sheldon area, in which the former gang further cut the price per barrel of beer.

As an additional inducement to buy their beer, the South Side O'Donnells invaded unwilling saloons north of Fifty-Fifth Street in September, smashing them up and slugging the operators in the process, including Jacob Geis's place on Fifty-First Street. The latter incursion was a daring act because Geis was actually a prominent member of the Saltis-Sheldon gang and his bar, later known as the "House of Death," was a Saltis headquarters.[11] Spike O'Donnell's opponents answered the fisticuffs with gunfire, killing Jerry O'Connor and wounding Walter O'Donnell on September 7 as they were saloon raiding. They also eliminated two O'Donnell gangsters, George Meegan and George Bucher, ten days later on Chicago's South Side. There was more mayhem in December when Frank McErlane and company murdered Thomas "Morrie" Keane and nearly killed "Shorty" Egan after intercepting an O'Donnell beer shipment coming from Joliet. Clearly, the South Side O'Donnells got the worst of it in the fall of 1923. However, at that point the two sides backed away from each other because there were no further incidents for eighteen months.

The standard conclusion about the South Side violence in 1923, that an intergang squad working as a cartel enforcement mechanism punished the South Side O'Donnells for their transgressions, is incorrect.[12] First, the Saltis-Sheldon gang was most likely behind the trouble. If anyone should have been penalized in order to keep the collusive peace, it was them and not the South Side O'Donnells. More importantly, all the shooters who hit the O'Donnells beginning in September 1923—whether McErlane, Saltis, Sheldon, Danny McFall, or Thomas Hoban—were in the united, at the time, Saltis-Sheldon gang.

Not a single Torrio-Capone hoodlum was involved, much less anyone from any other gang. Therefore, this was a *local* disturbance that was handled *locally*, and it shows that the cartel did not have an explicit device to penalize cheaters, an issue that would resurface again in 1924. In fact, Torrio capitalized on the confusion when he grabbed the O'Donnell-controlled Brighton Park police district, at the western edge of the city just north of New City, while Spike O'Donnell was busy elsewhere, which was hardly consistent with maintaining the cartel.[13] To help in the takeover, Torrio used his political connections to have O'Donnell-friendly police officers transferred out of Brighton Park and replaced them with policemen who would do his bidding.

As bad as things were in the Back of the Yards neighborhood, Chicago's underworld would have been a much different place during Prohibition, as well as possibly for decades afterward, if Dean O'Banion had been able to control himself. Or if he had at least been able to refrain from clashing with the Torrio-Capone gang. O'Banion was incensed when Genna booze showed up on the North Side, which was perhaps due to the large Italian community near Division Street, and he immediately quarreled with the Gennas.[14] Notice that, in terms of the preceding discussion about whether there was an intergang cartel enforcement squad in place to punish those who broke the rules, no one attacked the Gennas because they violated the North Siders' sovereignty. In fact, O'Banion was greatly upset because Torrio would *not* intercede on his behalf.

The North Side gang handled the problem themselves by hijacking Genna booze shipments. More importantly, they struck directly at Torrio. In an astounding double cross in May 1924, which was as bold as it was foolish, O'Banion offered to sell Torrio his interest in the Sieben brewery on N. Larrabee, claiming that he wanted to leave gangland and retire to Colorado.[15] What Torrio did not know was that the Sieben was going to be raided and padlocked, by Police Chief Morgan Collins himself, and that O'Banion, who had been tipped off, scheduled the closing of the sale for that same morning. He most likely did this over the objections of Weiss, Drucci, Moran, and Frank Gusenberg, all of whom understood what would follow from it.[16]

Fig. 4.1. The Sieben Brewery.

The problem between Torrio, Capone, and O'Banion was, as Capone stated less than two years later, "never over business. It was all bad feeling between one man and another."[17] In other words, O'Banion's volatile personality overwhelmed his business sense. If Samuel Jules "Nails" Morton had still been alive in 1924, perhaps he could have dissuaded the wild Irishman from such craziness. After the Sieben raid, Torrio was out half a million dollars, and he faced a mandatory prison term for a second bootlegging offense. He immediately smelled a rat. Along with the Gennas, he would gladly have killed O'Banion. However, Mike Merlo, the head of the Unione Siciliana in Chicago and a powerful voice in organized crime who was close to Torrio, Capone, and the Genna brothers, would not allow it. This has been attributed to his general policy of trying to maintain peace given the cost of conflict.[18] Merlo may also have been on good terms with O'Banion, who at one time lived on Surf Street, a mere stone's throw away from Merlo's home on Diversey Parkway.[19] They most likely had business dealings, if nothing more than an agreement to coexist, since one Unione alky-cooking stronghold was the Italian neighborhood near Division and Halsted, which was inside O'Banion's area on the North Side. Therefore, as long as Merlo lived, so did O'Banion.

Torrio and the Gennas showed considerable restraint during the remainder of 1924. The same, however, could not be said about O'Banion. He returned from a visit to Colorado that October with a small arsenal, including a machine gun, and drove around the Near West Side with it in search of the Genna brothers.[20] O'Banion never got a chance to use it; before he could find his intended targets, Mike Merlo died on November 9, 1924. The very next morning O'Banion was shot and killed in Schofield's flower shop on N. State Street, which

Fig. 4.2. The burial of Dean O'Banion. The pallbearers are Dan McCarthy (#1), Frank Gusenberg (#2), Louis Alterie (#3), Vincent Drucci (#4), Maxie Eisen (#5), George Moran (#6), Matt Foley (#7), and James Clark (#8). O'Banion's widow is standing next to the car (#9) with Hymie Weiss to her left.

he used as a headquarters, by three men who entered under the ruse that they were picking up flowers for Merlo's funeral. The killers were most probably Frankie Yale, again working for Torrio as a hired assassin, and Genna gangsters John Scalise and Albert Anselmi.[21]

Hymie Weiss succeeded O'Banion as the boss of the North Side gang. Contemporary writers were unanimous in their praise of him as a gang leader. James O'Donnell Bennett calls Weiss the "brainiest leader that [N]orth [S]ide boozedom has had," while Walter Noble Burns labels him as "far seeing, prudent, and diplomatic," and Hal Andrews notes that he was greatly respected in gangdom for his "brains, class, and courage."[22] Weiss possessed the latter quality in limitless quantity. He was completely unafraid of death, because, as revealed by recent research, he knew he was dying from cancer.[23] This made him an extremely dangerous enemy because he was totally fearless as well as extremely shrewd.

For example, during the summer of 1925 when the North Side gang's conflict with the Gennas was at its height, a police squad saw Weiss and George Moran walking up and down Taylor Street in the heart of the enemy lion's den.

"What are you birds doin' here?" one officer called out. "Don't you think it's pretty hot over here for you?"[24]

"Hell no," Moran replied. "I wish one of the [W]ops would show himself. I'm nuts to blow off some greaseball's head."

Obviously, there was no fear in Weiss or Moran. However, this episode shows some recklessness on their parts, more so in Moran than Weiss given the latter's life expectancy, because it was not in their best interests.[25]

Before discussing the North Side–Genna conflict further, it is necessary to return to the historical timeline. According to one newspaper account, Weiss made peace with the Genna clan in a meeting at a Loop hotel just after O'Banion's death.[26] While on the surface this admittedly appears, given what happened not long thereafter, to be implausible, on close examination it very much fits the facts. For example, in early 1925 Angelo Genna was living in a hotel in the heart of the North Side, on Belmont Avenue near the lake.[27] If there was no truce in place, this would have been an act of suicide. Also, there was no fighting between these two gangs until May 1925, some six months after O'Banion was slain. There would have been a truce, however, only if Weiss considered the Genna brothers to be the lesser of the two evils facing the North Siders at the time.

With some breathing room gained on the one front, Weiss and his gang went after Torrio and Capone. In January 1925 the North Siders shot up Capone's car, although he was not in it, and probably wounded some of his entourage in or near it at Fifty-Fifth and State Streets. More importantly, Weiss, Drucci, and Moran severely wounded Torrio outside his home later that month, although they failed to kill him by the narrowest of margins. As James O'Donnell Bennett accurately states, as a gang leader Torrio could dish out the violence, but he could not take it.[28] He stepped down at that point and returned to New York after a jail term due to his Sieben brewery arrest. Torrio gave the crown to Capone, surely in return for a regular stream of cash, while apparently maintaining a position equivalent to that of a stockholder in a legitimate business. The gang was now Al Capone's to lead, if he could hold on to it.

Not long after Torrio's departure Chicago plunged into an almost citywide gang war, which was unusual for the United States during Prohibition. In New York and other places, bootlegging gangs certainly fought one another, but rarely on such a scale and for so long. The Capone gang, the Gennas somewhat later in 1925, and soon thereafter the Sheldon-Stanton gang were the major players on the one side. Weiss wisely, given the numbers arrayed against the North Siders, allied his gang with the West Side O'Donnells, the Saltis-McErlane mob, and the GKW gang, along with possibly others.[29]

Regarding Capone, he is best described as a mixture of the characteristics of his three mentors: Frankie Yale, James Colosimo, and John Torrio. Personally he was gregarious, loud, and one of the best customers for many of the things his gang had to sell. He had a massive appetite for women, gambling, and the good life. Entertainer Rio Burke, who later married Dominic Roberto, met Capone at a picnic in the early 1920s and remembered him as "very, very drunk and throwing money around like confetti."[30] He was a lavish tipper, which was partly self-interested because it helped his public image, but separately did seem to indicate that he genuinely liked to be liked by people if he could help it. This is reminiscent of Colosimo. On a more personal level, Capone certainly was a doting father to his only child, Albert Francis "Sonny" Capone, even though he was less than a model husband.[31] On another dimension, Capone freely granted interviews to the press, which in the long run was not in his best interests because it made him extremely visible.

Like Yale, Capone had a wild, violent side. Admittedly this was within certain bounds a useful trait in gangland, especially during a major gang war. However, as with Yale, and to a lesser extent Colosimo, he took unnecessary risks when it would have been better to delegate the violence to others. For example, he personally killed Joe Howard in 1924, because Howard had slapped Jake Guzik around, and took part in the famous attack on the West Side O'Donnells in Cicero in 1926 that left three men dead. He is also believed to have been involved in murdering the White Hand Irish gangsters in New York City on Christmas Eve in 1925 as a hired killer, working for Yale.[32]

Capone's business sense and gangland diplomacy probably came largely from Torrio, including his philosophy that, if possible, "We don't want any trouble." In the words of Edward D. Sullivan, "Capone is an unusual 'hood.' He has concentration and executive ability beyond the ordinary. He is utterly fearless except when it is sensible to be afraid." Overall Capone, like Weiss, was an effective leader who could manage both the violent and the business ends of gangland.[33]

Regarding underworld leadership on the South Side, Laurence Bergreen asserts that from 1925 to his incarceration in 1931, Al Capone was not the boss of the gang in Chicago that bears his name.[34] Instead, Bergreen claims that Chicago Heights gangster Frank LaPorte, aided by Dominic Roberto and Jimmy Emery, was really in charge while Capone was a mere front man. He refers to them as "[t]he powerful Chicago Heights contingent—Roberto, Emery, and LaPorte—to whom Capone owed his position and for whom he served as figurehead."[35] Bergreen's claims are based on the reflections many years later of a man whose family moved from Chicago Heights to Lansing, Michigan, while he was still a young boy. Before he went to Michigan, this individual, who is given the pseudonym Anthony Russo by Bergreen, observed Capone walking around Chicago Heights with LaPorte and other gangsters and drew conclusions based on this.[36]

First, there is not a single word in the Chicago newspapers, the FBI or CCC files on LaPorte, or the Chicago Heights newspapers that closely followed gangland in the south suburban area even hinting that Capone was not the boss. In fact, the evidence is completely in the opposite direction. As discussed below, Capone aided Roberto, his business partner Emery, and LaPorte, who was third in command in Chicago Heights starting in 1926, in taking over the rackets in that suburb. They in turn swore fealty to Capone. Therefore, according to the far and away most credible accounts, LaPorte was not even the boss in Chicago Heights gangland, much less the boss of Capone, during Prohibition.

Second, none of the descendants of Roberto, Emery, or LaPorte claim that they outranked Capone, and they would be in a position to know because a number of the trio's male relatives (especially in LaPorte's case) were high-ranking members of the Chicago Heights crew for decades.[37] Instead, the relatives unanimously agree with the standard accounts that Capone was the man in charge of much of Chicago during Prohibition and Chicago Heights. If anyone had an incentive to make exaggerated claims about these three men, it would surely be their own relatives, yet they never did so. Therefore Bergreen's conclusions must be dismissed as the impressions of a young boy based on his casual observations of how Capone interacted with gangsters from Chicago Heights when he visited there during the 1920s.

Similarly, *Chicago Tribune* columnist John Kass claims that Paul Ricca was really Capone's boss. He states that the organization was so good at deception that "[t]hey had their front man, Al Capone, take all the media and federal heat, which is the way Paul 'the Waiter' Ricca wanted it" and that during the 1920s Ricca "was the real boss."[38] On one level it is hard to refute this claim because Kass provides no substantiation for it.[39] But therein is this assertion's great weakness. Suffice it to say that there is nothing in the Chicago newspapers during Prohibition to support this claim. In fact, in late 1926 after Capone had been the boss for well over a year, Ricca was still only a gunman in his gang.[40] Also, Kass's contention is treated with astonishment by Ricca's relatives.[41]

Returning to the Beer Wars, the North Side–Genna truce ended in April 1925 when Weiss learned that the Taylor Streeters were plotting with Capone to strike at him and his inner circle.[42] Infuriated by this betrayal, the North Siders launched a campaign of "Gennacide." Angelo Genna was killed on the Near North Side by Weiss, Drucci, Moran, and James Clark (whose real name was Albert Kachellek) on May 26, 1925, just before Weiss went to jail for six months on a bootlegging conviction.

The North Siders kept busy during Weiss's absence. On June 13, 1925, Moran and Drucci were wounded in an ambush just north of Taylor Street while they were searching for Genna gang targets. However, Mike Genna was eliminated that same day when he, Scalise, and Anselmi, who had shot at Drucci and Moran a few hours earlier, opened fire on a squad of Chicago police detectives on the Southwest Side. Less than a month later the Gennas lost a third brother when Anthony was gunned down by Drucci and Giuseppe (Joe) Nerone, the latter by then a disaffected former Genna hood, in the Grand Avenue neighborhood on the Near Northwest Side. Jim Genna, fearing for his life, fled the country, and "Samoots" Amatuna, who succeeded Angelo Genna as head of the Unione Siciliana in Chicago, took over the Genna mob.[43]

Under Amatuna's direction the gang also set up shop in west suburban Melrose Park, where the established Italian community was already extremely active in alky cooking.[44] There were several killings there in less than a year, including the murders of Lazzaro Clemente (February 1925), Aniello Taddeo (September 1925), and James Campanille (January 1926), which probably resulted from friction between the new arrivals and the incumbents.[45] When Patsy Dano was shot in October 1926, two days after his cousin John Dano was murdered, he blamed both incidents on "the Melrose Park alky racket."[46]

The Genna gang lost more men during the latter part of 1925 and in 1926, which ultimately removed it from the bootlegging landscape, when they were hit from essentially three sides. After a four-month quiet period, Drucci, working probably with Jim Doherty of the West Side O'Donnells, murdered Samoots Amatuna at the corner of Roosevelt Road and Halsted on November 10, 1925, and five days later he killed Eddie Zine (aka Zion), another Genna gangster. The damage having been done, it is fairly certain that the Genna remnants made peace once again with the North Siders. For example, in

January 1926 Genna brother-in-law Henry Spingola and five others were seen outside the Belden Hotel on the North Side, where Hymie Weiss lived.[47] In response, Weiss called Pete Genna and informed him, in no uncertain terms, "If you don't keep these guys off the North Side I'll come over there and blow your head off."[48] The warning would have been unnecessary, and inconsistent with his self-interest, if Weiss and the remaining Gennas were at war at the time.

The Gennas' compact with Capone would have been ended by their truce with Weiss, which sheds light on the second part of the gang's demise. From July 1925 to February 1926 two of the Vinci brothers and one of their cousins, all of whom were with the Gennas, were slain by the Annerino (also known as Genero or Genaro) brothers, who were with Capone, indicating definite problems between the two groups.

The third part of the fall of the Genna gang was due to the legal defense fund they created for Scalise and Anselmi after the murder of the Chicago police officers in 1925. Money was demanded from prominent Italian Americans, especially if they were connected to the rackets, and those who refused to pay (or to pay the second time the collectors came around when Scalise and Anselmi were retried) were killed, including Henry Spingola and the Morici brothers in January 1926.

What the extortionists failed to reckon with was that their targets were in some cases as dangerous as they were. One prominent Italian on the Near West Side encouraged a young man who was born as Vincenzo Gibaldi to avenge the death of his stepfather, Angelo De Mora (aka De Mory), an alky cooker with the Gennas who was murdered in 1923.[49] Gibaldi was also known as Vincenzo De Mora, later as James Gebardi, and most prominently by his name in the boxing ring, Jack McGurn.[50] The Italian gentleman revealed to McGurn the names of the killers, who were prominent collectors for the defense fund, and, as Hal Andrews implies, were also pressuring this gentleman to contribute.[51] In a span of *eight days* during February 1926, all three were killed by McGurn and his backup man, Johnny Armando.[52] This deprived the Genna gang of several important members and also demonstrated its weaknesses to interested observers.

Capone would not have been especially sorry to see the Gennas

Fig. 4.3. Jack McGurn.

go. When, with his help, their gang collapsed, he took over the important Taylor Street area. Capone had already gotten control of that rich prize, the Chicago chapter of the Unione Siciliana, in late 1925 when his man Tony Lombardo followed Amatuna as the head.

The Capone gang also picked up many valuable men from the Genna organization when that gang folded. For example, Scalise and Anselmi joined the Capone organization in 1925 or 1926. So did Frank Rio (aka Frank Kline or Cline), after a stint as a bootlegger around Taylor Street. Originally an actor and petty criminal, Rio was arrested as a pickpocket in Pittsburgh (1915), for burglary in Milwaukee (1917), for vagrancy in Louisville, Kentucky (1918), and for an unnamed offense in Cincinnati (1919). He was also suspected of many crimes in Chicago from 1913 to 1920. During the latter part of that period, the Chicago newspapers called him "Slippery Frank" due to his ability to avoid prosecution. His frequent partner in crime on the West Side, Nick Circella, likely went over to Capone at the same time.[53]

Fig. 4.4. A young Frank Rio. (Image from Chicago History Museum, ICHi-092807).

Fig. 4.5. Tony "Mops" Volpe.

Tony Volpe, known as "Mops," was a prominent Taylor Street gunman during the mid-1910s.[54] He rose to become the personal secretary as well as the brother-in-law of "Diamond Joe" Esposito. By 1927 at the latest Volpe was in the Capone ranks.[55] Paul "the Waiter" Ricca, whose real name was Felice De Lucia, was also in Diamond Joe's camp before coming under the Capone banner. A fugitive from justice in Italy, Ricca entered the country illegally and came to Chicago in 1920 after killing two men in the vicinity of Naples.[56] He went to work around Taylor and Halsted when he arrived and soon gravitated to Esposito.

Fig. 4.6. "Diamond Joe" Esposito.

A variety of evidence indicates that "Machine Gun" Jack McGurn went with the North Siders after he finished his vengeance in February 1926, because it was feared there would be reprisals against him by the Gennas. Hal Andrews describes him as a chauffeur for Weiss, which means that he was a driver and a bodyguard.[57] This is seconded by various other sources.[58] However, McGurn quickly fell out with the Weiss crowd and he may have been with the Capone gang as early as April 1926. The Chicago police believed that he was involved in the killing of the assistant state's attorney, William McSwiggin, and two West Side O'Donnell gang members in Cicero that month because the slugs taken from the bodies of McSwiggin and bootlegger Jim Doherty were eventually matched to a submachine gun police confiscated from McGurn at a later date.[59] McGurn went on to become the chief executioner for the Capone gang. The CPD listed him as a suspect in eighteen gangland killings between February 1926 and December 1928, and in at least a dozen of these murders he was definitely a Capone gunner when the crime occurred.

Fig. 4.7. Paul Ricca's wedding in 1927. Al Capone (standing second from the left) was the best man, and his sister Mafalda (seated second from the left) was the maid of honor. Jerry Gigante, the brother of the bride, is standing at the far left. According to Ricca family members, no one else in the wedding party was connected to organized crime.

Another Capone recruit was Louis "Little New York" Campagna. His nickname stems from his early days in New York City and the fact that he stood about five feet three inches tall. A one-time circus acrobat, Campagna arrived in Chicago before Prohibition and soon turned to robbery. When he was released from the penitentiary in 1925 he went to work for Capone.[60] Samuel McPherson "Golf Bag" Hunt probably joined the Capone gang during the mid-1920s, after a stint in Detroit. According to the 1910 US Census, Hunt was born in Alabama, and given his middle name he was likely at least partly of Scottish ancestry.[61] He was a volatile character, professionally as well as personally, who liked to carry his larger weapons around in a golf bag when he was on a gang hit.[62] The top killers in the Capone organization, circa 1930, included McGurn, Hunt, Volpe, Rio, Claude Maddox, and Tony Accardo—all of whom were experts with a machine gun.[63] Several of the aforementioned also served as

Fig. 4.8. Samuel McPherson "Golf Bag" Hunt (#4), Tony Accardo (#5), and other Capone hoodlums show quite a bit of attitude in this CPD photo.

Capone bodyguards and went on to become high-ranking members of his gang.

For a time after the Torrio shooting there was no fighting directly between the North Siders and the Caponeites. The only violence from February 1925 to July 1926 involving both groups was the murder of Capone man Frank Cremaldi, who was caught on the North Side, in May 1926.[64] However, the gangs behind the stockyards became involved in the North Side vs. South Side War when Ralph Sheldon, with most of the former Ragen's Colts, left Joe Saltis to form their own mob. Sheldon took the area roughly east of Halsted Street with him and allied himself with Capone.

Hal Andrews claims that the split occurred because Saltis was becoming too close to Hymie Weiss and the North Siders.[65] This makes sense because if Capone would have attacked the united Saltis-Sheldon gang, given its location, the Sheldon area would have taken the most punishment. The separation happened, at the latest, at the beginning of October 1925 because on the third day of that month the Saltis forces, certainly including Frank McErlane, cut loose with a submachine gun on the Colts' clubhouse on S. Halsted, killing Charles Kelly who was standing outside.[66] This created an on-again, off-again, three-sided conflict on the South Side over the next several years as the South Side O'Donnells and the Sheldon-Stanton gang separately battled the Saltis-McErlane forces, but did not fight each other.

The two newly opposed sides exchanged bullets and bombs for the next ten months. Joe Saltis was wounded in the shoulder in November 1925, most likely by Sheldon's crew, and two weeks later the Sheldon-Stanton gang invaded a McErlane-controlled saloon on S. Halsted, killing two police officers and another man.[67] In retaliation, Sheldon's car was riddled with bullets on December 2, 1925, a cigar store he owned at Sixty-Third and Ashland was bombed around the same time, and Danny Stanton was shot twice on December 15. More seriously, two Sheldonites, Joey Brooks and Cook County police officer Edwin Harmening, were killed by Saltis and McErlane on December 22, 1925. Sheldon's car took more punishment when it was bombed on February 5, 1926, and four days later Sheldon gangsters John "Mitters" Foley and William Wilson were wounded in a machine gun attack on a saloon on S. Halsted. On April 10, 1926, Saltis, McErlane, and "Dingbat" O'Berta killed Genna gangsters Frank De Laurentis and Jacomino Tuccillo (aka John Tuccello), who worked with Sheldon, and left the bodies in a car parked in front of the latter's home. Later that month, McErlane took an involuntary vacation from Chicago when he was arrested and extradited to Indiana to face a murder charge.

The Sheldon-Stanton crowd had been on the receiving end of most of the violence in its dispute with Saltis and McErlane. The gang responded in July 1926 when "Mitters" Foley killed Saltis gangster John Conlon in a saloon on S. Ashland. A few days later shots were fired at Walter Stevens outside his home. In turn, Foley was ambushed by Saltis, O'Berta, Frank Koncil, and "Big Earl" Herbert when he left his house in response to a phone call on August 6. After that point, things were peaceful for several months between these two groups. However, with McErlane away, Saltis indicted along with Koncil for the Foley murder, and Pete Kusanski dead, their gang was leaderless. During this period the Saltis-McErlane mob was set upon by its rivals.[68]

The Saltis-McErlane gang was more than just a detached North Side ally before October 1926. Although it has not been noted previously, on two occasions this mob likely struck directly at Capone or his allies other than the Sheldon-Stanton gang. When George Dietrich of the Valley Gang was killed in March 1926, Joe Saltis was the prime suspect. If the Valley gangsters were in the Capone camp at the time, they were fairly quiet participants because this was the only incident in the North Side vs. South Side War involving them before 1927.

More importantly for what happened not long thereafter, Saltis, McErlane, and O'Berta were believed by the CPD to have kidnapped and killed Capone driver Tony Cuirignone, also known as Tommy Ross, in August 1926. His body was found in southwest suburban Palos Township, which was Saltis territory and would have been an unusual place for the North Siders, who have usually been held responsible for this killing, to have dumped it.[69] Also, he was tortured before he died, a method the Saltis-McErlane gang was rather familiar with, but which was not otherwise associated with the North Siders.[70] Therefore, it appears that the Saltis crowd was at minimum involved in the murder of Tony Cuirignone, if not solely responsible for it.

On the other South Side front, the fighting between Saltis and the South Side O'Donnells flared up again when Walter O'Donnell and Harry Hassmiller were killed during an invasion of Evergreen Park in June 1925. O'Donnell lost another man, Anthony Campagna, in July 1925, and Edward Lattyak (aka Lottjak) and Pasquale Tolizotti, who some sources claim was an O'Donnell hoodlum, were killed during October. That same month Tommy O'Donnell was slightly wounded when he and his brother Spike were fired on as they drove near Ninety-Fifth Street and Western Avenue.[71] Overall, the South Side O'Donnells again took quite a few hits in the summer and fall of 1925 without getting on the scoreboard themselves. In contrast, there seems to have been at least a tacit truce between these two groups starting in November 1925 because there were no further incidents for about a year.

There were other major developments in suburban gangland during 1925 and 1926 that were connected to the North Side vs. South Side War. In early 1926, when the West Side O'Donnells encroached on the Capone-controlled section of Cicero, the retaliation was swift.[72]

"Fur" Sammons was wounded in a machine gun attack on April 23, 1926. Four days later a party of prominent O'Donnell gangsters was caught in front of the Pony Inn on Roosevelt Road in Cicero by a crew of Capone gunmen. Jim Doherty and "Red" Duffy were killed in this attack, along with Assistant State's Attorney William McSwiggin, who was a boyhood friend of some of the O'Donnell mobsters. Contemporary sources agree that Capone himself fired the machine gun in this triple homicide. He was most likely eager, in an almost juvenile way, to personally try out gangland's newest weapon. He surely did not recognize McSwiggin, who on that night was unfortunately at the wrong place at the wrong time. The public outcry and the official crackdown on gangland that followed the McSwiggin killing helped return Cicero to the status quo as the O'Donnells licked their wounds and Capone left Chicago for an extended period of time until things quieted down again.

In late 1925 Chicago Heights boss Phil Piazza became overly greedy. He collected protection money from the suburb's independent gangs even though they were frequently raided by the authorities. Dominic Roberto and Jimmy Emery lined up the groups that were incensed by this duplicity and approached Al Capone, who they already had a relationship with, for help in early 1926.[73] Capone agreed to assist them in toppling Piazza, and in return they became his men. What followed would be accurately termed the Summer of Death in the Heights area as the Roberto faction, which was so violent that it even killed women when they were in the way, quickly and efficiently eliminated the core of the opposition.

For example, Jim Lamberta, a Piazza top lieutenant, was killed on June 2, 1926, along with his lady friend, Mrs. Crystal Barrier, in a shotgun ambush outside a south suburban nightclub.[74] Frank Camera, another Piazza man, was murdered one week later. Phil Piazza died next when two gunmen shot him in front of his Milano Café in Chicago Heights on July 22, 1926.[75] By mid-September six more Piazza gangsters were dead: Joseph Salvo (August 3), Joseph Catanda (August 8), Joe "the Cavalier" Nerone (August 20), Frank Capello (August 29), Tony di Stefano aka Antonio Pelledrino (September 2), and Joseph Terman (whose body was identified on September 12).[76]

Not a single Roberto (or Capone) gangster was reported to have been wounded, much less killed, during the Piazza-Roberto war in Chicago Heights. Notice also how bloody this brief episode was, compared to the direct fighting between the North Side and South Side gangs at the time that, through September 1926, resulted in only two deaths. Similarly, the fatalities were much lower in the warfare between the Saltis and Sheldon gangs and the conflicts the Gennas had with opposing mobs, all of which took place over a much longer time period. After demolishing the opposition, Roberto and Emery merged the various groups in the Heights into one gang in early 1927, giving them control of the suburbs just south of Chicago.[77] This was a major victory for them and for Capone, who gained some important men, considerable revenue, and a safe haven to retreat to whenever the heat was on in Chicago. Capone also covered his flank ethnically, if not geographically at the time, by firmly establishing himself as the overlord of the alky cooking in the Heights, a signifi-

Fig. 4.9. From left to right: Albert Kator, Eddie McFadden, "Gloomy Gus" Schaefer, and Roger Touhy.

cant result in light of the struggle that was to come for control of the Unione Siciliana.

Roger "the Terrible" Touhy, whose last name was originally Towey, was a major player in suburban bootlegging after 1925. He got his start by pushing beer in Chicago in 1920 for Matt Kolb and Marty Guilfoyle.[78] The son of a Chicago policeman, Touhy and his several brothers were, contrary to what has been written, most likely all incorrigible before their mother died in a kitchen fire in 1908.[79] Specifically, in February 1907 Mary Touhy thrashed her ten-year-old son Joseph with a policeman's belt in court rather than see him go to trial for theft, and Tommy Touhy was sentenced to sixty days for vagrancy in 1909 (indicating that he had likely gone astray earlier).[80]

Roger Touhy stated that in the mid-1920s he formed his own gang and took control of a wide section of Cook County north of North Avenue and west of Harlem Avenue. Although this would not have been open territory at such a late date, previous research has not examined who had this area before the Touhy mob. It most likely belonged to the Valley Gang. A report by the Juvenile Protective

Fig. 4.10. Tommy Touhy.

Association (JPA) in 1929, which disguised the names of the groups involved, quoted a Wheeling roadhouse owner who told an investigator, "As far as the Des Plaines River goes, C— and his crowd are in control. The D— used to have it, but they went to jail, or something else happened to them."[81] "D—" in this statement was almost certainly the Druggan-Lake gang, since its leaders were in jail on contempt of court charges during most of 1925, they were active in the adjoining counties, and it would have been opportune for Touhy to strike around that time. The west suburban town of Maywood was also in the Touhy domain.[82]

By 1927 Matt Kolb of the GKW gang was Touhy's partner in his suburban beer business—together they grossed $1 million a year from beer sales alone—and the Touhys also had connections with prominent North Siders, at least partly because Edward and very possibly Tommy Touhy had worked with them before Prohibition.[83] Their position was strengthened by the fact that Kolb was the purveyor of protection in the county when William Graydon was sheriff from the end of 1926 to November 1928. While the Touhy mob had no use for vice, it did have slot machines throughout its area.

Roger Touhy's brothers Tommy, who was also called "the Terrible" by the newspapers, John, Joseph, and Edward were primary members of the gang. William "Buck" Henrichsen, a former Cook County police officer, and Leroy Marshalk, another product of the Valley Gang, were also at the forefront of the group. Basil "the Owl" Banghart, their ace machine gunner, most likely joined the Touhys in 1932. Earlier he had only been charged with stealing automobiles. Banghart was also an expert at escaping from the authorities. For instance, he and two other prisoners broke out of the federal maximum security penitentiary in Atlanta in January 1927, and Banghart, Roger Touhy, and others escaped from the Illinois state penitentiary at Joliet in 1942.[84]

According to Roger Touhy, his gang was actually a peaceful bunch, who pretended, in an elaborate series of charades done with the cooperation of the local police, to be armed to the teeth in order to frighten Capone gangsters who tried to intimidate them. This is nothing more than a self-serving fairy tale put out by Touhy during the 1950s when he was trying to obtain a pardon for his 1934 kidnap-

Fig. 4.11. Frank Foster. (Courtesy of Mario Gomes, MYALCAPONEMUSEUM.COM.)

ping conviction.[85] In reality, the Touhys could dish it out as well as take it, as the later history of the Beer Wars amply demonstrates. Otherwise they would not have held on to their area for a week, much less have kept the Capone mob out when push came to shove. To this point, *Chicago Tribune* ace crime reporter James Doherty states, "The Touhy gang had at least one hundred members, all men who would stop at nothing to achieve their ends."[86] And they had no need to borrow guns because they had plenty of their own. In 1933, police in Florida confiscated a machine gun, a shotgun, a pump gun, and two pistols when they raided a house Roger Touhy was staying at with his family.[87] In fact, federal agents believed that the Touhy gang owned at least six machine guns.[88]

A week after Tony Cuirignone's body was found in August 1926, the Capone gang, rightly or wrongly, went after the North Siders. Gunmen attacked a contingent of hoodlums including Hymie Weiss and Vincent Drucci as they walked along south Michigan Avenue near the Standard Oil building.[89] Drucci stood his ground, driving off the assailants, and police captured Paul Ricca at the scene, who on this occasion gave them the false name Paul Valerie. There are claims that Weiss and Drucci were fired on again, in almost the same spot, five days later, although contemporary newspapers made no reference to this incident.[90]

In retaliation the North Siders and their allies struck at Capone in the heart of Cicero. On September 20, 1926, a procession of ten vehicles sporting three or more machine guns and numerous shotguns fired on the Hawthorne Hotel and the surrounding buildings on Twenty-Second Street just west of Cicero Avenue, which Capone and his men frequented. They sprayed the premises and the automobiles parked in front with over 1,000 rounds.[91] The police believed the attacking party included Weiss, Drucci, the Gusenberg brothers, George Moran, Frank Foster, "Puggy" White, and Ernest and Ben Applequist. Allies of the North Side gang, such as Vincent McErlane, "Dingbat" O'Berta, and George Darrow also took part, as well as possibly John Touhy since he was arrested for questioning after several of the automobiles involved were identified.[92] The presence of a Saltis-McErlane crew, with their names reported in the newspapers, indicates that it was known at the time that this gang was firmly in the Weiss camp.

The only gangster wounded in the Hawthorne drive-by shooting was Paul Ricca, who gave the authorities the new alias Louis Barko. According to the standard accounts, on this occasion Frank Rio pulled Capone to the floor before the bullets flew. In contrast, a confidential source states that Ricca actually saved Capone's life in this attack.[93] However, Ricca was hit in the shoulder as he was *entering* the building.[94] Therefore, he most likely did not pull Capone down inside the restaurant.

Perhaps Ricca saw the caravan coming when he was outside and, disregarding his own safety, ran to the door to warn Capone and the others. As Ricca said at the time, "One of the men got out of the car and trained a machine gun on Capone in the restaurant, but Capone fled out the back way."[95] If Ricca risked his own safety to protect Capone and/or his gang mates as the North Side motorcade approached, he showed himself to be fearless, quick-witted, and utterly loyal to his boss, and Capone would have been very grateful.

This story certainly fits with the subsequent events. Capone was the best man at Ricca's wedding in early 1927, the only known instance when he so honored one of his men. Also, Ricca moved off the mean streets of gangland to the Capone mob's front offices to work with Frank Nitti not long after the attack on the Hawthorne Hotel, and he rapidly ascended the organization chart after that.

Capone countered the North Side gang's massive expenditure of ammunition in Cicero with a surgical strike. On October 11, 1926, Hymie Weiss and his entourage were fired on by a machine gun and a shotgun as they crossed from in front of Holy Name Cathedral, on the east side of State Street, to Schofield's flower shop on the opposite side. Weiss and Patrick Murray were killed, and several others were wounded. As in the O'Banion killing, once again the South Siders virtually penetrated the enemy's inner sanctum, with the gunmen

Fig. 4.12. Schofield's flower shop was in the two-story building in the center.

stationed in a second-floor apartment in the building next door to Schofield's. Capone's opponents would have found it difficult to get that good of a shot at him, given the extensive security measures he took, including ringing himself with bodyguards when he went out in public. According to the CPD, Jack McGurn was on the safe end of the machine gun that day, and Sam Hunt was likely stationed in a building around the corner, which would have provided fire from a second angle if necessary, where his signature golf bag was found with a shotgun in it.[96] Frank Nitti is credited with originating the idea of using a machine gun nest, which became a common stratagem in gangland over the next few years, to trap Weiss.[97] Vincent Drucci took over the reins of the North Side gang after Weiss's death with George Moran as his chief lieutenant.

Shortly after Weiss died, Capone stated, with diplomacy and most likely candor as well, "I told them I did not want to die. I didn't want them to die, either. I said it wasn't necessary. We could find a more sensible way to settle our difficulties. I had sent word to them many times before Hymie died. They thought I was kidding, but when they saw I was in earnest, they wanted to talk things over."[98] Drucci, Capone, and the other major players in the North Side vs. South Side War met on October 20, 1926, in a downtown hotel and made peace on the following terms:

1. No more killings or beatings.
2. All past murders and shootings attributed to gunmen affiliated with Chicago and Cicero mobs [were] to be looked upon as closed incidents.
3. All ribbing (malicious gossip) carried between the factions . . . prior to the peace treaty, shall be disregarded.
4. Leaders of factions are to be held responsible for any infractions of the peace pact and unfriendly activities of the rank and file shall be reported to the peace delegates for disciplining by the respective parties.[99]

One writer colorfully describes how the Capone gang would start rumors to rib an opponent: "[T]wo hoodlums [would] form an alliance and grow powerful enough to constitute a real menace to the

[Capone] Syndicate. The 'rib' is then applied. One of the hoodlums hears that his pal, jealous of him, is going around calling him a big punk, a jag-off, a big lug who never takes a bath, and who beats his wife every morning. And there you have it. And there is another war. . . ."[100]

The gangland map changed somewhat, if not dramatically, as a result of the first part of the North Side vs. South Side War. Capone took the Gennas' former territory, his allies were in control in Chicago Heights and the eastern part of what had been the Saltis-Sheldon domain, and at that time the Touhys grabbed the northwest section of Cook County. However, Capone was the clear winner overall: his two greatest rivals on the North Side were dead, including the extremely capable Weiss; he had, directly and indirectly, the largest territorial gains; and he now controlled the Unione Siciliana in the Chicago area.

William "Big Bill" Thompson, who had been disgraced four years earlier, resurfaced in 1927 and ran for mayor against William Dever. Thompson won handily, proving that Chicago was, neither for the first nor the last time, not yet ready for reform. Vice, gambling, and business racketeering flourished anew when Thompson was sworn in as mayor a third time. As US Attorney George E. Q. Johnson noted, "When Thompson defeated Mayor Dever for re-election it was on a platform of an open town. The hoodlums and criminals of other states took this literally and there was a great influx of law violators to Chicago."[101] The figures listed in the table in Fig. 1.3 of chapter 1 indicate that the laws against gambling and vice were enforced less vigorously in 1927 and 1928, in comparison to the two previous years. Ironically, while things were running wide open throughout the city, in June 1927 Thompson's chief of police suspended three police captains who had played important roles during the Dever administration, John Stege, Daniel Murphy, and Dennis Carroll, the latter two on charges that gambling and vice were rampant in their districts.[102]

Gambling places sprang up everywhere in 1927 with the aid of Chicago's top officials.[103] Of course, this competition led to minimal profitability. In response, two gambling syndicates formed in May 1927. One, which controlled the area north of Madison Avenue, was led by Christian "Barney" Bertsche, in cooperation with George

Moran. The other, south of the dividing line, was led by Al Capone. Both decreased the number of gambling places, generally squeezing out the newer operators in favor of the old hands, and demanded 40 percent of the receipts (gross revenues) from the places they themselves did not own. In Chicago itself, the biggest gambling district at the time was along Sixty-Third Street, from Cottage Grove west to South Park (now called Martin Luther King) Drive.[104]

The largest gambling houses in the northern syndicate, the Dells at Austin and Dempster and the Lighthouse at Waukegan and Dempster, were both in Morton Grove. The southern syndicate had major operations in Cicero, Stickney, Burnham, Lyons, and Chicago Heights.[105] Jessie Binford of the JPA states that gambling in Cicero was "the worst there is in the United States."[106] Daniel Russell reports that in the summer of 1927 every one of the 225 roadhouses in Cook County had gambling of one type or another.[107]

By August 1927 there was a different arrangement in gambling, probably because the major players in the two earlier syndicates—Moran and Capone—did not get along well, given their past differences in the bootlegging arena. One large syndicate replaced it, led by Jimmy Mondi who was the point man for Capone. South Side politician Dan Jackson assisted Mondi, along with Mont Tennes who came out of retirement and several other politicians, including "one of the men closest to Mayor Thompson in his present cabinet."[108] The other politicians, given later events, were almost certainly Thompson's cronies William "Doc" Reid and Charles Fitzmorris (see the discussion below), who was the city controller at the time. Therefore, the Thompson administration not only took protection money from the gamblers, but it helped operate the syndicate overseeing the business. The new syndicate's cut was 25 percent of the receipts from each gambling place.

Partly due to public pressure, the Chicago police shut down virtually all of the city's 1,500 or more gambling places in early November 1927. However, it was also done to reorganize gambling. According to one city hall politician, the shutdown was "just a temporary lull" until a new syndicate was set up.[109] The third gambling syndicate of 1927, which took a flat fee from each place rather than a percentage of the revenues, was up and running in December.[110] The major bootlegging gangs, and therefore also Jimmy Mondi, were not part of this group's management because fighting between them had resumed in late November. The previous arrangement had also suffered because politically influential gamblers were getting exemptions directly from city hall.

As well-informed politicians told the *Chicago Daily News* regarding gambling under Mayor Thompson and Charles Fitzmorris in late 1927, "The policies of the present administration called for the elimination of gambling factions. . . . Al Capone and other stalwarts of the old days were eliminated. In their place appeared individuals who were recognized spokesmen for the city hall and whom it was necessary to consult before opening any kind of game."[111] Frankie Pope represented the new syndicate on the North Side, dispensing gambling privileges and collecting the tithes, while Jack Lynch did the same on the West Side, and William Reid and Charles Fitzmorris handled the arrangements on the South Side.[112]

Dog racing, where the attendees bet on greyhounds, first appeared in the Chicago area in the spring of 1927. By June there were six dog tracks operating in Cook County, including the Laramie Kennel Club in Cicero owned by the Capone gang and the Fairview Kennel Club controlled by the North Side gang. A seventh, which was a joint venture between Danny Stanton and Spike O'Donnell, was planned for the South Shore neighborhood in Chicago. As opposed to the sport of kings (aka horse racing), the canine races were held at night and were especially popular with housewives and young working women, an audience they catered to in various ways.[113] The dog tracks were, however, in continual legal trouble and closed permanently in 1932 after the Illinois Supreme Court ruled against them.

Vice had decreased dramatically inside the city limits by the end of 1926, but in early 1927 it was running rampant again. A vice syndicate was in place, headed by "two politicians and a former saloonkeeper."[114] There was heavy activity along Clark Street, just north of the Chicago River, on the Near West Side, and also in the old Levee along Federal Street and near Twenty-Second and State.[115] To quote Jessie Binford, "It is impossible for a young man to travel from the river [up] North Clark Street without being accosted several times by women."[116] The suburbs most active in gambling at the time were almost all, with the exception of Cicero, centers of vice, with Burnham, Stickney, Chicago Heights, and Blue Island and the surrounding area along 119th Street at the top of the list.[117] Many of the people who had been in the forefront of the field four years earlier still dominated prostitution, such as Capone, through his lieutenants Jake Guzik and Dennis Cooney, and Jack Zuta.

After the very high-profile murders of the early 1920s, the labor union world was peaceful for several years. From 1925 through 1927 only one union man of any stature, Edward Dunn, was killed—on November 16, 1926—and his union seems to have been of minor importance at the time. Dunn was the vice president of the Afro-American Flat Janitors Union that had just broken away from the regular janitors' union.[118] In 1927, the bootlegging gangs were still only dabbling in labor racketeering.

Business racketeering took on a new dimension in January 1925 when Steve Sumner, the business agent of the Chicago Milk Wagon Drivers' union, organized the milk distributors into an association aimed at raising prices.[119] Threats, intimidation, strikes, and bombings were used in an attempt to force all the distributors into line. In fact, bombing, which was previously associated with the labor unions, was heavily used for the first time in 1925 by the business racketeers in Chicago.[120] However, the distributor's sale of substandard milk to school children drew the attention of the Employers' Association, a group of two thousand businessmen interested in business issues.[121] Through the efforts of Gordon L. Hostetter, the executive secretary of the group, and the Cook County

Fig. 4.13. Steve Sumner.

State's Attorney's Office, the milk distributors' organization disbanded in December 1925. This was a textbook example of how to defeat a business racket by using publicity and the legal system.

Business racketeering in Chicago increased dramatically after Mayor Thompson's third term began, and by the end of 1927 it was costing the citizens some $9 million a year.[122] This comes as no surprise because the mayor himself was running a racket through his political appendage, the America First association. "If you don't think that taking $10 a piece from 5000 policemen and as many firemen, as the America First people did, is a racket, you are badly mistaken," Earl Macoy of the Employers' Association stated after various city workers joined the group under duress.[123]

Unfortunately for Vincent Drucci, he did not live long enough to enjoy the change in political regime in the city. He was killed in an altercation with a Chicago police detective on April 4, 1927, stemming from election-related violence, and George Moran succeeded him. Moran was as fearless as the North Side leaders who preceded him, as his walk down Taylor Street with Hymie Weiss during the summer of 1925 demonstrates, and he had as much elan. He was hated by the Capone crowd, who called him "the Devil."[124] However, Moran seems to have lacked the business sense, diplomacy, and tact that Weiss and similarly Capone had.

Other North Side mobsters of note during the late 1920s included the aforementioned Gusenberg brothers and Frank Foster, who had been with the gang for a number of years, along with Willie Marks, Izzy Alderman, and Leo Mongoven, who was Moran's bodyguard. Edward "Ted" Newberry, another of the gang's Jewish members, lived on the same block as Dean O'Banion in the early 1920s, which was likely his entree into gangland.[125] Newberry, with his junior partner "Benny" Bennett, handled the whiskey business in Moran's North Side territory. Furthermore, Newberry, rather than Jack McGurn, owned the famous Green Mill club at Broadway and Lawrence on the North Side.[126]

Things continued to twist and turn on the South Side after the general peace was made in late 1926. Not long after Joe Saltis and Frank Koncil were acquitted of the murder of "Mitters" Foley in the first part of November 1926, Saltis was picked up on a gun charge and sentenced to sixty days in jail.[127] The violence synonymous with the Back of the Yards during Prohibition did not lie dormant for long either. On November 25, 1926, Tommy and Charles O'Donnell were wounded, along with Saltis hood Clarence Barrett, when Saltis gangsters attacked the South Side O'Donnells. On the other front, Sheldon-Stanton gangster Hillary Clements, who was at one time Foley's partner in crime, vanished around December 16, 1926, and his body was found near the end of the month in a building on W. Sixtieth Street.[128] The Saltis gang was suspected in the Clements killing.[129]

In March 1927 Koncil and Francis Hubacek were slain at Thirty-Ninth and Ashland by gunmen wielding pistols and shotguns. The South Side O'Donnell gang, or the Sheldon-Stanton gang, has usually been blamed for this double homicide. However, there is a variety of evidence to the contrary. The CPD, including Captain John Stege, attributed the killings to the Saltis-McErlane crowd, and several gangs protested loudly at the time that the 1926 peace was *not* broken by this incident.[130] This suggests, along with the double murder occurring only days after Frank McErlane returned to Chicago following his legal troubles in Indiana, that Koncil and Hubacek were responsible for the attack on the O'Donnells in November 1926, and their own gang, adhering to the peace treaty, punished the violators themselves. Consistent with this interpretation, there was no further mayhem behind the stockyards for almost sixteen months following this double homicide, including no retaliation by Saltis and McErlane for the killing of two of their own.

Joe Aiello, the disturber of the peace par excellence in Chicago after 1926, was by far a greater threat to gangland harmony. Born Guiseppe Aiello on September 27, 1890, in Bagheria, in the Sicilian province of Palermo, he came to the United States on July 27, 1907. Six of his brothers also lived in Chicago: Domenico (aka Dominic), who owned a bakery with Joe on W. Division Street; Nunzio, who ran a cigar store also on W. Division Street; Carlo, who operated a grocery on Oak Street; Tony, who worked for Joe; Mario, a tailor; and Andrew, a factory worker.[131]

Initially, Joe Aiello was Tony Lombardo's partner in a commission supply house that grew rich on bootlegging, as well as in a wholesale fruit business that also included Joseph Ferraro, another Unione

Siciliana official.[132] He was also a close colleague of Lombardo's in the Unione. Yet, the Aiello clan was inactive in underworld affairs before 1926. But with the demise of the Gennas, the rise of Tony Lombardo, and Tony Aiello's slaying of the much-feared Joe "the Cavalier" Nerone, they gained considerable prominence in gangland.

Despite their close ties earlier, Joe Aiello and Tony Lombardo had a serious falling out in late 1926 due to Aiello's ambitions and Lombardo's closeness to Capone and his position in Sicilian gangland.[133] What followed was initially a civil war inside the Unione and did not involve the bootlegging gangs, except for Capone's because Tony Lombardo was his man. Joe Aiello's power base consisted of his brothers, his dozens of cousins, and their multiple adherents, many of whom were Aiello paesani. The Aiello turf was around Division Street on the North Side, which distanced them from the Capone provinces, and they ran the alky cooking and the gambling in the area.[134] Lombardo was the power around Taylor Street and in the other southern Italian neighborhoods in Chicago controlled by the Capone gang and its allies. The split in the alky cookers union resulted in extreme competition and lower prices. In July 1927 a five-gallon can of alcohol was selling for about ten dollars in Chicago, compared to the eighteen to twenty dollars it had brought only a few months before.[135]

Fig. 4.14. Joe Aiello (right).

In mid-1927 Aiello's plans went into high gear with the encouragement of New York mobster Frankie Yale and George Moran.[136] He offered a chef in Cicero $35,000 to poison Capone and Lombardo, which was refused, and then put a bounty of $25,000 on each of them. According to the standard accounts, four out-of-town killers came to Chicago to try their luck and were promptly killed by Jack McGurn.[137] The four men were Antonio Tocci (aka Tony Torchio) from Bellwood, New York (killed May 25, 1927), Vincent Spicuzza and Tony Russo from St. Louis (killed August 9), and Salvatori Mezzapelle (aka Sam Valenti, whose body was found in Stickney on September 23).[138] The Aiello brothers' bakery was raked with machine gun fire, wounding Tony Aiello and another man, on May 28, the same day that the chef revealed the poison plot to Capone and three days after Tocci was murdered.[139]

Fig. 4.15. Tony Lombardo.

Between the beginning of June and the middle of July 1927 at least a dozen Italian American men were murdered gangland-style in Cook County, mostly in the Division Street and Taylor Street neighborhoods. These killings were largely due to fighting between the Aiello and Capone-Lombardo forces over the existing rackets, primarily the Unione, as well as expansion into new ones. For example, at the time Italian merchants were being forced into a business association (racket), apparently by the Aiello brothers.[140] Several of the dead men were, in fact, grocers or purveyors of food.

Interestingly, it was reported that the Sicilian hoodlums made peace in late July 1927. The meeting took place in Chicago Heights, following an initial parley in New York City, and the details covered not just Chicago, but the Heights and Melrose Park as well due to their immense alcohol production.[141] The peace, however, obviously did not last very long if Joe Aiello was dangling $50,000 in front of assassins in August and September. And, more importantly, in late 1927 the troubles in the Unione, which earlier that year had spread to the rest of gangland due to the Aiellos' involvement in gambling, ignited the second stage of the North Side vs. South Side War.

CHAPTER 5

THE BEER WARS: 1927–1930

"Chicago gangsters yesterday graduated from murder to massacre."

—*Chicago Herald and Examiner,* February 15, 1929

All was quiet in Chicago's underworld for some eight weeks until late November 1927, when Al Capone learned of new attempts by the North Siders to kill him and Tony Lombardo. It was revealed at the time that George Moran, who had earlier joined with Jack Zuta, "Barney" Bertsche, Billy Skidmore, and the Aiellos to form the North Side gambling syndicate, had created a broader, aggressively anti-Capone mob on the North and West Sides.[1] Moran, Joe Aiello, whose star had risen dramatically in gangland, and Zuta were the acknowledged leaders of the group, with Zuta serving as the chief strategist, Moran providing the muscle and the political connections, and Aiello supplying money (from the alky business) and troops of his own.[2] For Zuta, who "believed that money and scheming were far more powerful than a gang of powerful men," this was an opportunity to put his theories to the test.[3]

Fig. 5.1. Jack Zuta.

After making peace with Capone in 1926, why would Moran's gang resume hostilities a year later? The North Siders were frustrated that the recent arrangements made to control gambling citywide had left them with what they felt was the short end of the stick.[4] When Jimmy Mondi was the point man for the Capone-run syndicate, Moran's group was unhappy because they were paying protection money and investing large sums to set up gambling places only to have them raided by the police.[5] They were also stronger than they had been since the end of 1926 because they had put together a new coalition to replace the one that ended when Hymie Weiss was killed.

When the latest attempts on Capone and Lombardo became known, Capone hoods brazenly went after Joe Aiello and threatened him while he was in a cell inside the CPD's detective bureau. Aiello begged for his life and, along with his brothers, immediately fled Chicago.[6] Jack Zuta removed himself to Ohio at the time.[7] However, Zuta's business interests, located on the Near West Side somewhat north of Taylor Street, remained behind and were on the front lines of the conflict. Along with places controlled by gambler and Moran ally Billy Skidmore, they took considerable punishment during a vigorous bombing campaign over the next few months. During that time two of Zuta's men, Frank Carpenter and Isadore Goldberg, were killed.[8] The Genaro brothers and Rocco Fanelli led the Capone shock troops who, along with the Valley Gang, grabbed Zuta's West Side vice and gambling operations and put the previously displaced Mike Heitler and Joe Genaro in charge of the district.[9] Relatedly, Roger Touhy's brother John was killed in a beer runner's quarrel at the Lone Tree Inn in Niles on December 28, 1927, and around this time Matt Kolb was kidnapped by the Capone gang until

Fig. 5.2. Rocco Fanelli.

Fig. 5.3. Joe Genaro

Fig. 5.4. John Genaro.

Roger Touhy paid a $50,000 ransom to have him released.[10]

When Joe Aiello's brother Dominic returned to town, Caponeites Phil D'Andrea and Lawrence "Dago" Mangano walked into his bakery on Division Street in broad daylight on January 4, 1928, and riddled the walls with pistol and shotgun fire.[11] It was a dramatic warning to the Aiello brothers that if they did not stay out of Chicago, Capone gunmen could and would come for them no matter where they were. In March 1928 Aiello henchman Angelo Morreale was wounded, and not long thereafter there was an attempt to bomb the business offices of Capone's chieftain of the Unione Siciliana, Tony Lombardo, on Randolph Street.[12]

The Capone gang's retaliation continued in the spring of 1928 when a squad led by Jack McGurn flooded the lower North Side, where they had earlier established a beachhead, with slot machines. They were allied with the Gloriana gang, a group of criminals from around Division Street led by Dominic Nuccio, who pushed Capone booze in the East Chicago Avenue police district.[13] In response the

Moran-Aiello-Zuta gang aggressively hijacked Capone liquor shipments and the Gusenberg brothers wounded McGurn and Nick Mastro on March 7, 1928, in a machine gun attack inside the Hotel McCormick at Ontario and Rush, where McGurn was living. On April 17 McGurn was attacked by North Siders James Clark and Billy Davern, again with a machine gun, at the corner of Morgan and Harrison, just a few blocks north of Taylor Street.[14]

The North Side vs. South Side gang war heated up considerably during the following summer, most likely because Zuta slipped back into Chicago in April or May.[15] Three Capone-Lombardo men were killed in two separate incidents by the Aiellos on June 19, 1928. In retaliation, the Capone-Lombardo forces launched a three-pronged attack on Joe Aiello's support inside the Unione, at his closest followers, and at the local source of his power.

First, Capone struck against his New York City mentor Frankie Yale, who was the national president of the Unione Siciliana. An execution team using a variety of weapons killed Yale after a car chase in New York City on July 1, 1928. Aiello responded by setting up rival Unione branches in Melrose Park and Chicago Heights in an attempt to weaken Lombardo's power, but these efforts appear to have been completely unsuccessful.[16] Second, during July 1928 Aiello's bodyguard Tony Calafiore was wounded by shotgun fire and a Dominick Aiello, who was an uncle or cousin of Moran's partner in crime Joe Aiello, and Sam Canale were killed. Ballistics tests later established that a bullet removed from Dominick Aiello matched a .32-caliber Smith and Wesson taken by the police from Tony Lombardo.[17]

The third prong of the offensive attacked the Aiellos' bastion near Division Street. In the five weeks following August 1 some three hundred families moved out of the neighborhood after they received anonymous, threatening letters or phone calls, and an additional one hundred men fled, leaving their families behind. Almost all of the butcher shops in the area, most of which were owned by immigrants from the Aiello hometown of Bagheria, closed after they received demands that they pay $1,500, which they almost certainly did not have, or get out.[18]

The next major casualty was Unione head Lombardo. He was killed, along with Joseph Ferraro, by gunmen on September 7, 1928, on W. Madison when the Loop was full of people leaving from work. Although it has often been claimed that Moran and the Aiellos were directly responsible, the evidence favors the conclusion that it was revenge by Brooklyn gangsters, with Anthony Carfano (aka "Little Augie" Pisano) serving as the principal shooter, for the Yale murder.[19] Nonetheless, it furthered Aiello's cause by removing the man who held the position he coveted—the presidency of the Chicago chapter of the Unione Siciliana. In revenge, Peter Rizzito, a Chicago Unione official who was suspected of setting up Lombardo, was gunned down on October 27 by Capone affiliate Pasquale "Patsy" Lolordo.

Another conference, involving hoodlums from around the country, was arranged at the Hotel Statler in Cleveland, Ohio, in December 1928 to try and settle the nasty state of affairs in the Sicilian underworld in Chicago and beyond. Ten gangsters from the Chicago area and Gary, Indiana, were in attendance, including Lolordo, Joe Giunta, and Chicago Heights mobster Phil Bacino.[20] Lolordo was either named at this conclave to replace Lombardo as the head of the Unione Siciliana's Chicago chapter, or his choice by Capone was ratified by those assembled there. Aiello agreed to attend, but there

Fig. 5.5. Some of the attendees at the Hotel Statler conference in Cleveland, Ohio. The most prominent individuals are: Vincent Mangano (#8), Joe Giunta (#12), Joe Profaci (#13), and Pasquale Lolordo (#14).

was not a peaceful bone in his body. In another attempt to further his own ambitions, he disrupted the meeting by tipping off the police who arrested all those present.[21]

In December 1928 Capone's allies grabbed the bootlegging rights in the Cragin district from the GKW gang after a new police captain encouraged the change. Other Capone troops, including McGurn and Danny Vallo, working with the Circus Gang, moved eastward across the Chicago River into Moran's bailiwick.[22] The Circus Café was a perfect forward base, given its location just west of the river on North Avenue, for attacks by the Capone combine on the North Siders and their various allies inside Chicago. The two gangs also fought to control gambling at dog tracks (racing greyhounds) in the Chicago area, and Moran attempted to make inroads into other rackets.[23] At the end of 1928 it would be accurate to say that the Capone gang and the Moran-Aiello-Zuta mob were fighting on all fronts.

In January 1929 Joe Aiello returned to Chicago, pretending to make peace with Lolordo.[24] Under this false flag several North Side gunmen met with Lolordo in his home near North Avenue and Damen, a few doors from the Circus Café.[25] The unsuspecting Unione leader was murdered in his living room while his wife busied herself in the kitchen—where she was likely preparing food for her husband's "guests." Joe Giunta, another Capone man, succeeded Lolordo as head of the Unione in Chicago, a position that by now was clearly very hazardous to the holder's health.

Capone would have been incensed by this further duplicity on Aiello's part. His next move, however, was already well underway. In typical gangland fashion, the strike was aimed at the head, meaning at Moran and some of his most important followers. If Moran and several of his key men were eliminated, the core of the anti-Capone confederation would have been destroyed, and Aiello, Zuta, and the others would have been largely neutralized. On the morning of February 14, 1929, several carloads of men, posing as police officers, staged what appeared to be a raid on the SMC Cartage Company on N. Clark Street, which a section of the North Side gang used as a headquarters. Moran stalwarts Peter and Frank Gusenberg, James Clark, Adam Heyer, and Albert Weinshank were inside, along with John May, an ex-convict who worked there as a mechanic. Reinhardt (who sometimes spelled his name Reinhart) Schwimmer, an optometrist who had socialized with the North Side mobsters for years, was also present.[26] When the gunmen, who used two machine guns and two shotguns, were finished, all seven men inside the building were dead or mortally wounded. The death toll at the St. Valentine's Day Massacre included three of Moran's top killers and two of his other important operatives.

Some minutes before the killings, a lookout across the street from the garage had erroneously concluded that Moran was there and gave the execution squad the signal to proceed by telephone. Although it has been claimed that Weinshank was mistaken for the North Side leader, it is equally likely that a watcher may have incorrectly identified James Clark as Moran. There was a strong resemblance between them, as indicated in the photo of O'Banion's pallbearers that appears in Fig. 4.2 of chapter 4. Regardless of why the lookout committed this error, it led to a near miss because Moran was actually walking toward the garage with Willie Marks when a black Cadillac of the type used by Chicago detectives pulled up in front of the garage on N. Clark. The pair beat a hasty retreat down Clark Street in the belief that a police squad was entering the building.[27]

The enduring questions about the St. Valentine's Day Massacre are 1) who was behind the killings, and 2) who were the gunmen? The answers are interrelated. The consensus among researchers for many years has been that it was a Capone operation.[28] He certainly had an abundance of motive, given the continual troubles between his gang and the North Siders, including the never-ending, more recent problems with Aiello, and the fact that the North Siders were generally responsible for breaking the peace. However, the responsibility for the massacre also falls partly on the Circus Gang, which had much to gain from the demise of its enemies just across the Chicago River and was involved in various aspects of the planning and the logistics related to the perpetration of this multiple homicide.

There has been less than complete agreement, however, about the identities of the shooters. John Kobler leans heavily toward a roving, highly professional crew of robbers and killers for hire led by Fred "Killer" Burke, who grew out of the defunct Egan's Rats gang in St. Louis.[29] On the other hand, Laurence Bergreen names Burke, Gus

Fig. 5.6. Left to right: Norman Jones, Gus Winkler, and Fred Burke.

Winkler (born Gus Winkeler and also known as James Ray), who was a Burke confederate, Scalise, Anselmi, and Lolordo's brother Joe as the gunmen.[30] This is a Solomonic compromise that includes various people who were suspected at one time or another. Similarly, Robert Schoenberg favors Scalise, Anselmi, and two unnamed "Egan's Rats" from St. Louis, which is consistent with Burke and Winkler (or some of their ilk) having been involved.[31]

A considerable body of evidence, much of which has been known to organized crime historians for many years, indicates that the killers were Burke, Winkler, Fred Goetz (aka George Zeigler or Ziegler), Ray "Crane Neck" Nugent, and Bob Carey (aka Bob Conroy, Bob Newberry, and a multitude of other aliases).[32] Byron Bolton, Jimmy "the Swede" Johnson (aka Jimmy "the Swede" Moran or Morand), Jimmy McCrussen, and several others were the lookouts stationed on the east side of Clark Street in the days or weeks before the event.[33]

Fig. 5.7. Fred Goetz.

Fig. 5.8. Byron Bolton.

First, among the various pieces of evidence, Burke had the two machine guns used in the massacre. Second, he had clear connections to the Capone gang, including that he stayed with the families of Chicago Heights gangsters when he was in the Chicago area.[34] Third, the Heights guys were reported to have been involved in the killings.[35] Fourth, Burke was ultimately identified by three eyewitnesses as being one of the gunmen and named by the CPD as the chief suspect in the seven murders.[36] Fifth, the CPD found evidence in Circus Gang leader Claude Maddox's office that he brought Burke and his gun mates to Chicago to do the job.[37] Sixth, Jimmy Johnson, a close friend of Claude Maddox and a Circus gangster, was one of the lookouts, along with Byron Bolton, a Burke confederate who was identified in February 1929 by the CPD based on evidence found in the apartment they used to watch the garage. Seventh, the Circus Gang disposed of at least one and possibly two of the cars involved. Eighth, inside the Chicago Outfit and in the New York City underworld Burke and his crew are acknowledged as the killers.[38]

The last, but most important, piece of evidence is the confession by Bolton, who gave the FBI numerous details about the planning of the St. Valentine's Day Massacre and its execution after he was apprehended in 1935. This information is in two memos contained in the bureau's file on the massacre in which Bolton named Burke, Winkler, Goetz, Nugent, and Carey as the killers. Contrary to claims that Bolton never talked to the FBI about the crime, one of the two memos was written by J. Edgar Hoover to the US attorney general. Clearly, Bolton gave the FBI a full statement about the massacre and its planning, which that agency acknowledged in 1936, sometime after his arrest.[39]

Jonathan Eig disagrees with the standard view of the massacre. Based on claims by Chicagoan Frank T. Farrell, Eig concludes that William "Three Finger (or Three-Fingered) Jack" White, more commonly known as Jack White, planned and carried out the seven killings on Clark Street.[40] Farrell, a patronage worker with the state highway department at the time, wrote a letter to J. Edgar Hoover on January 28, 1935, to share with him the details of his "investigation" into the massacre.[41] The assertions in the Farrell letter include 1) North Side gangster William "Billy" Davern Jr. was shot (in November 1928) by members of his own gang, 2) before Davern died, he spoke to his cousin, Jack White, and told him the names of the men who shot him, and 3) White then planned a robbery in conjunction with Davern's murderers, but when they met at the garage on February 14, 1929, he killed the North Side gangsters to avenge Davern's death. Because this attempt to blame the St. Valentine's Day Massacre on Jack White has received considerable attention in the media, it merits further analysis.

Historians researching the St. Valentine's Day Massacre have been aware of this letter for many years. After careful examination it was dismissed because there are a number of problems with it and, therefore, the Farrell Assertion.[42] Several details in the Farrell letter, such as names, dates, and the specifics of how people were related to one another, are incorrect. For example, a detailed construction of Davern's family tree from newspaper obituaries and other genealogical sources indicates that Billy Davern's father's first wife was Anna L. Davern (née Gillespie), not Nellie Davern (née White) as Farrell claims. Nellie Davern was, in fact, the daughter of William J.

Fig. 5.9. "Three Finger Jack" White (circa 1920).

and Anna L. Davern and the sister of gangster Billy Davern. Anna L. Davern (Billy Davern's birth mother) was the sister of Jack White's mother, Mary Gillespie, rather than the sister of White's father. Furthermore, Billy Davern was shot on November 14, 1928, not the twenty-ninth or thirtieth of the month as Farrell states, and White was in jail in late 1928 because he had been convicted of murder, not manslaughter. The fifth basic error in this one-page letter is the claim that "White and Moran were pals." There is no evidence that Moran and Jack White were close to one another. Farrell was probably confusing Jack White with prominent North Side gang member Joseph "Puggy" White. The multiple inaccuracies about minor details call the letter's credibility into question before its assertions about the Clark Street killings are examined.

Moreover, the Farrell Assertion is inconsistent with the known facts about the Clark Street killings that are summarized above. Of greatest importance, the CPD, which was much better informed about a mass gangland homicide in its jurisdiction than a junior highway engineer, named Fred "Killer" Burke as the chief suspect, and three eyewitnesses identified him as the man they saw entering the garage. Also, White has not been mentioned in connection with the massacre by anyone other than Farrell.

Also, according to the CPD and another knowledgeable source, Capone's top executioner, Jack McGurn, rather than the North Side gangsters, was responsible for the murder of Billy Davern.[43] As previously noted, McGurn was shot in early 1928 by Davern and James Clark. In retaliation, Davern was, according to the only two contemporary sources who name the killer, slain by McGurn. This greatly weakens the Farrell Assertion because White's supposed motive for the massacre is completely eliminated.

Of greatest importance, White was in the Cook County Jail from March 1926 to July 1929, without bond, for murdering a Forest Park police officer.[44] Is it possible that he would have been able to leave the jail to commit the St. Valentine's Day Massacre? Also, one of the machine guns used on February 14, 1929, was also used to kill Frankie Yale in New York City in 1928. Did White then leave the Cook County Jail not once but twice to commit murder, in one case going to the East Coast to kill someone for Capone? It should be emphasized that White had no direct criminal association with Capone at the time, because when he was jailed in 1926 he was a freelance robber with no involvement in organized crime.

Regardless of his criminal résumé, is it plausible that White actually returned to the lockup on both occasions, in 1928 and 1929, rather than simply escaping, when he had been sentenced to life in prison in 1927? And would he have been able to return without being detected after he had been gone for days to do the Yale killing, if he had, in fact, committed that crime? White's incarceration from 1926 until the middle of 1929 would normally completely settle the issue of whether he was at the St. Valentine's Day Massacre.

The first (hardcover) edition of Eig's book makes no mention of the fact that White was in jail at the time, even though the Farrell letter explicitly states that he was incarcerated when Davern was shot in November 1928.[45] When White's imprisonment (and McGurn's responsibility for the Davern killing) were pointed out in a story on Chicago television by investigative reporter Chuck Goudie, Eig then asserted that there was an "open door" policy at the jail, which allowed Jack White to come and go as he pleased.[46] However, Eig has provided no evidence to support this new claim.

A check of the facts reveals that the exact opposite of an "open door" policy was in place at the Cook County Jail from late 1926 to the middle of 1929. In 1925 there were some abuses of the system at the jail. The most glaring was that Terry Druggan and Frankie Lake, who were under lock and key on the minor charge of contempt of court, bribed officials so that they could come and go on a regular basis. They were, based on detailed research on this issue, the only criminals with such privileges, and they were always accompanied by a jail official on their sojourns. Also, there is no evidence that they committed any crimes during their brief absences.[47] They went out for medical appointments as well as sometimes for meals, and then they returned.

The first thing that should be noted is that the situation with Druggan and Lake was completely different from that of White, a convicted cop killer sentenced to life in prison. White would obviously have fled if he was ever allowed to leave the jail on his own. Therefore, no warden or prison official in his right mind would have dared let him leave, much less without handcuffs, leg irons, and a guard detail, for fear of the consequences. On this dimension it is instructive to look at the repercussions from the Druggan-Lake affair that occurred several years before 1929. The newspapers had a field day with it once the information became known, and it caused a massive scandal. A federal judge sentenced Cook County sheriff Peter Hoffman to one month in the DuPage County Jail and Cook County Jail warden Wesley Westbrook to four months in the DeKalb County Jail in October 1925 for taking bribes from Druggan and Lake.[48] In fact, both Hoffman and Westbrook were ruined politically by their indiscretions.

A second and much larger problem for the Farrell Assertion is that the magnitude of the Druggan-Lake jail scandal caused, even in a place as politically tainted as Cook County, a tidal wave of reform. A blue ribbon citizen's committee brought in a professional penologist from Indiana, Edward Fogarty, as the new jail warden in September

1926. In Cook County, where politically appointed jobs were almost always filled by party hacks, outside hires happened only in times of crisis, such as when the politicians were forced by a scandal to give the reformers carte blanche. Relatedly, Orlando W. Wilson, the first police superintendent from outside the ranks of the CPD, was brought in after police officers at a North Side station were caught helping burglarize stores in the Summerdale Scandal in 1959.[49]

In this vein, the *Chicago Tribune* states that Sheriff Graydon, who replaced Peter Hoffman when he resigned, "allowed Fogarty a free hand and a virtual civil service system was set up. Grafting, dope smuggling, and other evils were promptly eliminated at the jail."[50] The *Chicago Evening Post* reports that Warden Fogarty "has raised the standards of the local jail to heretofore unknown high levels."[51] Even Cook County sheriff John Traeger, a product of Chicago politics who took office in 1928 and who was hardly reform-minded, said, "Mr. Fogarty is by all odds the best man we've ever had in the jail post."[52]

Therefore, during Fogarty's time as warden, which started in late 1926 and, more importantly, went well beyond February 1929, the earlier problems at the jail were nonexistent—meaning that White could not have walked out of his cell to commit the St. Valentine's Day Massacre or any other crime and then have walked back in again. Similarly, White would not have been able to plan or take part in such an attack that, given the number of men and the logistics involved, required intricate planning and military precision. Almost all of White's criminal associates, from his days of freelance robberies, were dead or under lock and key themselves by early 1929.[53] So White, regardless of whether he could work with them from inside the Cook County Jail, had essentially no resources outside the jail to call on.

Several other statements by Jonathan Eig about the St. Valentine's Day Massacre are worthy of further scrutiny. First, to bolster the contention that White was there on the morning of February 14, 1929, Eig states that a witness who saw the supposed CPD detective car at the front of the garage noted, "The fellow who stayed at the wheel had a finger missing. His hand was spread out on the steering apparatus, so the old amputation was apparent."[54] There are several reasons why this is actually inconsistent with White driving the car. "Three Finger Jack" White, as per his nickname, was minus two fingers on his hand, not one. Therefore the witness should have reported seeing two missing fingers. And a missing finger in that era was hardly rare, because industrial accidents were quite common, so that does not point to a particular individual in the way it might today.

Also, White's injury was on his right hand.[55] In a car with a manual transmission, the driver would have normally had his right hand on the stick shift and not on the wheel, so the right hand would not usually have been visible to someone standing outside the car. This is especially true if the man at the wheel had to be prepared to throw the car quickly into gear to leave the scene. Therefore, the driver's right hand was likely not on the steering wheel and was not seen by the witness.

The most important problem with this witness report is that White was *extremely* sensitive about his injured right hand. Fred Pasley notes that following his injury White "ever after wore a kid glove on the right hand, with the missing fingers stuffed."[56] For example, when he and other hoodlums were arrested in February 1930, police found in their overcoats a glove with pieces of cork in the exact places where White's fingers were missing.[57] In every identified photo this author has seen of him where, due to circumstances, White was not able to wear gloves, whether he is with his bride in their wedding photo, in pictures taken in court, or in police lineup photos, his deformed right hand is in his pocket or otherwise hidden from general view. Based on this evidence, if White had actually been at the wheel of the car in front of the garage on N. Clark Street that fatal winter morning, he would most likely have been wearing his specially equipped glove or he would have kept his hand out of sight to hide his injury from public view, as was his standard practice. Therefore, the eyewitness statement that the man in the car outside the massacre building was missing one finger on a hand on the steering wheel is strong evidence that he was not, in fact, Jack White.[58]

Eig also emphasizes the claim that Frank Gusenberg uttered the remark "Cops did it" before he died, which implies that he recognized some of the killers as actual police officers.[59] Although this statement appears in other books, it is not in any of the three CPD official reports on the St. Valentine's Day Massacre that discuss what Gusenberg said to the police before he died. And police officers were with him the entire time, from when he was found in the garage until he died in the hospital, just in case he made a dying declaration. Sergeant Thomas J. Loftus, who was the first officer on the scene at N. Clark Street and knew the Gusenberg brothers personally, states that in the garage Frank Gusenberg twice told him, "I won't talk" and similarly said, "I refuse to talk."[60] Lieutenant Otto Erlanson, who led the CPD investigation into the massacre, reports that at Alexian Brothers' hospital, "Sergeant Loftus, asked him 'Frank is that right, that three of the men wore police uniforms, and his answer was—yes. That was all that he would state."[61] This weaker remark is consistent with the testimony of Mrs. Alphonsine Morin, who saw several of the killers leave the garage in patrolmen's blue uniforms, but does not imply that Gusenberg knew the killers. Furthermore, in the police reports Gusenberg never says "Nobody shot me," as reported by Helmer and Bilek and others.[62]

Finally, Eig claims that there was no reason for the St. Valentine's Day Massacre because, if Capone had wanted to kill Moran, "[h]e could have put Jack McGurn in a car across the street and had him wait until he got a clean shot."[63] The obvious response to this claim is that if it was so easy to kill Moran, then why didn't the Capone gang do it long before 1929? It certainly had hated him at least since January 1925 when he nearly killed John Torrio.

The fuller answer is that Moran, the leader of one of the city's preeminent bootlegging gangs, was no easy target. And, more so than O'Banion and Weiss, he took precautions because he learned from their deaths. After O'Banion's murder, the North Siders were not going to let Italian faces, meaning Italia Americans who were not members of their gang, get too close to them again. They were doubly cautious after the killing of Weiss. Moran had bodyguards, who would have preceded him onto the sidewalk, and they would have scanned the street to make sure it was safe for him to venture out in public. His gang also used lookouts, such as on N. Clark Street. That is why the St. Valentine's Day killers pretended to be police officers and why they were non-Italians imported from out of town—men who the North Side gangsters would not recognize and would not arouse suspicion.

If the North Siders had spotted McGurn sitting in a car outside the garage on N. Clark or at any other location, they would have come up on him from behind with guns drawn while otherwise distracting him. When they were ready, they would have fired on him from several sides; for example, the north and the west, to avoid hitting each other in the crossfire. Or a carload of North Siders would have driven by and raked him and his vehicle with gunfire. McGurn, waiting in an automobile for Moran to show himself, would have had about as much chance of getting away alive as a sardine in a tin can. As discussed in chapter 7, the Prohibition Era gangsters were sure-thing killers rather than kamikazes. Their goal was to kill and get away to kill another day, as opposed to getting killed in the process.

It is instructive to note that McGurn spent much of 1928, as already noted, trying to *not* get killed by the North Siders, rather than hunting down their leaders. Also, Moran and company had dispatched several top Genna gangsters and had gone after Capone and Torrio on at least three occasions. Clearly the North Side gangsters were extremely dangerous, capable enemies, rather than clay pigeons waiting to be shot.

In sum, even if the other evidence that conflicts with the Farrell Assertion is ignored, the fact that White had neither a motive nor the opportunity to commit or plan the St. Valentine's Day Massacre invalidates what Farrell wrote in his letter to the FBI. At the end of the day, it is simply one of many random letters—and more broadly leads, tips, communications, and criminal confessions—in the hands of the authorities, purporting to solve a major crime, similar to other letters received by the FBI or the continual tips law enforcement receives about where Jimmy Hoffa is buried, which have no credibility. The leaders of the Capone gang, along with the Circus Gang, had the necessary motive, due to their lengthy conflicts with the North Siders and more recently with the Prince of Duplicity, Joe Aiello. They also had the opportunity (by not being in jail at the time) to bring in outsiders, who the lookouts inside the garage would not have recognized, to do the job.

It is a myth that the North Side gang broke up immediately following the St. Valentine's Day Massacre because Moran only had seven (or possibly eight) men working for him at the time, if the mechanic (John May) and the optometrist (Reinhardt Schwimmer) are included in the total.[64] This idea first appeared the morning after the event when the *Chicago Tribune* reports that the North Side mob had been "wiped out" and that "George (Bugs) Moran [was] a leader without a gang."[65] Similarly, a banner headline that day in another major Chicago paper exclaims, "Massacre Wipes Out Last of Powerful O'Banion Gang," and an article asserts, "The once powerful O'Banion gang was completely bordered in black. Two men, George ('Bugs') Moran and Billy Marks, remain alive, but the North Side gang is dead."[66] This contention has been repeated numerous times over the years, by contemporary sources, other newspapers, and various authors.[67]

It is quite simple to refute this claim. First, Moran could not have supplied beer to the North Side, much less have been involved in multiple additional rackets and kept other gangs out of the large area he controlled, with only five or so hardcore members plus a mechanic and a hanger-on. It would have been completely impossible. Second, it is straightforward to name more than seven important members of the Moran-Aiello-Zuta gang—Leo Mongoven, Willie Marks, Frank Foster, Dan McCarthy, Ted Newberry, "Benny" Bennett, Julian "Potatoes" Kaufman, Izzy Alderman, Sam Pellar, Charles "Ice Wagon" Connors, Grover Dullard (the former Valley gangster), Henry Finkelstein, the Applequist brothers, Joseph "Puggy" White, Solly Vision, Joe Aiello (and his brothers), Jack Zuta, Billy Skidmore, and "Barney" Bertsche—who were still alive after the St. Valentine's Day Massacre, much less to count the lower-ranking ones. At the time of his death, Weiss had two hundred gunmen in his employ, and, as shown in chapter 7, very few of them were killed between late 1926 and February 1929. Third, if the Moran gang folded in February 1929, why did the Capone gang not immediately take over the North Side area it controlled? As discussed in the next chapter, according to numerous other accounts, this did not happen until eighteen months after the St. Valentine's Day Massacre.

In reality, the massacre was not the end of the North Side gang, but it may have been the beginning of the end. Moran still had a large number of men who had been with the group for years, plus the contingents brought in by the 1927 marriage with the Zuta and, more importantly, the Aiello interests. However, Moran was shaken by the carnage on Clark Street, and it may have affected his judgment in the longer run. He checked into a hospital in Evanston, just north of Chicago, almost the same day as the massacre to deal with his mental state, and then he removed himself to Windsor, Ontario, with his inner circle before going to Europe for several months.[68]

There was at least a tacit truce between the Capone and North Side mobs immediately after the massacre, as evidenced by the lack of bloodshed involving these two gangs during the next few months. Both groups would have been distracted by the official response to the killings, a crackdown the likes of which the Windy City had probably never seen before, and the North Siders would have been regrouping. Capone was busy as well with internal housekeeping, including the difficult issue of eliminating Joe Giunta, John Scalise, and Albert Anselmi after he learned that they were plotting against him.[69]

The contemporary sources agree that a formal peace covering Chicago's underworld was negotiated in Atlantic City in May 1929 at the behest of Capone and/or Torrio. According to the *New York Times*, Capone stated that only a handful of other Chicago gangsters were present—including Moran (or his representatives) and possibly Joe Saltis.[70] Alternatively, the *Chicago Tribune* claims that it was "a nation-wide affair having to do with gangsters and racketeers in many cities," although it explicitly names only Capone, the North Side leaders, Torrio, Saltis, and McErlane as being in attendance or having a spokesman present.[71] According to Walter Noble Burns, Capone said at the time, "It wasn't an easy matter for men who had been fighting for years to agree on a peaceful business program. But we finally decided to forget the past and begin all over again, and we drew up a written agreement, and each man signed on the dotted line."[72]

Perhaps there were two sets of meetings in Atlantic City in 1929, one involving a limited group of Chicago gangsters to make peace locally, and a second series of conferences where Capone met with hoodlums from various eastern cities, since he was in the area, covering his business dealings with them. Regardless, Capone and the North Siders, as well as Chicago's underworld in general, reached an agreement. All violence between Chicago's bootlegging gangs was to stop, and a broad syndicate was formed with Torrio as the overseer. In this capacity Torrio flew to Chicago twice a month from New York City to meet with Capone's top lieutenants and the North Side gang leaders at a hotel in Evanston, Illinois.[73] As the arbitrator for the compact, he ruled on any disagreements between the members.[74]

Although the North Siders and the Capone gang did not actually merge at the time, they did effectively enter into a joint venture by pooling the profits from their activities and then dividing them based on predetermined percentages.[75] Pooling was a common device used by the railroad cartels in the United States in the late 1800s that decreased cheating on collusive agreements because it minimized the gains from self-interested behavior. Leaders of both gangs audited the books on a monthly basis to verify the figures. During Capone's stay in a Pennsylvania prison for carrying a concealed weapon, which roughly coincided with the time period that the agreement was maintained, Jake Guzik acted on his behalf in Chicago, as he had done previously when Capone wintered in Miami.[76] The other Chicago gangs were reportedly under Torrio's jurisdiction as well, although there was no discussion of them being part of a money pool.[77] Importantly, this was the first time that a syndicate of Chicago's bootlegging gangs had explicit mechanisms in place to try and uphold the arrangement and to minimize violence.

Little territory changed hands as a result of the second phase of the North Side vs. South Side War. The earlier dividing line at Madison Avenue between the two major factions was restored when the peace was made, although the GKW gang most likely lost the Cragin police district on the Northwest Side to Capone. Beyond the division of the relevant geographical areas, but important in terms of peace offerings, Joe Aiello was made the head of the Chicago chapter of the Unione Siciliana, succeeding the recently departed Joe Giunta. This occurred with Capone's blessing and was an explicit provision of the peace pact.[78] Therefore, although the second part of this gang war once again did not result in a complete victory by the Capone gang, it was a major one.

As a result, Capone got the peace he desired and Torrio had another opportunity to fashion a syndicate covering bootlegging and now other illegalities in Chicago. Capone probably believed that this would be a long-lasting peace between his gang and its worst enemies because they were working together closely, and he had made certain concessions to the North Siders even though they had been bested on the field of battle. Furthermore, the inclusion of the city's other gangs in the broader agreement would hopefully help maintain the peace by minimizing problems elsewhere in the area that entangled the biggest of the bootlegging mobs.

A variety of evidence indicates that there was, in fact, harmony and extensive cooperation between the Capone gang and the North Siders, as well as the city's other gangs, beginning in May 1929. Aiello returned to Chicago at the end of the month, which indicated that the agreement was "on the square."[79] A few months later Mike Heitler, James Belcastro, Jake Guzik, and other Capone stalwarts met with Jack Zuta and the Aiello brothers to oversee booze and gambling operations on the Near West Side.[80] In September 1929 Capone gangster "Mops" Volpe and North Sider Ted Newberry were jointly muscling in on bucket shops, which fraudulently sold common stocks to investors, and in December of that year Andrew Aiello, Dominick Aiello, and Leo Mongoven, all North Siders, and Capone gangster Frank Diamond were arrested together at the business headquarters of the North Side gang.[81]

Tellingly, Chicago's top hoods met at regular poker games during 1929 where they amicably discussed and settled their disagreements.[82] At the beginning of April 1930, shortly after Capone's release from prison, there were dinners in restaurants around the city where Guzik socialized with Zuta, Newberry fraternized with the Fischetti brothers, and Joe Aiello broke bread with his former sworn enemies.[83] Significantly, there was no visible fighting between the Capone gang and the North Siders from May 1929 until the middle of April 1930.

The North Side gang was, however, hit by internal problems as 1929 drew to a close. In November of that year, Moran, Aiello, and Zuta accused Newberry and "Benny" Bennett of shortchanging them on the revenues from hard liquor sales, and they took the business away from the pair. The meeting ended with snarled threats and promises to "get even." Newberry was wounded in an ambush on November 30, 1929, and quickly fled to Canada.[84] A few weeks later, Bennett received peace overtures, and, with his bodyguard John "the Billiken" Rito, he unwisely returned to the fold. Neither man was seen again until Rito's body, which rose to the surface because it had been improperly weighted down, was found floating in the Chicago River near Irving Park Road on March 16, 1930. This discovery spoke volumes about what had happened to Bennett. In spite of this, Newberry, probably after some solid assurances by Moran and other North Siders, had a change of heart and later rejoined the gang, but only for a short time.[85]

In terms of its broader geographical scope, by the early 1930s the Capone gang's tentacles reached not only to many parts of Illinois but to numerous other states as well, which laid the foundations for the Outfit's later activities in the United States. Closest to home, in the early 1920s Thomas Johnson was the point man for the Torrio-Capone gang in Northern Indiana.[86] He also dispensed protection to gambling and other illegal establishments in the vicinity in cooperation with the authorities in East Chicago, Indiana.

Separate from its gambling, the Calumet region around Gary, Indiana, was important to the Capone mob both as a major point on the imported Canadian whiskey highway that ran from Detroit to Chicago and, given its sizeable Sicilian community, as a center of alky cooking.[87] In 1924 alcohol manufactured on Chicago's South Side was also flowing into Gary, Hammond, and East Chicago, indicating that the local production was less than what was consumed in the area.[88] The Chicago Heights gangsters were suspected when the Gary home of Vito Schiralli, the "king of the bootleggers" in Northern Indiana, was bombed in January 1928. When Thomas Johnson was killed in 1928, Phil Collenger replaced him as the Capone gang overseer for the region around Gary, Indiana, working closely with local bootlegger Nick Sudovich. Collenger and Sudovich were found guilty of violating the Prohibition laws in January 1930, along with East Chicago mayor Raleigh Hale, Chief James Regan, Detective Sergeant Martin Zarkovich, who would later play a prominent role in the killing of John Dillinger, and ten others.[89]

Going far beyond the borders of Illinois, the Capone mob, through its Chicago Heights branch, had connections with Milwaukee during Prohibition. The Heights guys shipped pure alcohol to Wisconsin and Frank LaPorte's cousin on his mother's side, Frank Falvo, relocated there during the 1920s and became an important figure in the local mob. Additionally, the alky that was abundantly produced in the Heights went to Southern Illinois, Indiana, Iowa, Kentucky, and the cities of St. Louis and Kansas City in Missouri.[90]

Chicago Heights was well situated to export this commodity because the town was a railroad hub and it was also on the Lincoln Highway, a precursor to the modern interstate system.

More broadly, in the late 1920s a Capone ring based in Aurora, Illinois, sent alcohol to bootleggers located throughout northern and central Illinois, to towns such as Champaign and Springfield, and to Iowa, Minnesota, Nebraska, North Dakota, South Dakota, Wisconsin, Arkansas, and Oklahoma on the west and also to Indiana, Michigan, and New York on the east.[91] Most of this contraband was produced in the vicinity of Aurora, which was a low-cost way to supply Illinois outside of Cook County and the western United States. Many of the cities that received the Capone product were state capitals and/or the homes of the state university, and therefore they contained two very thirsty groups—college students and politicians. The pure alcohol produced in Cicero and Melrose Park tended to be consumed in the Chicago area.

By 1926 the Capone mob was already well established in Eastern Iowa, with Mike "Bon Bon" Allegretti owning a café in the "Little Cicero" section of Dubuque. In 1929 Ralph Capone visited faraway Dallas in an attempt to corner the city's liquor market.[92] This likely met with some success because by the mid-1940s the Chicago Outfit was active in Dallas and Oklahoma.[93] Furthermore, in 1931 Al Capone, working with local politician and gangland boss John Lazia, headed a major liquor combine operating out of Kansas City, and in 1932 the mayor of New Orleans was outraged because Capone-supported bootleggers were forcing their wares on speakeasy owners.[94]

Not long after Al Capone bought a winter home in Miami, Florida, his gang was in control of gambling in Dade County, including interests in the casino at the Floridian Hotel, the Palm Island Club, and the South Beach Dog Track, which involved slot machines, various table games, and dog racing.[95] He also had gambling interests in Hot Springs, Arkansas, in 1931. And in 1932, also through Allegretti, the Capone mob had a foothold in policy gambling in Cleveland, which may have been the first incursion by a bootlegging mob into this activity.[96] When the North Siders were syndicated with the Capone gang after May 1929, they supplied punch boards, a gambling device frequently found in stores and saloons, to most of the country.

By 1931 a score of Chicago mobsters "aided and encouraged

Fig. 5.10. Al Capone (left) and Nick Circella (right) at the Capone house in Miami, Florida, with Albert "Sonny" Capone in the background.

by Capone . . . moved on Los Angeles and sought to introduce the high pressure methods" there that had been so successful in Chicago.[97] In this capacity Frank Foster, after he went over to the Capone gang from the North Siders in the middle of 1930, and several other hoods were sent to Southern California to set up brewing operations to supply the West Coast. Foster soon moved to Reno, Nevada, and became involved in gambling.[98] Capone may also have had an interest in the Bank Club in Reno in 1931. Furthermore, John Roselli, another Capone emissary, operated a gambling boat outside of the Los Angeles harbor with Jack Dragna beginning in 1930.[99]

Returning to the South Side of Chicago, in late November 1927 there was still harmony between the Saltis-McErlane group and the Sheldon-Stanton gang.[100] When Frank McErlane appeared in court on various charges, Danny Stanton counseled him to avoid a particular judge and to ask for a jury trial instead. This may partially have been the result of the 1926 peace pact, but around this time Capone strengthened the bonds between the former enemies by agreeing to wholesale beer to the Saltis-McErlane gang on the condition that it left Sheldon and Stanton in peace.[101] Faced with continual problems on other fronts, Capone wisely covered one of his flanks with this move—and also shielded the Sheldon-Stanton gang, who had taken the worst of it in the earlier fighting, from further punishment.

Ralph Sheldon, who was afflicted with tuberculosis, was not involved in Chicago's underworld much longer. His men generously contributed money so that he could travel to the Southwest to recuperate.[102] While Sheldon was gone, they learned that he had been receiving bonus money from Capone each month that was meant for them—money they had never received. In a quarrel after Sheldon returned, one of his top men, Hugh "Stubby" McGovern, shot him in the leg, and Capone hoods reportedly shot him again not long thereafter. Sheldon soon permanently removed himself to the West Coast.[103] Stanton replaced him as the leader of the gang, and over the next few years they were drawn closer and closer to the Capone mob until they were for all practical purposes one unit.

In February 1928 Joe Saltis ran out of appeals on his 1926 weapons charge. Rather than go to jail, he went into hiding for almost a year, flitting in and out of Chicago while he lived primarily at his Wisconsin estate.[104] He was, however, still heavily involved in the rackets during the remainder of Prohibition, as the following discussion indicates, sometimes running the New City district directly and at other times operating it through a lieutenant when he was away from Chicago. Saltis finally surrendered to serve his sixty-day sentence on the gun charge in mid-December of 1928, more than two years after his initial conviction.

The disturbances behind the stockyards resumed when the Saltis troops made another attempt on Spike O'Donnell on June 29, 1928.[105] This was the first overt violent act between the two gangs that summer, although it was most probably in response to O'Donnell inroads on the Saltis-McErlane area during Saltis's frequent absences. At the beginning of July, Saltis dodged over a dozen bullets, and Joe Ruddy's saloon on W. Fifty-First Street, a Saltis-McErlane hangout, was bombed on September 21, 1928. October 1928 was another malicious month in the Back of the Yards area as more shots were aimed at Spike O'Donnell by Saltis, "Paddy" Sullivan, Willie Niemoth, and Nick Kramer; Steve O'Donnell's garage was bombed by the same gang; and Tommy O'Donnell lost his eyesight after apparently being poisoned. To punish Saltis for his flight from justice, the authorities soon put James Allman in command of the New City district. Captain Allman closed all the saloons in the area and raided the Saltis-McErlane sources of beer and whiskey, hitting the gang hard financially by squeezing at both ends of the hose.[106]

George Maloney, one of the top killers in Chicago's underworld, and Michael "Bubs" Quinlan left the Saltis mob in late 1928 to form their own South Side gang. They established themselves at the lower end of Stanton's area, in the vicinity of Halsted Street somewhat south of Fifty-First Street, which added a fourth major group to the mix behind the stockyards.[107] Maloney got his start in the Plumbers' Union and by 1923 had interests in a cigar store and a soft drink parlor, both of which were fronts for much heavier activities.[108] Quinlan, who earlier had links to the Ragen's Colts, was a labor slugger and a guard in a gambling house before joining the Saltis-McErlane gang.[109]

For obvious reasons, this incursion did not sit well with Stanton. Quinlan was wounded by machine gun bullets, and a man with him was killed in October 1928.[110] Maloney hit back on December 31, 1928, by killing two of Stanton's hard cases, Hugh "Stubby" McGovern and William "Gunner" McPadden, in front of two hundred people in the Granada Café at Cottage Grove and Sixty-Eighth Street, and Ray Cassidy was slain on March 22, 1929, by Maloney and Quinlan. In revenge, Quinlan was attacked again on March 27, not long after he returned from the hospital following the previous October's shooting, and businesses owned by his brothers Richard and Charles were bombed on April 7, 1929. Stanton aide Benny Butler was wounded later that month as well.

Around the same time the unimaginable happened in Chicago gangland. After gleefully trying to kill Spike O'Donnell and his men for years, Frank McErlane split with Saltis and joined the South Side O'Donnell gang. John Landesco notes that McErlane took numerous Saltis men with him when he moved on.[111] This demonstrates that Prohibition Era gangland in Chicago, like love and politics, sometimes made for extremely strange bedfellows—a point that is further illustrated by the Capone–North Side accord at the time. The earliest indication of the O'Donnell-McErlane union came at the start of June 1929 when the latter was on trial for carrying a concealed weapon. The verdict of "not guilty" was greeted by applause from a cheering section led by Spike O'Donnell himself.[112] McErlane's change in affiliation was due partly to the official clampdown on the New City district. But he also greatly disliked John O'Berta who Saltis had made a partner during his frequent absences from Chicago.[113]

This shift was facilitated, at least partly, by cooperation between the various gangs as peace reigned on much of the South Side following the Atlantic City peace conference in May 1929. Certainly the presence of Saltis and McErlane at the meeting, with Capone likely speaking for the newly appointed Stanton, indicates that affairs on the broader South Side were part of the discussion. His attendance at the meeting also shows the importance of Saltis, who has often been minimized in gangland histories of Chicago, in the scheme of things during Prohibition. Landesco reports at the time that "the O'Donnells and McErlane have been joined by Danny Stanton . . . and all others on the South Side. They are now one syndicate," which implies that there was a pooling arrangement covering the South Side bootleggers as well in 1929.[114]

If the Maloney-Quinlan gang belonged to the South Side syndicate, then the peace did not hold perfectly because Maloney was wounded by gunfire on July 5, 1929. Similarly, Quinlan's brother-in-law was shot about two months later.[115] Despite these occasional disturbances, the newest attempt at tranquility held up fairly well because through the middle of 1930 there were only two other reports of intergang violence on the South Side.

In January 1930 Frank McErlane was shot in a drunken quarrel by Marion Miller, aka Elfrieda Rigus or McErlane, who is usually described as his common-law wife.[116] Although this incident was not directly related to the Beer Wars, for McErlane, who had been involved in other drunken escapades, it was an indication of the state of his decline and of worse things yet to come. In late February, while McErlane was under medical care for his wounds, Saltis gangster Sammy Malaga and another gunman tried to kill him in the German Deaconess hospital on the South Side. When questioned about it by reporters, McErlane remarked ominously, "Look for 'em in a ditch. That's where you'll find 'em."[117] Omnisciently, Malaga was found on March 6, 1930, in a water-filled ditch near 103rd Street and Roberts Road, and O'Berta's bullet-torn body was in a car parked nearby, after Willie Niemoth reportedly did McErlane a professional favor.[118]

Saltis, who was still spending considerable amounts of time in Wisconsin, appointed gangster and saloonkeeper Jacob Geis to replace O'Berta as his chief lieutenant in the New City district.[119] There was no lasting animosity, however, between Saltis and McErlane; Saltis raced down from Wisconsin to provide a blood transfusion when his earlier partner's life was in jeopardy. After being released from the hospital in April 1930 McErlane convalesced at Saltisville.[120] Another important change in South Side gangland occurred on May 6, 1930, when the extremely dangerous Maloney died of pneumonia. His partner, Quinlan, most likely joined the O'Donnell-McErlane gang at this time, which would have contributed further to the serenity in the Back of the Yards.[121]

Elsewhere in the underworld, there were a number of major events after 1926. In 1927 Frankie Lake walked away from the rackets, and not long afterward he bought himself a posh estate on N. East Avenue in west suburban Oak Park where he lived with his mother. For example, the *Chicago Daily News* refers to him as an "erstwhile beer baron," and an article shortly thereafter calls Lake "the ex-beer baron and partner of Terry Druggan."[122] Oak Park was, however, not far enough from the city to let Lake escape his past, and he later moved to Detroit where he went into the ice business with a brother.

In the vicinity of Taylor and Ashland, one-time safecracker Joseph "Red" Bolton, who won his spurs during Prohibition with Druggan and Lake, formed his own small bootlegging gang in early 1929. Their headquarters was Bolton's saloon on Taylor Street near Ashland Avenue, and they were involved in beer distribution, gambling, and labor racketeering. This group included Bolton's brothers John and William, along with William Wilson, Frank Rein, William "Dinky" Quan, and various members of the 42 Gang.[123] The 42s, a street gang in the Taylor Street neighborhood who had a propensity for violence and criminality well beyond the average youth gang of the day, had not been involved in organized crime until that point. They provided the Bolton mob with a fair amount of muscle. By 1929 Capone appears to have taken control of the Twentieth Ward Jewish gang, or what remained of it, since various members had earlier joined the North Siders and others had moved their interests farther west to the Lawndale neighborhood.[124]

On the Near Northwest Side, there was a serious disagreement between the partners in the GKW gang in March 1928. Powerful politicians, protecting their cut of the proceeds, stepped in at the time lest it turn to violence, but the problems later led to a split. By early 1930 Al Winge may already have retired to California, and not long thereafter Marty Guilfoyle went over to Capone with his gambling enterprises.[125] This left Matt Kolb in control of the bootlegging in the former GKW area, and Jimmy Barry took on greater importance in Kolb's gang.[126]

In the south suburbs, Jimmy Emery oversaw the rackets around Chicago Heights during Dominic Roberto's visits to Italy in 1928, 1929, and 1931. In 1932 Roberto was convicted of making false statements on his naturalization papers and of several related offenses. After serving time in the US penitentiary in Leavenworth, Kansas, he was deported in 1935. This put Jimmy Emery permanently in charge of the area around the Heights, with Frank LaPorte as his chief lieutenant. LaPorte, and Roberto's brother John Roberts, watched over Roberto's interests during the subsequent years.[127]

By 1928 Joe Montana, a former Taylor Streeter who was Capone's man, had firm control of Melrose Park. That suburb boasted 119 illegal stills that turned out a million gallons of alcohol per annum worth about $5 million at the time. This output exceeded even what was produced in the Chicago Heights area.[128] Montana's operations reached into a number of areas west of Melrose Park, including Warrenville (just south of Wheaton). Circus gangster and Capone ally Rocco De Grazia took command of the Melrose Park rackets during the summer of 1931, aided by his brother Andrew. Their headquarters was the Lumber Gardens, a tavern and gambling den on N. Twenty-Fifth Street in Melrose Park. Around that time Rocco Passarella, who had vigorously raided stills in Melrose Park during his tenure as the chief of police in the late 1920s, vanished. The authorities concluded that he had been murdered and secretly buried by vengeful bootleggers.[129]

Elsewhere in the hinterlands, Joe Touhy was killed in October 1929 when he and several gunmen invaded a roadhouse at River Road and Irving Park in Schiller Park that was not buying their beer. This act, and the earlier death of John Touhy, was later blamed on the Capone mob.[130] If this interpretation is correct, the Atlantic City peace agreement did not cover the northern suburbs. Joe Touhy's death, and the killing of a saloonkeeper on Grand Avenue in Elmwood Park by the Touhy's in early November, indicates that in late 1929 there were incursions in the lower end of the Touhy's area by the Capone forces.

The 1929 peace treaty clearly did not cover Lake County, Illinois. In June 1929 the Moranites invaded the area, partly in response to the post-massacre crackdown in Cook County (discussed below), and were fighting with Druggan-Lake ally Ray Pregenzer for control of the rackets.[131] In short order they threatened resort owners, hijacked Pregenzer's beer trucks and slot machines, opened a gambling house in Waukegan, and set up a still.[132] The North Siders had their headquarters at a resort run by Elizabeth Cassidy near Antioch, Illinois, which was just south of the Wisconsin border. They practiced shooting at targets there with a machine gun—and accidentally hit the occasional farmer.[133]

Chicago's international reputation for gangland violence, which continued for many decades after Prohibition, was firmly established during the 1920s. It was due to the multiple shootings, bombings, and killings that occurred from 1920 to 1933 and the fascinating criminal characters, including Capone and the North Side gang leaders, who were involved—some of whom regularly spoke to the press. These plot elements were much more subdued, or close to nonexistent, in many other American cities during the Dry Era. One prominent Chicagoan noted in 1928, "Everywhere I went in Italy and the Riviera, I heard evil remarks about Chicago. . . . Judging from the reports in the papers, a European who had never visited our city would think every Chicagoan took his life in his hands when he stepped out of doors."[134] The *Chicago Daily News* jokingly lamented the situation with these words:

> Chicago and its quaint folkways [are] the subject for worldwide jest. Stories are told that no Chicagoan's wardrobe is complete without a bulletproof vest, two-pistols and a machine gun; that Chicago's children ride in armor-plated perambulators [baby carriages] and cut their teeth on cartridge belts; that the city's parks are used for target ranges and that championship gun battles are staged in the downtown streets with the police chief acting as referee and the mayor and the state's attorney acting as bottleholders for the respective battlers.[135]

In 1932 Invisible Textile Weavers, located on N. State Street, ran an ad in the Chicago papers that was widely quoted elsewhere.[136] It began,

> Bullet Holes
> Rewoven Perfectly
> In Damaged Clothes—Low Price

In terms of politics, not long after he regained control of city hall, Mayor Thompson's empire was irreversibly damaged, if not completely ruined, by his gangster alliances and political excesses. The Thompson machine's candidates were challenged in the famous April 1928 Republican "Pineapple Primary," so called because bombings were a frequent occurrence, by a slate backed by US senator John Deneen. The residences of Dr. William Reid and Charles Fitzmorris, two of Thompson's closest aides, were bombed on January 26. These two incidents were, however, due to problems with the new gambling syndicate that left out the bootlegging mobs, rather than party politics.[137]

The homes of Deneen and Judge John Swanson, the Deneen candidate for Cook County state's attorney, were rocked by explosions on March 26 that were unrelated to the status quo in the underworld, since both men were outside the Thompson machine and its syndication of the rackets. Incumbent state's attorney Robert Crowe stupidly claimed that the Deneen faction had bombed their own houses to garner voter sympathy, even though Swanson missed being killed by only three seconds when he drove into his garage at almost the same time as the bomb went off.[138]

Fig. 5.11. State's Attorney John Swanson.

The Capone gang's hand was clearly evident in the primary election, through the murder of "Diamond Joe" Esposito, a

Deneen loyalist who had been warned not to run for reelection as ward committeeman; the killing of Octavius Granady, an African American candidate for office in the Twentieth Ward; and the massive violence and voter fraud that was perpetrated in support of the America First candidates. In fact, the 1928 primary was a turning point in the organized crime–political relationship because it was the first time that the gangsters, meaning the Capones and the North Siders, visibly pushed the politicians in Chicago around, as opposed to filling their traditional role as hired muscle in local elections.[139]

Regarding the Capone gang's political evolution, Capone made noticeable inroads into ward politics in Chicago in the mid-1920s while he refined his skills by taking over various suburbs. Capone told the venerable First Ward aldermen in about 1925 that he was in charge of the Democratic ward organization, although for old time's sake he let Coughlin and Kenna remain in office.[140] Along with the

Fig. 5.12. Capone-linked politicians Dan Serritella, Albert Prignano, and Roland Libonati at the world's fair with Jimmy Durante (right).

First Ward, the Twentieth Ward, which included the Taylor Street neighborhood, was another early Capone bastion. By 1930 his gang had considerable political influence in other areas near the Loop, including the Twenty-Fifth Ward (slightly south and west of the Twentieth), the Twenty-Seventh Ward (just north of the Twentieth), the heavily African American Second and Third Wards (south of the First), and, with the aid of his ally at the time, Joe Aiello, the Forty-Second Ward (just north of downtown).[141] Several political office holders, including state senators James Leonardo, Roland Libonati, and Dan Serritella, along with newly elected US congressman Peter Granata, did Capone's bidding.[142] William Parrillo, an assistant US attorney and a product of the Twenty-Fifth Ward, was another Capone minion.[143]

There was a tremendous backlash by the voters against the Thompson-Small-Crowe machine in the 1928 primary election, and many of their candidates went down in flames. Not surprisingly, Swanson trounced Crowe by 120,000 votes and went on to win the general election in November 1928.[144] As the state's attorney, Swanson offset Thompson's open town policies for roughly the next two years and severely hindered organized crime for four years.

One of Swanson's first decisions was to appoint his staff of prosecutors based solely on merit, rather than through political patronage.[145] He named Frank Loesch as his first assistant and Patrick T. Roche as his chief investigator. The seventy-six-year-old Loesch was president of the Chicago Crime Commission (CCC) from 1928 to 1937 and a special assistant US attorney commissioned to investigate the local alliance between crime and politics. He brought virtually his entire staff from the latter appointment with him to Swanson's office.[146]

Fig. 5.13. Investigator Patrick T. Roche.

Roche joined the CPD in 1917, and in 1920 he was the

department's most productive officer.[147] After passing the civil service examination with the highest score, he continued to make a name for himself with the Special Intelligence Unit of the Internal Revenue Service (IRS) by apprehending bootleggers as well as crooked public officials. Roche was greatly feared by the gangster element because of his incorruptibility.

The new state's attorney enlisted or pressured the Cook County sheriff and the Chicago police to help him fight organized crime. His strategy was to strike at the gangs' sources of income. He stated just after the St. Valentine's Day Massacre,

> The police departments of the city and county, and by the latter is meant the sheriff's office, are directly responsible for the existence of all these means and sources of unlawful revenue.
>
> This, then, is stated to direct every commanding officer and every policeman in the city of Chicago, and the sheriff and county highway police, forthright [sic] and immediately to close and keep closed all places everywhere and anywhere, in which alcoholic liquor is sold; that all places wherein or where at gambling in any guise is carried on shall be closed and kept closed; that all disorderly houses shall be shut and stay shut, and that the continued conduct and operation of the "rackets" which have pestered and pillaged legitimate business shall be stopped and ended.[148]

Swanson threatened to indict any police commander who did not fully enforce the law, and he also helped establish a special rackets court to combat business racketeering.[149] Admittedly, some of this would have occurred in the aftermath of the St. Valentine's Day Massacre regardless of who was the county's chief prosecutor or the mayor, but under Swanson this was more than just a series of raids that lasted only as long as the public outcry after the latest outrage. This time it was a county-wide attack, as opposed to previous crackdowns that were largely inside the city, and the hoodlums had nowhere else to go.

Following in the footsteps of the Juvenile Protective Association (JPA) and the Committee of Fifteen, four additional citizens' groups were important in the battle against organized crime in Chicago during

Prohibition. All four of these organizations were established by prominent businessmen and other civic leaders. Three of them, the Better Government Association (BGA), the Employers' Association, and the Chicago Crime Commission (CCC), have already been mentioned. The more clandestine group known as the Secret Six was the fourth.

The Employers' Association was concerned primarily with labor racketeering and associated business rackets, both of which affected employers.[150] Founded in 1923, the BGA worked for better government, including exposing the links between elected officials and organized crime. The BGA's first president, the crusading Reverend Elmer Williams, was no shrinking violet. As discussed previously he personally led raids on gambling, and he once threatened Cook County sheriff Peter Hoffman with impeachment if he did not work to clean up the county.[151]

The CCC was established in 1919 to combat the crime wave threatening businesses, and the citizens of Chicago in general, at the time. It was apolitical in nature, concerned with the enforcement of existing laws, the passage of new legislation to fight crime, and the creation and maintenance of accurate records to document crime and criminals in the city, which was made necessary by abuses in the criminal justice system and the police department under reporting offenses at the district level.[152] The CCC (as opposed to the BGA) was not interested in electing candidates to office or apprehending criminals on its own. The commission's most widely publicized action during Prohibition was the creation of two non-overlapping Public Enemy lists in 1930 and 1931.[153] Twenty-eight gangsters, most of whom were active in bootlegging, were named each year, with Capone listed as Chicago's Public Enemy number one in 1930. Spotlighting these fifty-six individuals brought them under greater scrutiny by the public, the police, and the courts, and resulted in arrests and convictions, which hampered their activities in various ways.[154]

The Secret Six was so named because the identities of *six* of its leaders were kept secret while a seventh, Colonel Robert Isham Randolph, served as the public spokesman for the group. It was founded on February 7, 1930, after Philip Meagher was shot and wounded as a result of labor trouble at a construction site on the University of Chicago's campus.[155] Meagher's outraged employer, building contractor Harrison Barnard, went to the Chicago Association of Commerce (CAC), of which he was a prominent member, and called for vigorous action. The CAC funded the Secret Six, and, at John Swanson's urging, it became active in the pursuit of information about criminals that would lead to their prosecution, something the CCC, BGA, and the Employers' Association did not do. In fact, Swanson admitted his office sometimes had difficulty in doing so because his investigators were known to the underworld.[156]

Based on Dennis Hoffman's work, conversations I have had with Harrison Barnard's grandson Tom Barnard, and other sources, the six secret members were most likely Harrison Barnard, Julius Rosenwald (the chairman of Sears, Roebuck, & Company), public utility magnate Samuel Insull, investment banker George Paddock, accountant Edward Gore, and attorney Frank Loesch.[157] This group comprised some of Chicago's most esteemed citizens, and it overlapped with the leadership of the CCC, since Loesch, Gore, Paddock, and Rosenwald belonged to both organizations. This is not surprising because the CCC had also been established by the CAC.[158] Furthermore, the Secret Six worked closely with the Employers' Association.

The Secret Six hired federal agent Alexander Jamie as its chief investigator in October 1930 and maintained a large staff of operatives who initially investigated crimes in the Chicago area.[159] Unfortunately, it appears that the organization's activities have been misunderstood in several ways by later commentators. For example, Dennis Hoffman, based on statements by Colonel Randolph, describes the group as using "extralegal methods" and engaging in "vigilantism."[160] However, at one time six Chicago police officers—a lieutenant, a sergeant, and four detectives—were assigned by the mayor to the Secret Six, and four of the group's operatives were made Cook County sheriff's special deputies in the spring of 1930.[161] Therefore, these individuals not only had full police powers, but anyone aiding them in the performance of their duties, whether a private detective working for the group or an ordinary citizen, could legally use force, including deadly force, while doing so.[162]

The first appeal by a Chicagoan to the federal government, by US vice president Charles Dawes, for assistance in dealing with organized crime came in 1926.[163] This sparked an IRS investigation of Al

Capone for income tax evasion. In March 1929, after the St. Valentine's Day Massacre, a group of outraged Chicagoans asked President Herbert Hoover to expand these efforts.[164] Hoover did so with considerable enthusiasm. The second part of the federal response was the creation of a special squad of Prohibition agents, later referred to as "the Untouchables," at the end of October 1930 to strike at the Capone mob's revenues from bootlegging.[165] Because of his personal and political connections, Eliot Ness, a relatively junior Prohibition agent, was given the command of the unit.[166] Ness was born in Chicago on April 19, 1902, and graduated from the University of Chicago in 1925 before joining the Prohibition bureau in August 1926.[167]

Fig. 5.14. Alexander Jamie.

Fig. 5.15. Eliot Ness (at right).

In terms of the other rackets in Chicago, gambling flourished during 1928, with its citizens wagering an estimated $2.5 million per day on the horses and in table games.[168] The biggest place in the city, Gorman and Murphy's on S. Clark in the Loop, was sometimes packed with 1,500 bettors. In late 1928 the gambling syndicate that had been formed at the end of 1927 was still running, but by early 1929 two syndicates seem to again have been in place with Madison Avenue the likely dividing line between them.[169]

In September 1929 State's Attorney Swanson claimed that gambling was largely shut down within the city limits.[170] While this was surely an exaggeration, the enforcement of the law under Swanson was vigorous and, according to an unbiased source, "[t]he rackets have suffered considerably" and "gambling has suffered a severe setback" since Swanson's election.[171] Consistent with this assessment, the Gambling Index (see Fig. 1.3 in chapter 1) skyrocketed from an average value of forty during the years 1927 and 1928 to an average of 122 during 1929 and 1930. Mayor Thompson was certainly an unwilling participant in this crime fighting, but due to Swanson's insistence and the St. Valentine's Day Massacre, the CPD was forced to go along with this tidal wave of racket busting, just as had happened during the crusade against prostitution in the mid-1910s. The gamblers, unable to shift operations to the outer parts of Cook County, generally moved to a different place nearby whenever their main location was shut down. For various reasons, gambling was running strong again in the middle of 1930 with an estimated two thousand handbooks operating in Chicago, along with eight thousand other locations, such as cigar stores, barber shops, and newsstands where a bet could be placed, and it was active in the county as well.[172]

Slot machines, which had been around Chicago since the turn of the century, were omnipresent in Cook County in early 1928, with some six thousand of the devices operating in the city alone.[173] A syndicate, in which William "Doc" Reid was once again a major player and former saloonkeeper James "High Pockets" O'Brien was the graft collector, controlled this form of gambling. Various individuals, who were in charge of specific areas, granted speakeasies and other locations the right to house slots in exchange for 50 percent of the profits. The area controllers included, not surprisingly given the nature of the business and where the slots were placed, many prominent bootleggers and gamblers, such as Al Capone, Jake Guzik, Julius Anixter, Marty Guilfoyle, Joe Saltis, Dan Jackson, "Klondike" O'Donnell, "Red" Bolton, Willie Druggan, and Matt Kolb. The slots disappeared from sight not long after Swanson came into office. They did not resurface again until 1931, almost two years after a court case against the slot syndicate and various Chicago police captains collapsed when the star witness refused to testify.

Policy resurged in the African American community when Thompson returned to city hall in 1927. Walter Kelly, who was one of the operators of the Tia Juana, the biggest wheel in Chicago in early 1928, told his salesmen that they could run wide open because a deal had been struck with the Thompson-Crowe political machine. At the time there were fifty-seven policy wheels, which in aggregate handled $12 million in bets a year. Each wheel paid Kelly, who was the bagman for the politicians, $300 a week or almost $900,000 a year in total for political protection.[174] This game was so profitable that a number of African American men closed their legitimate businesses in order to run policy wheels instead.

Interestingly, the campaign manager for a young African American lawyer named William L. Dawson, who ran for Congress from the Near South Side in 1928, lashed out at the game and its protectors. "Our people are being kept in poverty by the gambling dens that may be found on every corner. . . . They have taken millions away in policy games. Even the men who run the games and the other resorts are complaining because so much has to go into the [L]oop. We don't know where the money goes, but Thompson has not helped our people. It has all been bunk," F. W. Smith protested.[175] Further pressure came from a grand jury indictment of Oscar De Priest and Dan Jackson in September 1928 for their roles in garnering bribes from vice and gambling on the South Side.[176] In December 1928 Swanson started to hit this type of gambling as well, with police raiding games on the South Side and "Big Jim" Martin's Oriental wheel on W. Lake Street.[177] Martin had brought policy to the black community on the West Side.

In early 1928, the vice syndicate continued to oversee prostitution, and the major brothel operators had little to fear from the law.[178] However, vice in general was hit hard by the authorities in 1929 and 1930, with the average value of the Vice Index climbing from 406 in 1927 and 1928 to 642 during the later time period. By 1929 bordellos had decreased by an order of magnitude throughout the county, but, like gambling, the operators reopened in 1930. Early in that year Jack Zuta transferred his vice interests from the Near West Side to Clark Street just north of the Chicago River, and he was also the vice overseer for the North Side mob he helped lead.[179] In this role he moved the gang heavily into prostitution.

For example, in 1930, over 50 percent of the vice activity in Chicago was found in five North Side neighborhoods (percentages in parentheses): Lake View (27.2), Uptown (14.5), Lincoln Park (5.4), Lower North (5.4), and Lower Northwest (0.5). Only 39 percent of Chicago's vice occurred in the four Near South Side neighborhoods where it had prospered for years, which was a noticeable change from the situation in 1924.[180] It was estimated that there were roughly two thousand brothels, call flats, and other vice dives running in the city in June 1930, generating revenues somewhat less than from gambling city wide.[181] According to the Committee of Fifteen, only three hundred of these places were traditional brothels, indicating once again that the industry had changed dramatically over the previous thirty years.[182]

Suburban roadhouses, which provided food, drink, and rooms to visitors on the major highways of Cook County, were investigated by the JPA in the summer of 1929. Many of them served liquor, hosted immoral behavior, ranging from lewd dancing to explicit prostitution, and conducted gambling on the premises.[183] According to the JPA, three large syndicates had iron-clad control of the sale of beer and liquor to the roadhouses and took a portion of the profits, from the places they themselves did not own, in return for protection. Roadhouse proprietors stated that they were told, as was also the case with speakeasy owners in Chicago, that they would be "blown up" or "taken for a ride" unless they obeyed the local syndicate's orders.[184]

One syndicate operated in the southern end of the county, another in the county's western portion, and the third in the northern part, with one section of that area, near Wheeling, still an open territory. Although the existing versions of the JPA reports do not explicitly name these groups, it is fairly easy to determine some of the kingpins based on who controlled illegal activities in each area. The northern syndicate was surely led by Matt Kolb and Roger Touhy, with the assistance of Moran and Zuta.[185] Regarding the south and the west, a candid roadhouse owner in Wheeling stated that "E— has the South and the West, and the F— are also in part of the territory."[186] "E—" was certainly the Capone gang, given its broad illegal activities south and west of the city. In the southern part of the county Capone would have operated in conjunction with his guys in Chicago Heights.

It is harder to identify the group referred to as "F—," partly because the sections of the county they were involved in are not made explicit in the preceding quote. However if "F—" does not designate the Heights group, it may well be Joe Saltis's gang. Saltis had the slot machine privileges in the southern end of the county and was also active southwest of Chicago. Separately, by 1929, he was also operating in the near north suburbs, which speaks of a very broad realm. For example, the Saltis mob owned the Orchard Inn near Dempster and Waukegan in Morton Grove and controlled the beer sales in the vicinity.[187]

Morton Grove had a large number of roadhouses that were located along or near Dempster Street, the major highway running east and west through the village. There were several reasons for this. First, Morton Grove is just north of Chicago as well as near the patrician, and in several cases traditionally dry, suburbs of Evanston, Wilmette, Winnetka, and Park Ridge. In fact many of its roadhouse keepers had earlier operated in Chicago, including in the South Side Levee before Prohibition, and were well connected politically. Second, the village initially had very low license fees for these businesses. The third, and perhaps the most important, reason was that "[t]he village authorities are regarded quite generally as friendly" to roadhouses housing illegal activity.[188]

In the sphere of racketeering, a group of West Side Irish American toughs, who had a long history of robbery, larceny, and union slugging in the service of others, entered the upper echelons of labor racketeering on April 15, 1928. On that date they muscled in on two coal teamsters' unions, which were part of the Chicago Teamsters, after shooting the business agent James "Lefty" Lynch.[189] As a further persuasive measure, the home of John Sheridan, a Lynch

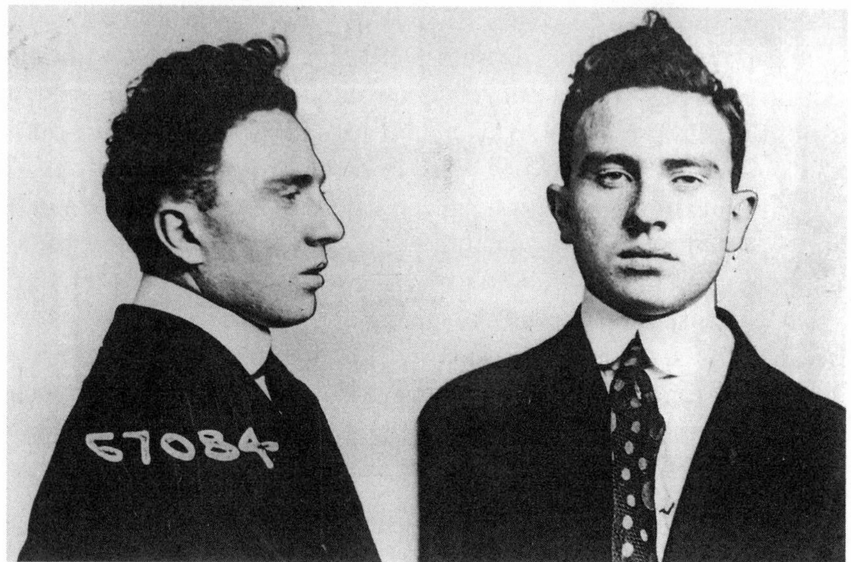

Fig. 5.16. George "Red" Barker.

ally, was bombed in August 1929 and again in May 1930. This group of upstarts was led by George "Red" Barker, Frank Cawley, William Clifford, Thomas McElligott, and Michael Reilley (whose last name is usually spelled Reilly).

The Barker gang moved into the business rackets as well when they took over the Midwest Garage Owners' Association by the simple expedient of shooting the president, David "Cockeyed Mulligan" Ablin (aka Albin), in June 1928.[190] After making a $7,000 contribution to Thompson's mayoral campaign in 1927, Ablin pressured garage owners to join his association. Next, his underlings slashed tires on cars parked on the streets throughout the city to convince the owners that their vehicles needed to be kept in the association's garages.[191]

Barker lost a number of his men in 1929, partly due to clashes with the West Side O'Donnell gang, and he cast his lot with that group in October 1929 when he returned from a six-month stint in the penitentiary.[192] Jack White joined Barker in early 1930, after his murder conviction was overturned and he was released from jail.[193] They were the point men for labor racketeering for the West Side

O'Donnells in the transportation-related unions, and in return the O'Donnells involved them in bootlegging.

In late 1929, due to the Great Depression and the clampdown after the St. Valentine's Day Massacre, the bootlegging gangs began to look more closely at a number of Chicago's unions.[194] Most prominently, Capone coveted more unions when he returned from prison in Pennsylvania.[195] In the spring of 1930 his gang controlled the street cleaners, the garbage handlers, and the plumbers, and an assault on the Pie Handler's Union was underway. The attacks by the Capone gang and the aforementioned West Side O'Donnells on Chicago's unions were the first large-scale moves by the bootlegging gangs into labor racketeering. By June 1930, "Klondike" O'Donnell's gang had joined with the Capone mob, making Barker the most important labor and business racketeer in the Capone organization.[196] At the time Barker, aided by White, controlled thirty-three union locals related to transportation.[197]

The business rackets in Chicago skyrocketed after 1927. In 1928, seventy-nine active rackets cost Chicago $136 million per annum, an increase of $125 million in one year![198] New rackets sprang up everywhere, including those controlling miniature golf courses and ice cream shops.[199] Business racketeering took on an entirely new dimension when some cleaning and dyeing establishments trumped the Master Cleaners and Dyers' violent methods by appealing to bootlegging gangs for assistance.[200] For example, a small breakaway group, the Central Cleaners and Dyers on the North Side, brought in Moran and friends as their partners in 1928. Around the same time, Morris Becker, an independent South Side cleaner who had been bombed repeatedly and forced out of business by the Master Cleaners and Dyers, formed a new business enterprise with Capone and Jake Guzik among the directors that had Frank Rio and Phil D'Andrea working in the background. When a representative of the Master Cleaners inquired with Capone about this arrangement, he was told in no uncertain terms, "Get the hell outta here! You try to monkey with my business and I'll toss you out of the window."[201]

Old-timer "Big Tim" Murphy returned from a spell in prison in 1928 and soon cast about for new things to plunder. He tried to take over the Master Cleaners and Dyers and also attempted to make inroads on the Hoisting Engineers union. The latter move put him on a collision course with Barker's gang. Murphy did not survive the collision—he was killed in a machine gun attack in front of his house in June 1928.[202] John Clay of the Teamsters, who was one of the leaders of the Master Cleaners and was trying to keep the bootlegging gangsters out of the industry, was murdered by North Siders Frank Gusenberg and Willie Marks in December 1928 due to their mob's involvement with the Central Cleaners and Dyers.[203]

Regarding the drug trade, it has been claimed that the Chicago Outfit, and, by extension its predecessors, had a firm "No Drug" rule prohibiting involvement by its members in the sale of illegal narcotics. This assertion seems to have originated with Cosa Nostra turncoat Joe Valachi, who testified in 1963 that Chicago mobsters were paid $250 a week *not* to handle narcotics.[204] Similarly, William Roemer alleges that, when Tony Accardo was the boss, Outfit members were forbidden to deal in illegal drugs.[205] Gus Russo repeats this claim.[206] In reality, the situation was quite different. However, before turning to the details, it is useful to discuss the history of illegal narcotics in the United States and more specifically in Chicago.

Opium, which comes from the poppy, and its first derivate, morphine, were popular in the country as early as 1840.[207] This consumption peaked in 1896, and then it declined as the associated dangers became widely known and as various states passed antidrug laws. Cocaine, which comes from the coca plant, was first widely used in the United States during the 1880s. However, by 1900 it was also considered to be dangerous. Heroin, another opiate, became popular in the nation after 1910 and soon began to replace opium and morphine in the illicit drug market.

In 1909 smoking opium was declared illegal in the United States, and in 1914 the first broad federal antinarcotic law, the Harrison Act, was passed by Congress. These national restrictions were the outgrowth of increased public intolerance toward drug use in the years after 1900. However, they put illegal narcotics in the hands of criminals and, in particular, made it the domain of organized crime.

Vigorous enforcement of the Harrison Act caused the street price of heroin to skyrocket from $6.50 to $100 an ounce in New York City in 1915.[208] Not surprisingly, illegal drug use in the United

States declined markedly in the early 1900s. There were roughly 375,000 addicts in the country at the turn of the century, but this figure dropped to less than 250,000 in 1915 and to about 110,000 in the mid-1920s.[209]

The figures for Chicago show a somewhat different pattern. Reliable estimates indicate that there were more than 35,000 addicts in Chicago in 1915. By 1918 this number fell to roughly 10,000, but it resurged to 18,000 in the middle of the 1920s.[210] While the initial decline was surely due to the Harrison Act, a second effect of the law was that addicts gravitated to large cities in the years that followed because illegal narcotics were more readily available.[211] For example, in the mid-1920s Elmer Irey, head of the Special Intelligence Unit of the Bureau of Internal Revenue, described Chicago as the "the source of supply for the entire country," a statement that speaks clearly of a well-organized activity.[212]

But who was behind the dope trade in Chicago during Prohibition? A variety of evidence indicates that it was the Torrio-Capone gang. For example, Hal Andrews summarizes Colosimo's operations before 1920 with the phrase, "No one dared molest the brothels, the gambling hells and opium joints owned or controlled by him."[213] Reporter Ed Doherty, in a discussion of their activities at the start of Prohibition, states, "Neither Torrio nor Capone knew much about booze or beer. They were concerned mostly with the businesslike operation and protection of gambling dens, hop joints [opium dens] and other sin dens."[214] The *Chicago Daily News* refers to a "horde of gunmen, bawdy-house keepers, dope peddlers, gyp gamblers and racketeers" who took their orders from Capone. Similarly, the *New Republic*, in a list of Capone's activities, emphasizes, "He has been closely allied with the most loathsome of all traffics, that in habit-forming drugs."[215] Martin Booth also notes that during Prohibition gangsters in the major cities, including Chicago, were trafficking in illegal drugs.[216]

It is not surprising that Colosimo's old gang was involved in selling narcotics—it was a major player in the Levee, where drug use was rampant, and the Levee was next to Chinatown, the center of the opium trade. Furthermore, George Turner notes that in 1906 cocaine was very popular among the city's prostitutes, and that "the chief markets for it in Chicago follow very closely the markets of prostitution" with the drug being sold in pharmacies and saloons.[217] During the 1920s much of the illegal narcotics sold in Chicago came in from Canada, and it was the usual practice to *combine* this contraband with liquor shipments, which suggests that bootleggers, at least in terms of the Torrio-Capone gang, were at the head of the business.[218]

Several higher-level Capone gangsters were clearly selling illegal narcotics. Guy Nichols reports that "Duke" Cooney, the Capone gang's South Side vice lord during the Prohibition Era, was dealing in narcotics, which is consistent with the traditional pairing of drugs and prostitution in and around the old Levee district.[219] West Side gambler Frankie Pope and his brother Willie ran a major narcotics operation in the Taylor Street area until they were convicted of dealing from Frankie Pope's restaurant on S. Halsted.[220] And in 1931 Joe Condi, who already had one conviction behind him, was the leader of a national drug ring that was based in Chicago.[221] Lesser Capone mobsters, such as Capone's chauffeur Louis Prisco, Max Tendler, and Frank Cremaldi were also actively selling illegal narcotics.

Finally, various New York mobsters dealt in narcotics, so it is not surprising that some of their Chicago counterparts did as well. The list includes Charles "Lucky" Luciano, Luciano's associate Augie "the Wop" Del Grazio, Meyer Lansky, Ben Siegel, Louis Buchalter, Dutch Schultz, and Waxey Gordon.[222] Luciano was arrested and convicted of selling heroin in 1916 and was arrested again on narcotics charges in 1926, when he was working with Arnold Rothstein, the kingpin of the Trans-Atlantic drug trade.[223]

Chapter 6

THE BEER WARS: 1930–1934

"When there's competition there's bound to be little tiffs at times. The cleanest way out of them is with a gun. We do not have them for ornaments."

—Rocco Fanelli, Capone gangster

The third and final stage of the North Side vs. South Side War began less than a month after Al Capone returned to Chicago from prison. The first shots were fired on April 16, 1930, when Druggan-Lake gangster Joseph Cameron (aka Joseph Blue) was killed in a machine gun attack near Taylor Street. According to the *Chicago Tribune*, this was an attempt by Jim Genna, who had recently returned from Italy, to reestablish himself in his old domain with the connivance of Joe Aiello and George Moran.[1] The dramatic decrease in gang profits in early 1930, due to police interference and severe economic conditions, caused the May 1929 peace agreement to collapse, with the North Siders once again the aggressors.[2]

The killings soon came in droves. On April 20 three Capone gangsters were shot down in the so-called Easter Massacre. The murder weapon was owned by Frank Del Bono, alias Frank Dale, who appears to have been a North Side gang member.[3] Peter Plescia, who was likely a Capone man, was murdered on Grand Avenue on May 25 by Aiello gunmen Jack Costa and Pete "Ash Can Pete" Inserra. On May 30 an Aiello gangster was wounded on the Near North Side, and the following day Jack McGurn, aided by Thomas Somnerio, fired on a car containing Jim Genna and four compatriots in retaliation for the Cameron murder. Filippo Abati (aka Gnolfo) was killed, and two others were injured in that attack. A day later two men reported to be Aiello mobsters, Sam Monestro (aka Monastero) and Joseph Ferrara, were murdered on N. Clark Street near Chicago Avenue.[4]

The North Siders perpetrated another multiple homicide, known as the Fox Lake Massacre, on June 1, 1930, when they fired on a party of bootleggers and their companions in the Manning Hotel in Lake County, Illinois. The hotel had just switched to Druggan-Lake beer from the Moran variety. Capone gangster Sam Pellar (a former Weiss bodyguard who had recently defected from the North Side mob), Joe Bertsche (a member of the Valley Gang), and Michael Quirk (a West Side O'Donnell gangster) were killed, and George Druggan and a lady he was friendly with were wounded by an eight-man team, which included five shooters armed with two submachine guns, two pistols, and a shotgun.[5] With two massacres in 1930 to their credit, the North Siders gained considerable revenge for the St. Valentine's Day killings.

Like Pellar, a number of prominent North Siders, as well as lower-ranking ones, had defected to Capone by this point in time, which seriously damaged the Moran-Aiello-Zuta gang. For example, Frankie Foster and Izzy Alderman were seen by the police with Frank Diamond on Twenty-Second Street on June 2, 1930.[6] A month later Foster was arrested in Los Angeles with a contingent of former Moran men who were working to extend the Capone gang's reach into California. Willie Marks also went over to Capone in early June.[7]

These defections were due at least partly to the disappearance and the certain murder of "Benny" Bennett in November 1929. Sometime after Bennett vanished, Moran held a meeting that was attended by Foster, Marks, Newberry, and others. Except for Joe Aiello, all those present spoke out against Jack Zuta, who, beyond his other activities, ran the whiskey business for the gang after it was taken away from Newberry and Bennett. Zuta had never been popular with the old-timers in the North Side gang, surely due to their long-standing aversion to prostitution. However, Moran would not throw Zuta out because he was backed by Aiello, and he sorely needed Aiello's troops and his money. Unfortunately for Moran, by siding with Aiello and Zuta, he alienated some of his staunchest long-time supporters who changed sides a few months later.[8]

While the Chicago newspapers credited the Fox Lake Massacre to the North Side gang, an alternative theory is that bank robber and outlaw Verne Miller was responsible for those killings.[9] According to this argument, Miller was a good friend of Chicago hoodlum Eugene "Red" McLaughlin and his brother Bob, and he did it to avenge McLaughlin's recent murder. If this theory is correct, Miller must have moved extremely quickly to learn who killed him and retaliate because McLaughlin had only gone missing around May 25 and his body was not found until June 7. Therefore, Miller could have learned of his murder at most eight days before the Fox Lake Massacre—assuming that it was clear on May 25 that McLaughlin was dead—and he would have had little time to reach Chicago, plan, and carry out the attack.[10]

Given that there was an eight-man execution team, Verne Miller, if he was involved, clearly did not do it single-handedly. Also, it is hard to imagine that Miller put together a large murder squad in Chicago on his own or that he had the "intimate knowledge of the hotel" possessed by the killers.[11] A previously neglected possibility, which fits the surrounding facts quite well, is that both theories are (to an extent) correct. Miller, eager to kill the killers of McLaughlin (who was listed by the CPD in one memo as a Moran gangster), may have joined forces with the North Siders. The Moran-Aiello-Zuta gang had its own reasons to attack the group in the Manning Hotel, they had the resources to carry it out, they were familiar with the hotel, and they may have already been planning such a strike. Certainly a team including Miller and the most dangerous of the North Siders would have been extremely lethal.

Rose Keefe further questions whether the North Side gang was responsible for the Fox Lake Massacre because Leo Mongoven was in the hotel that night.[12] She believes that Moran would not have put him in harm's way. One possibility is that Mongoven had changed sides by early June. A Fox Lake observer reported that Mongoven and Druggan were "the best of friends" at the time.[13] If Mongoven had already gone over to the Capone gang, then he was likely a target of the gunmen at the Fox Lake Massacre, which reinforces the conclusion that the Moran gang was behind the attack. Consistent with this, Moran remarked sarcastically in October 1930 that "Mongoven's dead as far as I'm concerned."[14] A second possibility is that Mongoven pretended to switch sides in early June, but his real intention was to set up the enemy at the Manning Hotel. A third possibility is that Mongoven had been grabbed by the Capone forces a few days before and the attack was a retaliation against them, which was also designed to allow Mongoven to escape in the confusion.[15] Furthermore, McLaughlin's brother Bob was reported to have been at the Manning Hotel that night. If Mongoven's presence, ignoring any further information, is evidence against Moran having been behind the attack, then Bob McLaughlin's presence must also weigh against Miller having committed the shootings.

Individual gang killings, such as the garroting of Thomas Somnerio on June 3 by the anti-Capone forces, were a matter of routine that summer. But the turbulence in the city's underworld increased by an order of magnitude when *Chicago Tribune* crime reporter Jake Lingle was murdered in downtown Chicago on June 9. Although it was unknown in the upperworld until after he died, Lingle was actually the bagman for Chicago's commissioner of police William Russell.[16] Russell seemingly chose well when he selected him for that role, because Lingle had important connections in both the upperworld and the underworld. In his regular job, he was familiar with an abundance of prominent police officers and public figures. He was also an intimate of Capone and various organized crime figures. According to the 1930 US Census, Lingle lived across the hall from Jimmy Mondi's brother Louis in an apartment building on W. Washington Boulevard; the Reverend Elmer Williams, in a public speech, claims that Lingle did so rent-free.[17]

Fig. 6.1. Jake Lingle.

Moreover, if an anonymous informant was correct, Lingle was more than just a dispenser of protection who collected the

Fig. 6.2. Cook County coroner Herman Bundesen (center) and Chicago police commissioner William Russell (right).

resulting money for Commissioner Russell. It was asserted in July 1930 that Lingle and Marty Guilfoyle were partners in the operation of gambling dens, vice houses, beer flats, and other forms of illegal entertainment in an area just north of Madison Avenue that abutted Guilfoyle's earlier operations.[18] The claim was that Lingle had obtained those concessions for Guilfoyle.

Eventually Lingle's sale of low-quality protection at high prices earned him the resentment of both the Capone and the North Side mobs.[19] The best explanation for Lingle's murder is that it was planned by Jack Zuta. Zuta hoped that doing away with the reporter in broad daylight in the Loop would, beyond punishing a double-crosser, also publicly expose Capone's ties to the police department and lead to the removal of Commissioner Russell and others who were under Capone's influence.[20] Ted Newberry was originally approached by the leaders of the North Side gang to do the killing, but he balked at the idea and switched to the Capone gang in early June 1930.[21] In the end, Lingle's killer used one of a dozen pistols Frank Foster and Newberry had purchased while they were still with the North Side gang that Zuta gave to the shooter to incriminate the pair.[22]

These machinations indicate the esteem in which Zuta held himself as a strategist; he attempted to kill three birds with one stone by getting rid of Lingle, damaging Capone's influence with the police, and framing Newberry and Foster. Although his moves on the gangland chessboard were somewhat sound tactically, the broader strategy of going to war with the Capone gang, without eliminating Capone first, and the killing of a high-profile individual such as Lingle in the Loop in broad daylight was unsound.[23] So was the tactic of using a gun purchased before Foster and Newberry bolted from the North Side because the pair ultimately shifted the blame meant for them back on Zuta.

Capone, incensed by the heat caused by the slaying of Lingle, sent the newly recruited Newberry, who needed little urging, after Zuta on July 1, 1930. On that occasion Zuta escaped unharmed, with the aid of a police officer who escorted him from the police station, but an innocent bystander was killed and another was wounded on State Street in the Loop during the ensuing gun battle. A month later he was not as lucky. Danny Stanton, along with most likely Sam Hunt—tellingly, a golf bag was discovered near the scene—and several other Caponeites tracked Zuta to a Wisconsin resort, where he was hiding, and executed him.[24]

Moran finally capitulated in early August 1930, giving up his holdings on the North Side of Chicago after several parleys with his enemies. Capone installed the renegade Newberry as his man in charge of the area, and Dominic Nuccio's Gloriana Gang was rewarded with a large swath of the beer rights on the lower North Side for its part in opposing the Moran-Aiello-Zuta gang.[25] All in all, it was a smashing victory that gave the Capone mob control of seven more police districts in terms of bootlegging, plus the Loop in its entirety, and almost completely removed the North Side gang from organized crime in the city itself. It also greatly exposed Moran's former allies to attack.

Moran lost because of the official heat in response to the Lingle killing, since the police department quickly attributed the murder to Zuta; the Capone retaliatory heat that occurred at the same time; the desertion of many of his most important associates and the men loyal to them in the middle of 1930; and the loss of his major allies. In the last category, Joe Aiello seems to have left the North Side alliance sometime after Zuta was killed because Moran publicly called him a "double crosser" in October 1930.[26] For Moran, Aiello's defection was one of the bitter fruits of defeat.

After Zuta's death, Moran went to Minnesota to regroup and rethink. If he was, as has been claimed, able to make peace with Capone in August 1930 it was because he had been viewed as the lesser of the North Side evils. In late 1931 Moran reportedly received a subsidy of approximately $25,000 a year from the Capone mob on the condition that he stay out of Chicago, which was money well spent for the peace and quiet it bought the Capone forces.[27] However, Moran was not ready to step out of the rackets completely—only to transplant himself outside Chicago.

On the other hand, the olive branch was not extended to Aiello because Capone rightfully perceived him to be a much larger problem at that point in time. Therefore, the violence north of Madison Avenue did not completely stop in August 1930. Danny Vallo, a Capone man who was working hand in glove with the Circus Gang, was killed (most likely by the GKW gang or the Touhys) when he incautiously ventured into the near north suburb of Niles Center (later renamed Skokie) on August 14, 1930. However, this was only a minor victory for the anti-Capone forces. Exactly one month later Aiello's bodyguard, Jack Costo, who was also known as Jack Costa and Angelo Spano, was gunned down in the courtyard of his apartment building on Sheridan Road just north of Irving Park Road by a rifleman shooting from the window of a flat on the third floor.[28] It was a well-planned and well-carried-out ambush, modeled after the killing of Hymie Weiss, and was the precursor to Aiello's own death.

In October 1930 Aiello, after he had returned to Chicago from an absence in Rochester, New York, was hiding in the West Side apartment of his business partner and friend "Patsy" Prestogiacomo. As he left the building on October 23 to board a taxi that would have taken him to a train bound for Texas, and possibly Mexico after that, Aiello was fired on by a machine gunner positioned across the street.[29] Personally brave until the end, Aiello reached for his own weapon as he tried to escape around the corner, only to come into the line of fire of another well-placed machine gun nest (and, showing the Capone gang's efficiency, there was evidence of a third gun nest that did not come into play that night).[30] In total, Aiello was hit by thirty-five bullets, causing Captain Patrick Collins of the Fillmore police station to remark that this gangland killing was "a work of art" and "there are only two gangsters in these parts who can do a job like that. Those two are Burke and McGurn."[31]

After the Moran-Aiello-Zuta triumvirate collapsed, a remnant of the gang, led by the Carr brothers and Sam Battaglia, took control of a section of the lower North Side east of the Chicago River (around Grand Avenue) and apparently also an adjacent area just west of the Chicago River (in the vicinity of Chicago Avenue and Racine).[32] The Battaglia-Carr gang was led by John "Red" Carr, his brother Willie Carr, and Sam "Teets" Battaglia. They were decidedly anti-Capone, which at the time took a tremendous amount of nerve, given that Ted Newberry and the Gloriana Gang were to the north of them, the Circus Gang was to the west, and the Capone gang was to the south.[33] John "Mule Ears" Wolek (aka Walek), John "T-Bone" Guida, Walter Guida, and Ted Virgillio were other members of this mob. The Battaglia-Carr gang paid for their transgressions against the Capone forces when "Red" Carr and Willie Carr were shot down by opposition gunmen in July 1931 and July 1933, respectively.

Meanwhile, building on the beachhead he had established in 1929, Moran took his remaining followers up to Lake County, Illinois, and intensified his struggle with Ray Pregenzer for domination of the local sins.[34] In early 1931 the former North Side leader had expanded into southern Wisconsin, and by September 1932 he had won the battle south of the state line; a newspaper article at the time reports that he "commands the vice, slot machine, and booze rackets in Lake County."[35]

After Capone ousted the Moran-Aiello-Zuta gang from the North Side, he moved against its various allies. In May 1931, ten carloads of hoods, led by Jack McGurn, Frank Rio, Claude Maddox, Tony

Accardo, and Rocco De Grazia, invaded Matt Kolb's districts in the city and the northern suburbs. Although the related political machinations in the city, if any, are unknown, a memo that *Chicago Tribune* ace crime reporter James Doherty sent to the *Tribune*'s editor outlines what happened in the county.[36] Doherty states that Sheriff William Meyering gave Jake Guzik the green light to take the north suburban area from Kolb, telling him to do so before he put his brother, Lieutenant James Meyering, in charge of that part of the county. The Capone shock troops went to forty-one booze emporiums, telling the owners, "Kolb is out. Hereafter we'd like you to handle syndicate stuff. We'll give you better service and set in at the same price." Kolb's slot machines were also removed. The interlopers also spent fifty dollars or more at each place they visited.[37] The takeover was accomplished without bloodshed, and Capone delegated Kolb's bootlegging districts in the city to the West Side O'Donnell branch of his organization, who worked closely with Marty Guilfoyle in this area, while Jake Guzik was put in charge of the newly acquired roadhouses in Morton Grove and Niles Center.[38]

However, Lieutenant Meyering was considerably disappointed when he found out that Guzik was paying off "downtown," meaning at the county building itself, rather than directly to him.[39] After Meyering told Kolb he could come back in again with his protection, Kolb reestablished himself in the northern suburbs. But the Capone mob decided that an example had to be made of Kolb—although they waited until the traditional gambling season was over at the places in northern Cook County.

On October 18, 1931, Kolb greeted two men he recognized at the Club Morton, his place near Ferris and Dempster in Morton Grove. The visitors joked with him at first—but then, as one shook his hand, the other pumped six bullets into Kolb's head. They fled the scene, but then one of them returned to shoot Kolb a seventh time. The Capone hoods next grabbed Kolb's man Leo Shaffer. After they gave Shaffer a terrible beating, he turned over to them a list of the suburban places that had been receiving Kolb beer and went to work for the Capone organization instead.[40]

Although there was considerable violence north of Madison Avenue starting in the middle of 1930, all was quiet behind the stockyards until 1931.[41] However, after the O'Donnell-McErlane gang split into three separate mobs in the spring of that year, there was a new round of South Side fighting.[42] A number of the troops, and six (out of nine) of the group's beer and alcohol districts, went with Frank McErlane. McErlane's chief lieutenant in his new gang was Eddie Kaufman. Spike O'Donnell kept the Gresham and Chicago Lawn districts, which were on the city's western edge, roughly between Fifty-Fifth Street and Ninety-Ninth Street. In what followed the South Side O'Donnell and McErlane mobs clearly remained on good terms because there were no reports of fighting between them and men from both groups lived in the Gresham neighborhood.

George "Yama" Downs, Daniel McGeoghegan, and Michael "Bubs" Quinlan, the earlier partner of George Maloney, led the third group that sprang from the breakup of the O'Donnell-McErlane gang. Downs, whose real name was George W. Downes, was arrested in 1924 for questioning in an attack on a young lady who was returning from singing with her church choir.[43] During the early 1930s he was running some gambling alongside his work in the field of bootlegging. McGeoghegan was a labor slugger and a bank robber during the 1920s. He was sentenced to death for the murder of an

Fig. 6.3. George Downs (#1).

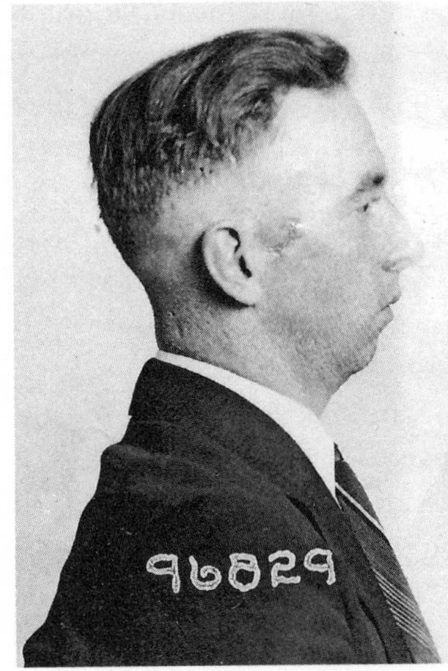

Fig. 6.4. Daniel McGeoghegan.

Fig. 6.5. Michael "Bubs" Quinlan.

officer of a building and loan association during a holdup in 1925, but his conviction was later overturned.[44]

The Downs-McGeoghegan-Quinlan (DMQ) gang controlled the Englewood police district, just south of Danny Stanton's area, and was backed by the Capone and, possibly at one time, the Saltis outfits.[45] The DMQs counted in their ranks Beer War veterans such as Joe Cainski, James "Daffy" Quigley, and Walter "the Terrible Pole" Zwolinski, all of whom got their start with Spike O'Donnell, as well as apparently a young Jewish lad from Lawndale named Lenny Patrick.[46] Zwolinski was so-called because he stabbed Steve O'Donnell's pet goat in a violent rage with a pitchfork when he left the O'Donnell-McErlane gang.[47]

Full of bravado, the DMQs quickly went on the offensive against both the O'Donnell and McErlane forces. The hostilities commenced on April 13, 1931, when shots were fired at Steve O'Donnell's car at Fifty-Fifth and Damen and into his house.[48] The latter type of attack, which endangered family members as well as the intended victim, was new to the South Side and to gangland in general. However, it soon became a standard tactic south of the stockyards.

Seven days later "Daffy" Quigley, Dominick Latronica, Joseph "Squint" Partell aka De Paola (whose real name was Michael J. Purtell), and a fourth man tried to force Edward Fitzgerald into a car outside a speakeasy on S. Peoria.[49] Fitzgerald was Eddie Kaufman's brother-in-law and a fellow McErlane gangster. Fitzgerald shouted, "Nix, you are not going to take me for a ride, Joey," as he attempted to flee before he was shot and killed in the street by one of his assailants.

This minor victory by the DMQs soon taught them what others, primarily dead men, already knew—that it was extremely dangerous to cross Frank McErlane. Although Walter Zwolinski's proficiency at goat stabbing gave him some notoriety in the underworld, he was far from being on the same level as Chicago's most vicious Prohibition Era killer. McErlane's vengeance, although it was not always immediate, was generally quite sure.

Harry Hyter, who was apparently the fourth man involved in the Fitzgerald killing, died first. His body was found in a wooded area near Torrence Avenue and 157th Street on May 12, 1931. Around that time, three separate attempts were made on Quigley's life, with shots fired into his home on two occasions.[50] In return, the DMQ gang sprayed the home of McErlane's brother-in-law with machine gun fire while McErlane was inside on March 26. The following day McErlane gave Zwolinski's house the same treatment.

On June 11, 1931, Dominick Latronica, the second of Fitzgerald's killers, was found near death in the vicinity of 107th and Archer in Willow Springs. Joseph Partell had been taken for a ride along with Latronica, but his corpse, which lay some two hundred feet away, was not discovered until June 29.[51] Two other DMQ gangsters were involved in a gun battle with enemies on June 16, and the McErlane gang tried unsuccessfully to kill George Downs on June 25. A day later the DMQs struck again at the South Side O'Donnells. Spike O'Donnell's house was riddled with machine gun bullets.[52] With a pistol in each hand, the plucky O'Donnell, who was probably the most fearless of all of Chicago's bootleggers, raced into the street to return fire. Perhaps fortunately for him, a car carrying the DMQ gunmen had already sped away.

In October 1931, death finally came for Quigley, who McErlane had openly threatened with revenge for his part in the Fitzgerald murder. After he was abducted, Quigley received a terrible beating before his assailants shot him three times. His body was found in a drainage canal near Lockport, Illinois, on October 11.[53] Despite his successes in the Beer Wars, Frank McErlane was increasingly stalked by his own demons, and his personal descent into hell accelerated during 1931. On June 6 he forced his way into his sister's home, knocked her down, and then bit her when she got up.[54] A few hours later the police found him in a completely drunken state at the corner of Seventy-Eighth Street and Crandon Avenue, where he blazed away a dozen times at imaginary enemies with two automatic shotguns. "They were trying to get me. But I drove 'em off," McErlane assured one arresting officer.[55] These related escapades earned him, after some finagling by his lawyer, a $225 fine, which he quickly paid before he left the courtroom in the company of a sympathetic Spike O'Donnell.

By the fall of 1931 McErlane was completely unhinged mentally. On October 8, 1931, his wife, Elfrieda, and her two pet dogs were found shot to death in her automobile on the South Side of Chicago.[56] Although "the McErlane touch," as described by the CPD, was clearly evident, her gangster husband was never prosecuted for these crimes. The police believed that the triple, if one counts the canines, slaying was due to yet another drunken quarrel between the couple, in which Frank McErlane was this time the victor.

Examining the broader picture, the bootlegging map of Chicago changed dramatically from January 1924 to January 1932, largely due to the events of 1930 and 1931.[57] At the start of 1932 (see Fig. 6.6), Capone's gang directly controlled eighteen police districts

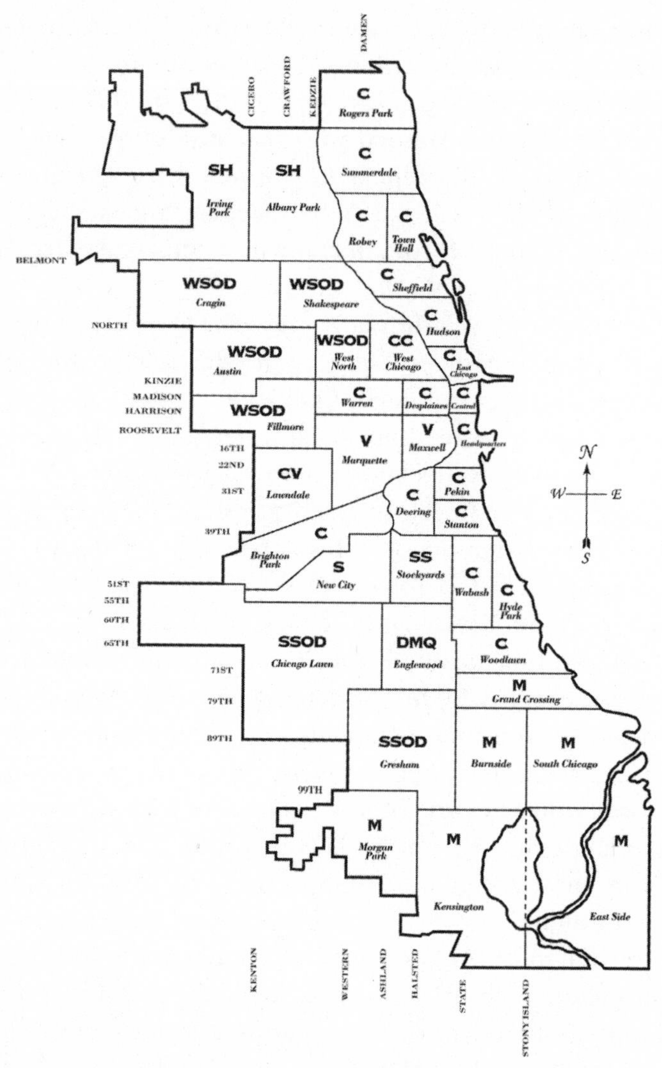

Fig. 6.6. Map of the major bootlegging gangs in Chicago, January 1, 1932.

Legend:
C = Capone
CC = Circus Café
CV = Cook-Vogel
DMQ = Downs-McGeoghegan-Quinlan
SH = Schultz-Horan
M = McErlane
S = Saltis
SS = Sheldon-Stanton
SSOD = South Side O'Donnells
V = Valley (Druggan-Lake)
WSOD = West Side O'Donnells

and indirectly ran another ten of the city's forty police districts through five gangs that were its subsidiaries or close allies: the West Side O'Donnells, the Circus Gang, the Sheldon-Stanton gang, the DMQs, and the Valley Gang. This gave the Capone mob control of 70 percent of the police districts in Chicago, which was a dramatic increase over the eight districts (and a major part of the Loop) John Torrio ruled over at the start of 1924 with at most three other districts in the hands of fairly independent allies. As has already been discussed, the Capone gang had also greatly extended itself in the suburbs over time.

Capone was eventually removed from Chicago by the federal government, rather than by his rivals or the local authorities. As has been well known for years, Prohibition agent Eliot Ness was not responsible for his conviction and imprisonment.[58] Based on the efforts of Ness and his squad of "Untouchables," Capone and his coworkers were indicted for five thousand Prohibition violations. However, the government chose—which was in no way the fault of Ness—not to proceed with that case. Instead, Capone was tried for income tax evasion, after the IRS meticulously built a case against him, and separately other Chicago mobsters were convicted of the same offense in what amounted to test cases. The prosecution was aided by 1) the fact that Capone had never paid a dime in income taxes or even filed a tax return and 2) the voluntary admissions he made about his negligible early income and wealth versus the large amounts that he later spent. Capone was convicted, and, as allowed by law, a federal judge sentenced him to ten years in federal prison for violating the internal revenue statutes.

Ness was an imperfect human being, and over time his reputation has been tarnished by his imperfections.[59] As Paul Heimel notes in his excellent biography, Ness's personal life was troubled.[60] Furthermore, like most bureaucrats, including J. Edgar Hoover, he was a self-promoter. Ness took newspaper men with him on raids, and in the process surely compromised their effectiveness.[61] Various false claims, including that Ness dried up Chicago or that he and his men were in constant danger, have been made about his career.[62] Paul Robsky, a member of Ness's squad, later noted that they were never in any real danger because Capone's men were ordered not to resist federal agents.[63] As Chicago's Prohibition Era violence indicates, bootleggers were very proficient killers, and while Ness's car was vandalized and other attempts were made to scare him, the fact that he and his men lived to tell about it indicates that there were no serious efforts to kill them.

Between his autobiography, which greatly embellishes the facts, and the various movies and television programs about him and the Untouchables, which further distort the story, the truth has been twisted to the point where there are more myths about Eliot Ness than there are about Loch Ness. In reality—and this cannot be overemphasized because he has been overly criticized in some quarters—Ness was an honest public servant. This is in stark contrast to Capone, a gangster who personally killed people and, directly or indirectly, ordered many others killed. Ness deserves credit for hampering Capone's bootlegging operations and inflicting on him considerable financial damage.

For example, US Attorney George E. Q. Johnson praised Ness and his men, and, in recognition of their work, three of them were part of the detail that escorted Capone from the Cook County Jail to a train bound for Atlanta in 1932.[64] Ness noted that the breweries his unit shut down produced $9 million worth of beer a year. However, this is an extreme estimate of the actual damages done by his unit's raids because this is revenue as opposed to profit, and the Capone gang would have opened other breweries or imported beer from elsewhere in the vicinity to replace the flow that was disrupted. Therefore, the gang would not have permanently lost the monies from the locations the Untouchables closed. At the other end of the spectrum, Ness calculated that the beer and equipment that was seized in the raids was worth roughly $500,000.[65] This estimate does not, however, take into account the net revenues lost by Capone and his gang until they could set up other breweries or the effect on their costs if they were forced to buy beer at the wholesale price for a period of time instead. The true monetary effect of Ness and his unit on the Capone gang is a number between the preceding figures.

While Capone's income tax problems might seem excusable, since many of his contemporaries in Chicago committed the same offenses, not everyone in his shoes refused to pay the government, and he should have followed that example. In 1923 almost five thousand bootleggers around the country paid income taxes.[66] John Torrio, Hirshie Miller, Maxie Eisen, and Frankie Lake did so in 1924, and it was front-page news.[67] Eddie Waters, a zealous internal revenue agent in Chicago, pestered various bootleggers, including Capone's brother Ralph, about filling out their tax returns. He even helped them do it in a way that did not reveal their sources of income.[68] Certainly the federal government had charged several bootleggers with income tax evasion as early as 1925, and in 1927 the US Supreme Court ruled that it was legal for the government to collect income taxes from illegal activities. Robert Schoenberg, for one, is astounded that by 1929 Al Capone did not simply settle up with the government for the previous years' tax liabilities, which would probably have closed the issue.[69]

Although the legal points at the time were rather tricky, when Capone was indicted the statute of limitations, under one interpretation of the law, had run out for the tax years from 1924 to 1927. These years represent the major counts Capone was convicted on and added the most years to his sentence. It might have been a much weaker case if those charges were invalid. His lawyers were primarily responsible for dropping the ball on this matter, because they never argued that parts of the indictment were moot during the original trial.[70] Admittedly this may seem like a more minor point against Capone, but if he had been paying attention to what was going on around him, he would have caught this on his own since the details appeared in the newspapers before his trial. For example, when Terry Druggan and Frank Lake were indicted in 1928 for income tax violations pertaining to the years 1924 and 1925, the *Chicago Daily News* reports, "The indictments were rushed through today as the charges would be outlawed by March 15 if no definite federal action had been taken."[71]

In the early 1930s officialdom was ecstatic over the convictions of Al Capone, Ralph Capone, Jake Guzik, Frank Nitti, Druggan, and Lake for income tax evasion. At the time the authorities declared that the war against organized crime in Chicago was over. Frank Loesch of the Chicago Crime Commission (CCC) asserted, "Organized law enforcement has fought it out with organized crime and we have won. The gangster has been conquered."[72] Similarly, the *New York Times* claims that the Capone gang had been smashed and that only small, fragmented gangs remained in Chicago.[73] Nothing could have been further from the truth, because the Capone mob, although it had been hit the hardest by the authorities, found new leaders and also got out from under the federal government microscope that had led to the convictions of so many top hoodlums.

Admittedly, when Capone was removed from Chicago his gang faced its worst leadership crisis to date.[74] Earlier, Torrio had smoothly replaced James Colosimo, after disposing of him, and Capone fairly easily took over the reins when Torrio stepped down in 1925. But who was to take Capone's place? It has been assumed that 1) Frank Nitti was Capone's underboss in 1931 and 2) he became the top man when he returned from prison in early 1932, which implies a seamless transition. Yet this does not appear to have been the case.[75] For example, in 1927 and 1931 the CCC refers to Tony "Mops" Volpe as Capone's "chief lieutenant" and names him as Public Enemy number two in 1930, while Nitti does not even appear on that list or the one released in 1931.[76] The *Chicago Tribune* describes Volpe, who was soon placed under a deportation order, in December 1930 as "ranked second to Capone."[77] In the same vein, Hal Andrews calls Volpe "one of the most important" members of the gang and states that he "was a candidate for the Capone throne and might have occupied it except for the fact that, until recently, he faced deportation to Italy."[78]

Jake Guzik, who filled in for Capone during his earlier incarceration in Pennsylvania, was also out of the running to replace him. He did not have the martial abilities required to be the boss, and he was unacceptable to the top men in the gang because of his ethnicity. Also, he was headed to federal prison just as Capone was going away and Nitti was returning to Chicago.

Frank Rio, who had a strong combat record in the Beer Wars, reportedly served briefly as the top man after Capone went to federal prison. On this point, Guy Murchie states that Rio "became the boss after Capone was imprisoned."[79] Similarly, in November 1932 the *Chicago Daily News* refers to him as "Frank Rio, public enemy and Capone gang leader," and the *Chicago Tribune* calls him the "Capone gang chief."[80] He was, however, most likely lacking in administrative skills, having spent too much time on the front lines. Rio was also with Capone and away from Chicago for several extended periods of time, which removed him from the pulse of the organization.[81] Due to Rio's inadequacies, the seeming unavailability of Volpe, and the shortcomings of Guzik, Nitti took charge of the gang at the end of 1932.[82]

Nitti was a compromise of sorts, because while he had solid front office experience directing the business activities of the gang, he was never personally involved in the mayhem, although he had directed the shock troops at various times. However, Rio was at his side to consult with him on all matters of violence. In fact, it is quite possible that Rio became the underboss when Nitti took the boss's position, since both spots had become open (due to Volpe's legal problems) and as a team they had all the requisite leadership skills. Consistent with this interpretation, in April 1934 when the Outfit's upper echelon met with labor fakers George Browne and Willie Bioff, Nitti and Rio did most of the talking, as they had on previous occasions, which befitted the boss *and* the underboss of the organization.[83]

Undeniably, Nitti had a difficult job.[84] By 1932 the end of Prohibition was in sight, which would take away gangland's crown jewel, the bootlegging racket. Plus, Chicago's underworld had just gone through a period of intense federal and local scrutiny that resulted in the convictions of numerous Chicago mobsters for income tax evasion and a variety of other offenses. Also, when Nitti took over, the gang's revenues from all sources had declined dramatically compared to what they were during the prosperity of the late 1920s. And the number of men trying to feed at the trough had not changed greatly.

For example, beer and whiskey sales dropped by two-thirds from their heyday in the late 1920s to the fall of 1931. Gambling and prostitution slumped similarly. The Capone gang's leaders responded by decreasing the wages and salaries of lower-level members, and the money received by the higher-level hoods also diminished.[85] Specifically, by December 1932 various gangs were selling their beer to speakeasies for twenty-five or thirty dollars a barrel, as opposed to the long-time retail price of fifty-five dollars; although this price cut appears to have started in March of that year.[86] In early 1933, the Capone bootlegging syndicate, which sold beer to speakeasies in its own provinces and wholesaled it to non-enemy gangs, dropped retail prices to between twenty-five and fifty dollars a barrel, depending on the area it was sold in, after holding the line at fifty-five dollars for several months.[87] However, in March 1931 independent hard liquor dealers were forced to buy from the Capone syndicate, and by early 1932 most of the gangs in the city, with the exception of a few South Side areas, were also buying beer from it.[88]

On the other hand, as the Dry Era wound down so did the Beer Wars. This took the Capone mob out of the spotlight because the number of gangland killings greatly decreased. The negative effects of the demise of Prohibition were also offset by the addition of large parts of the North Side and the nearby suburbs to the Capone kingdom, without the need to completely merge the incumbent hoodlums into the mob, as well as the expansion into other activities that began earlier. The growing dominance of the underworld by the old Capone gang would pay it further dividends at the end of Prohibition.

In terms of management style, Frank Nitti was in many ways the complete opposite of Al Capone, whose persona and loud manner targeted him and the organization. Nitti was a low-key businessman, who ascended to the throne when strategic thinking was increasingly required and battlefield leadership was relatively less important because the Beer Wars were coming to an end.[89] In 1932 the gang, given the intense scrutiny it was under, needed to go below the radar, and Nitti was just the man to take it there.

Regarding the Capone mob's administrative structure in the early 1930s, it has been assumed that the gang was organized along geographical lines because in the 1960s the Chicago Outfit's street crews controlled all the rackets within their designated areas, led by a head (the equivalent of a capo in the Cosa Nostra structure on the East Coast) who reported directly to the underboss and boss.[90] However, the street crew structure appears to be a more recent innovation, because the Chicago newspapers do not even mention street crews until the 1960s. As noted in chapter 3, during the 1920s the bootlegging gangs, including the Capone mob, were organized by function. Different individuals directed specific activities throughout the gang's domain, as opposed to one person running everything in a particular geographic area.

One source, which discusses the 1930s, states, "It is generally believed that shortly after Al Capone went to the penitentiary . . . there was a complete re-organization in compliance with a plan set up primarily by Tony Accardo. The various enterprises which the outfit was interested in were put on a departmental basis with experts in each field placed at the head of the various sections or departments."[91] Certain questions must be addressed, however, before sense can be made of this memo because the Capone gang was earlier organized on just such a departmental basis, meaning by function.

As has been previously noted, over time the Capone gang had absorbed several other allied mobs, such as the Chicago Heights hoodlums, the West Side O'Donnells, the Sheldon-Stanton mob, and most probably the DMQs. Each gang leader controlled a variety of rackets in his area because those activities had belonged to this gang before it merged with the Capones. Similarly, Ted Newberry and his successors had control of the North Side gang's territory starting in late 1930. This evolution created a mixed structure because in the Capone gang's original domain things were organized differently. Accardo's suggestion was then to return to the earlier form of organization with a given activity once again reporting to one individual throughout the gang's domain, who in turn reported to the underboss.

This would not necessarily have caused serious problems in the Capone gang because the same activity was still run by the same person in each local area—after the change he just answered to someone else above him. As an illustration, Dominic Roberto and Jimmy Emery controlled the illegal activities in the Chicago Heights area when they joined the Capone mob and did so for the next several years. After Accardo suggested reorganization, Emery (or Roberto, depending on when it took place) was still the overseer of all gambling, for example, in that neck of the woods, but he now reported to the mob's gambling czar with regard to that racket.[92]

In terms of the gang's operating divisions at the beginning of 1932, Charlie Fischetti appears to have been in charge of the higher-end gambling places and nightclubs. Guzik had the handbooks and the horse race betting. "Red" Barker oversaw the labor and business rackets. Liquor distribution was under Joe Fusco. Eddie Vogel ran the slot machines and other coin-operated devices, such as pinball machines and jukeboxes. Vice operations were under Duke Cooney, as they had been for a number of years.[93]

Big Bill Thompson was permanently removed from Chicago politics in 1931 when Anton Cermak, a skillful politician who created the modern Democratic party machine in Cook County, trounced him in the mayoral election. Although he was an unabashed foe of Prohibition, Cermak soon called for a "complete cleanup of vice and gambling resorts."[94] He made organized crime's greatest enemy, Captain James Allman, the city's police commissioner. However, Cermak's war on organized crime hit the policy operators disproportionately, as is discussed further below, because one of its main goals was to turn them from good Republicans into loyal Democrats.[95]

In 1931 the elite Scotland Yard unit was established as part of the CPD's detective bureau to investigate major crimes and gather intelligence.[96] Many years later it became the CPD's vaunted Intelligence Unit. A special "hoodlum squad" was created by Cermak within the Scotland Yard detail in November 1932 to "harass and drive out of Chicago all known hoodlums."[97] On December 19, 1932 Nitti's office was raided by members of the mayor's own police detail, including Harry Lang and his partner Harry Miller. The overzealous Lang shot Nitti when he tried to destroy evidence. Within days Miller was given command of a detail of his own in the "hoodlum squad" as a reward.[98] One of the forces driving these interconnected events was the world's fair that was coming to Chicago in 1933. With Chicago's public image heavily blackened by Prohibition, the city's administration strove to make the best impression possible by clamping down on crime before the Century of Progress Exhibition opened.[99]

Fig. 6.7. Chicago police captain John Allman (left) and Mayor Anton Cermak.

After Cermak was killed in Miami in early 1933, Edward Kelly became Chicago's mayor due to his close connections to West Side political heavyweight Pat Nash, who replaced Cermak as chairman of the Cook County Democratic Party. The Kelly-Nash tandem soon took the concept of an unholy alliance to a new level by making the party—the political machine that Cermak had built—a virtual partner with the hoods in gambling and apparently vice as well.[100] Although there is no way to know for certain, because Cermak died before his true aims were apparent, perhaps this was another objective of his attack on organized crime.

Specifically, during his early days in office, Mayor Kelly met with Murray Humphreys and obtained underworld support for several bills that passed the Illinois General Assembly. In exchange, a blind eye was turned toward gambling in the city and the county.[101] The Kelly-Nash political power was absolute for a number of years because after the Democratic landslide in the November 1932 general election they held all the major positions in city and county government, including the offices of state's attorney and sheriff.[102]

Fig. 6.8. Mayor Edward Kelly (seated) is surrounded by admirers.

Instead of bothering the sanctioned gambling under Nitti's direction, the police, except for the occasional token raid on the syndicate houses, focused on closing unsanctioned places that opened up. Both sides greatly benefitted from this arrangement. The party was allowed to put key people from the various ward organizations in gambling houses and other mob establishments at lucrative salaries. Of course, they and the other employees were given time off so they could work for the party's candidates on election days.[103] In return, the money paid by the old Capone mob helped fund the Democratic machine's campaign efforts. In 1934 the gambling places turned over 50 percent of their profits to the politicians, which in aggregate put about $1 million a month in the hands of the Democratic Party in Cook County. Forty percent of that was retained by the specific ward organizations for their use, while the remaining $600,000 went to the party apparatus.[104]

Although this rake-off by the politicians might appear to have been rather high, in exchange the gamblers and vice operators received virtual immunity from the law. The *Chicago Daily News* observes, "Not for many a year has the city been so wide open with respect to police and political protection of gambling and other forms of vice."[105] Similarly, Virgil Peterson states, "Never had the gambling business flourished to a greater extent than during the Kelly administration. Never had the gamblers received better protection," and, "The political-gambling organization under the Kelly-Nash regime exceeded anything Mike McDonald had ever dreamed of a half-century earlier."[106]

The various private agencies, once they realized that the Hydra known as the Capone mob had not been destroyed in 1931, continued to fight organized crime in Cook County for many years after that. The notable exception was the Secret Six. For a short period of time it basked, more than anyone or anything else, in the glow of the spotlight that illuminated the downfall of Al Capone. Capone told Ted Tod of the *Chicago Herald and Examiner*, "The Secret Six has licked the racket. They've licked me. They've made it so there's no money in the game anymore."[107] Obviously, this was an exaggeration because the IRS ultimately took down Capone, and his gang prospered long after his conviction. Although, if Capone was speaking figuratively, this statement is somewhat accurate because Chicago's civic leaders, most of whom were prominent members of the business community, were at the helm of the CAC, the CCC, and the Secret Six, and they were also the impetus for the federal assault on him and his gang.

Citizens' groups modeled on the original Secret Six quickly sprang up elsewhere. For example, between April 1930 and December 1932 similar organizations were founded in the Rogers Park neighborhood on the North Side of Chicago, in Lake County, Illinois, and in New York City, Kansas City, Missouri, Omaha, Nebraska, and Atlantic City, New Jersey.[108] In fact, the group's investigators were soon combatting bank robbery, kidnapping, and other crimes around the state of Illinois as well as in various other parts of the country.

The Secret Six's fall was as spectacular as its rise, which ironically parallels Capone's own career. In September 1932 it was revealed that the group had been investigating the Cook County State's Attorney's Office, run by John Swanson, who had been its strongest supporter. Alexander Jamie charged, "I . . . have found that a political-criminal cabal exists."[109] In return, Swanson's men had tapped the phone line in a clandestine office maintained by the Secret Six and were monitoring the activities of Mrs. Shirley Kub, one of its agents. The state's attorney was exonerated by a grand jury when no evidence was produced to support Jamie's charges.[110] This episode put the Secret Six in an extremely bad light. Although Mrs. Kub was discharged by the group in January 1933, that month Mayor Cermak withdrew the Chicago police officers who were assigned to the agency. In March the CAC stopped funding the Secret Six and Colonel Randolph severed his connection with it, effectively killing the organization.[111]

Returning to the world of gambling, as noted in the previous chapter, games of chance mushroomed when the North and South Side mobs went to war in the summer of 1930. By the middle of 1931, broad control of gambling was restored under a new Capone-led syndicate that oversaw illegal betting throughout the city and the county.[112] In the city, five major groups, which had been in place for several years, were at the head of the setup. They were led by the following individuals: 1) Jake Guzik, who directed the majority of the Capone places and spoke for Capone overall, 2) Johnson, Anixter, and Skidmore, 3) Marty Guilfoyle, 4) "North Side" Frankie Pope, and 5) "Dago Lawrence" Mangano and "West Side" Frankie Pope, who were Capone's men on the Near West Side. The thousands of independently owned establishments paid the Capone syndicate for the right to operate. Handbooks were for the first time generally also offering table games such as blackjack and craps, as opposed to their previous focus on horse races.

Gambling was running openly in greater Cook County in mid-1931. Guzik was the overseer for the syndicate in the northern part of the county, as well as in the south and west where the Capone gang had always been strong. Roadhouses that had previously been without table games were encouraged to add them to the menu. If the owner provided the premises and the basic amenities, the syndicate took care of everything else, including bankrolling the game, while the roadhouse received 40 percent of the profits.[113]

In late 1931 Mayor Cermak's crusade against illegal gaming appeared to be hitting the independents disproportionally hard, indicating that the big gamblers had reached an accommodation with city hall while the minnows were still being targeted. For example, one small operator complained, "There's no reform stuff in this pitchin'. . . . They'll push guys around until we see somebody. Or else they'll chase us into the alley and the business will go to the big boys."[114] In search of new gambling revenues, the Capone gang added the ancient sport of cockfighting to the list of its wagering activities in 1932. "West Side" Frankie Pope was arrested for running these matches, which were augmented by hula dancers and plenty of beer to entertain the bettors, on W. Adams Street near Halsted.[115]

The Gambling Index had an average value of ninety-three during 1931 and 1932 (when Anton Cermak was the mayor), which was down noticeably from 122 during the preceding two years. However, this at least partly reflected the Great Depression's negative effects on economic activity, legal or illegal, and therefore a decrease in related arrests. The index dropped considerably during Kelly's first years in office, equaling thirty-eight in 1933 and dropping to thirteen in 1934, which was the all-time low for the period from 1875 to 1973. The Democratic machine's blind eye toward gambling is perfectly illustrated by these figures. Equally consistent with this laxity in enforcement of the gambling laws, in 1933 beat cops in Chicago reported that gambling places were popping up faster than they could be closed.[116]

The syndicate kidnapped and held for ransom gamblers who were outside the agreement, which was a signal to them to clear out. For example, James Hackett, the major force in illegal gambling in Blue Island, was taken on May 1, 1931, and again on May 27, 1933. "Cully" Flanigan, the king of the Gary, Indiana, gambling syndicate, was snatched on August 7, 1931, and Jack Lynch, who was as big as anyone in illegal betting in Chicago, was abducted later that month and reportedly paid a $50,000 ransom.[117] According to gambler James Ragen, the Capone mob was behind the kidnappings of Hackett, Lynch, and others, with Red Barker in one case personally pointing the target out to the freelance criminals who actually committed the act on the Capone gang's behalf.[118]

Cermak's initial efforts against policy gambling achieved only minimal success. But, in late 1931, he assigned Captain John Stege to the Wabash station with "strict orders to wipe out policy."[119] Stege immediately hit hard at the game and its owners, including the biggest operators. Play was also hurt by the Great Depression. In consequence, the amount of money bet annually in Chicago on policy games dropped by about two-thirds from 1928 to only $4.2 million in 1931.[120]

But even in the earliest days of the police crackdown there were whispers in the African American community that its real purpose was to "make way for a new regime that has been formed and is to be controlled by men who supported the mayor."[121] Consistent with this explanation, when Stege was suddenly and without explanation transferred from the South Side to the Desplaines Avenue district on the Near West Side in March 1932, the word went out that all might soon be well again with policy.[122]

The new regime was a syndicate known as the Big 12, which was "in" with Mayor Cermak. Initial meetings regarding its creation were held in December 1931, and the arrangement was finalized in September 1932.[123] The members of the Big 12 were Eddie Jones, "Big Jim" Martin, "Mack" Jones, George Jones, Jim Knight, Bill Driver, Julian Black, Walter Kelley, Ily Kelley, Leon Motts, Henry Young, and Charlie Ferrill. Eddie Jones and Jim Martin served as its leaders.[124] The group sanctioned who could operate and collected protection

Fig. 6.9. Eddie Jones (left) grabs his attorney.

money that was passed on to "Billy" Skidmore, the bagman major-general for policy as well as for all of gambling in Chicagoland, who in turn paid the police and the politicians.

Several violent incidents occurred in the previously peaceful world of policy in 1931 and 1932. Specifically, David Giles was killed on December 1931, "Mack" Jones, one of the Jones brothers, was kidnapped for ransom in February 1932, and Wynn McCullough was shot eight months later. Informed sources disagree on who was behind these attacks. Nathan Thompson places the blame squarely on the Capone gang.[125] However, the *Chicago Defender*, the leading contemporary source in the African American community, makes no mention of this and notes that one of the gunmen in the Giles slaying, who was seen by an eyewitness, did not appear to be Caucasian.[126] Consistent with the interpretation that the problems were internal to policy gambling and were due to the growing pains associated with the formation of the Big 12 syndicate as opposed to inroads by the Capone forces, this violence was sporadic and there is no evidence that the latter took over a wheel at the time or drove one out of the business.

The Committee of Fifteen, reporting on recent vice conditions in September 1930, states, "It is obvious that vice resorts have been opening more rapidly than they have been closed. This condition is due partly to reduced profits of late from liquor and gambling."[127] On the other hand, by the middle of 1931 the Uptown neighborhood on the North Side was largely free from vice. Local businessmen had come up with an effective solution to the problem; they bought several blocks of property for the sole purpose of closing the vice dens.[128] The

Vice Index fell to an average value of 338 during 1931 and 1932 from 642 two years earlier, and by 1933 it had dropped to 259.

The vice syndicate re-formed in 1932, obviously without Jack Zuta, after the gang wars ended. It controlled the parlor houses on the Near South Side, which operated openly and now charged two dollars.[129] According to the Juvenile Protective Association (JPA), some forty-nine traditional brothels were operating in Chicago at the time.[130] While ten to fifteen of these were higher-priced establishments, which were outside the narrow bounds of the group, the rest were syndicate joints. For example, an investigator for the JPA (posing as a potential customer) was told laughingly by a roper in front of a brothel on S. Wabash, when he intimated that he was worried about it being raided, "Why don't you know that these are all [Murray] Humphrey's places? . . . They are all protected. You've got nothing to worry about."[131] Furthermore, potential customers were assured that the women were inspected twice a week for venereal disease and that anyone who could prove he was infected at a syndicate place would be treated for free.[132]

Vic Shaw, the oldest of the old-timers, ran a house on Prairie Avenue in the early 1930s. It was reported to contain six quite attractive women who charged five dollars—three performed straight sex, and three were "French," that is they performed oral sex. Three women, all supposedly beautiful, operated at the Lexington Hotel at Twenty-Second and Michigan, where a bellboy instructed potential customers to rent a room for $1.50 and a woman would come to him for an additional three dollars.[133] Streetwalkers and more clandestine bordellos predominated on the North and West Sides, which is a clear indication that the vice syndicate controlled only a piece of the city's sex trade.

The 1933 world's fair, which was intended to diminish the city's gangster reputation, was nonetheless expected to be a great boon to prostitution, especially to the Near South Side houses closest to the fairgrounds that geared up for it. Harlots from other cities were migrating to Chicago as well. For example, brothel owners in Buffalo, New York, lamented that "many girls have left for Chi[cago]" and that if the trend continued "[t]here won't be any girls (prostitutes) left in Buffalo!"[134] Taxi dance halls, which had been eliminated in the city a few years earlier, were springing up again for the fair.[135] One such establishment was the Century Dancing Club on S. Wabash, which was partly owned by Ralph Capone.[136]

A new twist in vice that flourished at the time was the massage parlor, where the "masseuses" performed sex acts. When thirty-one operators in twenty-six establishments were canvassed, twelve offered to only do local treatments (masturbations), five agreed to perform sexual intercourse, and fourteen were willing to engage in sexual intercourse or oral sex. The going massage parlor rate was three dollars.[137]

Capone's guys also profited on the grounds of the world's fair. The gang's beer was served there, and Paul Ricca apparently had a heavy investment in the Italian Village section of the fair, where Sally Rand and Jimmy Durante performed.[138] Ricca's brother-in-law, Jerry Gigante, and his lawyer, Joseph Imburgio, were on the payroll.[139]

In the broader sweep of time, as the old-time brothels were increasingly driven out of business by reform, their male employees were absorbed by the Torrio and Capone enterprises (and before that by Colosimo's empire). They went to work in bootlegging during Prohibition and later in gambling.[140] Some of these men, for example Hymie Levin and the Guzik brothers, as well as Ralph Capone and Al Capone himself, rose to high rank in the gang. Others, such as Nick Juffra, followed the same path but never achieved close to the same stature.

The underworld made deeper inroads into organized labor, and relatedly in business racketeering, in the early 1930s, but not without a struggle. Decency struck back in March 1931 when the earlier deposed James "Lefty" Lynch ousted Red Barker and his cronies, with the aid of the Cook County state's attorney, in a special meeting of the Coal Teamsters.[141] This was a short-lived victory, however, because a judge quickly stopped the Lynch group from taking office.

Barker's next move, against the Outlaw Teamsters west of Crawford, was initially thwarted when two of his underlings, Bernard McCone and Herman "the Kid" Diehm, were killed in a Forest Park saloon on July 16, 1931. The killers were in the employ of Chicago Teamsters leader Timothy Lynch (not to be confused with "Lefty" Lynch). In retaliation Timothy Lynch was murdered outside his home in Maywood on November 9. Daniel Tognotti (aka Tagnetti or Tagnatti), a Barker adherent, was found dead in North Riverside on

December 22 in what was seen as revenge for Lynch's murder. Nonetheless, Lynch's successors relinquished the area in the city between Crawford and Austin Boulevard to the Barker-controlled union, limiting the former group's domain to suburban Cook County.[142]

The hoods also sought to take over the International Brotherhood of Teamsters (IBT) locals. To that end, union leader Patrick Berrell and his bodyguard, former North Side gangster Willie Marks, were killed in Shawano, Wisconsin, on July 22, 1932, and Richard Roberts, a business agent of IBT local 705, was murdered the following October.[143] In May 1933 the home of Lake Forest Teamsters' official Arthur Metzger was bombed during a union meeting.[144] He had received numerous threats from the Outlaw Teamsters—whose Lake County muscleman was none other than George Moran, working closely with Jack White and Murray Humphreys—to step aside.[145]

Barker's dream was not just to control the truck drivers. He wanted a stranglehold over the entire coal industry and possibly all transportation in the metropolitan area. As the chief of detectives William Schoemaker explained,

> Barker was seeking to gain supreme control of every branch of the teamsters' and chauffeurs' unions in the city and the county. If he had gained his objective, he would have complete power over all delivery services in the city. . . . On top of that, he would have had the mastery over 90,000 teamsters and chauffeurs who would pay dues of $10 a month, a total of nearly a million dollars a month. . . .[146]

To further that goal, he and Jack White organized the Trucking and Transportation Exchange (TNT), which worked hand in glove with John Sheridan's Chicago Teamsters. Contractors wishing to employ drivers were forced to join the exchange, which received $400,000 in total initiation fees and dues of approximately $500,000 a year.[147] At the other end of the process, TNT helped fix the prices coal dealers charged their customers, including the city of Chicago.[148] However, action by State's Attorney Thomas Courtney and Mayor Kelly derailed the TNT after about two years of operation.[149] The same two men were also instrumental in bringing a number of the

Chicago Teamsters' locals back into the IBT by the end of 1933 in an attempt to remove them from the hands of the hoodlums.[150]

The Capone outfit pursued other uses for its fleet of trucks as the end of Prohibition drew near. It decided that "the milk industry was the simplest to organize along the lines of the beer business," which was at least partly due to the fact that a racket association had appeared earlier in the industry.[151] Control of the business was the main goal, but the milking of the Milk Wagon Drivers' Union, which had a $700,000 treasury and was part of the IBT, was a lucrative objective as well. Its president Robert Fitchie was kidnapped in December 1931, and he was released when the organization's treasurer, Steve Sumner, delivered a $50,000 ransom to Barker and Murray Humphreys.[152] In June 1932, Humphreys, Marcus "Studdy" Looney, Barker, and "Klondike" O'Donnell, all heavily armed, invaded the milk drivers' headquarters on S. Ashland Avenue.[153] During this brief visit Humphreys took it upon himself to instruct Sumner, an old-timer who had been at the group's forefront since 1902, on how a labor union should be operated: "You're just letting a gold mine get away from you. . . . Unions are a great thing if run right, but you are not running your[s] right."[154] The hoods demanded half of the spoils that would flow from their control of the milk drivers, and Humphreys explained how the money would be obtained:

> Tribute? If you want it from the milk companies a few sticks of dynamite will do the trick. If you want it from the mugs out driving the wagons a pair of brass knuckles and a blackjack will get it. We'll get the tribute all right and if you don't want to split with us, we'll give you a hundred grand [$100,000] to get out.[155]

However, Sumner and Fitchie were not easily frightened and blocked the takeover. The union offices soon became a bombproof fortress with armor plate and bulletproof glass while Chicago police officers were stationed in a window across the street with a machine gun. A bulletproof vehicle was also purchased to drive Sumner to and from work.[156]

The Capone gang opened Meadowmoor Dairies, Inc., with Humphreys as a silent partner, in competition with the milk association members in February 1932.[157] The new dairy was bombed in May, but it nonetheless started selling milk at nine cents a quart in June, undercutting the association price of eleven cents. Refused drivers by Fitchie's union, Meadowmoor hired men who belonged to a new labor group organized by Barker.

In other labor violence, Elija Orr, secretary of the Newspaper Wagon Drivers' Union, was murdered in July 1931 as the West Side O'Donnells tried to regain control of the organization. William Rooney, boss of the Sheet Metal Workers' Union and active in the Meat Cutters' and Flat Janitors' unions as well, was gunned down in March 1931. Carmelo Lucchesi of the Macaroni Workers and Charles Argento of the Italian Master Bakers, both of whom were business agents, were killed in January and August 1932, respectively. The following February Dennis Ziegler, secretary of the Hoisting Engineers, was murdered, and John Pippan, secretary of the Italian Bread Drivers' Union, was shot down six months later. Although the motives in these killings, except in the Orr murder, were not clear at the time, Gordon Hostetter commented later that most of these crimes were due to "professional hoodlums" seeking union control.[158]

Other unions caved in more easily. For example, by 1930 Capone affiliate Danny Stanton had worked his way into the Motion Picture Operators' Union.[159] It soon benefited from favorable Illinois legislation and experienced increased violence as dissident members Jacob Kaufman and Fred Oser were murdered in 1931 and 1933, respectively. The painters' union was targeted, as were others, because of its large treasury, and its secretary, Francis Carr Jr., was killed in February 1931. According to Roger Touhy, in 1932 the boss of the painters, Art Wallace, paid Frank Nitti $40,000 in the mistaken belief that his organization would no longer be troubled.[160] Touhy also stated that the Building Janitors' Union surrendered to the Capones. The Cook County State's Attorney's Office estimated that in 1932 the Capone gang received tribute, in one fashion or another, from *two-thirds* of the unions in the Chicago area with Barker personally controlling between forty and fifty unions.[161] In a few short years the bootlegging mobs, and most prominently among them the Capone gang, had gone from a minor presence in organized labor to dominating the field.

The Master Cleaners and Dyers Association attempted to clean its own house in December 1930 when it brought Dr. Benjamin Squires, an arbitrator and lecturer in economics at the University of Chicago, in as the head of the newly formed Cleaners and Dyers Institute.[162] The institute included about 90 percent of the cleaning establishments in Chicago. Squires was installed as the czar of the group with the power to set prices and wages and also to control individual plants. However, the prices he set were still high enough that independents offered the same service at a lower charge.

Al Capone showed his true colors, which dry cleaner Morris Becker, who regarded him as a savior, never saw, when he approached Squires in May 1931. Capone offered to enforce the association's agreement in return for 1 percent of the industry's gross revenues—an offer that Squires promptly refused.[163] Undeterred, the Capone gang, through Murray Humphreys, operated the Drexel Cleaners and Dyers on the South Side and tried to organize other shops as well. Despite Squires's well-meaning efforts to legitimize the industry, bombs were thrown, plants were attacked by goons, employees were slugged, and acid was poured on the customers' clothing. Some of the violence may have happened behind Squires's back because the long-time players in the industry were not yet ready for reform, but the Capone gang was involved as well. In August 1931 several Capone hoods with machine guns invaded the International Cleaners and Dyers, which competed directly with Humphreys's shop. Two hoodlums were soon arrested, but the manager of the business, Benjamin Rosenberg, was murdered in January 1932, a few days before he would have testified against them.[164]

Disgusted by the violence, Squires resigned his post in August 1932. His troubles were not over yet because a year later he was indicted with seventeen others, including Capone and Humphreys, for racketeering.[165] Squires and the other defendants were eventually acquitted, but the cleaning and dyeing industry was for years tainted by the gangster elements.

In the broader picture, the number of business racket associations fell to fifty-three in 1931 due to vigorous counter measures by the authorities, although the overall cost to Chicagoland was still $165 million per annum.[166] In 1932 the cost had dropped to $145 million a year. However, the fundamental nature of this criminal enterprise was changing for the worse. As Gordon Hostetter noted, "Whereas several years ago organizations of business men and organized labor were principally responsible, with the criminal acting merely as tool or an agent, the criminal is now gaining the ascendancy."[167] The "criminal" Hostetter referred to was, in the plural sense, the Capone gang and, in the singular meaning of the word, Humphreys, who in 1933 led the Capone mob efforts in the cleaning and laundry fields and in business racketeering overall and was involved with the TNT as well.[168] The Capone organization was certainly adept at working all the angles, such as when it forced bars throughout almost all of Cook County in 1931 to buy from them not only their alcoholic beverages, but also the ginger ale, soda, carbonated water, pretzels, towels, table cloths, and other peripherals they used.[169]

The Capone gang was faced with various internal problems during the early 1930s. Some were due to the age-old issue of members who were dissatisfied with their situation or otherwise violated the rules. In other cases, people in the recently absorbed areas were unwilling to go along with the new order. The Applequist brothers were shot down in their saloon on N. Paulina Street on the Near West Side in April 1932 for peddling their own needled beer instead of handling the Capone brew. Another ex–North Sider, Joseph "Big Rabbit" Connell, was killed on Goose Island in October 1932 for making and selling beer in competition with the Capone syndicate.[170]

Among the disgruntled members of the Capone gang, Mike Heitler was killed in April 1931 for sending a detailed letter to the authorities describing the workings of vice on the Near West Side after he had been removed from his position as overseer. Similarly, Salvatore (Agostino) Loverde (aka Frank LaCort) was shot down in Cicero in November 1931. Long prominent in alky cooking, he had followed Joe Aiello as the real boss of the Chicago section of the Unione Siciliana, while serving as the treasurer of a new importing company that was formed on Aiello's death and was a continuation of Tony Lombardo's original enterprise.[171] He was also the pioneer in the macaroni (pasta) manufacturing racket in Chicago. Capone's one-time bodyguard Phil D'Andrea replaced Loverde as the head of the Unione's Chicago chapter, and unusually, given the fate of his seven most recent predecessors, he lived through it.[172]

In the days and months after the Capone-appointed boss of the North Side, Ted Newberry, was found slain in Northern Indiana on January 7, 1933, several theories circulated about why he had been killed. The most tantalizing is that Newberry had conspired with Anton Cermak to kill Frank Nitti and set up a new crime syndicate in Chicago that he would lead in conjunction with Roger Touhy. Cermak, while accompanying President Franklin D. Roosevelt in February 1933 in Miami, was shot by Giuseppe Zangara and died of his wounds in March. It has been asserted that Newberry and Cermak were killed for their roles in this attempted coup, and that Zangara was paid by the Capone gang to assassinate the mayor.[173] As is typical of conspiracy theories, there is no hard evidence to support these claims. Furthermore, it appears that a woman standing next to Zangara bumped into the chair he was standing on and jarred it when he started to fire—Zangara admitted as much—so it is uncertain that his bullets struck the intended target, and it is quite possible that his goal was to kill the president. In fact, Zangara maintained that Roosevelt was the target.[174] Also, organized crime is a tight-knit cabal that uses people it trusts to do the dirty work, as opposed to hiring deranged outsiders as assassins. Therefore, these extreme claims are unproven and Newberry was most likely killed for some other reason, as the Chicago newspapers suggest the next day.

Tony Marino aka Dominick Russo, a major Capone alcohol dealer in Cicero, was killed on August 1, 1933. Newberry's replacement on the North Side, Gus Winkler, was slain on October 9. Winkler was most likely murdered because he still dabbled in the world of ordinary crime; he had recently been involved in and he was suspected of helping authorities regarding two major robberies. Louis Cowen, another prominent hood with long-standing ties to Capone, was murdered in Cicero on October 27, 1933, in an attack that left his bodyguard wounded.[175]

Returning to the South Side bootlegging wars in 1932, the DMQs ambushed Spike O'Donnell's brother, Charles, outside his apartment on W. Ninety-First Street on March 6, 1932, and filled him full of bullets and shotgun pellets. They also invaded the O'Donnell brothers' Gresham district that month, smashing saloon windows to convince the owners to change their beer supplier.[176] The DMQs had previously taken the Chicago Lawn district from the South Side O'Donnells.[177] When Charles O'Donnell died from his wounds on April 2, 1932, his brother Spike finally called it quits after over twelve years of beer selling and beer warring.

Frank McErlane made peace in 1932 with the Capone gang, agreeing to buy beer from them, which gave the Capone beer syndicate control, at the wholesale level, of virtually the entire city.[178] This did not, however, save Walter Zwolinski or his business partner Thomas Kane. Zwolinski was found dead in his automobile, shot six times in the head, on September 2, 1932. Kane died similarly on October 19, 1932.[179]

Death came for McErlane in October as well—on the eighth, exactly a year after his wife's dead body was found. He died in Beardstown, Illinois, where he maintained a lavish houseboat on which he had spent a considerable amount of time during the previous year. Surprisingly, McErlane's death was from natural causes. Suffering from pneumonia and in a delirious state, with imaginary enemies once again pursuing him, McErlane managed to punch a nurse into unconsciousness before he expired in the hospital. One of his former associates accurately summed up the gunman's existence when he said, "I don't know that he ever did anything good in his life."[180] Denied the rites of the Catholic Church, McErlane's wake and funeral were sparsely attended.

Joe Saltis's gang was not visibly involved in the Back of the Yards Wars during the early 1930s, which allowed him to dart in and out of Chicago as he pleased. For example, in late 1930 he avoided a vagrancy charge by spending several months in Wisconsin.[181] However, Saltis still ran the New City bootlegging business by "remote control," through "Paddy" Sullivan, who oversaw the beer end of it, aided by Nick Kramer, and Joe Pollak, who ran the hard liquor sales until his own death in July 1932.[182] Saltis returned to Chicago bootlegging on a more permanent basis in September 1932 when he finished building a new home on Irving Avenue in the city's posh Beverly (sometimes called Beverly Hills due to its elevation) district. He allied himself once again with McErlane.

After McErlane's death, Saltis most likely ran his far South Side areas as well, at least until the legalization of real (3.2 percent alcohol) beer was imminent in early 1933. A newspaper article at that time refers to him as the "erstwhile beer boss of the *[S]outheast* [italics added] Side" and notes that Saltis had visited McErlane in Beardstown before he died.[183] What was left of illegal retail beer sales on the South Side, in terms of brew with alcohol content higher than 3.2 percent, beyond what the Capone gang controlled itself, essentially fell to the DMQ gang. On that point, one Chicago newspaper describes Daniel McGeoghegan in the middle of 1933 as the "successor to Saltis."[184]

In mid-1932 the Touhy brothers reportedly entered into a compact with the Moran gang. They had recently lost ground to Rocco De Grazia, Claude Maddox, and Tony Capezio, the Capone gang's spearheads in the invasion of the northern and northwestern sections of Cook County.[185] Defiant as ever, the Touhys pointedly refused all peace offers from Frank Nitti, Frank Rio, and their associates, and, after new recruits arrived, they went on the offensive.[186]

The *Chicago Daily News* calls the Touhy gang at the time "as choice a collection of desperadoes as the town has seen for many a day. It is made up of fugitives from justice from a dozen states. The common bond seems to be their dislike for Italian gangsters. For months, it is said, they have been hi-jacking every syndicate truck of beer or 'alky' they encounter. The driver and his aid[e]s are pulled from the truck seat, given insulting messages to deliver to the leaders of the syndicate and forced to walk back."[187] On June 16, 1932, Roger Touhy's men killed Red Barker in a machine gun ambush outside of the hotel he lived in near Crawford and North Avenue on Chicago's Northwest Side, apparently narrowly missing Claude Maddox, Willie Heeney (another transplant from St. Louis to the Capone gang), and Jack White who were in the street with him at the time.[188] White succeeded Barker as the head of the gang's labor racketeering department and was aided by the O'Donnell brothers from the West Side, "Fur" Sammons, and Murray Humphreys. That same day, Touhy gunmen led by Roy Marshalk invaded the Dells, the posh gambling house at Austin and Dempster in Morton Grove, and shot to death Freddie "the Cowboy" Di Giovanni, a Capone killer and bodyguard. In the fall of 1932 the Touhy gang moved in on the far northwest corner of Chicago "formerly controlled by the Capone gang," which it appears to have quickly captured.[189]

On September 26, 1932, a guard at a De Grazia gambling house near Melrose Park was killed by invaders, most probably the Touhys. Four days later the Touhy gang murdered a waiter in an invasion of a Niles roadhouse. In October 1932 they killed Tony Jerfita, who was probably a Capone man. By December 1932, however, the Touhys had been pushed north of Irving Park Road, three miles beyond North Avenue that had earlier been the southern boundary of their area.[190] The gang killed Joseph Provenzano on December 1 and John Liberto on December 6, both of whom were connected to Jerfita and were, therefore, most likely Capone gangsters. The Touhys eliminated alcohol peddlers Anthony Persico and Nicholas Maggio in a double homicide the following day at Irving Park Road and Cumberland Avenue. John Rinella, who owned a roadhouse just south of River Road and Higgins, which was quite a bit north of the Irving Park Road dividing line, was slain on December 16 because he was buying beer from De Grazia.[191]

This string of unanswered killings by the Touhy mob was unprecedented, in terms of fighting between the Capone gang and its various enemies. However, the Capone forces struck back, using methods other than violence, probably because Frank Nitti was intent on keeping them out of the spotlight as much as possible. In December 1932 William Collins, chief of the county sheriff's police, and Lieutenant Meyering closed all the speakeasies in the northwest section of the county, telling the owners, "The Touhys must go."[192]

One of the most unusual incidents in the Beer Wars occurred on February 2, 1933, when a carload of Touhy gangsters ambushed an auto heading south on Harlem Avenue at North Avenue on the western edge of Chicago. The second car, which was armored, reportedly contained Capone gunman Fur Sammons who was wearing a woman's hat and a short fur coat as a disguise as he tried to slip through enemy territory.[193] The attackers, at least one of whom had a Thompson submachine gun, were aware of the target vehicle's protective steel plate and fired at the tires and radiator to disable it. A machine gunner in the second car, mostly likely Sammons, returned the fire and wounded an adversary believed to have been Tommy Touhy.

Sammons's now useless car was abandoned in Oak Park, and its occupants took control of another vehicle at gunpoint to make their escape. River Forest police officers, who responded to the gun battle, were fired on by Touhy mobsters before the gang escaped into Elmwood Park. This is the only known incident in Chicago's Beer Wars (and elsewhere during Prohibition) where machine gunners fired at each other, and ironically no one was killed, as opposed to the hundreds of other gang hits in which there were fatalities.[194] Five days later the Capone gang most likely killed William O'Brien, a Touhy mobster, at a location on N. Clark Street in Chicago, less than a block from the St. Valentine's Day Massacre garage.

On a different front, Roger Touhy entered the battle for control of the teamsters' unions in the metropolitan area, in opposition to the Capone hoodlums. On April 28, 1933, Touhy and five of his gang mates, wielding machine guns, took over the Chicago Teamsters' headquarters on S. Ashland, telling the men they found in the building that they had come to "clean the Dago syndicate out of the union."[195] Jack White, Murray Humphreys, and "Klondike" O'Donnell avoided certain death by failing to appear that evening, so the invaders kidnapped two minor union officials who were soon released unharmed.

From the Capone gang's perspective something clearly had to be done about the Touhy gang. Nitti and company continued to respond with brains and political influence rather than with brawn, which the Touhys had in abundance. The leaders of the Capone gang had stock swindler Jake Factor stage his own kidnapping on July 1, 1933, after he and his party left the Dells roadhouse in Morton Grove, where Fred Di Giovanni had been killed almost a year earlier. Captain Daniel Gilbert, of the State's Attorney's Office, who was later revealed to be an appendage of organized crime and surely received a bag of silver coins for it, quickly blamed the supposed crime on the Touhys. He harangued a multitude of suburban police chiefs to drive them out by hitting at their slot machine operations with the intent of crippling the gang's revenues.[196]

By the middle of 1933 the end was near for the Touhy mob. Roger Touhy, "Gloomy Gus" Schaefer, and Edward McFadden were jailed in July 1933 for allegedly kidnapping a brewer in St. Paul, Minnesota. In November the same trio, along with Albert Kator and several others, were indicted for the Factor kidnapping. Touhy, Schaefer, and Kator were ultimately convicted in the Factor case in February 1934. At that point, with a number of their comrades dead, several gang members already in prison, and others on the way to jail for a variety of different crimes (including Tommy Touhy, who was suffering from Parkinson's disease), the Touhy gang was broken.[197] Using all the weapons at its command, the Capone gang had rid itself of an implacable and extremely difficult enemy. The Touhy gang ranked near the top, right after the North Side gang, on the list of the Capone mob's most dangerous Prohibition Era foes. It is, among other things, the only rival mob to have taken a beer district away from the Capone forces.

By the mid-1930s George Moran had drifted out of the Lake County rackets and the world of organized crime entirely, concentrating for a time on his Chicago dry cleaning business. With the Touhys smashed, Moran out of the picture, and the South Side dominated by the Capone gang once Joe Saltis retired from bootlegging, gangland rivalries in Chicago came to an end at about the same time as Prohibition, which was fully repealed in December 1933.

As the Dry Era came to a close, the bootleggers considered what they should do next. The seemingly obvious answer was to try and control the distribution of legal beer, just as they had monopolized it when it was illegal. Although a few breweries put Dry Era musclemen on their sales force in an attempt to garner customers, the gangsters were now largely fish out of water in the liquor business because illegal activity was no longer tolerated.[198] Just to be safe, in early 1933 the Cook County sheriff assigned fifty additional deputies to protect legitimate beer shipments by traditional brewing concerns from hijacking. The retail price for a barrel of legal beer was sixteen dollars in 1933, which included five dollars in federal taxes, a drop of 70 percent from the rate during the heyday of the bootlegger.

The Capone gang won the various gang wars it had been involved in during the Dry Era. The other bootlegging mobs in Chicago at the tail end of Prohibition were essentially all its allies, several of which had already been merged into the main entity. It had finally syndicated gambling countywide, had over time expanded greatly in the areas of labor and business racketeering, had control of the sale of illegal narcotics, and was in charge of the admittedly small syndicated portion of vice. Thus, in early 1934 Capone's old gang was the preeminent force in the local underworld with almost all of organized crime in Chicagoland under its umbrella. At this point the Chicago Outfit, spelled with an uppercase "O" to denote the gang with essentially a monopoly on organized crime in the Chicago area as opposed to the term outfit with a lowercase "o," which the Capone hoodlums used to describe their gang, was born.[199]

The process was made easier by the retirement from the underworld of various prominent Chicago bootleggers, who would trouble Nitti and the Outfit no more. Many of these men were "temporary" gangsters who had ventured into that world due to the easy money bootlegging offered—unlike the "permanent" gangsters in the Capone mob—and they withdrew from organized crime in the Chicago area when Prohibition ended. A survey in 1943 of the fifty-six men the CCC designated as a public enemy during Prohibition notes that Saltis had retired at the end of the era in the hope of living as a country gentleman off his accumulated millions.[200] Spike O'Donnell, who survived in the very dangerous profession of bootlegging from the beginning of the Dry Era to almost its end, drifted into other activities. Ten years after Prohibition, George "Dutch" Vogel was living in Wisconsin where he owned a brewery. Terry Druggan had also retired, to his gigantic farm near Lake Zurich in Lake County, Illinois. Several big-name hoodlums reverted to ordinary crime, such as Daniel McGeoghegan, who served a lengthy prison term for a 1933 bank robbery in Indiana and was later convicted of robbing a Chicago currency exchange. Similarly, Willie Niemoth, who was ostensibly a boilermaker, was sentenced to life in prison in 1945 for his part in a multimillion-dollar robbery in Chicago.

Other prominent Dry Era bootleggers receded into the shadows over time as small players in the Outfit. For example, in 1943 Klondike and Bernard O'Donnell had two gambling places in Cicero, and "Paddy" Sullivan also had a handbook. George Downs and his earlier enemy Eddie Kaufman worked in the gigantic Chicago Dodge war plant on the South Side where they were also involved in bookmaking. In a few cases old enemies, such as "Teets" Battaglia and his various gang mates, who read the handwriting on the wall and were aware of the Capone mob's practice of letting bygones be bygones, came in under the umbrella.[201]

But the upper echelon of the Chicago Outfit in the mid-1930s, as was also true during the 1940s, 1950s, and 1960s, was heavily staffed with men who worked for Capone during Prohibition, such as Frank Nitti, Paul Ricca, Tony Accardo, Jake Guzik, Murray Humphreys, Louis Campagna, Claude Maddox, Tony Capezio, the Fischetti brothers, Jimmy Emery, and Frank LaPorte. They made the Outfit, through a combination of criminal cunning, corruption, and political chicanery, the most successful of the Cosa Nostra crime families.[202]

In summary, the Chicago Outfit was created by Capone and his henchmen, building on the foundation laid by James Colosimo and John Torrio. Since the end of Prohibition it has tainted Northern Illinois and many other parts of the United States with crime and corruption, which in some cases continues to this day. This, as opposed to what appears in movies and some other works, is the real legacy of Alphonse Capone.

The next chapter examines over seven hundred gangland-style killings in the Chicago area during Prohibition. Although it tabulates a variety of data about these incidents, the purpose of the analysis is to understand the broader aspects of gangland murders during the Dry Era and to compare the results to previously drawn conclusions about the Beer Wars in Chicago (and gangland violence elsewhere during this time period). The book concludes with an examination of how the Capone gang came to rule organized crime in the Chicago area and beyond in 1934, which is a remarkable transition because at the start of Prohibition the Torrio-Capone mob was one of some twelve major bootlegging mobs in the city.

Chapter 7

THE FACE OF BATTLE: GANGLAND KILLINGS IN CHICAGO

"When gangsters kill, they only kill each other."

—Arthur V. Lashly, *Illinois Crime Survey*

"A real goddam[n] crazy place! Nobody's safe in the streets."

—Charles "Lucky" Luciano, discussing Chicago during Prohibition[1]

According to the Chicago Crime Commission (CCC), 729 people were slain gangland-style in Cook County, Illinois, including the city of Chicago, from 1919 to 1933, which is essentially the Prohibition Era. This accounts for 15 percent of the murders in the county during this time period.[2] While data for other cities in the United States are incomplete, Chicago was clearly the *gangland* murder capital of the country during Prohibition.[3] Various authors draw numerous conclusions about these 729 murders, including that all (almost all) the victims were members of the major bootlegging gangs in Chicago and, consequently, that the Beer Wars were incredibly violent.[4] Although Prohibition ended over eighty years ago, this data set has only recently been carefully analyzed. Therefore, the earlier conclusions about gangland violence during the Dry Era are based on at best a cursory examination of the evidence, and they often conflict dramatically, as the opening quotations indicate.

This chapter is based on research by this author and Mars Eghi-

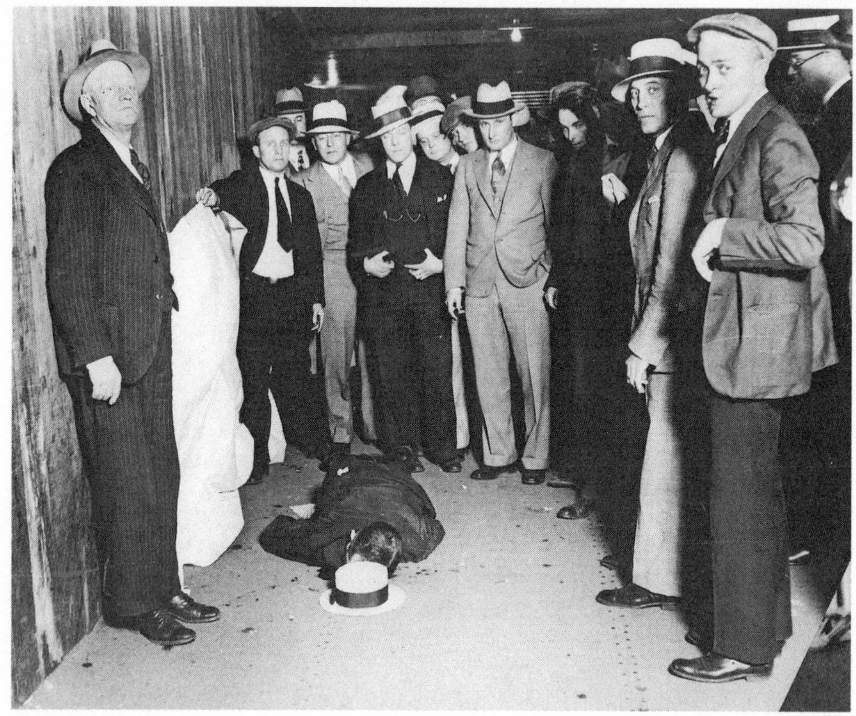

Fig. 7.1. The body of Jake Lingle.

gian.[5] They examined all 729 of the murders on the CCC list using the CCC records, CPD homicide reports, and newspaper accounts, and they collected a variety of data about the victims and these incidents.[6] The sample was stratified by the major reasons for the killings, such as bootlegging, gambling, labor racketeering, vice, or other criminal disputes, and each type of killing was examined as well as the full sample. The great majority of the results contradict the conventional wisdom about Prohibition Era violence in Chicago. In fact, almost every conclusion that has been drawn previously about gang murders in the Chicago area during Prohibition is incorrect.

For example, a large number (43 percent) of these murders were unrelated to organized crime. Also, only 41 percent of the killings were due to bootlegging, and the victims belonged to the major bootlegging gangs in the Chicago area in only about 40 percent of those cases. In other words, only 138 of the people slain between 1919 and

1933 on this well-known list were members of the major bootlegging gangs. Therefore, while various bootleggers in the major gangs were killed during the Prohibition Era, those casualties are much smaller than is expected based on the total of 729 victims or the phrases "Beer Wars" or "gang wars" that are often used to describe the conflicts during this era.

The CCC enumeration of gangland killings begins with the slaying of Frank Poroino (aka Porcino or Focino) on January 4, 1919, and continues to the new millennium. Unfortunately, there is nothing in the CCC's files or in the Chicago newspapers at the inception of the list detailing the criteria used to classify a murder as a gangland killing. However, the CCC's typed list of victims is entitled "Gangland Style Killings," and in a newspaper article in 1962 long-time CCC operating director Virgil Peterson referred to them as "gang style."[7] While the CCC's exact definition of "gang style" murder is also not known, contemporary and later definitions are available. These definitions are consistent with what the criteria for the CCC list appear to be, based on the details of those killings from 1919 to 1933.

Arthur V. Lashly defines a gangland killing as a murder committed by a gang of organized criminals that is consistent with gang methods.[8] These killings were premeditated, did not involve robbery or other common motives, and were carried out in a manner that allowed the killer(s) to usually escape. From the extant CCC files, the agency's determination appeared to be based on evidence presented at the coroner's inquest into each slaying, the verdict of the coroner's jury, and information developed by the CCC. In fact, one recently discovered CCC memo listing some of these murders has the phrase "based on coroner's verdicts" in its title.[9] The Cook County coroner and the CCC had trained investigators on staff during this era, so the designation reflected more than just witness testimony at the inquest.

All the victims on the list were found in Cook County. Therefore, the CCC did not include killings outside this area even though Chicago gangsters sometimes dumped their victims elsewhere and even committed murders outside the state. These omissions do not, however, appear to be serious. Organized crime historian Jeff Thurston's files on gangland killings from 1931 to 1933 reveal only eight victims found outside Cook County—five in Indiana, two in Wisconsin, and one near Lockport, Illinois—whose deaths were related to organized crime in Chicago. This indicates that the CCC killings (which total 119 for these three years) are understated by about 7 percent due to the geographical focus.[10]

Beyond basic details related to each incident, such as when the killing occurred, how many victims there were, how many people were accidentally killed or wounded, and how many slayings resulted in an arrest or conviction, information was also collected related to who the victim was, why she was killed, how she was killed, and where the body was found.[11] Regarding the victim's identity, data were collected on gender, age, ethnicity, occupation, and whether he belonged to one of the major bootlegging gangs in the area. The killings were broken down by cause, which ranges from organized criminal activities synonymous with the era, for example, bootlegging and gambling, to other organized crime, such as Chinese Tong Wars or business racketeering or political disputes or feuds/vendettas in the city's Italian community. Regarding how the victim was killed, the type(s) of weapon(s) used, and whether the victim was taken on a "one-way ride" or killed in a "drive-by shooting" were tabulated. The location of the body was defined in terms of political units, for example, the city of Chicago versus various suburban areas, in terms of police districts in Chicago, and also with respect to whether the victim was found indoors or outside.

Arthur V. Lashly's study of the years 1926 and 1927 is the only other systematic examination of gangland killings during Prohibition.[12] Lashly, however, examines only the ethnicity of the victim, where the body was found, how many victims were killed by guns, and the legal disposition of the case. His results may also be specific to the years he studied. The results in this chapter are compared and contrasted to Lashly's findings and to the conclusions drawn elsewhere in the literature on gangland during Prohibition.

The data used came from three main sources: the CCC files on gangland killings (which were found for only the years 1927, 1928, 1930, 1931, and 1932), the CPD homicide records (which are available online and on microfilm), and newspaper articles (primarily from the *Chicago Tribune*).[13] The CPD records go through the year 1930 while the *Chicago Tribune* is available for all the years in the study. The general rule in the data collection was to try and obtain two sources for each killing; at least one official source (CCC or CPD) and one newspaper, or two newspapers for 1933 because the CCC and CPD records are not available.[14]

The CPD and CCC records provide good information on basic details, such as the age of the victim, the method of killing (at least in terms of the type of weapon used), and what happened at the crime scene. However, they provide little information on the victim's occupation (especially if he was a criminal) or why he was killed.[15] The newspapers provide much better information on who the victim was and the motive for the murder. Of course, a few killings were not found in the newspapers, partly due to weaker reporting of events outside the city, and in some cases the articles are brief and not overly informative. Nonetheless, the sources cover the vast majority of the 729 murders. For example, no information was found on the killing in the CCC files, CPD records, or in the newspapers in only nine cases (less than 2 percent of the sample), and no newspaper article was found in only twenty-nine cases (4 percent of the sample).

Given the relative strengths of the various sources, the CCC was the primary source for most of the data, followed by the CPD and then the newspapers.[16] That is, if the sources conflict, information from the primary source was used. However, the newspapers were the primary sources for data on who the victim was, and why he or she was killed, followed by the CCC, and then CPD.

The number of gangland-style killings per annum is reported in the first panel of the table in Fig. 7.2.[17] From initially less than thirty such murders a year, the total exceeded thirty from 1922 to 1933. There were at least fifty gangland-style killings every year from 1923 to 1930, with a maximum of seventy-five in 1926. While the figure for 1931 (forty-eight) is roughly comparable to the low during the preceding several years, the number of killings declined to under forty in 1932 and 1933.

The killings are broken down by causes related to organized and also ordinary crime. The results are reported in the second panel of the table. The first eight causes are part of organized crime, such as bootlegging, the related struggle for the control of the Unione Siciliana, gambling, labor union control or labor racketeering, business

	1919	1920	1921	1922	1923	1924	1925	1926	1927	1928	1929	1930	1931	1932	1933	Total
Total CCC Killings	24	23	29	37	52	56	64	75	58	72	56	64	48	39	32	729

	1919	1920	1921	1922	1923	1924	1925	1926	1927	1928	1929	1930	1931	1932	1933	Total
Boot-legging	0	2	1	6	11	6	29	41	38	29	16	21	11	21	3	235
Unione Siciliana	0	0	0	0	0	0	1	0	12	8	1	3	0	0	0	25
Gambling	0	0	0	0	2	2	2	0	2	1	2	3	3	3	3	23
Labor Union or Rackets	0	5	1	4	2	7	0	2	1	3	6	5	9	8	2	55
Business Rackets	0	0	1	0	1	4	1	2	3	4	2	2	0	1	0	21
Taxi Cab Wars	0	0	1	0	1	4	1	1	0	1	1	2	0	0	0	12
Vice	0	0	0	0	0	0	0	0	1	4	0	0	1	0	0	6
Tong Wars	0	0	0	0	0	0	0	0	3	2	1	0	0	0	0	6
Organized Crime Related	0	7	3	10	16	16	31	45	45	38	27	30	23	29	8	328
Italian Feud	3	3	6	8	3	1	5	7	3	1	0	2	0	0	1	43
Black Hand	4	2	4	9	9	12	3	2	4	7	0	9	1	0	1	67
Politics	0	0	13	2	1	2	0	1	0	4	0	0	0	0	0	23
Gang Related–Other	7	2	1	1	0	0	2	3	1	1	3	5	3	3	4	36
Other Causes	6	9	2	5	10	15	12	21	9	14	11	5	9	3	9	140
Cause Unknown	5	1	6	9	18	11	17	3	6	13	17	14	15	7	12	154

Fig. 7.2. Gangland killings per annum and by cause.

All Unione-related killings are also counted as bootlegging killings. All killings in the Taxi Cab Wars are also counted as business rackets killings. Totals for a year may exceed the number of actual killings because often there were multiple reasons for the killing.

racketeering, the Taxi Cab Wars in Chicago, vice, and the Chinese Tong Wars. All killings related to the control of the Unione—given its involvement in bootlegging—were counted in the bootlegging killings and are also listed separately. Killings related to the control of labor in a field are grouped under the heading "Labor Union or Rackets." The Hip Sing and On Leong tongs were American-born organizations that fought to control organized crime in the Chinese community.[18] The Taxi Cab Wars were a little-known episode in Chicago's history, which related to the Checker and Yellow cab companies. The Checker drivers belonged to the Teamsters' Union, and the company was mutually owned. Teamster intimidation of Checker drivers in an attempt to control the company, and the rivalry between the two companies' drivers for the choicest cab stands, resulted in considerable violence.[19] All Taxi Cab War killings are also counted in the category of business racketeering.

Many murders, according to the newspapers, had nothing to do with organized crime. Some were due to feuds or personal disagreements in Chicago's Italian community. Blackhanders, who were blamed for many of the killings on the CCC list, were freelance extortionists who preyed heavily on Italian immigrants and murdered the victims if they did not comply with their demands. Other killings resulted from political struggles, especially the battle for control of the Near West Side Nineteenth Ward Democratic organization in the early 1920s. Various murders stemmed from disputes among common criminals. Often multiple reasons were given by the sources for a slaying, while in 154 cases the cause was not reported.

Bootlegging was the stated reason for 235 of the 575 killings where a cause was given, or about 40 percent of the total. Rivalries related to the Unione Siciliana accounted for twenty-five murders. While bootlegging was the most frequent cause of gangland killings during this era, 60 percent of the CCC killings were unrelated to bootlegging. This contrasts markedly with the statement by Gus Russo that "[t]wo thirds of the deaths in Chicago are due to the beer running trade" during Prohibition.[20]

The first bootlegging killing on the CCC list was the murder of James Colosimo on May 11, 1920. There were few bootlegging murders until 1923, when three South Side O'Donnell mobsters, among others, were slain. The bootlegging total dropped to six in 1924, but the murder of Dean O'Banion on November 10, 1924, ignited the North Side vs. South Side gang war. The number of bootlegging killings after 1924 ebbed and flowed largely with the Beer Wars, reaching a height of forty-one in 1926 when the North Side vs. South Side War, the Back of the Yards Wars, and the battle for control of the Chicago Heights area were at their worst. The gangland peace after the death of Hymie Weiss in October 1926 helped decrease bootlegging killings in 1927, although this was quickly offset by the revolt of the Aiello brothers inside the Unione Siciliana. Similarly, the almost citywide peace after the St. Valentine's Day Massacre, even though that event was responsible for seven deaths, kept the bootlegging killings below twenty during 1929. The demise of the North Side gang in late 1930 and the waning of Prohibition led to fewer alcohol-related murders per annum on average in the 1930s than in the period from 1925 to 1929, with only three in 1933.

Fig. 7.3. James "Big Jim" Colosimo lies dead in his café.

The various gambling operators coexisted fairly peacefully during much of this period. Until 1930 there were never more than two gambling-related killings a year, and only three a year thereafter. Capone and others made greater inroads into gambling as the bootlegging wars waned and the independent gamblers, outgunned by the bootlegging mobs, knew the odds they faced and usually went along quietly. For example, there were only twenty-three gambling-related killings, as many as were due to politics and a tenth of what was related to bootlegging, from 1919 to 1933.

There were fifty-five labor-related killings during this period, which reflects Chicago's long history of union-related violence. In fact, the first high-profile victim on this list is Maurice "Mossy" Enright, who was gunned down by rival labor racketeers on February 2, 1920. As the bootleggers and others moved in on the unions more heavily around 1929, the labor killings increased. Business racketeering was responsible for twenty-one deaths, mostly from the Taxi Cab Wars. Killings related to vice activities were minimal (six in total) because for years the vice operators in the city generally got along well with each other. The Tong Wars accounted for six deaths in Chicago.

Of the 575 killings with a known cause, 328 were due to organized crime. That is, at least one of the stated reasons for the killing was bootlegging, gambling, labor union activity or labor racketeering, business racketeering, vice, or war among the tongs. This means, however, that 43 percent of these killings (247 of 575) were unrelated to organized crime, which is again inconsistent with the standard wisdom. For example, Lashly states, "Bootlegging and gambling are directly responsible for practically all Cook County gang murders."[21]

Regarding other types of slayings, feuds in the Italian community caused forty-three murders in total, and these were more prevalent during the early part of the period. Sixty-seven murders were due to Black Hand extortion, the most frequent reason after bootlegging for gangland-style killings. This type of murder decreased noticeably during the early 1930s and is explored further in the appendix. Political struggles accounted for twenty-three killings, mostly during the early 1920s. Barring a few cases, the victims were usually followers rather than political leaders. Problems among ordinary criminal

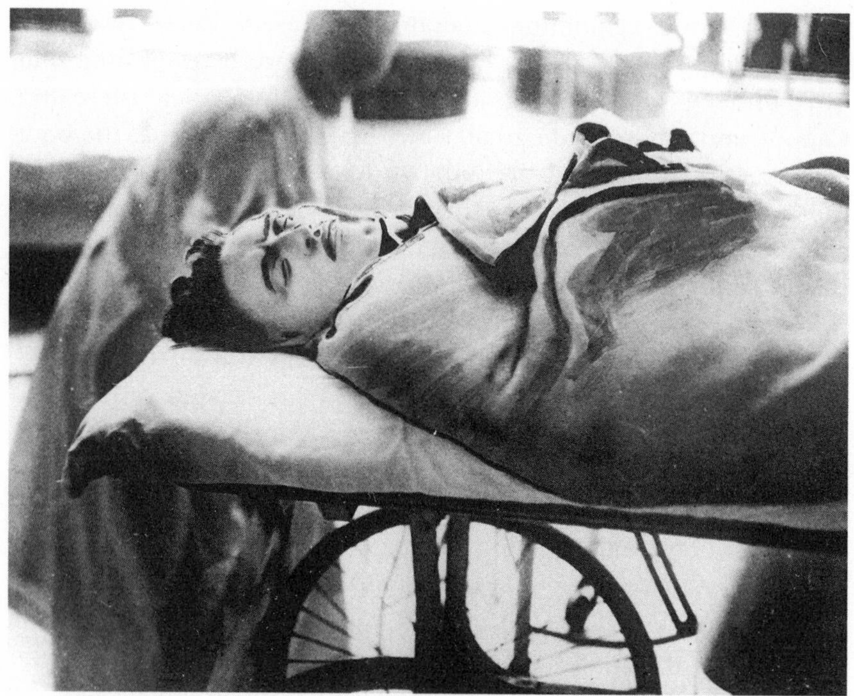

Fig. 7.4. Tony Genna in the hospital after being shot.

gangs led to thirty-six killings, while 140 murders were caused by various other factors.

Leigh Bienen and Bradley Rottinghaus speculate that organized crime was responsible for the noticeable increase in homicides in Chicago during Prohibition.[22] Analysis of the CCC killings sheds further light on this issue. There were 4,392 non-accidental homicides in Chicago from 1919 to 1930 as opposed to 2,236 during the preceding twelve years.[23] Based on the CCC's list, an estimated 239 murders *in* the city of Chicago were due to organized crime from 1919 to 1930.[24] Even if the number of organized crime killings from 1907 to 1918 is arbitrarily set to zero, the increase in this type of murder over the next twelve years (239) accounts for only about 10 percent of the increase in non-accidental homicides. This indicates that organized crime was not the major reason for the increase in murders in Chicago during the Prohibition Era.

Fig. 7.5. The funeral of "Diamond Joe" Esposito.

It is interesting, and important, to examine how many of the victims belonged (at the time they were killed) to the major gangs in the Windy City whose primary focus was bootlegging. The results are reported by gang, for eighteen gangs (including two in the suburbs), and by year in the table in Fig. 7.7. The first thirteen gangs, ignoring the fact that the Saltis-McErlane and Sheldon-Stanton organizations were initially one unit, were operating from essentially the start of Prohibition. The other five gangs arose later. The approximate years each gang was in existence are shown in the table.

The North Side gang had the most members killed, twenty-five in total, which includes Aiello and Zuta gangsters who joined with George Moran in late 1927. The Capone gang is second with twenty-three dead, and the Genna gang is third with sixteen. Fourth on the list, with thirteen victims, is the Sheldon-Stanton mob, which had to deal with Frank McErlane and Joe Saltis in the mid-1920s after they separated from the latter, and the various Chicago Heights gangs. The Druggan-Lake gang, which is almost invisible in previous his-

Fig. 7.6. Six victims of the St. Valentine's Day Massacre: Reinhardt Schwimmer (#1), John May (#2), Adam Heyer (#3), Albert Weinshank (#4), Peter Gusenberg (#5), and James Clark (#6).

tories of the violence during the Beer Wars, is noticeable with ten casualties.

For the remaining gangs, the number of victims ranges from seven for the South Side O'Donnells to zero for the GKW gang. The South Side O'Donnell members fell largely in two brief episodes during 1923 and 1925. The GKWs appear to have stayed out of the shooting in the North Side vs. South Side gang war, and their remnants capitulated quietly when Capone moved against them in 1931. Six members of the Saltis gang were killed, the last two in retaliation for the attempt on the life of Frank McErlane. The large number of DMQ gangsters killed per year also testifies to the difficulty of being on the wrong side of McErlane. The DMQ mob figure of 1.33 members killed per annum is fourth behind the North Siders (2.08 per annum), the Gennas (1.77), and the Capone gang (1.53).

The total number of major bootlegging gang members slain each year is reported in the last line of the table. The previously discussed

	1919	1920	1921	1922	1923	1924	1925	1926	1927	1928	1929	1930	1931	1932	1933	Total
Torrio-Capone	0	1	0	0	0	0	0	2	0	5	1	4	6	1	3	23
Sheldon-Stanton	NA	NA	NA	NA	NA	NA	5	3	0	2	1	1	1	0	0	13
Saltis-McErlane	0	0	0	0	0	0	0	1	2	0	1	2	0	0	0	6
South Side O'Donnell	0	0	0	0	3	0	3	0	0	0	0	0	0	1	NA	7
Genna	0	0	0	0	0	0	8	8	0	NA	NA	NA	NA	NA	NA	16
Druggan-Lake (Valley)	0	1	0	0	0	1	1	3	0	0	0	3	1	0	0	10
West Side O'Donnell	0	0	0	0	0	1	0	3	0	0	0	0	NA	NA	NA	4
North Side	0	0	0	0	1	2	3	2	0	4	6	7	NA	NA	NA	25
Schultz-Horan	0	0	0	1	0	0	0	0	0	0	0	0	0	0	0	1
Chicago Heights	0	0	0	0	0	1	0	7	2	1	0	2	0	0	0	13
Twentieth Ward	0	0	0	0	0	0	0	2	0	2	NA	NA	NA	NA	NA	4
Circus	0	0	0	0	0	0	0	0	0	0	0	1	0	0	2	3
Guilfoyle-Kolb-Winge (GKW)	0	0	0	0	0	0	0	0	0	0	0	0	NA	NA	NA	0
Downs-McGeoghegan-Quinlan (DMQ)	NA	NA	NA	NA	NA	NA	NA	NA	NA	NA	NA	NA	2	2	0	4
McErlane	NA	NA	NA	NA	NA	NA	NA	NA	NA	NA	NA	NA	1	0	0	1
"Red" Bolton	NA	NA	NA	NA	NA	NA	NA	NA	NA	NA	1	1	0	0	1	3
Battaglia-Carr	NA	NA	NA	NA	NA	NA	NA	NA	NA	NA	NA	1	1	0	0	2
Touhy	NA	NA	NA	NA	NA	NA	0	0	1	0	0	0	1	0	1	3
Total	0	2	0	1	4	5	20	31	5	14	10	22	13	4	7	138

Fig. 7.7. Number of members of major bootlegging gangs killed—all killings.

NA = Not Applicable because the gang did not exist at the time.

underworld truces are clearly evident, with only five such killings in 1927 and ten, including the five North Side mobsters murdered in the St. Valentine's Day Massacre, in 1929. So are the years when the Beer Wars were at their hottest; 1925 (twenty killed following O'Banion's death), 1926 (thirty-one killed), and 1930 (twenty-two killed). Finally, Fig. 7.7 provides insight into several interesting questions regarding Chicago's gang wars, such as which of them was the bloodiest. A rough estimate for the North Side vs. South Side War is obtained by summing the casualties for the Torrio-Capone and North Side gangs, which yields forty-eight dead. However, this is an imprecise estimate for two reasons. First, it does not differentiate intergang killings from intra-gang killings. For example, in the Torrio-Capone gang the slayings of James Colosimo and Mike Heitler were internal matters. Second, it ignores the deaths of allied gangsters, such as, at times, the West Side O'Donnells, the Saltis crowd, the Circus Gang, Druggan and Lake, the Sheldon-Stanton gang, the Gennas (at least in 1925), and perhaps the Touhys. Also, some killings around Chicago Heights after 1926 may have been a part of that war because the Aiellos tried to install a dissident Unione chapter there at the time.

The only other conflict that might be comparable is the revolving

Fig. 7.8. "Dingbat" O'Berta in the car in which he was killed.

battle south of the stockyards. The sum of the Sheldon-Stanton, Saltis, South Side O'Donnell, DMQ, and McErlane gang dead equals thirty-one, which is much smaller than the estimate for the North Side vs. South Side War. The difference would be even greater if the allied dead were included in the latter figure. Therefore, the battle between the Torrio-Capone forces and North Side gang was clearly the major Prohibition gang war in Chicago.

How dangerous were the Beer Wars for the members of Chicago's important bootlegging gangs? The total count of 138 dead is surprisingly low, compared to this author's expectation and those of other authors and gangland historians familiar with the CCC count of 729 killings during this time period. To put the figures into perspective, the Capone gang had five hundred gunmen in about 1931, but it suffered only twenty-three casualties during the fifteen-year period in question. Similarly, in 1924 and 1926 the North Side gang had two hundred gunmen, but only twenty-five North Siders—including the Aiello and Zuta gangsters who joined Moran later—were killed during a decade and a half. On the one hand, the figure of 138 killed is understated because it does not include bodies found outside Cook County. Increasing the total by 17 percent, based on reasonable estimates of the bodies that were dumped elsewhere to adjust for these omissions, still yields only 161 victims.[25] On the other hand, a number of the killings were due to internal gang discipline or other reasons, so the figures overstate the gang war casualties.

There is, however, a simple explanation for the low total. The phrase "gang war" or "Beer War" exaggerates what really happened. As the preceding chapters indicate, pitched battles between the major gangs in the Chicago area during Prohibition were *extremely* rare. Rather, the organized crime–related killings were largely a series of executions. The victims were usually caught off guard, generally one or two at a time, and they rarely returned fire or killed their killers.

A significant fraction—15 of 138—of the bootlegging gang members killed can be categorized as gang leaders, meaning they were at the top of their gang. If the second-tier leaders are included, this figure would be quite a bit larger. This is also not surprising. The main objective in a gang war is to "strike at the head" by killing the opposition's leaders. They are the most capable individuals, and killing them is the easiest way to defeat the other gang and, in the extreme, to take it over. Therefore, the rank-and-file members of the bootlegging gangs were in less danger than their leaders.

John Landesco argues that the election of reform mayor William Dever in 1923, which broke up the centralized system of protection instituted by Big Bill Thompson, caused the Prohibition Era gang wars. He states that "the union of each for the good of all" ended and "[t]he war of each against all" began.[26] The data do not, however, support this conclusion. The three CCC-listed deaths (and a further one outside of Cook County) of South Side O'Donnell gangsters in 1923 hardly constitutes a citywide gang war. Instead, it was a minor disturbance. Similarly, only five members of the major bootlegging outfits were killed gangland-style in 1924 (see Fig. 7.7), and none of these, until O'Banion was murdered, can be described as due to gang warfare. Therefore, O'Banion's death in November 1924—which resulted from enmity between gang leaders—and the resulting violence, which began eighteen months after Dever came into office, set off the Beer Wars. Twenty members of the major bootlegging gangs were killed during the next year (1925) alone.

The table in Fig. 7.9 reports the occupations of the victims by year, and the table in Fig. 7.10 shows the victims' occupations by the type of killing and also for the members of the major gangs. Often more than one occupation was reported for the deceased, especially if he was a criminal. For example, given his activities James Colosimo was recorded as a bootlegger, gambler, vice operator, and labor racketeer. Eighty-one of the victims (the second-largest number) were businessmen, meaning they apparently had some ownership in the business they operated, and many of these killings were related to bootlegging or the Black Hand. Over fifty of the dead were common criminals, and between twenty and forty victims were gamblers, labor leaders, or racketeers. Eighteen individuals in law enforcement were killed gangland-style during this time period, most frequently for reasons related to bootlegging, and seventeen blackhanders were killed. Although only a few politicians and vice operators were killed, eight officials of the Unione Siciliana were slain. In 145 cases the victim's occupation was outside these categories, and in 122 cases it was unknown.

	1919	1920	1921	1922	1923	1924	1925	1926	1927	1928	1929	1930	1931	1932	1933	Total
Bootlegger	0	4	3	4	8	6	25	42	21	27	18	31	16	17	11	233
Gambler	0	1	0	0	2	2	3	1	0	1	2	2	3	5	2	24
Vice operator	0	1	0	0	0	0	0	2	0	2	0	0	1	0	0	6
Unione official	0	0	1	0	0	0	2	0	0	2	1	1	1	0	0	8
Labor/ Business Racketeer	0	1	0	0	2	5	3	3	0	1	8	2	3	2	0	30
Labor Leader	0	4	1	1	1	2	0	3	0	5	2	2	7	5	2	35
Businessman	2	0	4	5	5	9	6	10	13	6	3	7	3	7	1	81
Black Hander	0	2	1	5	0	0	3	0	0	0	2	2	1	0	1	17
Law Enforcement	0	0	0	2	1	1	4	1	2	3	3	1	0	0	0	18
Politician	0	0	1	0	0	2	0	0	0	1	0	0	0	0	0	4
Criminal (Non-organized crime)	7	2	1	3	0	0	2	4	4	5	5	4	6	2	8	53
Other	6	5	9	7	9	15	8	11	15	14	8	14	10	6	8	145
Unknown	9	8	10	10	24	17	16	5	3	11	6	1	1	1	0	122

Fig. 7.9. Occupation of the victim—all killings.

Totals for a year may exceed the number of killings because the victims often had multiple occupations.

	N	Boot-legger	Gambler	Labor Leader	Busi-nessman	Vice oper-ator	Unione official	Black-hander	Rack-eteer	Law Enforcer	Politician	Criminal (other)	other	unknown
Bootlegging	235	164	8	3	20	4	7	2	7	6	2	7	23	12
Unione Siciliana	25	17	0	0	3	0	5	0	0	0	0	0	4	1
Gambling	23	4	12	1	3	0	0	0	1	0	0	2	2	0
Labor Union/ Rackets	55	8	2	29	0	0	1	0	12	2	1	0	7	0
Business Rackets	21	1	0	2	6	0	0	0	5	0	0	0	7	0
Taxi cab wars	12	1	0	0	1	0	0	0	4	0	0	0	6	0
Vice	6	1	0	1	1	3	0	0	1	1	0	0	0	0
Tong wars	6	0	0	0	0	0	0	0	0	0	0	6	0	0
Italian Feud	43	5	0	0	6	0	0	2	1	0	0	5	14	11
Black Hand	67	6	0	0	22	0	0	4	0	1	0	0	20	15
Politics	23	6	0	1	4	0	1	0	0	0	2	1	8	2
Gang Related–other	36	13	2	1	1	0	0	3	0	0	0	18	3	0
Major Gang Members	138	132	10	3	0	5	6	2	11	0	1	1	0	0

Fig. 7.10. Occupation of the victim—by cause of killing and for members of the major bootlegging gangs.

The sum of the occupation figures may exceed the total number of killings (N) because the victims often had multiple occupations.

Fig. 7.11. The last ride of Blue Island rackets boss Lorenzo Juliano.

Not surprisingly, 233 of the victims were engaged in bootlegging, and this was most often the reason they were killed. Of the 235 killings in Fig. 7.10 *due* to bootlegging, only ninety-seven of the dead were members of the major beer and liquor mobs (which is not reported directly in the table). Instead, most of the victims were independents who had the temerity to operate where they should not have, or businessmen, such as bar owners or wholesale merchants, who may have supplied bootleggers with ingredients or who refused to buy from the gang that controlled the area where they were selling alcoholic beverages.

These results conflict markedly with the conventional wisdom, including the opening quote by Lashly, that the gangsters only killed each other. The clearest contradiction of this statement is that eighteen members of law enforcement were killed gangland-style during this time period. More broadly, of the 607 victims in Fig. 7.9 who had a known occupation, 45 percent (274) of them were not reported to be involved in any illegal activity.

Fig. 7.12. CPD officer Harold Olson, who was murdered by Genna gangsters in 1925, with his mother Gertrude Olson (circa 1924).

Regarding ethnicity, six of the victims were Chinese, and they were all murdered in the Tong Wars. Eight, or roughly 1 percent of the victims, were African American, which is low relative to homicides overall in Chicago during this time period.[27] However, the gambling and vice operators in Chicago's small African American community coexisted fairly harmoniously for years, and there was little black involvement in organized labor and none in bootlegging, resulting in no liquor-related deaths in these eight cases. About 54 percent of the victims (394 in total) were Italian Americans. However, this figure gives a false impression about how many of Chicago's gangsters during Prohibition were of Italian extraction. Many of these victims were non-criminals; they were targeted for one reason or another by the bootlegging gangs, the blackhanders, or other criminal groups.

In terms of age and gender, eight females were murdered gangland-style, three of whom were killed accidentally. The 729 victims were on average 34.6 years old, with their ages ranging from six to seventy-two years. The bootlegging casualties were slightly younger (33.6 years of age on average) than the victims in general, and the major bootlegging gang members killed were even younger (32.1 years of age on average).[28]

The tables in Figs. 7.14 and 7.15 report the types of weapons used in the CCC slayings and, in the last column, how many victims were taken on a "one-way ride."[29] In a few cases more than one type of weapon was used. For example, in the St. Valentine's Day Massacre John May and Reinhardt Schwimmer were shot by a machine gun

Fig. 7.13. Frank McErlane's wife, Elfrieda, and her two dogs after he shot them.

and a shotgun. In the full sample, 208 victims were shot with a pistol, 174 were apparently shot with a handgun, and, based on the cases where the weapon was known and the circumstances of the other killings, the 182 cases where the victim was shot with an unknown weapon most likely involved a pistol. Summing these figures, in 564 of 729 slayings a handgun was apparently used. In twenty-nine instances the caliber of the pistol(s) used is reported by the newspapers. The Prohibition Era killers favored large caliber handguns—a .45 was used twelve times, as was a .38, and a .32 was used in the other five killings. A shotgun figured in about 15 percent (109) of the killings, making it the second most frequently used weapon. Therefore, Dry Era gunmen eliminated their victims largely as their predecessors had done, with handguns and shotguns.

	N	Pistol	Pistol (Probably)	Shotgun	Machine Gun	Gun (other)	Gun (unknown)	Stabbing	Strangulation	Explosion	Beating	One-way Ride
All Killings	729	208	174	109	29	4	182	18	6	5	12	142
Bootlegging	235	69	48	52	15	2	56	3	4	0	2	69
Unione Siciliana	25	3	4	11	1	1	5	0	1	0	0	2
Gambling	23	10	4	3	3	0	3	0	0	0	0	2
Labor Union/Rackets	55	26	15	9	6	0	1	1	0	0	0	5
Business Rackets	21	9	2	2	3	0	6	0	0	0	0	1
Taxi Cab Wars	12	4	2	2	0	0	4	0	0	0	0	1
Vice	6	1	3	1	1	0	0	0	0	0	0	1
Tong Wars	6	2	2	0	0	0	2	0	0	0	0	0
Italian Feud	43	14	10	4	0	0	13	2	0	0	0	6
Black Hand	67	18	16	13	0	0	18	3	0	1	0	5
Politics	23	13	4	3	0	0	4	0	0	0	0	5
Gang Related -other	36	10	15	5	1	0	5	0	0	0	1	17
Major Gang Members	138	47	30	28	15	3	20	1	2	0	1	42

Fig. 7.14. Method of killing—for all killings, for members of major bootlegging gangs, and by cause of death.

All Unione-related killings are also counted as bootlegging killings. All killings in the Taxi Cab Wars are also counted as business rackets killings. The sum of the category figures may exceed the total number of killings (N) because in some cases multiple weapons were used.

	1919	1920	1921	1922	1923	1924	1925	1926	1927	1928	1929	1930	1931	1932	1933	Total
one-way Ride	6	2	2	1	2	5	6	22	17	17	10	17	17	10	8	142
Total CCC Kill-ings	24	23	29	37	52	56	64	75	58	72	56	64	48	39	32	729

Fig. 7.15. One-way rides—all killings.

In twenty-seven cases it is unclear whether the victim was taken on a one-way ride.

Saltis-Sheldon gangster Willie Dickman was shot several times on September 3, 1925, and shortly thereafter his body was thrown from an automobile on S. Troy Street.[30] In the letter Herman Bundesen wrote to Calvin Goddard, the bullets taken from Dickman are denoted as "45 Tho."[31] This is the standard abbreviation in this document for a .45-caliber bullet fired by a Thompson submachine gun, as opposed to the same round fired from a pistol. It appears, therefore, that Frank McErlane had a machine gun with him when Dickman was taken for a ride, and he fired three rounds into his head.[32] If the Bundesen letter is correct on those details, the Dickman slaying was the first time a submachine gun was used in a gangland hit in Chicago or anywhere else in the United States. It occurred twenty-two days before what had been thought to be the first use of a machine gun in gangland and a month before the previously documented first such killing in the country, both of which were also in Chicago.

Although the Thompson submachine gun figured in many of the most famous Prohibition Era events, even after 1925 it was used sparingly. For instance, analysis of the killings from 1926 to 1933 indicates that this weapon was used in only twenty-seven of the 444 CCC killings during those eight years. It was also seldom used in bootlegging killings in Cook County after 1925. This is inconsistent with the statement by Robert Schoenberg that the submachine gun "would displace the shotgun as the weapon of choice" in gangland and Frederick Thrasher's conclusion that "[t]he machine gun became the standard weapon of Chicago gangs . . . in 1926."[33] As already noted, the pistol was the weapon of choice, followed by the shotgun, by Chicago's bootleggers before 1926, and the machine gun displaced neither during the later period. Although the bootlegging gangs most likely all owned at least one submachine gun, there is a simple reason why they used them infrequently; when fired on full automatic, such weapons are difficult to control and the gangsters were extremely wary of accidentally hitting bystanders. To minimize this risk, gunmen tended (see below) to shoot their victims at close range, in which case a handgun or shotgun was sufficient.

Other guns, like rifles, were used in only four killings. Eighteen victims were stabbed or hacked to death, six were strangled, twelve were beaten, and five were killed in explosions. Although bombings were very common in Chicago during this period, the bombers focused on destruction of property, and few deaths resulted. Lashly's claim that "[n]o recent bombing in this community has resulted in loss of life" is, however, incorrect, unless he is referring only to the two years that he investigated.[34]

The machine gun was used more frequently in bootlegging killings than in general and most heavily in murders due to labor racketeering, business racketeering, and gambling and when the victim was a member of one of the major bootlegging gangs. The shotgun was used more heavily in bootlegging, labor-related, and Black Hand killings and in the murders of established bootlegging gang members than in the CCC killings overall. It was used most frequently (in percentage terms) in the Unione-related killings. While there is an impression that the shotgun was an "Italian weapon," according to various newspaper accounts numerous other bootlegging mobs owned them in abundance and used them regularly.

Another common belief is that the one-way ride was used extensively in gangland killings during Prohibition.[35] A killing is categorized as a one-way ride if the evidence indicates that the victim was killed in the car or at the spot where the body was found after having been driven there.[36] The one-way ride was not uncommon, occurring in about 20 percent (142) of the cases, but it was far from the preferred method of eliminating the victim. About one-third of the bootlegging-related killings and the murders of members of the major bootlegging gangs were rides that did not result in a round

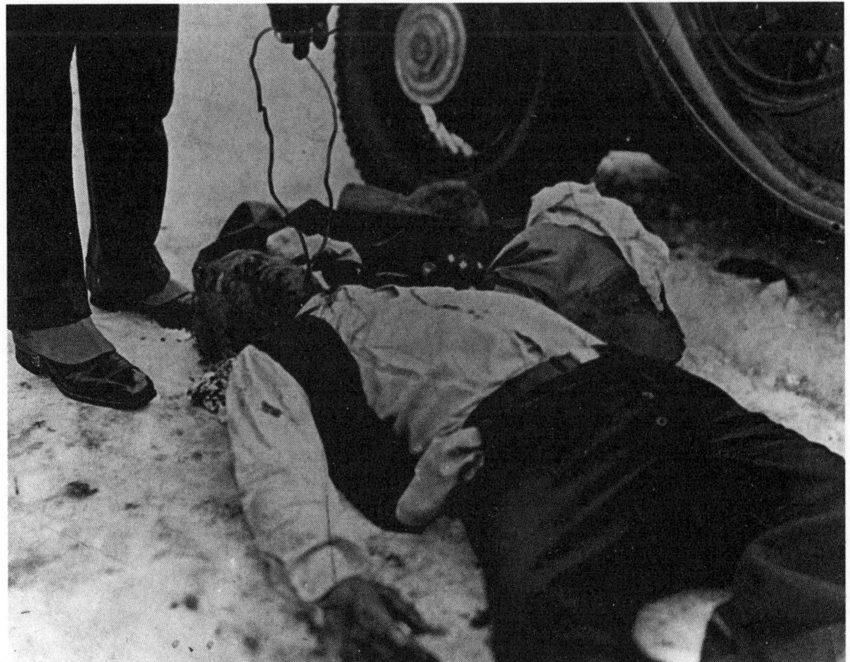

Fig. 7.16. Bootlegger Otto Froneck was shot, stabbed, and strangled.

trip. At the extreme, almost half of the CCC killings of common criminals were one-way rides. In terms of the CCC list of killings, the common criminals in Chicago first used this method, with six of the one-way-ride victims in 1919 and 1920 killed due to disputes between common criminals.[37]

The number of one-way rides per annum is reported in the table in Fig. 7.15. Excluding the initial flurry in 1919, the figures represent only 10 percent or less of the total number of CCC killings each year before 1926. There is a noticeable change in 1926 when the proportion increases to around 25 percent. What caused this shift? It is at least partly the result of the increase in bootlegging killings and the greater propensity of the bootleggers to use this method to dispose of their victims. The bootleggers adopted this practice more heavily starting in 1924. The widespread purchase of automobiles in the United States, due to increased prosperity in the 1920s, is the most likely explanation for the change in this method of gangland killings.

Overall, twenty-one of the victims on the CCC list were unintentionally killed and sixty-one people were unintentionally wounded during the 729 killings. This is at odds with Lashly's conclusion that states, "In the two years passed only two innocent bystanders were killed in Cook County and neither was killed by gangsters."[38] In fact, there were six such unintentional killings in 1926 and 1927. However, 1.4 accidental murders and 4.06 accidental woundings per year in gangland killings among some four million people in Cook County at the time yield a probability of one in 2,857,143 of being accidentally killed and one in 983,607 of being accidentally wounded per year in this time period during this type of attack. Although this is greater than the probability of being killed by lightning, overall these risks were not especially large.[39] Further analysis finds that only four accidental deaths and fourteen woundings (the first in 1926) were related to bootlegging, indicating that the bootleggers were more careful than gangland killers in general.

What of Charles "Lucky" Luciano's remark that Chicago was a crazy place and no one was safe in the streets? By the standards of New York or other major cities, Chicago during Prohibition may have seemed crazy due to the large number of underworld killings and also bombings, which were largely unheard of in gangland outside the Midwest. On the other hand, the data indicate that the gangland killers were fairly proficient at getting their intended victims while not hurting or killing bystanders. Although this is slight consolation to the people who were accidentally killed or wounded in the process, residents of Cook County who were not involved with organized crime were in little danger during Prohibition, especially if they avoided, as discussed below, certain areas in Chicago.

After the original research by this author and Eghigian was completed, the online CPD records were examined to determine how many of the CCC killings that took place in Chicago were due to "drive-by" shootings.[40] The number of drive-bys and the number of CCC killings in the CPD dataset each year are reported in Fig. 7.17. Based on the evidence for the city of Chicago, overall about 10 percent of the gangland-style murders were the result of a drive-by shooting. At the start of the time period, this method of killing was virtually unknown. It became much more common after 1923, and during some years almost 20 percent of the CCC killings were drive-bys. This was again likely due, at least partly, to increased automobile ownership. The evidence does not, however, support the conclusion that after the submachine gun was introduced in late 1925 "the drive-by shooting becomes the center piece of gangster recrimination."[41] The drive-by became popular slightly earlier, and it was never the dominate method of killing in the underworld.

	1919	1920	1921	1922	1923	1924	1925	1926	1927	1928	1929	1930	Total
Drive-by shootings	0	0	1	0	0	5	8	8	7	4	3	8	44
CCC Killings in Chicago	23	20	22	30	37	42	54	45	38	55	44	48	458

Fig. 7.17. Number of drive-by shootings—CCC Killings in Chicago.

In twenty-seven cases it is unclear whether the victim was taken on a one-way ride.

Where the killings occurred, defined in terms of geographic area as well as the type of structure or place the body was found, was also examined. For this purpose, suburban Cook County was divided into three zones: north of Irving Park Road, south of the current Interstate 55, and the western area between these two dividing lines. Overall, 551 of the 729 killings (about 75 percent) occurred in Chicago, fourteen (2 percent) in the northern suburbs, seventy (about 10 percent) in the western suburbs, and ninety-one (about 12 percent) in the southern suburbs. Because less than one in eight residents in Cook County lived outside of Chicago in 1927, the figures for the outer county are higher than expected based on population alone.[42] The gang battles in some suburbs and Chicago gangsters taking their ride victims to the hinterlands to frustrate apprehension contributed to this higher proportion. Of the 551 CCC murders in Chicago from 1919 to 1933, only fifty-eight were one-way rides. Five of fourteen north suburban victims, thirty of seventy west suburban victims, and forty-nine of ninety-one south suburban victims were taken for a ride.

Fig. 7.19 shows the locations of the CCC murders in Chicago from 1922 to 1933 by police district, based on the district boundaries from late 1921 to January 1928. The number of killings in each district appears next to the district name. The killings were concen-

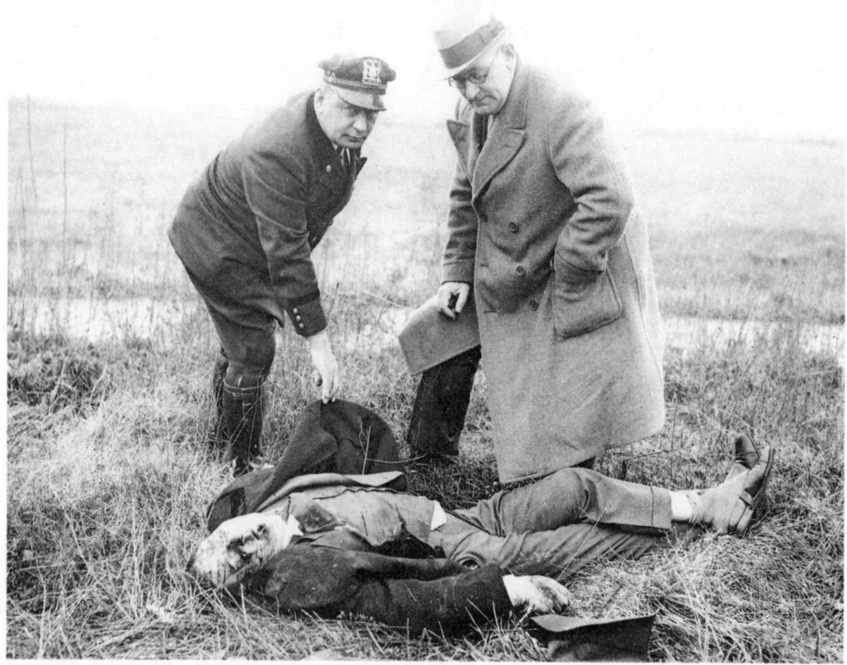

Fig. 7.18. Dan Tagnatti rests in peace.

trated in the center of the city, occurring most heavily between North Avenue and Thirty-Ninth Street and east of Kedzie Avenue. There were more than fifteen killings in only one district outside this area, Englewood, where the Back of the Yards Wars raged. There were few killings on the far North or South Sides.

Killings in the Loop, which during this period extended to Roosevelt Road, were uncommon since there were only fifteen in the Central police district. This is not surprising because historically crime was kept out of the downtown, even by the hardcore criminals. Most of the killings occurred in the city's major southern Italian neighborhoods: Taylor Street, Division Street, Grand Avenue, and Twenty-Sixth Street. The Maxwell (seventy-five killings), Marquette (thirty-eight killings), Desplaines (eighteen killings), and Warren Avenue (twenty-five killings) police districts contained parts of the Taylor Street neighborhood. Division Street was the northern boundary of the East Chicago district (forty-seven killings), so that

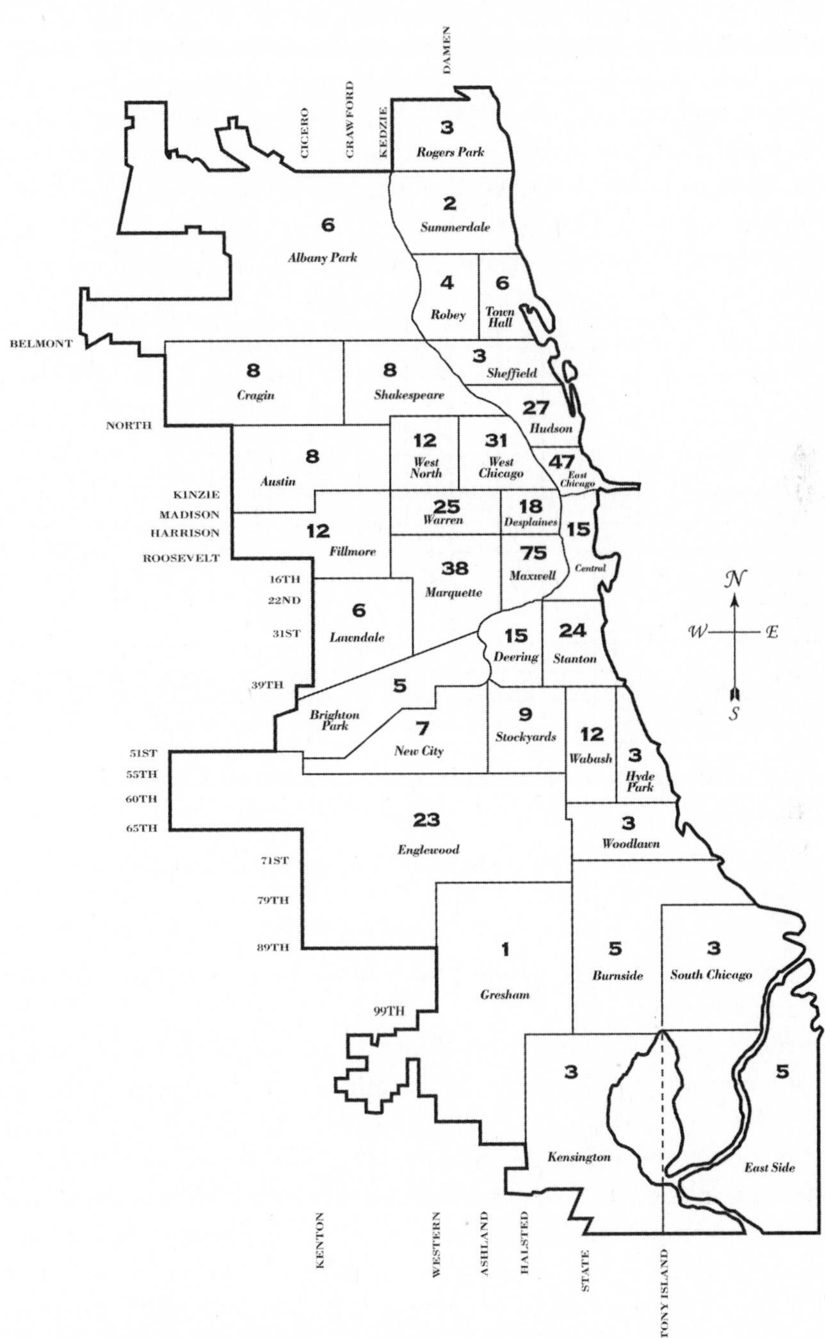

Fig. 7.19. Gangland killings in Chicago, 1922–1933.

neighborhood's murders occurred in the Hudson district (twenty-seven killings) as well. The Grand Avenue neighborhood was in the West Chicago district (thirty killings), and the Twenty-Sixth Street neighborhood, just east of Chinatown, was in the Stanton Avenue district (twenty-four killings). The location of the bodies is consistent with John Drury's statement that gangland killings were mostly committed in the "Sicilian" (meaning southern Italian) areas of the city.[43]

	1919	1920	1921	1922	1923	1924	1925	1926	1927	1928	1929	1930	Total
Building	5	6	5	7	11	14	12	11	12	20	21	12	136
Home	0	0	2	0	1	1	8	2	2	5	1	4	26
Restaurant/saloon//soft Drink Parlor	0	3	0	1	5	4	0	6	2	5	6	5	37
Other	5	3	3	6	5	9	4	3	8	10	14	3	73
Auto	1	0	1	1	2	0	6	10	3	6	5	8	43
Street/Alley/Gangway/Sidewalk/Yard	17	14	16	22	24	27	35	23	22	29	18	26	273
Vacant Lot/Prairie	0	0	0	0	0	1	1	1	1	0	0	1	5
Body of water	0	0	0	0	0	0	0	0	0	0	0	1	1
Killings in Chicago	23	20	22	30	37	42	54	45	38	55	44	48	458

Fig. 7.20. Location of the killing (by type of structure, etc.)—CCC killings in Chicago.

The data, which cover the period through 1930, are from the CPD homicide records online.

In terms of the type of place the murders occurred, the results for Chicago are summarized in Fig. 7.20. In 136 of 458 cases where the murder was found in the CPD homicide records, the killing occurred inside a building. This was a restaurant or other establishment that probably served alcohol in only thirty-seven cases, a private residence in twenty-six instances, and some other type of building, usually a business, in seventy-three murders. In forty-three killings the victim was found in an automobile, and fourteen of these murders were due to a drive-by shooting. Not one body was found in the trunk of a car, as opposed to the common practice in Chicago gangland after Prohibition. This is because autos in the Dry Era generally did not have a separate trunk space. More than half of the victims (273 of 458) were found outside where the body was plainly visible, such as in the street, an alley, or a yard. Five victims were found in areas where the body was not as visible, such as a prairie or vacant lot. Only one victim, North Side gangster John Rito, was found in a (permanent) body of water, contradicting the belief that the Chicago River was a major depository for gangland victims.[44]

To summarize these results, most of the gangland-style murders in Chicago from 1919 to 1933 were committed in open view, such as a public place (when the killing occurred in a building), or outside on the street, which indicates that Prohibition Era killers made little effort to conceal the bodies of their victims. The vast majority of the killings were done at close range, as opposed to a gunman firing from concealment at a distance. This is because the killers were generally not very good shots, were concerned about hitting innocent bystanders, and there was little cost to approaching the victims because witnesses were generally mute. This contrasts with the earlier statement by this author that "[m]ost gangland killings during Prohibition were quiet affairs" such as one-way rides where there were no witnesses.[45]

The CPD database reports arrests and convictions for the killings in Chicago. The police made arrests in 132 of the 458 gangland-style murders in the city from 1919 to 1930, yet only eight convictions were obtained. This differs from the zero convictions reported by Lashly and the Citizen's Police Committee, in the latter case for gangland killings in Chicago from 1923 to 1929.[46] However, even these figures overstate the efficiency of the criminal justice system in Chicago during Prohibition because convictions were often overturned on appeal. According to the CCC, thirty-two of these 729 gangland killings went to trial, just nine trials resulted in a conviction, and in only six killings was a conviction the final outcome after appeal.[47]

What can be learned from gangland violence during Prohibition? Gangland killings greatly increased during Prohibition because, as noted in an earlier chapter, the killers operated under virtual "immunity" from the law.[48] Due to bribery and other factors, witnesses refused to testify, police officers sometimes "looked the other way," prosecutors and judges failed to show the necessary zeal, and jurors were reluctant to find the defendants guilty, which explains the minimal number of convictions in these murders.

Interestingly, mayoral policy did not have a major effect on gangland violence. Ignoring the brief term of Anton Cermak, the era can be divided into three periods: the earlier term of Big Bill Thompson (April 1919 to April 1923), the administration of William Dever (April 1923 to April 1927), and Thompson's last term (April 1927 to April 1931). As discussed in the preceding chapters, the Thompson and Dever policies with respect to crime were radically different. The table in Fig. 7.2 indicates that there were fewer gangland killings (in total as well as ones related to organized crime) during Thompson's earlier term than during his final one and on average less killings during the Thompson years overall than during the Dever years. However, this is because the North Side vs. South Side War did not begin until late 1924.

A more accurate measure of mayoral impact compares the gangland killings per month during the Dever administration and the last four years under Thompson, excluding periods of peace in the North Side vs. South Side War. Based on these data, there were 6.00 CCC killings per month under Dever and 5.83 per month during Thompson's last term. The average number of organized crime–related killings per month is 3.13 during the Dever years compared to 3.33 for the Thompson period, a difference of about two and half killings per annum. The Dever and Thompson policies impacted gangland violence similarly because the actual enforcement of the law was essentially the same under both mayors. Bootleggers and other operators paid for protection from the police under either mayor; the only difference was who they paid. Simply put, there was no way Dever could fire all the police officers on the underworld payroll and replace them with incorruptible ones. It was also impossible for him to remove elected officials such as ward committeemen who had considerable power over the police commanders. He had no control over the state's attorney or the governor.

If mayoral policy was unimportant, what did restrain gangland during Prohibition? The preceding results indicate that the gang leaders behaved fairly rationally because they used violence in ways consistent with their self-interest. For example, unintentional killings and woundings were minimal and the murders of the members of other bootlegging gangs were fairly infrequent. Also, the major gangs, despite their issues, coexisted peacefully for lengthy periods of time.

Recognizing this, and that individual gang homicides were virtually unsolvable, during Prohibition the authorities used other methods to combat gang violence. First, they flooded trouble zones with additional police officers to prevent further killings to the extent possible. Second, they penalized the gangs' business operations by shutting down all bars, gambling houses, and other underworld activities in the problem areas or sometimes across the entire city. If violence persisted in a district, the lid was kept on for months. Consistent application of this policy deterred future killings because the hoodlums recognized they would be severely hurt economically whenever violence escalated.

In summary, Chicago was the gangland murder capital of the United States during Prohibition. Although a variety of research has examined homicides in the city in general, until recently there has been no systematic study of gangland-style murders during this period, beyond the investigation by Lashly of a few aspects of this type of homicide in 1926 and 1927.[49] A detailed analysis of 729 gangland-style killings from 1919 to 1933 yields conclusions that in almost *every* case contradict the conventional wisdom about the gang wars and gangland murders around Chicago. For example, many of these killings had nothing to do with bootlegging or more broadly organized crime, the gangsters did not just kill each other, the submachine gun was not the dominant weapon in the underworld after its introduction, and relatively few members of the major bootlegging gangs were killed during Chicago's Beer Wars.

Chapter 8

CONCLUSION

"To the victor belong the spoils of the enemy."

—William L. Marcy (D-NY), US senator

"Cut off gang revenues and the gang disintegrates."

—George E. Q. Johnson, US attorney

Chicago's Prohibition Beer Wars were a complicated series of conflicts over more than ten years in which the Capone mob was the great winner. At the start of the Dry Era, the Torrio-Capone gang was one of a dozen major bootlegging groups in the city of Chicago. By the early 1930s it dominated the battlefield, leading to the creation of the Chicago Outfit, which controlled Cook County's underworld in 1934 and had important connections throughout the country as well. It is worthwhile to examine the reasons for this striking victory.[1]

First, this gang got off to an excellent start because it was built on the foundation laid by James Colosimo and John Torrio during the two decades preceding 1920. With seven police districts, plus a good part of the Loop and a variety of suburban areas under its control, the Torrio-Capone mob was certainly Chicago's biggest bootlegging gang at the dawn of Prohibition. The gang's geographical spread allowed it to profit from the generally laxer enforcement in the rest of Cook County versus that in Chicago and to easily switch between the city and the county when it encountered problems that were not countywide.

Second, it had a much larger initial presence in vice, narcotics, gambling, and (probably) labor racketeering than the other liquor mobs, and it expanded in most of these areas over time. This additional cash flow helped finance the Capone group's growth and also allowed it to keep a large number of gunmen on the payroll. Toward the end of Prohibition this advantage was very useful because it was able to easily expand into other rackets and to redefine the organization.[2]

Third, the gang had very capable leaders who possessed good business sense as well as an understanding of when to use violence in pursuit of their goals. This was not true for a number of Chicago's other gangs. Also, the Capone forces had several strong individuals just below the level of the boss. While Jake Guzik readily comes to mind, the same can be said of, for example, Paul Ricca, Tony Accardo, Louis Campagna, and the Fischetti brothers based on their later roles in the Chicago Outfit.

As befits a university professor, in summary final grades will be assigned to the gang's leaders to evaluate their work in their chosen profession. James Colosimo receives an overall grade of B+. His efforts before Prohibition produced admirable underworld results, in particular his move into the suburbs, and he would have gotten a much higher grade if he would only have been able to see the opportunities bootlegging presented. This was Colosimo's major shortcoming. John Torrio earns an A–. He was a superb strategist and an excellent leader who, as the boss from 1920 to 1925, greatly expanded the criminal kingdom Colosimo had created. He was such a strong leader that he was called back into service while Capone was in prison in Pennsylvania to oversee the cartel set up in 1929. Torrio was, however, deficient as a warlord because he lacked fortitude, and this flaw keeps him from earning a higher grade.

In my opinion, Al Capone also deserves an A–. He had strong business sense and excellent martial skills. By the time he left Chicago for the US penitentiary in Atlanta in early 1932, the hotly contested Beer Wars were largely over and a large amount of additional territory in the city and suburbs had come under his gang's control. He also extended its operations, primarily through the sale of pure alcohol, into many other states. However, there are two major criticisms of Capone's performance. First, his public behavior, especially the frequent statements he gave to reporters, put him in the spotlight. In contrast, Torrio and later mob leaders, such as Frank Nitti, Paul Ricca, and Tony Accardo in Chicago, and New York gangsters such as Carlo

Gambino, avoided calling attention to themselves and their organizations at all costs. Second, Capone should have filed his income tax returns every year and declared income equal to what he thought the authorities could attribute to him. Regarding Nitti, because this book only covers the period through the end of Prohibition, he receives an incomplete grade despite his exemplary work after 1933.

The higher degree of "professionalism" exhibited by the Torrio-Capone mob, compared to other bootlegging gangs in Chicagoland, is also of importance. Due to tight security and an excellent intelligence network, the gang avoided disarray by keeping its leaders, in the cases of Capone and Nitti, safe. To a lesser extent, the delegation of the dirty work by the upper echelons to lower-level members shielded not only Torrio, Capone, and Nitti, but also many of the higher-level hoods, from the authorities. At the direction of their leaders, the lower-level Capone hoodlums also devoted themselves to organized crime and never delved into robbery, safecracking, and other types of ordinary crime. Admittedly, the almost complete breakdown of law and order in Cook County during the 1920s made an attractive payroll robbery less problematic than it otherwise would have been, but there were still difficulties associated with such criminal capers, and the Torrio-Capone gang avoided them, unlike the other bootlegging mobs.

They also were extremely lucky at least once. If George Moran had not run out of bullets and had not been recalled to the vehicle used by the North Side hit squad before he could reload, Torrio would most likely have been killed in January 1925. Instead, he was available to counsel Capone later and to return as the overseer of Chicago gangland during the broad peace in 1929 and 1930. Similarly, if the North Side gunners had caught Capone in or near his car in January 1925 or at the Hawthorne Hotel in Cicero in September 1926, gangland history might have been quite a bit different.

Other gangs had serious problems in these areas. For example, the downfall of the Gennas was largely due to the deaths of three of the most important of the brothers in 1925. Dean O'Banion and Hymie Weiss died at least partly due to what could be termed lax security, at least in comparison to the extensive precautions that Capone himself took, and Vincent Drucci might have lived to a ripe old age if he had left the election-related violence in 1927 to his subordinates. Similarly, two of the Touhy brothers and one of the South Side O'Donnells were killed during saloon invasions that Capone would have left to his underlings. While in the case of the Touhys these deaths took enemies out of Capone's way, in terms of the Genna brothers it also greatly opened doors for him. If the Genna gang had not collapsed, the Capone gang would not have gotten control as early as it did of the Unione Siciliana's alky-cooking racket and the millions of dollars of revenues from supplying alcohol to the Upper Midwest and beyond, if it ever would have.

The fact that Chicago was at various times engulfed in broad fighting between the bootleggers aided the Capone mob because it was the major winner in those conflicts. Several gangs lined up as its allies and were gradually, peacefully merged with it. Other gangs were its enemies and were absorbed by conquest. If peace had reigned throughout the city during Prohibition, it is much less likely that such an amalgamation would have occurred.

The Capone gangsters were also innovators. Although they were not the first to use the Thompson submachine gun, they quickly adopted it and introduced the machine gun nest to gangland in the killing of Hymie Weiss. After O'Banion and Weiss were slain, the North Siders were on their guard against further attacks. Therefore, Capone used gunmen from out of town, who posed as police officers, to get into the garage on N. Clark Street. On the same point, the Chicago Heights gangsters pioneered an odorless method of distilling that avoided detection and was copied by others.[3] Other innovations were less dramatic and were more about seeing the angles and exploiting them, at which Capone and his men were experts. For example, if Jewish congregations in New York were not using all the sacramental wine they were allowed under the law, the Capone gang was happy to buy the federal permits from the rabbis and redirect the wine to other locations.

Furthermore, there is the role of ethnicity. The Colosimo gang was an inclusive, multi-ethnic group, and Torrio and Capone continued this policy. Therefore, from the earliest days their gang greatly benefitted from the likes of Jake Guzik and Murray Humphreys and readily embraced other non-Italians, such as Sam Hunt and Willie Heeney, when they gravitated to Chicago. Capone was also willing to cooperate with and eventually merge with other gangs as things evolved, as opposed to fighting them and then expelling them from the areas they controlled, even though these other gangs were not heavily Italian in membership. In that respect the Sheldon-Stanton, Circus, West Side O'Donnell, Valley, and the DMQ gangs are important examples. On the other side of the ledger, the immigration to the United States by numerous southern Italians in the years up to and including Prohibition provided Torrio and Capone, who by 1929 controlled three of Chicago's four largest southern Italian neighborhoods, with a number of men as the ethnic face of America's underworld changed.

Therefore, the Capone gang triumphed due to its superior initial position in the underworld, the business and military aptitude of its leaders, the shortcomings of some of its enemies, and, as is true in much of life (and sometimes death), a bit of luck.

Finally, a few words are in order regarding the fight against organized crime by the upperworld. The standard approach by law enforcement, which has been used against all criminal activity since time immemorial, is to apprehend and punish specific offenders. This removes them from society for the period they are incarcerated, which under the current RICO statute can be for many years. In the extreme, convicting numerous members of a gang could break it up, although that happened in the past far less often with organized crime than with bank robbery gangs and other groups of common criminals. However, in consensual activities such as gambling, bootlegging, and vice, where the consumers consented to gamble, drink, or visit prostitutes, as long as the demand for the product was there, someone was willing to supply it. Witness the results of the war on drugs over the last one hundred years, where each time one criminal group was put out of business by the authorities, it was replaced by another one.

During Prohibition whenever the hoodlums did not behave themselves the CPD hit at their revenues as a form of punishment after the fact. Eliot Ness and State's Attorney John Swanson took this approach further. They struck at the gangs' sources of income in an attempt to cripple them. A third, even stronger approach would be to legalize the underlying activities and take them permanently out of the hands of the mobsters. This would effectively destroy organized crime and eliminate the violence and corruption that goes along with it.

In the broad sweep of time, this has worked very well in the city of Chicago, the state of Illinois, and elsewhere in the United States, even though the impetus of such legalization was not always to damage organized crime. Instead, it seems that the state has been motivated most often by a desire to increase its tax revenues. For example, the end of Prohibition took away gangland's crown jewel (and increased federal and local monies from liquor taxes). More recently, Illinois created a state-run lottery, introduced legal casinos, and legalized video poker machines outside of casinos. This has taken a large bite out of the Chicago Outfit's revenues while also putting money into the state's coffers.[4]

Admittedly, this is not a simple solution because legalization comes with its own problems. The voting populace, given its morals and attitudes, has not been in favor of decriminalizing everything that the underworld purveys. National Prohibition and various anti-gambling laws were unpopular, and eventually the electorate saw those laws in an unfavorable light. Prostitution, however, has not been viewed the same way. Similarly, American society for years has tended to see the sellers of illegal narcotics as "evil pushers" who turn youngsters into drug abusers. There is also the concern, because so many drug users are criminals, that drug use drives people to commit criminal acts. In terms of public policy, this requires society to weigh the cost of the increase in crime (to the extent it is true) against the decrease in murders and corruption and the increased government revenues that would result from the legalization of narcotics and other illegal activities. These are not easy to estimate, and all the effects of legalization would have to be taken into account before it is implemented. But, decriminalizing the activities of organized crime would clearly strike massively at the heart of what it does.

Appendix

BLACK HAND MURDERS IN CHICAGO

Humbert Nelli and Robert Lombardo argue that Black Hand killings in Chicago essentially ended by 1920.[1] Nelli attributes this to three factors: federal government prosecution of extortion, blackhanders becoming bootleggers during Prohibition, and restrictions on foreign immigration that decreased the supply of victims. Yet, the CCC list contains more than sixty murders in Chicago that occurred from 1920 to 1933 that were Black Hand related. Therefore, further examination of this issue is warranted.

Unfortunately, in his analysis Nelli apparently misquotes the original sources. For example, Nelli's overall conclusion that Black Hand activity virtually ceased by 1920 is based on a statement by John Landesco that due to federal prosecutions of letters sent by mail, "[e]xtortion by mail has ceased and little more is heard of the 'black hand,' but extortion by violence or gun and the bomb has not ceased."[2] While Landesco argues that Black Hand letters largely stopped, he clearly states that this type of extortion and the related violence continued:

> If, in late years, bombing and murders have not been ascribed to "black hand," it is not because threats of extortion have not been common, but because the *modus operandi* has been changed and the threats do not come by letter. One of the probable reasons for the present rarity of the threat by letter is that the perpetrators lay themselves open to prosecution in the Federal Courts, which have occasionally succeeded in convicting such criminals. In Sicily, where telephones are even now rare, the threat was usually communicated by letter. In the earlier days it was thus in Chicago. The

> letter has partly disappeared because other ways of communication have become available.[3]

The demands for money could have been communicated by telephone or by a secretly hand-delivered note if mail was too risky. For example, the *Chicago Tribune* reports in 1925 that Black Hand notes in the Taylor Street neighborhood "are prone to be as common as rent bills."[4] Also, one blackhander in the late 1920s sent at least twenty-eight extortion notes and, according to the victims, received money from twenty-four of them.[5]

Similarly, Landesco is the source for Nelli's conclusion that the blackhanders became bootleggers during Prohibition. Landesco notes that bootlegging provided a less risky way to make money than ordinary crime, but he argues elsewhere that criminals who entered bootlegging continued "to engage in the same types of crime in which they have already specialized."[6] Also, for Nelli's conclusion to hold, there must have been a limited supply of extortionists, or new entrants would simply have replaced the ones who became bootleggers. This effectively leaves one justification for Nelli's conclusion, that the supply of victims was depleted by 1920. Given Chicago's large Italian community, whose wealth increased during the economically prosperous years from 1920 to 1929, this does not seem likely. Also, this would, if anything, have caused a gradual decrease in the number of victims over time, as immigration slowed and the blackhanders worked their way through the existing individuals and their wealth, rather than an abrupt end to the activity starting with Prohibition. On the same point, the federal government's new restrictions on immigration did not fully take effect until 1924.

Regardless of Nelli's arguments, this is ultimately an issue that must be resolved based on the evidence. Although neither Nelli nor Lombardo collect data to support their theory, other contemporary data support the conclusion, based on analysis of the CCC killings, that Black Hand extortion continued into the 1920s, which agrees with Landesco's own statements. On this point, the CPD *Annual Report* lists 216 Black Hand killings in Chicago from 1919 to 1931, about three times as many as the CCC total, with no clear decrease until 1931.[7] The Citizens' Police Committee reports totals for the years 1923 to 1929 that are similar to those of the CPD, and Frederick Thrasher states that there were twelve Black Hand murders in Chicago during the first six months of 1925 alone.[8]

It is also useful to more carefully examine the evidence supporting the Black Hand categorization for the sixty-seven CCC killings. This result is more than just the opinion of the writer of the newspaper article about the murder. In fifty-six cases the articles explicitly state that the CPD, CCC, or some other crime-fighting agency was the source of this conclusion, and the CPD is mentioned in the vast majority of the cases. During this period the CPD had a special Black Hand squad that included knowledgeable Italian American officers, which lends credence to the police department's findings.

On the other hand, Landesco claims that the Chicago police labeled every Italian murder whose cause was unknown as a Black Hand killing, implying that CPD classification alone is not sufficient to warrant such a logical result.[9] The fact that sixty-five of the sixty-seven victims were Italian is equally consistent with this bias or the fact that the Italian community was the center of Black Hand activity. However, about one-third of the victims (see Fig. 7.10 in chapter 7) were businessmen, meaning they had some wealth, which is indicative of extortion being behind their murders. Also, there are seventy instances on the CCC list where an Italian was killed, and no reason was given by the newspapers for the killing, indicating that Landesco's claim about the CPD's blanket use of the Black Hand designation is far from accurate.

More importantly, in fourteen of the sixty-seven CCC Black Hand killings, there was direct evidence of Black Hand activity: the victim received extortion letters, he had testified against a blackhander, or he was a blackhander killed by someone he was extorting money from. While this accounts for only 20 percent of the sample, the authorities were unable in many cases to obtain any information from witnesses or relatives when the victim was Italian, so the absence of clear evidence in 100 percent of these cases is hardly surprising. Similarly, if only cases where there was clear-cut evidence that bootlegging activity caused the murder were categorized as bootlegging related, we would conclude that there were few such killings during Prohibition. As Chicago police chief Morgan Collins stated, "Many of our unsolved crimes of today are committed in the Italian black hand district, where the police are confronted with walls of silence. . . . Even the relatives and intimates of victims, though they know the murderers, refuse to name them to the police."[10] For example, when Ciro Compino was killed in front of hundreds of people on July 18, 1923, not a single witness provided the police with information.[11]

While Black Hand extortion in Chicago did not stop in 1920, it did essentially vanish around 1931. There were only two Black Hand murders among the CCC gangland killings from 1931 to 1933, and a similar drop is found in the CPD *Annual Report,* which reports only two such murders in 1931, compared to eleven in 1930, six in 1929, and fourteen in 1928. It is unlikely that a police bias toward the Black Hand designation suddenly disappeared.

In fact, there is a simple explanation for the sudden decrease in reported Black Hand murders in the early 1930s. When the North Side vs. South Side gang war ended in late 1930, the Capone forces took control of organized crime in the Italian neighborhood around Division Street, just as they had done earlier around Twenty-Sixth Street, Grand Avenue, and Taylor Street. Division Street east of Halsted was the center of Black Hand activity in Chicago.[12] Once the Capone gang was in charge, ordinary crime and violence were no longer tolerated. Landesco notes that when they took over along Taylor Street, "Capone interests with the cooperation of the police cleaned up the neighborhood. Life became much more difficult for the unattached hoodlum."[13] In what was partly a magnanimous gesture, because his gang did not directly profit from it, Al Capone stamped out crime in general and, according to the *Chicago Tribune,* Black Hand extortion in particular, in these areas.[14]

SELECT BIBLIOGRAPHY

BOOKS

Abadinsky, Howard. *Organized Crime.* Chicago: Thompson-Wadsworth, 2003.

Abbott, Karen. *Sin in the Second City.* New York: Random House, 2007.

Allsop, Kenneth. *The Bootleggers and Their Era.* Garden City, NY: Doubleday, 1961.

Andrews, Hal. *X Marks the Spot.* n. p.: Spot Publishing, 1930.

Andrews, Wayne. *Battle for Chicago.* New York: Harcourt, Brace, 1946.

Asbury, Herbert. *Gem of the Prairie.* Garden City, NY: Garden City Publishing, 1942.

Balsamo, William, and John Balsamo. *Young Al Capone.* New York: Skyhorse Publishing, 2011.

Bergreen, Laurence. *Capone.* New York: Simon and Schuster, 1994.

Bilek, Arthur J. *The First Vice Lord.* Nashville: Cumberland House, 2008.

Biles, Roger. *Big City Boss in Depression and War.* DeKalb: Northern Illinois University Press, 1984.

Binder, John J. *The Chicago Outfit.* Charleston: Arcadia Publishing, 2003.

Blecha, Jon L. *Cigars and Wires.* Omaha: Jon L. Blecha, 2012.

Booth, Martin. *Opium.* New York: St. Martin's Press, 1996.

Brashler, William. *The Don: The Life and Death of Sam Giancana.* New York: Harper and Row, 1977.

Burns, Walter Noble. *The One-Way Ride.* Garden City, NY: Doubleday, 1931.

Citizen's Police Committee. *Chicago Police Problems.* Chicago: University of Chicago Press, 1931.

Corsino, Lou. *The Neighborhood Outfit: Organized Crime in Chicago Heights.* Urbana: University of Illinois Press, 2014.

Cowdery, Ray R. *Capone's Chicago.* Lakeville, MN: Northstar Maschek Books, 1987.

Drake, St. Clair, and Horace R. Cayton. *Black Metropolis.* New York: Harcourt, Brace, 1945.

Drury, John. *Chicago in Seven Days.* New York: Robert M. McBride, 1928.

Eghigian, Mars, Jr. *After Capone: The Life and World of Chicago Mob Boss Frank "The Enforcer" Nitti.* Nashville: Cumberland House, 2006.

Eig, Jonathan. *Get Capone: The Secret Plot That Captured America's Most Wanted Gangster.* New York: Simon and Schuster, 2010 (hardcover), 2011 (paperback).

Gosnell, Harold F. *Negro Politicians: Rise of Negro Politics in Chicago.* Chicago: University of Chicago Press, 1935.

Gusfield, Jeffrey. *Deadly Valentines.* Chicago: Chicago Review Press, 2012.

Heimel, Paul W. *Eliot Ness: The Real Story.* Coudersport, PA: Knox Books, 1997.

Helmer, William J., and Arthur J. Bilek. *The St. Valentine's Day Massacre.* Nashville: Cumberland House, 2004.

Hoffman, Dennis E. *Scarface Al and the Crime Crusaders.* Carbondale: Southern Illinois University Press, 2010.

Hortis, C. Alexander. *The Mob and the City.* Amherst, NY: Prometheus Books, 2014.

Hostetter, Gordon L., and Thomas Q. Beesley. *It's a Racket.* Chicago: Les Quin Books, 1929.

Illinois Association for Criminal Justice. *The Illinois Crime Survey.* Chicago: Illinois Association for Criminal Justice, 1929.

Irey, Elmer L., and William J. Slocum. *The Tax Dodgers.* New York: Greenberg, 1948.

Johnson, David R. *American Law Enforcement: A History.* St. Louis: Forum Press, 1981.

Johnson, Wayne. *A History of Violence: An Encyclopedia of 1400 Chicago Mob Murders.* McLean, VA: LLR Books, 2012.

Jonnes, Jill. *Hep-Cats, Narcs, and Pipe Dreams.* Baltimore: Johns Hopkins University Press, 1996.

Keefe, Rose. *Guns and Roses.* Nashville: Cumberland House, 2003.

———. *The Man Who Got Away: The Bugs Moran Story.* Nashville: Cumberland House, 2005.

Kobler, John. *Capone.* New York: G.P. Putnam, 1971.

———. *Ardent Spirits.* New York: G.P. Putnam, 1973.

Landesco, John. *Organized Crime in Chicago. Part III of The Illinois Crime Survey.* Chicago: Illinois Association for Criminal Justice, 1929.

Lindberg, Richard. *Chicago by Gaslight.* Chicago: Academy Chicago, 1996.

———. *The Gambler King of Clark Street.* Carbondale, IL: SIU Press, 2009.

Lombardo, Robert. *Organized Crime in Chicago: Beyond the Mafia.* Urbana: University of Illinois Press, 2013.

Luzi, Matthew J. *The Boys in Chicago Heights.* Charleston: History Press, 2012.

Lyle, John H. *The Dry and Lawless Years.* New York: Prentice-Hall, 1960.

Lyon, Chriss. *A Killing in Capone's Playground.* Holland, MI: In-Depth Editions, 2014.

McPhaul, John. *Johnny Torrio: First of the Gang Lords.* New Rochelle, NY: Arlington House, 1970.

Murray, George. *The Legacy of Al Capone.* New York: G.P. Putnam, 1975.

Musto, David F. *The American Disease: Origins of Narcotic Control.* Oxford: Oxford University Press, 1999.

Ness, Eliot, and Oscar Fraley. *The Untouchables.* New York: Julian Messner, 1957.

Newell, Barbara W. *Chicago and the Labor Movement.* Urbana: University of Illinois Press, 1961.

Pasley, Fred D. *Al Capone: The Biography of a Self-Made Man.* New York: Garden City, 1930.

———. *Muscling In.* New York: Ives Washburn, 1931.

Perry, Douglas. *Eliot Ness: The Rise and Fall of an American Hero.* New York: Viking, 2014.

Peterson, Virgil W. *Barbarians in Our Midst.* Boston: Atlantic-Little, Brown, 1952.

Picchi, Blaise. *The Five Weeks of Giuseppe Zangara.* Chicago: Academy Chicago Publishers, 1998.

Reckless, Walter C. *Vice in Chicago.* Chicago: University of Chicago Press, 1933.

Roemer, William F. *Accardo: The Genuine Godfather.* New York: Donald I. Fine, 1995.

Royko, Mike. *Boss.* New York: E.P. Dutton, 1971.

Schoenberg, Robert J. *Mr. Capone.* New York: William Morrow, 1992.

Sullivan, Edward D. *Rattling the Cup on Chicago Crime.* New York: Vanguard, 1929.

———. *Chicago Surrenders.* New York: Vanguard, 1930.

Thompson, Nathan. *Kings: The True Story of Chicago Policy Kings and Numbers Racketeers.* Chicago: Bronzeville Press, 2003.

Thrasher, Frederic M. *The Gang.* Chicago: University of Chicago Press, 1937.

Touhy, Roger. *The Stolen Years.* Cleveland: Pennington Press, 1959.

Tuttle, William M., Jr. *Race Riot.* New York: Atheneum, 1984.

The Vice Commission of Chicago. *The Social Evil in Chicago.* Chicago:

Gunthrop-Warren Printing, 1911.

Washburn, Charles. *Come into My Parlor.* New York: Knickerbocker Publishing, 1936.

Wendt, Lloyd, and Herman Kogan. *Lords of the Levee.* Indianapolis: Bobbs-Merrill, 1943.

———. *Big Bill of Chicago.* Indianapolis: Bobbs-Merrill, 1953.

Wiltz, Christine. *The Last Madam.* Boston: Da Capo Press, 2001.

ARCHIVES, JOURNALS, MAGAZINES, AND OTHER SOURCES

Ashley, Frederick J. "Power of Aroused Citizens Bigger than Al Capone." *Chicago Commerce* (December 1931): 39–41.

Basil Hugh Banghart. Admission Summary, US Penitentiary, Alcatraz Island. October 1, 1943.

Beall, C. R. F. *40886–Capone, Alphonse: Neuro-Psychiatric Examination.* US Penitentiary, Atlanta, GA. May 18, 1932.

Becker, Gary S. "Crime and Punishment: An Economic Approach." *Journal of Political Economy* 76 (March/April 1968): 169–217.

Bennett, James O. *Chicago Gangland.* Chicago: Chicago Tribune, 1929.

Bienen, Leigh B., and Bradley Rottinghaus. "Learning from the Past, Living in the Present: Understanding Homicide in Chicago, 1870–1930." *Journal of Criminal Law and Criminology* 92 (Spring/Summer 2002): 437–554.

Binder, John J. "Eliot Ness," in *The American Midwest: An Interpretive Encyclopedia.* Edited by Richard Sisson, Christian Zacher, and Andrew Cayton. Bloomington, IN: Indiana University Press, 2006.

———. "The Transportation Revolution and Antebellum Sectional Disagreement." *Social Science History* 35 (March 2011): 19–57.

Binder, John J., and Mars Eghigian, Jr. "Gangland Killings in Chicago, 1919–1933." Unpublished manuscript (February, 2008).

———. "Gangland Killings in Chicago, 1919–1933." *Journal of Contemporary Criminal Justice* 29 (May 2013): 219–232.

Binder, John J., and Matthew J. Luzi. "Al Capone and Friends." *Criminal Organizations* 10 (Winter 1996): 16–22.

Binford, Jessie F. *Brief Summary of the Report Submitted to the Board of Directors of the Juvenile Protective Association.* n.d.

Brown, Joseph. "The Unwelcomed Visitor: Al Capone in Miami." *South Beach Magazine* (August 13, 2007). http://www.southbeachmagazine

.com/the-unwelcomed-visitor-al-capone-in-miami/ (accessed July 22, 2013).

Bundesen, Herman N. Letter to Major Calvin Goddard. April 1, 1929.

Capone, Alphonse, alias Al Brown. Cook County Jail booking record. July 28, 1926.

Capone, Ralph. *Hearings before the Special Committee to Investigate Organized Crime in Interstate Commerce. Part 5. Illinois.* Washington, DC: US Government Printing Office, 1951.

Case Summary of Federal Parolee: Jack Gusick. United States penitentiary, Leavenworth. November 29, 1933.

"Changing Origins of Metropolitan Chicago's Foreign-Born Population." *Encyclopedia of Chicago.* http://www.encyclopedia.chicagohistory.org/pages/2278.html (accessed March 15, 2013).

Chicago Crime Commission Archive. CCC, Chicago, IL.

Chicago Police Department. *Annual Report.* Chicago: CPD, various years.

Committee of Fifteen Papers. University of Chicago, Joseph L. Regenstein Library, Department of Special Collections.

Cooney, Jackie. "Men of Violent Means: The Chicago Circulation War and Its Effects on Chicago Prohibition." Unpublished course paper, LEJ230, Harper College, IL (2012).

"Crime: Smart Young Men." *Time* (March 21, 1927). http://content.time.com/time/magazine/article/0,9171,730120,00.html (accessed September 5, 2011).

Doherty, James. "Gangsters: Drive to Control Food, Drink Sale Told: Stanton Plots to Rule Union Members." *Chicago Tribune.* May 12, 1942.

Doherty, James and Mr. Lee. "Letter to Mr. Lee" (private letter to the editor). *Chicago Tribune,* October 20, 1930.

Evans, Wainwright. "Fighting a Crime Organization." *Nation's Business* 8 (December 1920): 17.

Everleigh Club Illustrated 2131-2133 Dearborn Street. n.p.: n.p., 1911.

Federal Bureau of Investigation. *Murray Humphreys. File 92-3088, CG 92-795.* January 28, 1960, p. HH.

Federal Bureau of Investigation. *Re: St. Valentine's Day Massacre.* October 26, 1936.

Gomes, Mario. "The Farrell Letter (or Assertion)." In *Discounted Valentine Massacre Theories,* http://www.myalcaponemuseum.com/id173.htm.

Goudie, Chuck. "Dead Wrong." Chicago: ABC Television, Channel 7. June 3, 2010.

Gunther, John. "The High Cost of Hoodlums." *Harper's* 159 (October 1929): 529–40.

Haller, Mark. Introduction to *Organized Crime in Chicago*, by John Landesco. Chicago: University of Chicago Press, 1968.

———. "Policy Gambling, Entertainment, and the Emergence of Black Politics: Chicago from 1900 and 1940." *Journal of Social History* 24 (Summer 1991): 719–739.

Heitler, Michael. *Standard Certificate of Death.* State of Illinois. May 1, 1931.

Hoffman, Dennis E. *Business vs. Organized Crime: Chicago's Private War on Al Capone, 1929–1932.* Chicago: CCC, 1989.

"Homicide in Chicago." Northwestern University School of Law. http://homicide. northwestern.edu/ (accessed in 2008).

Hoover, J. Edgar. *Memorandum for Mr. Joseph B. Keenan, Acting Attorney General.* August 27, 1936.

Illinois Bureau of Criminal Identification and Investigation. Letter to the Chief of Police, Oak Park, Illinois, March 30, 1953.

Juvenile Protective Association papers, University of Illinois at Chicago, Richard J. Daley Library, Department of Special Collections.

Kass, Sarah, Jonathan Gruber et al. "Al Capone and the Machine Gun Massacre." *Man, Moment, and Machine.* Dir. Michael McInerney et al. Aired November 7, 2006. Bay Area, San Francisco, CA: History Channel.

Keefe, Rose. "The Bate Auto Murder." Unpublished manuscript (2008).

Landesco, John. Letter to Ernest W. Burgess. June 26, 1929.

Landesco, John. "Prohibition and Crime." *Annals of the American Academy of Political and Social Science* 163 (September 1932): 120–129.

Lashly, Arthur V. "Homicide (in Cook County)." *Illinois Crime Survey, chap. XIII.* Chicago: Illinois Association for Criminal Justice, 1929.

Lombardo, Robert. "The Black Mafia: African-American Organized Crime in Chicago 1890–1965." *Crime, Law, and Social Change* 38 (July 2002): 33–65.

———. "The Black Hand: Terror by Letter in Chicago." *Journal of Contemporary Criminal Justice* 18 (November 2002): 393–408.

Lurigio, Arthur J., and John J. Binder. "The Chicago Outfit: Challenging the Myths about Organized Crime." *Journal of Contemporary Criminal Justice* 29 (May 2013): 198–218.

Luzi, Matthew J. "From the Boys in Chicago Heights." Unpublished article (2006).

McCormick, Robert R. *Memoirs: Thompson, Part II: Address by Colonel Robert R. McCormick.* Chicago: n. p., July 17, 1954.

McCullough, Robert. *Hearings before the Special Committee to Investigate*

Organized Crime in Interstate Commerce. Part 5. Illinois. Washington, DC: US Government Printing Office, 1951.

Meyne, Gerhardt F. Letter to Judge John P. McGoorty et al. June 4, 1931.

Moran, George C. US Department of Justice, Bureau of Prisons, Classification study. February 13, 1957.

Morey, Bryan. "Problems of Evidence in the Saint Valentine's Day Massacre." Unpublished course paper, History 500, Hillsdale College, Hillsdale, MI (April 20, 2015).

Murder of Seven Men at 2122 N. Clark Street, Report—Lieut. Otto Erlanson & Squad 41A. CPD report, February 14, 1929.

Nelli, Humbert. "Italians and Crime in Chicago: The Formative Years, 1890–1920." *American Journal of Sociology* 74 (January 1969): 373–91.

Ness, Eliot. *Civil Service Papers.* April 6, 1942.

Nichols, Guy L. "Report." *Wickersham Report: Seventy-First Congress: Enforcement of the Prohibition Laws: Official Records of the National Commission on Law Observance and Enforcement: A Prohibition Survey of the State of Illinois:* Part II, vol. 4. Washington, DC: US Government Printing Office, 1931.

People of the State of Illinois v. John Scalisi et al. 324 Ill. 131. December 23, 1926.

Peterson, Virgil W. "The Career of a Syndicate Boss." *Crime and Delinquency* 8 (October 1962): 339–354.

———. *A Report on Chicago Crime for 1964.* Chicago: CCC, 1965.

"Philadelphia Justice for Chicago's Al Capone." *Literary Digest* 101 (June 15, 1929): 32, 34.

Reedy. *Gang War Memo. Chicago Tribune* files, October 1, 1926.

Record of Alphonse Capone. US Penitentiary Atlanta, August 19, 1934.

Report of the Hartford Vice Commission. Hartford: Connecticut Woman Suffrage Association, July 1913.

Roth, Walter. "Frankie Foster: Did He Really Murder Jake Lingle?" *Chicago Jewish History* 28 (Winter 2005): 8–9.

Russell, Daniel. "The Road House: A Study of Commercialized Amusements in the Environs of Chicago." Master's thesis, University of Chicago (1931).

Schneider, Richard L. *Information on Matthew Hoffman/Roger Touhy.* April 9, 1990.

Selective service registration card. "Dennis F. Cooney." September 12, 1918.

———. "Frank R. Nitto." September 9, 1918.

———. "Maurice Enright." September 12, 1918.

———. "Sam Genna." September 12, 1918.

Simpson, George E. "The Chicago Crime Commission." *Journal of Criminal Law and Criminology* 26 (September 1935): 401–420.

Sims, Edwin W. "Fighting Crime in Chicago: The Crime Commission." *Journal of the American Institute of Criminal Law and Criminology* 11 (May 1920): 21–28.

Skogan, Wesley G. "Chicago Since 1840: A Time-Series Data Handbook." Unpublished manuscript, Champaign, IL: University of Illinois (1976).

Statement of Sergt. Thomas J. Loftus, 36th District. CPD report. February 14, 1929.

Stewart, Harold. Letter to Nathan Levin. November 20, 1931.

Turner, George K. "The City of Chicago: A Study of Great Immoralities." *McClure's* 28 (April, 1907): 575–92.

Vaccaro, Courtney. "Red Light Districts and Segregated Prostitution in Progressive Era Chicago: A Demographic Survey of the Levee in 1910." Master's thesis, University of Nebraska at Kearney (December, 2013).

White, Owen P. "Looting the Loop." *Collier's* (May 12, 1928): 10–11, 54.

Williams, David C. *Hearings before the Permanent Subcommittee on Investigations.* Washington, DC: US Government Printing Office, 1988.

Williams, Reverend Elmer. "Lingle and Lee Pick Russell" (speech, WCFL-AM). Reverend Elmer Williams papers, Chicago History Museum, August 1930.

World's Annual Sporting Records 1905. n. p.: n. p., 1905.

NOTES

PREFACE

1. Gus Russo, *The Outfit* (New York: Bloomsbury, 2001).

2. Robert M. Lombardo, *Organized Crime in Chicago: Beyond the Mafia* (Urbana: University of Illinois Press, 2013). However, Lombardo presents a variety of information on the other rackets. John J. Binder, *The Chicago Outfit* (Charleston: Arcadia Publishing, 2003) contains about 20,000 words and 180 photos and therefore only very broadly discusses Prohibition.

3. John Landesco, *Organized Crime in Chicago: Part III of the Illinois Crime Survey* (Chicago: Illinois Association for Criminal Justice, 1929).

4. Mark Haller, introduction to *Organized Crime in Chicago,* by John Landesco (Chicago: University of Chicago Press, 1968), pp. vii–xviii.

5. Walter Noble Burns, *The One-Way Ride* (Garden City, NY: Doubleday, 1931); Edward D. Sullivan, *Rattling the Cup on Chicago Crime* (New York: Vanguard, 1929); Sullivan, *Chicago Surrenders* (New York, NY: Vanguard, 1930).

6. Hal Andrews, *X Marks the Spot* (n.p.: Spot Publishing, 1930).

7. Herbert Asbury, *Gem of the Prairie* (Garden City, NY: Garden City Publishing, 1942); Virgil W. Peterson, *Barbarians in Our Midst* (Boston: Atlantic-Little, Brown, 1952).

8. Kenneth Allsop, *The Bootleggers and Their Era* (Garden City, NY: Doubleday, 1961).

9. Fred D. Pasley, *Al Capone: The Biography of a Self-Made Man* (New York: Garden City, 1930); John Kobler, *Capone* (New York: G. P. Putnam, 1971); Robert J. Schoenberg, *Mr. Capone* (New York: William Morrow, 1992); Laurence Bergreen, *Capone* (New York: Simon and Schuster, 1994); Jonathan Eig, *Get Capone: The Secret Plot That Captured America's Most Wanted Gangster* (New York: Simon and Schuster, 2010).

10. Rose Keefe provides a much fuller treatment of the North Side gang initially led by Dean O'Banion than is found in the Capone biographies. Rose Keefe, *Guns and Roses* (Nashville: Cumberland House, 2003); Keefe, *The Man Who Got Away: The Bugs Moran Story* (Nashville: Cumberland House, 2005).

11. Mars Eghigian, *After Capone: The Life and World of Chicago Mob Boss Frank "The Enforcer" Nitti* (Nashville: Cumberland House, 2006).

CHAPTER 1: BEFORE PROHIBITION

1. The expletive has been redacted from the poem by the author.

2. Colosimo's origins were largely a mystery until Arthur Bilek shed new light on his early years. Arthur Bilek, *The First Vice Lord* (Nashville: Cumberland House, 2008).

3. For a general treatment of the seamy side of Chicago before Prohibition, see Richard Lindberg, *Chicago by Gaslight* (Chicago: Academy Chicago, 1996).

4. John J. Binder, "The Transportation Revolution and Antebellum Sectional Disagreement," *Social Science History* 35 (March 2011): 19–57.

5. Herbert Asbury, *Gem of the Prairie* (Garden City, NY: Garden City Publishing, 1942), p. 29.

6. Ibid., pp. 31–36.

7. Richard Lindberg, *The Gambler King of Clark Street* (Carbondale: Southern Illinois University Press, 2009) chronicles McDonald and his machinations.

8. Asbury, *Gem of the Prairie*, p. 41.

9. *Chicago Tribune*, January 11, 1882.

10. Asbury, *Gem of the Prairie*, p. 144.

11. Ibid., p. 148.

12. CPD, *Annual Report* (Chicago: CPD, various years). The population figures are from Table 1 of Wesley G. Skogan, *Chicago Since 1840: A Time-Series Data Handbook* (Champaign, IL: University of Illinois, 1976).

13. If enforcement was constant over time, then the index would show the changes in the amount of the activity per capita, such as gambling.

14. John Landesco, *Organized Crime in Chicago: Part III of the Illinois Crime Survey* (Chicago: Illinois Association for Criminal Justice, 1929), p. 894.

15. *Chicago Tribune*, November 28, 1911.

16. Asbury, *Gem of the Prairie*, chap. 5; Landesco, *Organized Crime in Chicago*, chap. XIX; Virgil W. Peterson, *Barbarians in Our Midst* (Boston: Atlantic-Little, Brown, 1952), pp. 86–91.

17. George K. Turner, "The City of Chicago: A Study of Great Immoralities," *McClure's* (April 1907), pp. 575–92.

18. Peterson, *Barbarians in Our Midst*, pp. 82–84.

19. Landesco, *Organized Crime in Chicago*, p. 873.

20. *Chicago Tribune*, November 6, 1909.

21. Asbury, *Gem of the Prairie*, p. 166.

22. Peterson, *Barbarians in Our Midst*, p. 89.

23. *Chicago Tribune*, September 15, 1911, November 23, 1911; Landesco, *Organized Crime in Chicago*, pp. 882–83.

24. *Chicago Tribune*, July 13, 1914.

25. Ibid., September 17, 1911.

26. Landesco, *Organized Crime in Chicago*, pp. 893–95 discusses the profits from the news bureau and the handbooks. The average monthly profit of $4,500 for Tennes's operations is used to obtain the annual figure for his handbooks.

27. According to Landesco, *Organized Crime in Chicago*, p. 881, Tim Murphy, a one-time partner of Mont Tennes, claimed in 1911 that some three hundred gambling establishments of all types in Chicago together handled more than $500,000 per day in bets. Using exactly half a million dollars and 360 operating days per year yields $180 million wagered per year. If the ratio of profit to the amount bet was the same as in Tennes's handbooks (see the preceding note), 2.3 percent of this amount ($4,140,000) would have been the annual profit for all the gambling places in the city.

28. This point is also made by Mark Haller, "Policy Gambling, Entertainment, and the Emergence of Black Politics: Chicago from 1900 and 1940," *Journal of Social History* 24 (Summer 1991): ftnt. 2.

29. *Chicago Tribune*, January 5, 1924, May 26, 1875.

30. *Chicago Inter Ocean*, September 18, 1875, May 2, 1877.

31. St. Clair Drake and Horace R. Cayton, *Black Metropolis* (New York: Harcourt, Brace, 1945), p. 472, among others, report this figure.

32. *Chicago Tribune*, May 16, 1886.

33. It also ignores the fact that operators lowered the payoffs if some numbers were bet especially heavily, due to chance, regular betting patterns, or superior information on the part of the bettors (due to the drawing being fixed by employees to aid certain wagerers), because it might bankrupt the wheel. If a particular number was in the news due to a natural or human-made disaster—for example, Engine 123 crashed with great loss of life on a railroad line—it would have been heavily played and the wheel operators would have lowered the payoff on that number. Similarly, some combinations were always popular with bettors, such as the washerwoman's gig 4-11-44, and carried a lower payoff.

34. *Chicago Tribune,* May 26, 1875, November 21, 1875, August 20, 1876.

35. *Chicago Tribune,* April 4, 1890.

36. Ibid., October 31, 1898.

37. Ibid., May 3, 1903. At that time "Policy Sam" Young was described as a messenger for Patsy King.

38. *Chicago Tribune,* February 24, 1901.

39. Ibid., May 4, 1903.

40. Ibid., February 15, 1906. The number of shops and runners is estimated based on one hundred shops open in 1908.

41. William Brashler, *The Don: The Life and Death of Sam Giancana* (New York: Harper and Row, 1977), p. 83.

42. *Chicago Daily News,* October 2, 1923; Herbert F. Gosnell, *Negro Politicians: Rise of Negro Politics in Chicago* (Chicago: University of Chicago Press, 1935), especially chap. 6; Robert Lombardo, "The Black Mafia: African-American Organized Crime in Chicago 1890–1965," *Crime, Law, and Social Change* 38 (July 2002): 33–65.

43. *Chicago Tribune,* April 3, 1905.

44. John H. Lyle, *The Dry and Lawless Years* (New York: Prentice-Hall, 1960), chap. 4.

Landesco, *Organized Crime in Chicago,* chap. XXII discusses the early labor racketeers to a minor extent.

45. *Chicago Tribune,* July 23, 1912.

46. Ibid., March 24, 1911.

47. Ibid., February 20, 1909, January 2, 1910.

48. *Chicago Tribune,* January 2, 1910, March 26, 1910, March 28, 1910.

49. This information was obtained from Enright's selective service card, dated September 12, 1918.

50. *Chicago Tribune,* March 24, 1911.

51. Ibid., May 24, 1911.

52. Ibid., June 27, 1919, May 11, 1922.

53. *Chicago Tribune,* November 6, 1942.

54. Ibid., September 18, 1923.

55. Ibid., October 11, 1922.

56. Ibid., February 20, 1931.

57. Ibid., October 17, 1911.

58. *Chicago Daily News,* May 20, 1921.

59. Ibid., June 5, 1919, January 13, 1929.

60. Roger Touhy, *The Stolen Years* (Cleveland: Pennington, 1959), p. 56.

61. *Chicago Tribune*, April 19, 1936; Barbara W. Newell, *Chicago and the Labor Movement* (Urbana: University of Illinois Press, 1961), p. 95.

62. *Chicago Tribune*, May 11, 1922.

63. *Chicago Tribune*, October 23, 1923.

64. See the *Report of the Hartford Vice Commission* (Hartford, CT: Connecticut Woman Suffrage Association, 1913).

65. Asbury, *Gem of the Prairie*, pp. 64–65.

66. *Chicago Inter Ocean*, March 25, 1876.

67. The 1861 England Census provides details on Roger Plant Sr.'s ancestry and shows him married to Ann Maria Plant. US Census records list her name as Anna or Annie. Under the Willow was closed by 1866 at the latest.

68. . *Chicago Tribune*, May 23, 1864.

69. Ibid., December 22, 1880.

70. *Los Angeles Times*, February 20, 1894.

71. *Chicago Tribune*, July 5, 1887.

72. *Chicago Inter Ocean*, January 15, 1895.

73. *Chicago Tribune*, January 22, 1868.

74. *Rockford Republic*, October 25, 1900.

75. *Chicago Inter Ocean*, November 25, 1900.

76. Ibid.

77. Ibid.

78. *Chicago Inter Ocean*, November 25, 1900.

79. Asbury, *Gem of the Prairie*, p. 96.

80. Americus [pseud.], *Chicago Inter Ocean*, March 18, 1882.

81. *Chicago Inter Ocean*, January 15, 1895.

82. Turner, "City of Chicago."

83. Americus [pseud.], *Chicago Inter Ocean*, January 14, 1882.

84. Officer 666 [pseud.], *Chicago Tribune*, July 20, 1914, May 6, 1903.

85. *Chicago Tribune*, November 5, 1903.

86. Asbury, *Gem of the Prairie*, chaps. 4, 8, and 9.

87. Officer 666 [pseud.], *Chicago Tribune*, July 25, 1914.

88. Norma Lee Browning, *Chicago Tribune*, March 14, 1949.

89. Eli Bogardus (known as E. B. or Ebie) Shaw, son of William W. Shaw, who owned the Dake Bakery, did in fact elope with actress May Yohe in 1888, the star performer at the Chicago Opera House. There are no reports that he ever eloped with Emma Fitzgerald, so she most likely concocted the story based on Shaw's episode with Yohe. *Chicago Tribune*, July 4, 1888.

90. The photo is in the Vic Shaw Family Album, Department of Special Collections, Lawrence J. Gutter Collection of Chicagoana, University of Illinois at Chicago Library.

91. Karen Abbott, *Sin in the Second City* (New York: Random House, 2007).

92. These physical features are from the sisters' 1909 passport applications.

93. Abbott, *Sin in the Second City*, p. 43, footnote; Charles Washburn, *Come into My Parlor* (New York: Knickerbocker Publishing Company, 1936).

94. This date appears in the club's famous brochure and is confirmed by its listing in the Chicago City Directory in 1900 on Dearborn. George Hankins, likely the husband of bordello keeper Effie Hankins, is shown at that address in 1899. The house was originally built at a cost of $125,000 by Lizzie Allen, whose consort and heir, Christopher Columbus Crabb, rented it to the Everleighs. *Chicago Tribune*, January 26, 1936.

95. According to the 1900 US Census, two separate households were at this particular location on S. Dearborn, indicating that the Everleigh Club might have initially occupied only one floor of the building. If the census is in error and this was really one household, then there were eight additional women at the club, although one of them—given her age—was probably a cook or staff member as opposed to a working prostitute. The sisters' occupations are listed as housekeeper while the women's professions were marked as artist, bookkeeper, and cashier.

96. The 1910 US Census lists Minna Everleigh as the resort keeper in a house of ill repute and describes the women as inmates.

97. *Chicago Tribune*, March 1, 1902.

98. Ibid., February 26, 1902.

99. Ibid., February 25, 1902.

100. Abbott, *Sin in the Second City*, pp. 73–77. As splendid as the Everleigh Club clearly was, it was not without its tragedies. For example, eighteen-year-old Della Watson died there on March 20, 1903, of maemic poisoning, with pelvic peritonitis—which sounds like it was caused by an occupational injury. She was buried in Thornton, Illinois, on March 22, 1903.

101. The Vice Commission of Chicago, *The Social Evil in Chicago* (Chicago: Gunthrop-Warren Printing, 1911), pp. 104–105; *Chicago Tribune*, February 2, 1936.

102. Asbury, *Gem of the Prairie*, pp. 247–56.

103. *Chicago Examiner*, October 25, 1911.

104. *Everleigh Club Illustrated 2131–2133 Dearborn Street* (n.p.: n.p., 1911).

105. Washburn, *Come into My Parlor*.

106. *Chicago Examiner*, July 27, 1914.

107. Ibid., July 22, 1914. In the 1910 US Census, twenty-year-old Amie Leslie was still working at the Everleigh Club.

108. Abbott, *Sin in the Second City*, p. 43.

109. Kate J. Adams, *Chicago Examiner*, August 19, 1916.

110. Vice Commission of Chicago, *Social Evil in Chicago*, p. 113. Excluding the sale of liquor, the profits from prostitution were estimated at around $8.5 million for the year.

111. Henry M. Hyde, *Chicago Tribune*, January 13, 1916, describes the segregated vice district as a "huge blackmail plant."

112. Walter C. Reckless, *Vice in Chicago* (Chicago: University of Chicago Press, 1933), Table 57. The Committee of Fifteen, a private group founded in 1908 to combat vice in Chicago, kept statistics on addresses where commercialized vice was operating, broken down by forty geographical areas in the city. These percentages are based on their reports.

113. Vice Commission of Chicago, *Social Evil in Chicago*, pp. 166–70.

114. Ibid., pp. 84–87.

115. Ibid., pp. 99–100.

116. Ibid., p. 97.

117. After completing this research, I became aware of Courtney Vaccaro's excellent master's thesis, which also studies the Levee in 1910. The results reported here are similar to what emerges from her analysis, although she examines several other aspects of the census data. See Courtney Vaccaro, "Red Light Districts and Segregated Prostitution in Progressive Era Chicago: A Demographic Survey of the Levee in 1910" (master's thesis, University of Nebraska at Kearney, 2013).

118. The census taker for district 160, which contains these two parts of Armour Avenue, did not use the same terminology as his colleague just to the east. However, it is well known (see the map in Asbury, *Gem of the Prairie*, p. 264) that this stretch of Armour was filled with brothels. According to the 1910 US Census, all the buildings there contained unmarried women, almost all between twenty and thirty-five years old, whose occupation is listed as "none." The other buildings in district 160 were occupied by families, male lodgers, or young women with legal occupations, so the western boundary of the Levee was clearly Armour Avenue. To the east of State Street (district 165), the census taker used the term "prostitute" rather than "inmate," but only for two locations: the saloon of vice lord Harry Hopkins on E. Twentieth Street and another bar on S. Wabash. There is no evidence of open vice in district 168, which

lies just south of district 162, and little or nothing beyond Vina Field's house on Dearborn in district 161 to the north. Therefore, little is lost by counting the prostitutes in census district 162 plus those on the west side of Armour on the two blocks just mentioned, which was also the traditional definition of the Levee. This tight containment of prostitution is consistent with the concept of a tolerated, segregated vice district.

119. Vaccaro, "Red Light Districts," p. 43. Ms. Vaccaro kindly shared her map with me.

120. Reckless, *Vice in Chicago*, pp. 25–31.

121. Although two bordellos are shown in the usual maps of the area as Chinese houses, these appear to be Chinese-owned rather than containing Chinese women. Asbury, *Gem of the Prairie*, p. 264.

122. In 1910, 3,662 people who were born in France lived in the metropolitan area out of a total population of about 2.8 million. Michael P. Conzen, "Changing Origins of Metropolitan Chicago's Foreign-Born Population," Encyclopedia of Chicago, http://www.encyclopedia.chicagohistory.org/pages/2278.html (accessed March 15, 2013).

123. Abbott, *Sin in the Second City*, p. 156.

124. Landesco, *Organized Crime in Chicago*, p. 817, footnote 1. Jews were not recorded as a separate nationality as no Jewish state existed at the time. They were therefore counted largely with the Germans (10.55 percent of Chicago's population) and even more so with the Russians (8.55 percent) due to the recent waves of Eastern European immigration. It is likely that a large part of the Russian population of Chicago was Jewish, giving the city a large Jewish contingent, as evidenced by the number of synagogues and sizes of the neighborhoods where this group predominated.

125. The theory of ethnic succession predicts that one ethnic group will displace another in organized crime as the first group's members prosper and raise their children in middle-class surroundings, leading their descendants to choose legitimate careers. It would perhaps be better recast as the "theory of economic success" because the factors that lead the subsequent generation(s) to avoid crime are the relatively higher earnings they expect (as opposed to their fathers or grandfathers) from noncriminal careers. If economic success does not occur over time, then that ethnic group would likely be mired in crime for years. See Howard Abadinsky, *Organized Crime* (Chicago: Thompson-Wadsworth, 2003) and Gary Becker, "Crime and Punishment: An Economic Approach," *Journal of Political Economy* 76 (March/April 1968): 169–217.

126. Asbury, *Gem of the Prairie,* pp. 313–18; Jack McPhaul, *Johnny Torrio: First of the Gang Lords* (New Rochelle, NY: Arlington House, 1970), pp. 69–71; Peterson, *Barbarians in Our Midst,* pp. 106–10.

127. *Chicago Tribune,* April 18, 1901.

128. Ibid., April 24, 1901.

129. John Kobler, *Capone* (New York: G. P. Putnam, 1971), p. 43.

130. Officer 666 [pseud.], *Chicago Tribune,* July 25, 1914.

131. The Chicago police also took bribes from common criminals. For example, pickpockets paid ten dollars a day whereas safecrackers paid fifty dollars a day when they were working. *New York Times,* June 10, 1903.

132. Lloyd Wendt and Herman Kogan, *Lords of the Levee* (Indianapolis: Bobbs-Merrill, 1943), pp. 320–21.

133. *Chicago Tribune,* November 12, 1912.

134. Landesco, *Organized Crime in Chicago,* p. 850.

135. The cozy relationship between the vice lords and the police is illustrated by a photo taken at a banquet at Colosimo's café. Colosimo, John Torrio, Unione Siciliana power (and later head) Mike Merlo, Nineteenth Ward Republican committeeman "Diamond Joe" Esposito, and Colosimo gangster Joey D'Andrea are seated with former policeman (and Colosimo associate) Harry Cullet, Detective Sergeant Ed Murphy, and Detective John Howe. At the time, Howe and Murphy were the right-hand men of Captain Ryan, who was in charge of the Twenty-Second Street police station. Cullet had tried to bribe Police Inspector W. C. Dannenberg of the Morals Squad, offering him $2,200 a month to lay off the Levee. *Chicago Tribune,* July 24, 1914; Landesco, *Organized Crime in Chicago,* p. 848.

136. Asbury, *Gem of the Prairie,* p. 278.

137. A newspaper ad for the Colosimo Hotel and Buffet on Archer Avenue, which is the same location as the Victoria, stated, "The premises have been renovated completely so that now they are considered the most elegant on the South Side. Italians who desire wines and liquors of the finest brands will find them at Signor Colosimo's." Perhaps "Big Jim" renamed the place after his ardor for Victoria subsided. *L'Italia,* December 19, 1908.

138. As shown on the cover of *World's Annual Sporting Records 1905,* Colosimo operated a poolroom on E. Twenty-Second Street (whose address changed to W. Twenty-Second Street when the city renumbered the streets in 1909). A subsequent owner told authorities in 1909 that the rooms on the second floor had been used for poker games before he bought the place. *Chicago Tribune,* January 7, 1909.

139. *Chicago Daily News,* June 21, 1922.

140. *L'Avanti,* May 22, 1920.

141. Asbury, *Gem of the Prairie,* pp. 312–13; Robert J. Schoenberg, *Mr. Capone* (New York: William Morrow, 1992), p. 41.

142. Vanilli was convicted of second-degree murder in Billings, Montana, on January 25, 1908, and was paroled in the spring of 1914. *Newark Advocate,* July 22, 1914. Robert Vanella (aka Rocco or Roxie Vanilli) was John Torrio's first cousin and was a witness on his citizenship papers in 1923. In turn, Torrio was the best man at Vanella's wedding in New York City in 1921. I am grateful to Joan Kiernan, the granddaughter of Robert Vanella, for sharing this information with me.

143. Hal Andrews, *X Marks the Spot* (n.p.: Spot Publishing, 1930), p. 4; Eliot Ness and Oscar Fraley, *The Untouchables* (New York: Julian Messner, 1957), p. 41.

144. *Chicago Tribune,* December 11, 1907.

145. *Chicago Tribune,* November 29, 1909; Asbury, *Gem of the Prairie,* pp. 268–69.

146. Wayne Johnson, *A History of Violence: An Encyclopedia* of *1400 Chicago Mob Murders* (McLean, VA: LLR Books, 2012), p. 27; *Chicago Tribune,* November 23, 1911; *The Day Book,* November 23, 1911. The spellings of the victims' names are from their death certificates.

147. *Chicago Tribune,* November 23, 1911.

148. McPhaul, *Johnny Torrio,* chap. 5; Kobler, *Capone,* p. 51.

149. *Chicago Tribune,* May 29, 1919.

150. Reckless, *Vice in Chicago,* pp. 3–7.

151. Officer 666 [pseud.], *Chicago Tribune,* July 20, 1914. There were also a number of independent operators, although they were frequently closely tied to one of the three main rings. For example, the Guzik brothers mentioned by the anonymous officer were likely connected to the Colosimo group. This was before Charles Maibaum was deported to France in November 1914. See *Chicago Tribune,* November 22, 1914.

152. *Chicago Tribune,* July 23, 1914.

153. Vanilli was arrested for the crime, although he was not indicted due to a lack of evidence. The aforementioned "Officer 666" states that Colosimo gangster W. E. Frazier fired the first shot that night. Frazier was allegedly brought to Chicago to kill Inspector Dannenberg of the Morals Squad but shot at the wrong man. Officer 666 [pseud.], *Chicago Tribune,* July 21, 1914.

154. Reckless, *Vice in Chicago,* table 57.

155. This was largely a return to 1874, when an attempt to regulate prostitution by the city led to the introduction of "pretty waiter girls" in saloons. It was estimated that at the time 75 percent of the lovely waitresses were prostitutes. *Chicago Inter Ocean*, August 7, 1874.

156. Kate J. Adams, *Chicago Examiner*, October 22, 1917.

157. Landesco, *Organized Crime in Chicago*, p. 852, ftnt. 1.

158. Reckless, *Vice in Chicago*, chaps. 1, 3, 5, and 6; Landesco, *Organized Crime in Chicago*, pp. 852–53.

159. *Chicago Tribune*, December 30, 1915.

160. Asbury, *Gem of the Prairie*, p. 310; McPhaul, *Johnny Torrio*, chap. 7.

161. *Chicago Tribune*, November 14, 1939.

162. Ibid., August 12, 1914.

163. Ibid., July 20, 1918.

164. Ibid., April 20, 1919.

165. Committee of Fifteen, *#10-Speedway Inn: Research Observations*, volume 10, part 2, University of Chicago, Joseph L. Regenstein Library, Department of Special Collections (April 21, 1918).

166. Committee of Fifteen, *10 Gostlin St. (Speedway Inn). Research Observations*, Volume 10, Part 2, University of Chicago, Joseph L. Regenstein Library, Department of Special Collections (May 5, 1918).

167. *Chicago Tribune*, January 28, 1917.

168. Lloyd Wendt and Herman Kogan, *Big Bill of Chicago* (Indianapolis: Bobbs-Merrill, 1953), pp. 329–30.

169. *Chicago Tribune*, April 9, 1931.

170. Ibid.

171. Unless otherwise noted, the details of Colosimo's murder are from articles in the *Chicago Tribune*, May 12, 1920, May 13, 1920, and May 14, 1920.

172. William Balsamo, telephone conversation with the author, 1996.

173. Asbury, *Gem of the Prairie*, p. 317 and Peterson, *Barbarians in Our Midst*, p. 108 state that Yale was hired by Torrio, but they assert that Colosimo was killed because of Torrio's ambitions to become the boss. However, the timing of his death, coming shortly after the start of Prohibition and his marriage to Dale Winter, indicates that there was more going on here than just Torrio's personal goals. Schoenberg, *Mr. Capone*, pp. 60–62 also backs this conclusion. Although Torrio did become the boss by removing Colosimo.

174. Landesco, *Organized Crime in Chicago*, p. 857.

175. Ibid., p. 1033.

176. *Chicago Tribune*, May 14, 1920.

177. Walter Noble Burns, *The One-Way Ride* (Garden City, NY: Doubleday, 1931), p. 19.

CHAPTER 2: BOOTLEGGING

1. John Kobler, *Ardent Spirits* (New York: G. P. Putnam, 1973), chap. 1; Daniel Okrent, *Last Call: The Rise and Fall of Prohibition* (New York: Scribner, 2010).

2. Herbert Asbury, *Gem of the Prairie* (Garden City, NY: Garden City Publishing, 1942), pp. 43–48.

3. George K. Turner, "The City of Chicago: A Study of Great Immoralities," *McClure's* (April 1907).

4. Although a street, hospital, and medical school in Chicago are named after Dr. Rush, the city seems to have otherwise ignored his views on temperance. In fact, Rush Street is the heart of the Near North bar district that was long a center of Outfit activity.

5. Kobler, *Ardent Spirits*, chap. 7.

6. Ibid., p. 203.

7. *Chicago Tribune*, April 2, 1919.

8. Ibid., March 31, 1932.

9. Ibid., June 16, 1925.

10. James O. Bennett, *Chicago Gangland* (Chicago: Chicago Tribune, 1929), pp. 63–69; George Murray, *The Legacy of Al Capone* (New York: G. P. Putnam, 1975), pp. 52–53.

11. *Chicago Tribune*, July 16, 1924.

12. Bennett, *Chicago Gangland*, pp. 67–68.

13. *Chicago Tribune*, March 20, 1932.

14. Ibid., May 17, 1930.

15. *New York Times*, July 9, 1928; *Chicago Tribune*, February 7, 1931, February 4, 1932.

16. Robert J. Schoenberg, *Mr. Capone* (New York: William Morrow, 1992), pp. 195, 202.

17. *Chicago Tribune*, September 26, 1924.

18. Ibid., February 21, 1926.

19. *New York Times*, April 3, 1932.

20. *Chicago Tribune*, November 22, 1927.

21. Federal prosecutor Richard Ogilvie estimates that the profits of the

Chicago Outfit were 15 percent of its revenues. Richard B. Ogilvie, "How Syndicate Rakes in Billions from Gamblers," *Chicago American*, March 3, 1961.

22. *Chicago Daily News*, June 13, 1930.

23. It should be remembered that these are rough estimates and there often is little or no detail provided about how they were derived. Therefore it is sometimes difficult to compare them over time or to reconcile estimates from different sources at a similar point in time.

24. James O'Donnell Bennett, *Chicago Tribune*, April 8, 1926.

25. In 1925, the Cicero Lions' club suggested, based on criminal conditions there, renaming Cicero Avenue after Terry Druggan or some other important bootlegger. *Chicago Tribune*, December 1, 1925.

26. *Chicago Tribune*, June 27, 1924, July 25, 1924.

27. John H. Lyle, *Chicago Tribune*, November 27, 1960, p. 51; Guy Murchie, *Chicago Tribune*, February 9, 1936.

28. Ibid., June 13, 1931. Richard Enright estimates the Capone gang's gross revenues for 1931 as $300 million. This figure appears to be dramatically overstated, given the estimates for 1925 and 1927, the estimate for all of Chicago organized crime in 1930, and the extent of Capone's domination of the underworld at the time. Enright's booklet was reprinted as Ray R. Cowdery, *Capone's Chicago* (Lakeville, MN: Northstar Maschek Books, 1987).

29. *Chicago Tribune*, August 27, 1929.

30. Ibid., December 30, 1926.

31. Ibid., September 25, 1921.

32. Ibid., September 27, 1921.

33. Ibid., March 21, 1924.

34. Ibid., April 6, 1923.

35. *Chicago Examiner*, July 29, 1917.

36. *Chicago Tribune*, February 23, 1921.

37. Ibid., September 23, 1921.

38. *Chicago Daily News*, April 14, 1928.

39. *Chicago Tribune*, January 16, 1932.

40. Ibid., November 15, 1927.

41. Ibid., March 17, 1924.

42. Ibid., March 7, 1930.

43. Ibid., August 29, 1928.

44. Ibid., December 4, 1926.

45. Sandy Smith, *Chicago Tribune*, February 2, 1960 provides a later description of these arrangements.

46. *Chicago Tribune*, April 8, 1924.

47. Illinois Association for Criminal Justice, *The Illinois Crime Survey* (Chicago: Illinois Association for Criminal Justice), p. 1091.

48. *Chicago Tribune*, January 30, 1923.

49. *Chicago Daily News*, April 25, 1930.

50. *Chicago Tribune*, February 17, 1931.

51. At the time, Thompson was convalescing after surgery at a sanatorium in Wedron. Because this event was only a few months before the 1931 primary elections in Chicago, the attendees, whether part of the Republican political machine or the Capone mob, were almost certainly there to raise funds and discuss election strategy. Obviously there was much at stake in the 1931 mayoral election for the Capone gang.

52. Schoenberg, *Mr. Capone*, chap. 18.

53. *Chicago Tribune*, February 22, 1929.

54. Ibid., May 25, 1928.

55. Ibid., May 7, 1928.

56. Illinois Association for Criminal Justice, *The Illinois Crime Survey*, chap. VI.

57. Illinois Association for Criminal Justice, *The Illinois Crime Survey*, p. 329.

58. *Chicago Tribune*, January 22, 1924.

59. Ibid., December 15, 1925, May 5, 1926.

60. Ibid., May 8, 1926.

61. Ibid., September 10, 1924.

62. Ibid., May 6, 1926.

63. Bennett, *Chicago Gangland*, p. 80.

64. *Chicago Tribune*, August 31, 1930.

65. Guy Murchie, *Chicago Tribune*, February 9, 1936.

66. Bennett, *Chicago Gangland*, pp. 84–85.

67. *Chicago Tribune*, October 13, 1926, August 3, 1947.

CHAPTER 3: THE GANGSTERS

1. Robert Lombardo, *Organized Crime in Chicago: Beyond the Mafia* (Urbana: University of Illinois Press, 2013), pp. 91–92; Guy Murchie, *Chicago Tribune*, February 9, 1936.

2. Frederic M. Thrasher, *The Gang* (Chicago: University of Chicago Press, 1937), chap. 20.

3. Jackie Cooney, "Men of Violent Means: The Chicago Circulation War and Its Effects on Chicago Prohibition" (unpublished course paper, LEJ230, Harper College, IL, 2012); *The Day Book*, December 16, 1911, April 16, 1916, and December 11, 1916. I am grateful to Jackie Cooney for sharing her research paper on the Circulation War with me.

4. Wayne Andrews, *Battle for Chicago* (New York: Harcourt, Brace, 1946), p. 232.

5. Cooney, "Men of Violent Means," p. 12.

6. Lou Corsino, *The Neighborhood Outfit: Organized Crime in Chicago Heights* (Urbana: University of Illinois Press, 2014).

7. Murchie, *Chicago Tribune*, February 9, 1936.

8. *Chicago Tribune*, August 25, 1930.

9. James Doherty, *Chicago Tribune*, April 1, 1951.

10. See the reprint by Ray R. Cowdery, *Capone's Chicago* (Lakeville, MN: Northstar Maschek Books, 1987).

11. *Chicago Tribune*, November 11, 1924. The gang had a similar number of goons in late 1926 at the time of Hymie Weiss's death (*Chicago Daily News*, October 12, 1926).

12. If the leadership duties were shared by two individuals or several brothers, the leaders' pronouncements to their subordinates were still law.

13. Robert Fuesel, conversation with the author, December 16, 2005.

14. Guy L. Nichols, "Report," *Wickersham Report: Seventy-First Congress: Enforcement of the Prohibition Laws: Official Records of the National Commission on Law Observance and Enforcement: A Prohibition Survey of the State of Illinois: Part II, Vol. 4.* (Washington, DC: US Government Printing Office, 1931), p. 311.

15. *Chicago Herald and Examiner*, May 22, 1932.

16. Herman N. Bundesen to Major Calvin Goddard, April 1, 1929. I am grateful to Chuck Schauer for sharing the Bundesen letter with me.

17. Rose Keefe, conversation with the author, July 30, 2011.

18. Robert J. Schoenberg, *Mr. Capone* (New York: William Morrow, 1992), p. 166; Craig Eisen, conversation with the author, November 9, 2011.

19. The map in Murchie, *Chicago Tribune*, February 16, 1936, which has frequently been reprinted, contains many errors and inconsistencies. Some of the gangs shown did not exist at the same time, other gangs are not included in it, the territories they controlled are not all correctly located, and in some cases gangs were not aligned with or against Torrio and Capone as claimed.

20. Hal Andrews, "Gangsters Grip Chicago!" *Real Detective* 26

(September 1932): 28; Cowdery, *Capone's Chicago*, p. 35; Nichols, "Report," pp. 309, 325–28. Admittedly, the various sources sometimes disagree about who controlled a particular neighborhood at a point in time, and the bootlegging areas did not exactly match the police districts in every case. For example, Jack Schaller, the ninety-year-old owner of Schaller's Pump on S. Halsted, stated that, to the best of his recollection, his establishment and the surrounding area in the Bridgeport neighborhood were supplied by Danny Stanton's gang. Jack Schaller, conversation with the author, April 22, 2014; Sue Weber, conversation with the author, April 18, 2015. Although this is part of the Deering police district, this does not necessarily negate the claims by other sources that this area was controlled by the Capone gang because, by about 1928, the Sheldon-Stanton gang was essentially a subsidiary of the Capone mob.

21. The discussion of the North Side gang is based heavily on Rose Keefe, *Guns and Roses* (Nashville: Cumberland House, 2003); Keefe, *The Man Who Got Away: The Bugs Moran Story* (Nashville: Cumberland House, 2005).

22. Chicago Crime Commission, "In Re: Case #28982," July 20, 1922.

23. A number of these details are confirmed by O'Banion's draft registration card for World War I.

24. Oscar Hewitt, *Chicago Tribune*, January 22, 1924.

25. James O. Bennett, *Chicago Gangland* (Chicago: Chicago Tribune Co., 1929), p. 8.

26. Hal Andrews, *X Marks the Spot* (n.p.: Spot Publishing, 1930), p. 14.

27. *Chicago Tribune*, November 11, 1924.

28. John Kobler, *Capone* (New York: G. P. Putnam, 1971), p. 80.

29. Keefe, *Guns and Roses*, pp. 125–26.

30. Ibid., June 25, 1920; Robert Koznecki, conversation with the author, 1994.

31. Chicago Crime Commission, "Bulletin #45," November 17, 1926.

32. Chicago Crime Commission, "Bulletin #38," April 5, 1926; Chicago Crime Commission, "In re: Vincent Drucci," November 16, 1926.

33. Keefe, *Man Who Got Away*, p. 14.

34. *The Pantagraph*, April 21, 1913.

35. Schoenberg, *Mr. Capone*, pp. 80–81.

36. *Chicago Tribune*, June 5, 1927.

37. Ibid., November 8, 1932.

38. Ibid., February 20, 1923.

39. *The Sentinel*, September 27, 1918.

40. Chicago Crime Commission, "Known Chicago Gangsters for the Past 12 Years and Their Activities," May 25, 1931, p. 2.

41. *Chicago Herald and Examiner*, February 15, 1929.

42. Chicago Crime Commission, "Known Chicago Gangsters," p. 2; *Chicago Tribune*, August 31, 1935. Professor Joe Kraus of the University of Scranton first brought to my attention that there were two Maxie Eisens, based on information he received from Craig Eisen.

43. The newspapers of the era refer to one of the Eisens as "North Side" Maxie Eisen and the other as "West Side" Maxie Eisen, although it is not clear who bears which label. The Eisen who joined the O'Banion gang (Eisen #2) grew up on the West Side, while (Eisen #1) seems to have grown up on the North Side.

44. Walter Roth, "Frankie Foster: Did He Really Murder Jake Lingle?" *Chicago Jewish History* 28 (Winter 2005): 8–9. Detailed genealogical information about Frankie Foster can also be found in his family tree on http://www.ancestry.com, which was created by his relative, Mike Karsen. Foster was lost for three days during the San Francisco earthquake of 1906. Mike Karsen, conversation with the author, October 11, 2016.

45. *Chicago Tribune*, August 30, 1922; Chicago Crime Commission, "Re: Frank Lake," September 8, 1930, p. C.

46. *Chicago Daily News*, September 28, 1923.

47. *Chicago Tribune*, August 25, 1930; *Chicago Daily News*, June 19, 1931.

48. *Chicago Tribune*, November 19, 1925.

49. Ibid., September 2, 1919.

50. Ibid., December 23, 1925.

51. Ibid., July 16, 1926.

52. Chicago Crime Commission, "Re: George 'Bugs' Moran," October 22, 1930, p. D; *Chicago Tribune*, October 18, 1931.

53. *Chicago Tribune*, January 10, 1933.

54. Chicago Crime Commission, "Known Chicago Gangsters," p. 3.

55. "Klondike" O'Donnell relative, conversation with the author, April 17, 2012.

56. Chicago Crime Commission, "Re: Myles O'Donnell," n.d., p. C.

57. *Chicago Tribune*, July 8, 1927.

58. Ibid., November 8, 1933.

59. Ibid., February 7, 1931.

60. Chicago Crime Commission, "Re: Anthony Capezio," March 3, 1945, p. 2.

61. Chicago Crime Commission, "Re: John Edward Moore alias

Johnny Moore, John 'Screwy' Moore, Claude Maddox, Joseph Manning," October 10, 1946.

62. Ibid.; *Chicago Tribune*, August 28, 1922.

63. Chicago Crime Commission, "Re: Claude Maddox alias John Moore," October 17, 1930; *Chicago Tribune*, November 5, 1924, June 23, 1925.

64. Chicago Crime Commission, "Re: Anthony Capezio," March 3, 1945, p. 1.

65. Virgil W. Peterson, "The Career of a Syndicate Boss," *Crime and Delinquency* 8 (October 1962): 340.

66. Chicago Crime Commission, "Accardo, Tony alias Joe Batters alias Anthony Joseph Accardo," n.d., pp. 1–2.

67. No one with the name Antonino or Tony Accardo (or a similar first name and surname) whose age is even close to that of the gangster Tony Accardo is listed in Chicago in the 1930 US Census. However, a Joseph Batters, who was born in Illinois of Italian parents and whose age is correct, was living in a hotel on W. Jackson on Chicago's Near West Side at the time. Consistent with this being Tony Accardo, no such Joseph Batters is found in the 1920 Census, while young Tony Accardo is listed as living that year with his parents at the place of his birth. Similarly, when Accardo was an owner of the Owl Club in Calumet City in the early 1940s he gave his name as "Joe Batters."

68. Confidential source, conversation with the author, March 17, 2008; Illinois Bureau of Criminal Identification and Investigation, March 30, 1953. According to Chicago Crime Commission, "Re: Capone Syndicate," July 19, 1955, Johnson was a pallbearer at Louis Campagna's funeral in 1955 and attended Tony Accardo's Fourth of July party on Franklin Avenue in River Forest that same year, which confirms his prominence in organized crime in Chicago during and following Prohibition.

69. Confidential source, conversation with the author, 1993.

70. This information is from Salvatore Genna's WWI draft registration card and Mike Genna's death certificate.

71. *Chicago Tribune*, July 10, 1925. A later article states that Angelo, Mike, and Tony Genna were the leaders. *Chicago Tribune*, January 12, 1926.

72. *Chicago Tribune*, November 19, 1922.

73. Ibid., October 9, 1926.

74. Schoenberg, *Mr. Capone*, p. 129.

75. *Chicago Tribune*, June 14, 1930.

76. Walter Noble Burns, *The One-Way Ride* (Garden City, NY: Doubleday, 1931), p. 131.

77. George Murray, *The Legacy of Al Capone* (New York: G. P. Putnam, 1975), pp. 188–89; *New York Times*, October 25, 1935.

78. John J. Binder, *The Chicago Outfit* (Charleston: Arcadia Publishing, 2003), p. 12.

79. *Chicago Tribune*, October 18, 1931.

80. Schoenberg, *Mr. Capone*, p. 129.

81. *Chicago Tribune*, November 14, 1924.

82. Ibid., February 23, 1928.

83. Ibid., March 20, 1928; Schoenberg, *Mr. Capone*, chap. 18.

84. Virgil W. Peterson, *Chicago Tribune*, October 7, 1956.

85. People v. Scalisi, 324 Ill. 131 (December 23, 1926).

86. Kobler, *Capone*, pp. 89, 164.

87. *Chicago Daily News*, August 17, 1931.

88. *Chicago Tribune*, February 16, 1919. In 1930 the *Chicago Daily News* reports that Cook and Vogel "had the beer concession in Lawndale for seven years." This raises the distinct possibility that they grabbed this area from Spike O'Donnell in 1923—just as John Torrio (see the discussion in chapter 4) took Brighton Park from the South Side O'Donnells in the fall of that year. *Chicago Daily News*, June 18, 1930.

89. *Chicago Tribune*, February 18, 1919.

90. Ibid., April 28, 1926.

91. Walter Noble Burns, *Chicago Tribune*, September 1, 1917, p. 1.

92. *Chicago Tribune*, June 27, 1920.

93. The name is spelled Drugan in various censuses, Cook County death records, obituaries, selective service records, and Social Security records. This is also the spelling the family uses currently.

94. Chicago Crime Commission, "Re: Frank Lake," p. A.

95. *Chicago Tribune*, September 3, 1927.

96. Ibid., September 12, 1923. The addresses were obtained from a variety of other newspaper articles.

97. Interestingly, when this operation was leased from Druggan in 1933 by a new Gambrinus brewing company, its officers and directors included the nephew of West Side congressman Adolph Sabath and Alderman John J. Lagodny, *Chicago Tribune*, June 27, 1933.

98. *Chicago Tribune*, December 6, 1923.

99. Ibid., September 12, 1923.

100. Ibid., April 29, 1924.

101. Ibid., January 19, 1926.

102. Ibid., April 6, 1923, April 29, 1924.

103. Ibid., April 28, 1924.

104. Ibid., April 15, 1924.

105. Ibid., November 18, 1924.

106. Ibid., September 27, 1924.

107. Ibid., December 4, 1927.

108. Chicago Crime Commission, "Known Chicago Gangsters," p. 2; *Chicago Tribune*, March 5, 1924.

109. *Chicago Tribune*, August 24, 1920.

110. Ibid., July 1, 1925.

111. This section has benefitted from the comments of Professor Joe Kraus, who very graciously shared his extensive research on Chicago's Jewish gangsters with me while working on his own book.

112. *Chicago Daily News*, May 18, 1943.

113. *Chicago Tribune*, May 12, 1942.

114. *Chicago Tribune*, September 18, 1930.

115. Ibid., March 2, 1925.

116. Ibid., December 23, 1925.

117. *Chicago Examiner*, July 2, 1916; *Chicago Tribune*, August 6, 1927.

118. *Chicago Examiner*, April 13, 1918.

119. *Chicago Tribune*, August 18, 1926.

120. Ibid., February 1, 1927.

121. Ibid., March 22, 1915.

122. Ibid., January 3, 1918.

123. Northwestern University School of Law, "Homicide in Chicago," https://homicide.northwestern.edu/database/ (accessed February 24, 2006).

124. *Chicago Tribune*, March 8, 1926.

125. William M. Tuttle Jr., *Race Riot* (New York: Atheneum, 1984), pp. 32–33.

126. *Chicago Tribune*, September 20, 1925.

127. Ibid., September 1, 1920, January 24, 1925.

128. Reedy, *Gang War Memo* (Chicago: *Chicago Tribune* files, October 1, 1926); *Chicago Tribune*, May 9, 1912, December 14, 1924.

129. *Chicago Herald and Examiner*, January 17, 1927. Original source entirely omitted whatever expletive Saltis may have used.

130. *Chicago Tribune*, September 11, 1926, October 12, 1928.

131. Edward Soltis, conversation with the author, February 3, 1994.

132. Chicago Crime Commission, "Re: Joe Saltis alias 'Polack Joe,'" October 4, 1930.

133. Chicago Crime Commission, "Re: Frank McErlane," October 9, 1930, p. A.

134. *Chicago Tribune*, October 13, 1931.

135. Ibid., January 23, 1913, June 14, 1916.

136. Ibid., August 3, 1932.

137. Ibid., October 23, 1926.

138. Chicago Crime Commission, "Re: Vincent McErlane," n.d., p. A.

139. See, for example, Kobler, *Capone*, p. 101, and, more strongly, Schoenberg, *Mr. Capone*, pp. 84–87.

140. Chicago Crime Commission, "Re: Edward 'Spike' O'Donnell," September 27, 1930; *Chicago Tribune*, December 14, 1922. The preceding details also appear in Keefe, *Man Who Got Away*.

141. *Chicago Tribune*, August 27, 1919.

142. Ibid., May 20, 1924, May 9, 1922.

143. *Chicago Tribune*, May 24, 1923.

144. *Chicago Daily News*, September 20, 1923.

145. *Chicago Tribune*, January 30, 1924; *Chicago Daily News*, September 12, 1923.

146. See Cowdery, *Capone's Chicago*, p. 35; Nichols, "Report," p. 309. Fred D. Pasley, *Al Capone: The Biography of a Self-Made Man* (New York: Garden City, 1930), p. 144 is an exception, although he may refer to the situation around 1926 when the South Side O'Donnells were most likely Capone allies. Or to 1929 when for a time there was broad cooperation among the South Side gangs under the direction of Capone ally Danny Stanton. A third possibility is that he is discussing the Capone-led syndicate that controlled gambling on the entire South Side at one time.

147. Nichols, "Report," pp. 325–28 concurs with "John Law's" analysis of the situation. At the time, the Woodlawn police district extended to Seventy-First Street on the south.

148. Andrews, "Gangsters Grip Chicago!"

149. Ibid., p. 90.

150. Again, it would have been foolish for O'Donnell and his gang to have lived in the Gresham neighborhood when he was fighting with Saltis if the latter controlled the area.

151. *Chicago Tribune*, September 20, 1923.

152. Ibid., July 31, 1924.

153. His name and birth date are confirmed by his tombstone, draft records from both World Wars, and Social Security death records.

154. Chicago Crime Commission, "Re: Edward 'Spike' O'Donnell."

155. *Chicago Tribune*, February 17, 1918.

156. Bennett, *Chicago Gangland*, pp. 28–29; Jack McPhaul, *Johnny Torrio:*

First of the Gang Lords (New Rochelle, NY: Arlington House, 1970), pp. 32–37. This description comes from his second wife, Anna Jacobs, who was herself married at least once before she met Torrio. Despite claims to the contrary, she was a Protestant girl of English ancestry from Kentucky, whose family had earlier lived in Virginia. I am grateful to Jim Jacobs for clarifying Anna Jacobs's background. Torrio's first wife, Helen, helped him manage a house of prostitution on Armour. *The Day Book*, August 24, 1912. Although little is known about Helen Torrio (aka Turio), it is safe to conclude that she met John Torrio in the underworld.

157. McPhaul, *Johnny Torrio*, p. 32; Schoenberg, *Mr. Capone*, p. 68.

158. John Landesco, *Organized Crime in Chicago: Part III of the Illinois Crime Survey* (Chicago: Illinois Association for Criminal Justice, 1929), pp. 918; *Chicago Tribune*, May 20, 1924.

159. William Balsamo and John Balsamo, *Young Al Capone* (New York: Skyhorse Publishing, 2011), chap. 10; Schoenberg, *Mr. Capone*, p. 36. According to McPhaul, *Johnny Torrio*, p. 460, Capone fled a murder charge in New York and arrived in Chicago in 1918. McPhaul has him working for Torrio at the Four Deuces for thirty-five dollars a week when he arrived.

160. "Capone, Alphonse, alias Al Brown," Cook County jail booking record (July 28, 1926).

161. *Record of Alphonse Capone*, US Penitentiary Atlanta, GA (August 19, 1934).

162. C.R.F. Beall, *40886–Capone, Alphonse: Neuro-Psychiatric Examination* (Atlanta, GA: US Penitentiary, May 18, 1932).

163. Laurence Bergreen, *Capone* (New York: Simon and Schuster, 1994), pp. 56–58. The claim that Capone was a bookkeeper in Baltimore seems to fill a need by some researchers for Capone to have had a background in business before he became the leader of a multimillion-dollar illegal enterprise in Chicago. Actually, bookkeeping (accounting) is to business leadership what filling out a scorecard is to managing a baseball team. It records the results of the decisions that were made, but it does not teach anyone how to run a business, including how to make strategic decisions. So even if Capone had worked as a bookkeeper for several years, this is not the missing link that explains how a Brooklyn street tough became the savvy boss of a criminal empire. Similarly, a number of America's most successful gangsters, including James Colosimo, Frankie Yale, John Torrio, Lucky Luciano, Paul Ricca, Tony Accardo, and Carlo Gambino had no formal business training.

164. Kobler, *Capone*, 1971, p. 67; *Chicago Tribune*, March 14, 1949.

165. Pasley, *Al Capone*, pp. 17–18.

166. I am grateful to organized crime historian Mark Levell for his insightful comments on this issue. Of course, Torrio might have seen Capone after 1909, when he returned to visit New York, but this is hardly the type of relationship that would have led a gang leader to bring in a twenty-year-old from out of town as his full partner.

167. Schoenberg, *Mr. Capone*; Balsamo and Balsamo, *Young Al Capone.*

168. "Capone, Alphonse."

169. Beall, *40886–Capone, Alphonse.*

170. *Chicago Tribune*, October 28, 1931 quotes this editorial.

171. Ibid., January 21, 1921, April 15, 1921.

172. Ibid., August 31, 1922.

173. Ibid., November 3, 1924.

174. Ibid., June 21, 1919.

175. Robert McCullough, *Hearings before the Special Committee to Investigate Organized Crime in Interstate Commerce. Part 5. Illinois* (Washington, DC: US Government Printing Office, 1951).

176. Chicago Crime Commission, "Re: Frank Diamond," October 1, 1930.

177. Mike Martin, conversation with the author, 2012; Balsamo and Balsamo, *Young Al Capone.*

178. Ralph Capone, *Hearings before the Special Committee to Investigate Organized Crime in Interstate Commerce. Part 5. Illinois* (Washington, DC: US Government Printing Office, 1951).

179. While official records disagree on the year of Dennis Cooney's birth, his World War I draft card and the 1880 US Census both list it as 1878, as does his twin brother's death record.

180. *Chicago Tribune*, June 1, 1900.

181. Selective service registration card. "Dennis F. Cooney" (September 12, 1918).

182. *Chicago Tribune*, January 20, 1942.

183. The obituaries of his wife, father, and brother spell the name Guiffra. *Chicago Tribune*, June 8, 1938, July 6, 1957, and November 21, 1966.

184. *Chicago Tribune*, June 14, 1931.

185. Ibid., May 28, 1924.

186. Schoenberg, *Mr. Capone*, p. 18, like Kobler, *Capone*, pp. 17–18, concludes that Ralph Capone was born in the United States in 1893. However, immigration records indicate that he arrived from Italy with his mother and older brother on the Werra on June 18, 1895. The

booking records at McNeil Island penitentiary, Capone's World War II draft registration form, and the Social Security Death Index show his date of birth as January 12, 1894. The two former records, which contain information on the location of birth, report that he was born in Italy.

187. Ralph Capone, *Hearings before the Special Committee*; Chicago Crime Commission, "Capone, Ralph alias 'Bottles' Capone," n.d.; Chicago Crime Commission, "Re: Ralph Capone," October 4, 1930.

188. "Case Summary of Federal Parolee—Jack Gusick," November 29, 1933.

189. Ibid.; *Chicago Tribune*, April 20, 1919.

190. *Chicago Examiner*, August 21, 1909.

191. This paragraph is based heavily on Eghigian, *After Capone*.

192. New York crime historian William Balsamo believes that Al Capone and Frank Nitti were second cousins and that both families stemmed from the village of Angri. William Balsamo, conversation with the author, 2012.

193. Eghigian, *After Capone*, pp. 14–17; Balsamo and Balsamo, *Young Al Capone*, chap. 1.

194. Eghigian, *After Capone*, p. 39.

195. *Chicago Tribune*, July 30, 1930.

196. *Chicago Daily News*, September 21, 1923.

197. Juvenile Protective Association, *Cicero, Illinois*, University of Illinois at Chicago, Richard J. Daley Library, Department of Special Collections (December 6, 1923).

198. *Chicago Tribune*, September 22, 1926.

199. Ibid., May 3, 1926.

200. Ibid., September 22, 1926.

201. Ibid., November 17, 1929.

202. Ibid., May 21, 1926.

203. Ibid., April 17, 1935. Specialville was later renamed Dixmoor.

204. Ibid., July 26, 1913.

205. Ibid., June 2, 1921.

206. Ibid., May 3, 1926; Juvenile Protective Association, *Leyden, Illinois, A-100*, University of Illinois at Chicago, Richard J. Daley Library, Department of Special Collections (August 15, 1929).

207. After breaking with the Small-Thompson machine in 1921, State's Attorney Crowe conducted numerous gambling raids. However, this was a political move rather than a serious reform effort, and it dissipated when he returned to the party fold. *Chicago Tribune*, November 11, 1921.

208. John R. Schmidt, "William E. Dever: A Chicago Political Fable," in *The Mayors*, ed. Paul M. Green and Melvin G. Holli (Carbondale: Southern Illinois University Press, 1987), pp. 82–98.

209. *Chicago Tribune*, May 7, 1923, October 6, 1923.

210. Ibid., July 4, 1926; Craig Eisen, conversation with the author, November 9, 2011.

211. For years, the Outfit's Chicago Heights street crew was the least understood of the organization's five traditional crews. Due to research during the last twenty-five years by Matthew J. Luzi and Lou Corsino, the situation has been completely reversed. The discussion of Chicago Heights gangland in this book is based largely on Matthew J. Luzi, "From the Boys in Chicago Heights" (unpublished manuscript, 2006); Luzi, *The Boys in Chicago Heights* (Charleston: History Press, 2012).

212. John J. Binder and Matthew J. Luzi, "Al Capone and Friends," *Criminal Organizations* 10 (Winter 1996): 16–22; Luzi, *Boys in Chicago Heights*; *Southtown Economist*, April 9, 1924.

213. *Chicago Tribune*, May 4, 1929.

214. Luzi, "From the Boys," pp. 13–14.

215. *Chicago Tribune*, August 9, 1924, November 18, 1924.

216. Ibid., August 9, 1924.

217. Ibid., December 2, 1923.

218. Ibid., January 11, January 20, and January 30, 1923; Walter C. Reckless, *Vice in Chicago* (Chicago: University of Chicago Press, 1933), p. 91.

219. Juvenile Protective Association, *Commercialized Prostitution*, University of Illinois at Chicago, Richard J. Daley Library, Department of Special Collections (December 10, 1922), p. 8; *Chicago Tribune*, February 22, 1923.

220. Juvenile Protective Association, *Commercialized Prostitution.*

221. Juvenile Protective Association, *Parlor House, Rex Hotel*, University of Illinois at Chicago, Richard J. Daley Library, Department of Special Collections (November 24, 1922); Juvenile Protective Association, *Parlor House, 2222 S. Wabash*, University of Illinois at Chicago, Richard J. Daley Library, Department of Special Collections (December 22, 1922).

222. Committee of Fifteen, *4453 N. Winchester. Records, Volume I, Part I*, University of Chicago, Joseph L. Regenstein Library, Department of Special Collections (April 24, 1922).

223. Juvenile Protective Association, *Law Enforcement and Police, Columbia Hotel, 8 W. 31st Street*, University of Illinois at Chicago, Richard J. Daley Library, Department of Special Collections (December 2, 1922);

Juvenile Protective Association, *Commercialized Prostitution*; Juvenile Protective Association, *Syndicate Houses Reported by Cheatham Hunter*, University of Illinois at Chicago, Richard J. Daley Library, Department of Special Collections (March 7, 1923).

224. Juvenile Protective Association, *Parlor House, Rex Hotel*, p. 2.

225. *Chicago Tribune*, January 25, 1923.

226. Juvenile Protective Association, *Commercialized Prostitution*, p. 7.

227. Juvenile Protective Association, *Syndicate Houses*.

228. Michael Heitler standard certificate of death (State of Illinois, May 1, 1931).

229. Reckless, *Vice in Chicago*, pp. 70, 77, and 83.

230. *Chicago Tribune*, June 1, 1921.

231. *Chicago Daily News*, January 10, 1923.

232. *The Day Book*, July 28, 1914.

233. Juvenile Protective Association, *General Summary*, University of Illinois at Chicago, Richard J. Daley Library, Department of Special Collections (December 10, 1923).

234. Walter C. Reckless, *Vice in Chicago* (Chicago: University of Chicago Press, 1933), Table 57.

235. Ibid., pp. 25–30.

236. *Chicago Tribune*, November 2, 1924.

237. Ibid., December 4, 1926; *Chicago Daily News*, September 23, 1931.

238. *Chicago Tribune*, July 21, 1924.

239. Ibid., April 1, 1904.

240. Ibid., September 12, 1907, January 18, 1917.

241. Ibid., October 10, 1926.

242. *Chicago Daily News*, October 2, 1923, January 25, 1924, and August 13, 1924.

243. Landesco, *Organized Crime in Chicago*, p. 900.

244. *Chicago Tribune*, July 22, 1924.

245. Landesco, *Organized Crime in Chicago*, p. 901.

246. Kent A. Hunter, *Chicago Daily News*, September 20, 1923; Hunter, *Chicago Daily News*, September 22, 1923.

247. *Chicago Tribune*, June 25, 1924, August 29, 1924.

248. Robert Lombardo, "The Black Mafia: African-American Organized Crime in Chicago 1890–1965," *Crime, Law, and Social Change* 38 (July 2002): 15.

249. *Chicago Defender*, June 29, 1918.

250. *Chicago Daily News*, January 9, 1923, June 29, 1923.

251. Lombardo, "The Black Mafia," p. 16.

252. *Chicago Tribune,* January 16, 1945.

253. *Chicago Defender,* June 29, 1918.

254. Nathan Thompson, *Kings: The True Story of Chicago Policy Kings and Numbers Racketeers* (Chicago: Bronzeville Press, 2003), chap. 6.

255. *Chicago Tribune,* February 4, 1920.

256. Ibid., November 28, 1920.

257. These labor union murders are listed by the CCC among the gangland-style murders in Chicago from 1919 to 1933. See chapter 7 for further details.

258. Ibid., April 23, 1920, April 24, 1920.

259. Ibid., February 4, 1924.

260. Ibid., April 23, 1923.

261. Ibid., May 10, 1922.

262. Ibid., May 12, 1922.

263. John Gunther, "The High Cost of Hoodlums," *Harper's* (October, 1929): 529–40; Gordon L. Hostetter and Thomas Quinn Beesley, *It's a Racket* (Chicago, IL: Les Quin Books Inc., 1929), p. 29.

264. *Chicago Tribune,* September 6, 1921.

265. Ibid., November 14, 1928.

266. Landesco, *Organized Crime in Chicago,* p. 990; *Chicago Tribune,* October 8, 1927.

CHAPTER 4: TORRIO, CAPONE, AND THE BEER WARS: 1922–1927

1. For example, John Kobler, *Capone* (New York: G. P. Putnam, 1971); Robert J. Schoenberg, *Mr. Capone* (New York: William Morrow, 1992); Laurence Bergreen, *Capone* (New York: Simon and Schuster, 1994); and Rose Keefe, *The Man Who Got Away: The Bugs Moran Story* (Nashville: Cumberland House, 2005).

2. Herman N. Bundesen to Major Calvin Goddard, April 1, 1929.

3. *Chicago Tribune,* September 2, 1922.

4. Ibid., September 14, 1923, September 20, 1923.

5. John Landesco, *Organized Crime in Chicago: Part III of the Illinois Crime Survey* (Chicago: Illinois Association for Criminal Justice, 1929), chaps. XX and XXI; Schoenberg, *Mr. Capone,* chap. 7.

6. *Chicago Tribune,* June 9, 1922.

7. Ibid., February 24, 1923; *Chicago Daily News*, February 9, 1923; *Chicago Examiner*, September 21, 1923. Another beer runner was killed by rivals in July on Archer Avenue near the Cal-Sag Channel, between Joliet and Chicago, although his gang affiliation is not known. See *Chicago Tribune*, July 4, 1923.

8. *Chicago Daily News*, September 21, 1923.

9. *Chicago Tribune*, December 5, 1923; n.p., September 10, 1923; *Chicago Tribune*, September 12, 1923; *Chicago Examiner*, September 21, 1923.

10. *Chicago Tribune*, October 19, 1923; Schoenberg, *Mr. Capone*, p. 87.

11. *Chicago Tribune*, October 22, 1925.

12. *Chicago Daily News*, October 24, 1925; Schoenberg, *Mr. Capone*, pp. 90–91.

13. *Chicago Daily News*, September 9, 1923.

14. Walter Noble Burns, *The One-Way Ride* (Garden City, NY: Doubleday, 1931), p. 93; Rose Keefe, *Guns and Roses* (Nashville: Cumberland House, 2003), p. 180.

15. Burns, *One-Way Ride*, pp. 94–95.

16. Ibid., p. 97. Alternatively, Keefe, *Guns and Roses*, p. 184 believes that Weiss not only supported O'Banion in this maneuver, but he most likely was responsible for it.

17. *Los Angeles Times*, October 23, 1926.

18. Schoenberg, *Mr. Capone*, p. 11.

19. *Chicago Daily News*, November 10, 1924.

20. Ibid., November 12, 1924; Maureen McKernan, *Chicago Tribune*, November 13, 1924, p. 4.

21. The CPD's list of suspected killers has Joseph Giunta as the third gunman, rather than Anselmi. See Bundesen to Goddard.

22. James O. Bennett, *Chicago Gangland* (Chicago: Chicago Tribune Co., 1929), p. 55; Burns, *One-Way Ride*, p. 184; Hal Andrews, *X Marks the Spot* (n.p.: Spot Publishing, 1930), p. 30.

23. Rose Keefe, *Man Who Got Away*, p. 163.

24. Andrews, *X Marks the Spot*, p. 23.

25. By his own admission, during Prohibition George Moran was shot on the right side of his neck and in the right thigh in 1925 and 1929, respectively. See *Moran, George C.* (US Department of Justice, Bureau of Prisons, Classification study, February 13, 1957). The former injury almost certainly happened on June 13, 1925, when Moran and Drucci were attacked by Genna gunmen. The 1929 wound occurred in January during an attempt on Moran's life. See also Keefe, *Man Who Got Away*, pp. 232–33.

26. Genevieve Forbes Herrick, *Chicago Tribune,* January 12, 1926, p. 1.

27. Kobler, *Capone,* p. 160.

28. Bennett, *Chicago Gangland,* p. 23.

29. According to the *Chicago Herald and Examiner,* September 21, 1926, the South Side O'Donnell clique was allied with Capone at the time. If so, this is a classic example of the old principle that the enemy ("Spike" O'Donnell) of my enemy (Joe Saltis) is my friend. This article also has the Cook-Vogel gang lined up with the North Siders, probably for the same reasons as the West Side O'Donnells—namely, that a Capone defeat would open up the western suburbs to both groups. The Touhy gang, which was in the northwestern suburbs and is discussed later in this chapter, was also most likely in the North Side coalition in 1926.

30. Anne Bowhay, *Daily Southtown,* September 7, 1993, p. A6.

31. Diane Capone is finishing her own book about her famous grandfather, his wife Mae, and their family. It is a factual account of Al Capone's personal life based on Diane's unique access to her grandmother, other family members, and various documents and photos.

32. William Balsamo, conversation with the author, 2005.

33. Edward D. Sullivan, *Chicago Surrenders* (New York: Vanguard, 1930), pp. 157–58.

34. Bergreen, *Capone.* Much of the material in this section first appeared in Arthur J. Lurigio and John J. Binder, "The Chicago Outfit: Challenging the Myths about Organized Crime," *Journal of Contemporary Criminal Justice* 29 (May 2013): 198–218.

35. Bergreen, *Capone,* p. 406.

36. Matthew J. Luzi, conversation with the author, 1994.

37. Matthew J. Luzi has conducted numerous interviews with relatives of the south suburban bootleggers over the past twenty-five years.

38. John Kass, *Chicago Tribune,* June 11, 2002, September 12, 2003.

39. Lurigio and Binder, "Chicago Outfit," pp. 209–10.

40. *Chicago Tribune,* August 11, 1926.

41. Paul Ricca relative, conversation with the author, 2009.

42. Herrick, *Chicago Tribune.*

43. Kobler, *Capone,* p. 164.

44. *Chicago Tribune,* November 21, 1923, November 11, 1925.

45. Ibid., January 8, 1926.

46. *Melrose Park Leader,* December 10, 1926.

47. *Chicago Daily News,* January 11, 1926.

48. Herrick, *Chicago Tribune.*

49. Andrews, *X Marks the Spot*, p. 26.

50. Jeffrey Gusfield, *Deadly Valentines* (Chicago: Chicago Review Press, 2012).

51. Andrews, *X Marks the Spot*, p. 26.

52. In the case of Edward "Eco" Baldelli, a bullet from his body was ballistically matched to a gun later taken from Jack McGurn (see Bundesen to Goddard). Andrews, *X Marks the Spot* attributes a fourth such killing to McGurn as well.

53. Chicago Crime Commission, "Re: Frank Rio," May 7, 1930.

54. *Chicago Tribune*, February 3, 1916.

55. Ibid., April 30, 1921; Chicago Crime Commission, "Re: Anthony 'Mops' Volpe," October 4, 1930.

56. Chicago Crime Commission, "Re: Paul De Lucia with Aliases; Paul Ricca, Paul Viela, Paul Salvi, Paul Magleo," June 17, 1966.

57. Andrews, *X Marks the Spot*, p. 30.

58. *Chicago Daily News*, March 8, 1928, July 17, 1933; *Chicago Tribune*, February 28, 1929.

59. Bundesen to Goddard. On the other hand, McGurn may have entered the Capone ranks after the McSwiggin murder, and he could have gotten the machine gun involved after the fact.

60. Eghigian, *After Capone: The Life and World of Chicago Mob Boss Frank "The Enforcer" Nitti* (Nashville: Cumberland House, 2006), pp. 119–20.

61. Chicago Crime Commission, "Re: Samuel McPherson Hunt," February 12, 1946.

62. Christine Wiltz, *The Last Madam* (Boston: Da Capo Press, 2001), chap. 5.

63. *Chicago Tribune*, October 25, 1930.

64. Although there was no mention of it at the time, such a long period without any murders or other violence is at minimum consistent with a truce between the North Siders and Capone's gang after John Torrio was shot. Also, Vincent Drucci was arrested by police in a Cadillac dealership on S. Michigan Avenue—across the street from the Metropole Hotel in the heart of Caponedom—in November 1925, which was the last place he would have been if the two gangs were at war. See *Chicago Tribune*, November 15, 1925.

65. Andrews, *X Marks the Spot*, p. 24.

66. Schoenberg, *Mr. Capone*, p. 141. One newspaper account (*Chicago American*, January 26, 1926) blames the rift on the killing of gangster Willie Dickman on September 3, 1925, which was supposedly an internal Saltis-Sheldon matter that irked Sheldon. A different source (*Chicago Daily*

News, October 20, 1925) has Dickman already separated from the gang, indicating that Sheldon had previously left Saltis. If the latter account is correct, then Sheldon went his own way at least a month before the attack on the Ragen Colts' clubhouse.

67. *Chicago American*, January 26, 1926.

68. *Chicago Tribune*, March 12, 1927.

69. Kobler, *Capone*, p. 138.

70. Ibid., p. 139; Chicago Crime Commission, "Re: Jacob Guzik," April 19, 1955, p. 2.

71. *Chicago Tribune*, October 17, 1925.

72. Schoenberg, *Mr. Capone*, pp. 150–51.

73. Luzi, *Boys in Chicago Heights*, chaps. 2 and 3.

74. Similarly, Mrs. Katherine Jones and her lover, alky cooker Frank Passani, were killed in separate shootings on October 12, 1927, after she passed information Passani gave her about illicit stills to authorities in exchange for reward money. *Chicago Tribune*, October 15, 1927. The Chicago Heights gangsters also almost certainly killed Leroy Gilbert, the police chief of South Chicago Heights, on December 6, 1928.

75. *Chicago Daily News*, August 20, 1926.

76. *Chicago Tribune*, August 21, 1926, September 3, 1926, and September 13, 1926.

77. At one time the Heights guys were also reported to be operating in the Kensington police district on the far South Side of Chicago, through Lorenzo Juliano. *Chicago Tribune*, April 1, 1928.

78. Chicago Crime Commission, "Re: Martin F. Guilfoyle, aka 'Marty' Guilfoyle," October 10, 1946; *Chicago Tribune*, September 19, 1952, March 9, 1958; *Chicago Sun-Times*, September 19, 1952.

79. Warren Baker, *Chicago Tribune*, October 11, 1942; *Chicago Tribune*, September 3, 1908.

80. *Chicago Tribune*, February 17, 1907, November 18, 1909.

81. Juvenile Protective Association, *Wheeling, Illinois, A-139* (August 24, 1929), University of Illinois at Chicago, Richard J. Daley Library, Department of Special Collections.

82. *Chicago Tribune*, October 12, 1929.

83. Ibid., May 5, 1918, December 9, 1920; Oscar Hewitt, *Chicago Tribune*, January 22, 1924; *Franklin Park Beacon*, December 30, 1927; Roger Touhy, *The Stolen Years* (Cleveland: Pennington Press, 1959), p. 66.

84. *Basil Hugh Banghart*, Admission Summary, US Penitentiary, Alcatraz Island, California (October 1, 1943).

85. Touhy, *Stolen Years*, chap. 6.

86. *Chicago Tribune*, April 29, 1934.

87. Ibid., March 17, 1933.

88. Ibid., August 27, 1933.

89. Keefe, 2005, pp. 191–92.

90. For example, Kobler, *Capone*, p. 190; Keefe, *Man Who Got Away*, p. 237.

91. *Chicago Tribune*, September 22, 1926; Schoenberg, *Mr. Capone*, pp. 159–60.

92. *Chicago Tribune*, September 22, 1926. The *Tribune* also has Dominic Nuccio of the Gloriana gang and Danny Vallo among the shooters. This is highly unlikely because Vallo was not otherwise associated with the North Siders and, in fact, is usually described as a Capone ally. Nuccio's inclusion on this list may be a simple misunderstanding. His nickname was "Libby," and Earl "Hymie" Weiss's girlfriend, whose car was used in the attack, went by Josephine Libby. See Reedy, *Gang War Memo* (Chicago: *Chicago Tribune* files, October 1, 1926). Neither of Nuccio's wives was named Josephine, although there was another Dominic Nuccio living in Chicago whose wife was named Josephine, which may be part of the broader confusion on who owned this particular car.

93. Confidential source close to Ricca family, conversation with the author, 2009.

94. *Chicago Daily News*, September 20, 1926; Kobler, *Mr. Capone*, p. 191.

95. *Chicago Daily News*, September 20, 1926. According to other accounts (see, for example, *Chicago Tribune*, September 22, 1926), Capone was not inside the Hawthorne at the time of the attack, but was in a restaurant a few doors away. Perhaps Capone ran out the back door of the Hawthorne during the shooting and went to a building a few feet away where he was found after the attack.

96. Bundesen to Goddard.

97. Eghigian, *After Capone*, p. 124.

98. *Los Angeles Times*, October 23, 1926.

99. *Chicago Tribune*, October 21, 1926.

100. Hal Andrews, "Gangsters Grip Chicago!" *Real Detective* 26 (September 1932): p. 89.

101. *Chicago Tribune*, December 15, 1930.

102. Ibid., June 12, 1927.

103. *Chicago Daily News*, July 25, 1927.

104. Jessie F. Binford, *Brief Summary of the Report Submitted to the Board of Directors of the Juvenile Protective Association* (n. d.).

105. *Chicago Daily News*, June 20, November 22, 1927.

106. To aid Cicero's gambling fraternity, in 1927 the Western State bank at Twenty-Second Street and Cicero Avenue installed an after-hours deposit chute so gambling house proprietors would not have to take the winnings for the day home late at night and risk being robbed. *Chicago Tribune*, April 3, 1927.

107. Daniel Russell, "The Road House: A Study of Commercialized Amusements in the Environs of Chicago" (master's thesis: University of Chicago, 1931), p. 92.

108. *Chicago Daily News*, August 20, 1927.

109. *Chicago Tribune*, November 8, 1927, November 9, 1927.

110. *Chicago Daily News*, November 29, 1927, December 22, 1927.

111. Ibid., January 26, 1928.

112. Ibid. In January 1928 the syndicate was taking 50 percent of the net revenue on horse race betting from each gambling place, while table games were allowed to run without paying off. The police crackdown on gambling in Chicago continued into January.

113. Ibid., June 24, 1927, June 25, 1927.

114. *Chicago Tribune*, November 20, 1928. The two politicians were almost certainly once again Charles Fitzmorris and William Reid. "Barney" Bertsche, the leader of the North Side gambling syndicate in early 1927, once operated a saloon. Other articles refer to a citywide vice and gambling syndicate, indicating that the same people were involved in both.

115. Jessie Binford, *Report Submitted to the Board of Directors*; *Chicago Tribune*, May 22, 1928. The data on vice operations in Walter C. Reckless, *Vice in Chicago* (Chicago: University of Chicago Press, 1933), table 57 indicate that from 1924 to 1927 activity had shifted away from the Near South Side, although it still was the busiest area in the city, and toward the Near North Side and to Uptown and Lakeview, which were even farther north.

116. *Chicago Tribune*, July 24, 1927.

117. Russell, "Road House," p. 51.

118. *Chicago Tribune*, November 17, 1926.

119. Ibid., January 21, 1925.

120. Ibid., December 4, 1925.

121. Ibid., September 16, 1925.

122. Thomas Wren, *Chicago Tribune*, November 13, 1927.

123. *Chicago Tribune*, December 17, 1927, February 22, 1929.

124. Ibid., October 15, 1926.

125. Walter Roth, "Frankie Foster: Did He Really Murder Jake Lingle?" *Chicago Jewish History* 28 (Winter 2005): 8–9.

126. James Doherty, March 4, 1951, March 11, 1951.

127. *Chicago Tribune*, November 10, 1926, December 18, 1926, February 21, 1928.

128. Ibid., January 1, 1927.

129. An article about two years later asserts that Clements was actually killed inside the Ragen's Colts' clubhouse by Michael "Bubs" Quinlan. See *Chicago Tribune*, October 18, 1928. This claim, along with where the body was found—east of Halsted in the Sheldon-Stanton lands—suggests that the Clements murder was an internal gang matter. Unless, of course, Quinlan killed him at the behest of the Saltis-McErlane gang before he went over to them. Calvin Goddard matched a slug taken out of the body to a gun that was confiscated from either Hugh "Stubby" McGovern or George Maloney, which suggests that the Saltis gang was directly involved in the slaying of Clements.

130. *Chicago Tribune*, March 13, 1927.

131. Fred J. Schlotfeldt to Henry Barrett Chamberlain, November 25, 1930.

132. *Chicago Tribune*, September 12, 1926.

133. *Chicago Herald and Examiner*, November 22, 1927.

134. *Chicago Tribune*, November 27, 1927.

135. Ibid., July 1, 1927.

136. Burns, *One-Way Ride*, p. 226.

137. Ibid., p. 271.

138. It is worth noting that the CPD (see Bundesen to Goddard) attributes only the Torchio killing to McGurn. Several contemporary sources claim that Spicuzza and Russo were Capone men who were killed by the Moran gang and Valenti was reportedly from Taylor Street and most likely an Aiello gunman. *Chicago Daily News*, August 11, 1927; Andrews, *X Marks the Spot*, p. 38; *Chicago Tribune*, September 25, 1927.

139. *Chicago Tribune*, September 8, 1928.

140. Ibid., July 14, 1927, July 18, 1927.

141. Ibid., July 27, 1927. There were a number of gangland killings around Chicago Heights during 1927 and early 1928. However, most of these deaths appear to have been related to disciplining hijackers and others who broke the rules of the underworld, rather than due to the war for control of the Heights. *Chicago Tribune*, January 19, 1928. An exception is Joe Martino, the last of the pre-1926 gang leaders in the Heights, who was murdered on November 30, 1928.

CHAPTER 5: THE BEER WARS: 1927–1930

1. *Chicago Tribune,* November 22, 1927; *Chicago Daily News,* November 22, 1927.

2. *Chicago Daily News,* July 14, 1930.

3. Chicago Crime Commission, "Re: Jack Zuta," n.d., p. A.

4. *Chicago Daily News,* November 21, 1927.

5. Ibid., December 22, 1927.

6. *Chicago Tribune,* June 21, 1928.

7. Ibid., March 25, 1930.

8. There were rumors of a truce on November 23, but this appears, in light of the violence that soon followed, to be incorrect or to have been extremely short-lived. *Chicago Tribune,* November 24, 1927.

9. *Chicago Daily News,* July 16, 1928; *Chicago Tribune,* March 25, 1930.

10. *Chicago Tribune,* September 19, 1952. Beer-runner Charles Miller was supposedly selling in the Touhys' bailiwick, and John Touhy was most likely accidentally shot by his own men in the gun battle at the Lone Tree Inn that killed Miller. According to Rose Keefe, *The Man Who Got Away: The Bugs Moran Story* (Nashville, TN: Cumberland House, 2005), pp. 216–18, this was a Capone invasion of Touhy territory, and the death of John Touhy enraged George Moran and brought him into a new conflict with the Capone gang.

11. *Chicago Daily News,* January 5, 1928.

12. *Chicago Tribune,* September 8, 1928.

13. Chicago Crime Commission, "Re: Dominick Nuccio, alias Dominic Nuccio, Dominick Nutcchio, 'Libby' Nuccio, Hoodlum and Gambler," June 27, 1951; *Chicago Tribune,* September 5, 1930.

14. Walter Noble Burns, *The One-Way Ride* (Garden City, NY: Doubleday, 1931), pp. 270–71.

15. *Chicago Tribune,* May 7, 1928.

16. Ibid., October 24, 1930.

17. Herman N. Bundesen to Major Calvin Goddard, April 1, 1929.

18. *Chicago Tribune,* August 28, 1928, September 8, 1928, and September 9, 1928.

19. Bundesen to Goddard; William Balsamo, conversation with the author, 2001; *Chicago Tribune,* September 8, 1928; Robert J. Schoenberg, *Mr. Capone* (New York: William Morrow, 1992), p. 205.

20. Although his last name is usually spelled Guinta, his monument in Mt. Carmel Cemetery in Hillside, Illinois, bears the name Joseph Giunta. I am grateful to Mario Gomes for helping clarify this issue.

21. *Chicago Tribune*, January 10, 1929.

22. Ibid., February 28, 1929.

23. Schoenberg, *Mr. Capone*, p. 206.

24. *Chicago Tribune*, January 10, 1929.

25. The CPD lists Pete Gusenberg, James Clark, and Frank Foster as the killers (Bundesen to Goddard). Other sources claim that Mrs. Lolordo definitely identified Joe Aiello as one of the gunmen, although this was later retracted. *Chicago Tribune*, January 9, 1929. Although Lolordo's wife blamed Aiello for her husband's murder, she later described the shooters as non-Italians. *Chicago Tribune*, March 5, 1929. However, Aiello was surely involved, because it is hard to imagine Lolordo meeting with a contingent of Moran gunsels to discuss underworld matters unless he arranged it.

26. In the 1910 US Census and on his tombstone his first name appears as Reinhart.

27. Keefe, *Man Who Got Away*, p. 235.

28. John Kobler, *Capone* (New York: G. P. Putnam, 1971), chap. 17; Robert J. Schoenberg, *Mr. Capone* (New York: William Morrow, 1992), chap. 20; Laurence Bergreen, *Capone* (New York: Simon and Schuster, 1994), chap. 7.

29. Kobler, *Capone*, chap. 17.

30. Bergreen, *Capone*, chap. 7.

31. Schoenberg, *Mr. Capone*, chap. 20.

32. William J. Helmer and Arthur J. Bilek, *The St. Valentine's Day Massacre* (Nashville: Cumberland House, 2004) compile, extend, and analyze this material. Unless noted otherwise, the evidence that follows can be found in their book.

33. Some authors, such as William F. Roemer, *Accardo: The Genuine Godfather* (New York: Donald I. Fine, 1995), p. 51, minimize the criminal careers of Burke and his associates. In reality they were at the top of the game as robbers and guns for hire. For example, Burke was labeled by the police as "the most dangerous criminal in America" in 1931, and one crime-fighting group asserted that his gang was responsible for about 25 percent of the daylight bank robberies in the country. *Chicago Tribune*, April 20, 1931, September 14, 1931. Although the latter claim may be somewhat exaggerated, if it is even half true it shows that Burke and his henchmen were highly professional and important in the criminal world. For a full history of Burke's nefarious deeds, Chriss Lyon, *A Killing in Capone's Playground* (Holland, MI: In-Depth Editions, 2014) is highly recommended.

34. John J. Binder and Matthew J. Luzi, "Al Capone and Friends," *Criminal Organizations* 10 (Winter 1996): 16–22; Matthew J. Luzi, *The Boys in Chicago Heights* (Charleston: History Press, 2012), p. 51.

35. Binder and Luzi, "Al Capone and Friends."

36. *Chicago Daily News*, December 23, 1929; *Chicago Tribune*, April 3, 1929.

37. *Chicago Tribune*, March 5, 1929, October 10, 1929.

38. John J. Binder, *The Chicago Outfit* (Charleston: Arcadia Publishing, 2003), p. 38; Confidential source, conversation with the author, 2003.

39. J. Edgar Hoover, *Memorandum for Mr. Joseph B. Keenan, Acting Attorney General* (August 27, 1936); FBI, "Re: St. Valentine's Day Massacre," October 26, 1936.

40. Jonathan Eig, *Get Capone: The Secret Plot That Captured America's Most Wanted Gangster* (New York: Simon and Schuster, 2010, 2011).

41. Frank T. Farrell to J. Edgar Hoover, January 28, 1935, FBI file on the St. Valentine's Day Massacre. Regarding Farrell's middle name, Hoover's brief response was addressed to "Frank F. Farrell." While the middle initial in Farrell's handwritten signature on the letter to Hoover looks like an "F" or a "T," the writer was clearly Frank Thomas Farrell. For instance, the signature on his draft registration card in 1918 matches that on the Farrell letter. Also, Frank T. Farrell lists himself in the 1940 US Census as a self-employed private detective who works on major US crimes.

42. Much of the following discussion was originally written by the author as a section of an article on Mario Gomes's website. See Mario Gomes, "Discounted Valentine Massacre Theories," http://www.myalcaponemuseum.com/id173.htm (accessed 2011). It appears more recently in Arthur J. Lurigio and John J. Binder, "The Chicago Outfit: Challenging the Myths about Organized Crime," *Journal of Contemporary Criminal Justice* 29 (May 2013): 198–218.

43. Bundesen to Goddard; Burns, *One-Way Ride*, pp. 271–72.

44. *Chicago Tribune*, March 25, 1926, July 11, 1929; Chicago Crime Commission, "In Re: William (Three Fingered Jack) White, Public Enemy," May 2, 1930.

45. Eig, *Get Capone* (2010).

46. Chuck Goudie, "Dead Wrong," (Chicago: ABC television, Channel 7 investigative report, June 3, 2010). Eig later added this sentence to the paperback edition of his book *Get Capone* (2011), p. 252: "White was supposed to be locked up in the county jail at the time, according to Farrell, but bribed his way out whenever business or personal matters required."

47. *Chicago Tribune,* September 19, 1925.

48. Ibid., October 15, 1925.

49. Mike Royko, *Boss* (New York: E.P. Dutton, 1971), chap. 6.

50. *Chicago Tribune,* June 12, 1929.

51. *Chicago Evening Post,* June 11, 1929.

52. *Chicago Daily Journal,* June 11, 1929.

53. As discussed below, White joined George "Red" Barker in early 1930. By that time Barker was with the West Side O'Donnell gang, working as its point man on labor racketeering, most likely because Barker's earlier associates were all dead or gone.

54. Eig, *Get Capone,* p. 253.

55. Chicago Crime Commission, "Re: William 'Three Finger Jack' White," August 8, 1930.

56. Fred D. Pasley, *Muscling In* (New York: Ives Washburn, 1931), p. 22.

57. *Chicago Tribune,* February 13, 1930.

58. Furthermore, Eig, *Get Capone* (2010), p. 252 claims, "White knew both the Gusenberg brothers. They'd worked together in 1926 on the $80,000 robbery of the International Harvester factory," and he cites the *Chicago Tribune,* March 8, 1926, as the source of this information. On March 7, 1926, the *Tribune* actually states that eighteen men were picked up as suspects in that case and, although Peter and Frank Gusenberg resembled two of the robbers, "There were no positive identifications." *Chicago Tribune,* March 7, 1926. The article Eig directly references distances them even further from the crime, stating that "all efforts so far to connect them with the crime have failed." *Chicago Tribune,* March 8, 1926. In fact, the Gusenbergs were never tied to that robbery.

59. Eig, *Get Capone* (2010), p. 252.

60. *Statement of Sergt. Thomas J. Loftus, 36th District* (February 14, 1929), CPD report; Ron Koziol and George Estep, *Chicago Tribune,* February 14, 1983. This paragraph owes much to the insightful article by Koziol and Estep, which they wrote when the original police reports were discovered. I have also had numerous discussions with Bryan Morey, which took place while he was writing a term paper on the use of original source material—and carefully searching for the relevant documents—in the study of the St. Valentine's Day Massacre. See Brian Morey, "Problems of Evidence in the Saint Valentine's Day Massacre" (course paper, History 500, Hillsdale College, April 20, 2015).

61. *Murder of Seven Men at 2122 N. Clark Street, Report—Lieut. Otto Erlanson & Squad 41A* (February 14, 1929), CPD report.

62. Helmer and Bilek, *St. Valentine's Day Massacre,* pp. 7–8.

63. Eig, *Get Capone,* p. 250.

64. This author was the first to explicitly dispel this notion. See Binder, "Chicago Outfit," p. 40.

65. *Chicago Tribune,* February 15, 1929.

66. *Chicago Herald and Examiner,* February 15, 1929.

67. *Chicago Tribune,* October 10, 1929; *New York Times,* August 2, 1932; Pasley, *Muscling In,* p. 38; John H. Lyle, *The Dry and Lawless Years* (New York: Prentice-Hall, 1960), p. 227; Bergreen, *Capone,* pp. 305, 309, and 315.

68. Keefe, *Man Who Got Away,* p. 238.

69. Schoenberg, *Mr. Capone,* pp. 233–34.

70. *New York Times,* May 18, 1929; "Philadelphia Justice for Chicago's Al Capone," *Literary Digest,* June 15, 1929, pp. 32, 34, states that this was a meeting of Chicago gangsters.

71. *Chicago Tribune,* May 18, 1929.

72. Burns, *One-Way Ride,* p. 307.

73. *Chicago Daily News,* September 9, 1929.

74. *New York Times,* May 18, 1929; "Philadelphia Justice for Capone," *Literary Digest.*

75. n.p., April 7, 1930.

76. Ibid.; *Chicago Daily News,* September 9, 1929, February 7, 1930, and March 4, 1930; *Chicago Tribune,* January 22, 1928.

77. "Philadelphia Justice for Capone," *Literary Digest.*

78. Ibid.

79. *Chicago Tribune,* May 30, 1929.

80. Ibid., September 17, 1931.

81. Ibid., September 12, 1929, December 30, 1929.

82. Ibid., August 27, 1929.

83. n.p., April 7, 1930.

84. *Chicago Tribune,* December 3, 1929.

85. *Chicago Daily News,* July 14, 1930.

86. Archibald McKinlay, "Calumet Roots: Price of Protection Added Up for East," *Northwest Indiana Times,* March 16, 1997, http://www.nwitimes.com/uncategorized/calumet-roots-price-of-protection-added-up-for-east/article_ce98664b-62a3-5043-925b-410d9d6d3326.html (accessed July 22, 2013).

87. *Chicago Tribune,* January 14, 1923.

88. Ibid., August 4, 1924.

89. Ibid., January 18, 1930.

90. Binder, "Chicago Outfit," p. 28; Luzi, *Boys from Chicago Heights*, p. 31; *Chicago Tribune*, July 26, 1927.

91. *Chicago Tribune*, June 6, 1931, July 5, 1931, and January 16, 1932. The Capone links to places as far away as Nebraska are not surprising. In 1925 the Gennas had connections to Omaha bootlegger Charlie Hutter, and in 1927 the Capone gang helped Gene Livingston build a massive still in that city. Jon L. Blecha, *Cigars and Wires* (Omaha: Jon L. Blecha, 2012), pp. 32, 40.

92. *Chicago Tribune*, March 26, 1929.

93. Ibid., December 20, 1946.

94. Ibid., May 29, 1931, April 14, 1932.

95. Ibid., February 28, 1929, March 15, 1930; Joseph Brown, "The Unwelcomed Visitor: Al Capone in Miami," *South Beach Magazine*, August 13, 2007, http://www.southbeachmagazine.com/the-unwelcomed-visitor-al-capone-in-miami/ (accessed July 22, 2013).

96. I am grateful to organized crime historian Allan May for bringing this to my attention.

97. *Chicago Tribune*, December 23, 1931.

98. Walter Roth, "Frankie Foster: Did He Really Murder Jake Lingle?" *Chicago Jewish History* 28 (Winter 2005).

99. *Los Angeles Times*, October 8, 1950.

100. *Chicago Daily News*, November 28, 1927.

101. Andrews, *X Marks the Spot*, p. 47.

102. *Chicago Daily News*, July 23, 1928; Andrews, *X Marks the Spot*, p. 47.

103. *Chicago Daily News*, July 23, 1928; n.p., July 23, 1928; *Chicago Evening Post*, December 31, 1928.

104. John Landesco to Ernest W. Burgess, June 26, 1929.

105. Curiously, Capone gangster Thomas Johnson was, based on later ballistic tests, killed by Saltis-McErlane gunner George Maloney on March 31, 1928. *Chicago Tribune*, March 31, 1928. It is possible that in this case the Saltis gang was again involved in the North Side vs. South Side gang struggle, but given the surrounding events it seems more likely that this was not related to the bootlegging wars.

106. *Chicago Tribune*, February 9, 1929; Landesco to Burgess. Guy L. Nichols, "Report," *Wickersham Report: Seventy-First Congress: Enforcement of the Prohibition Laws: Official Records of the National Commission on Law Observance and Enforcement: A Prohibition Survey of the State of Illinois: Part II, Vol. 4* (Washington, DC: US Government Printing Office, 1931), pp. 301–302 states that when it was announced that Allman would take over the

Stockyards police district in April 1929, where Danny Stanton controlled the bootlegging, all liquor shipments ceased and as soon as Allman was in charge, before any raids occurred, all saloons closed.

107. Andrews, *X Marks the Spot*, pp. 48, 51. The De Coursey gang had either drifted out of the picture by this point in time or it was focused on the production of alcohol rather than the selling of beer and was possibly part of Stanton's (Capone's) operations. Certainly by 1930 Thomas De Coursey was, according to the US Census, living on a farm in Wisconsin.

108. *Chicago Tribune*, September 21, 1923.

109. *Chicago Daily News*, December 31, 1928.

110. Ibid., October 18, 1928.

111. Landesco to Burgess.

112. *Chicago Daily News*, June 1, 1929.

113. *Chicago Tribune*, November 17, 1929; Andrews, *X Marks the Spot*, p. 47.

114. Landesco to Burgess.

115. *Chicago Tribune*, September 1, 1929.

116. *Chicago Daily News*, October 8, 1931; *Chicago Tribune*, October 9, 1931.

117. *Chicago Tribune*, March 6, 1930.

118. Andrews, *X Marks the Spot*, p. 52; *Chicago Tribune*, March 7, 1930.

119. *Chicago Tribune*, March 9, 1930.

120. n.p., March 25, 1930; n. p., April 29, 1930.

121. When shotgunners fired on July 16, 1930, at a house two doors north of Spike O'Donnell's residence the police were convinced that the buckshot was meant for O'Donnell. *Chicago Tribune*, July 16, 1930. This appears, however, to have been unrelated to the Beer Wars or to have been an isolated, unimportant incident because there were no other attacks on the South Side O'Donnells from November 1928 through March 1931.

122. *Chicago Daily News*, November 22, 1927; *Chicago Tribune*, February 5, 1928.

123. *Chicago Daily News*, February 7, 1930.

124. For example, in 1928 Johnny Armando and Sammy Kaplan from this group are described as Capone gangsters. There is also evidence of friction between the Valley Gang and the Twentieth Ward Jewish crowd, which would have hastened the demise of the latter as a separate entity. *Chicago Daily News*, November 30, 1927; *Chicago Tribune*, August 10, 1928.

125. *Chicago Daily News*, March 4, 1930.

126. *Chicago Tribune*, September 27, 1930.

127. Luzi, *Boys in Chicago Heights,* pp. 44–45.

128. *Chicago Tribune,* June 2, 1928.

129. Ibid., September 14, 1931.

130. Ibid., December 18, 1932.

131. Based on one account, Binder, *Chicago Outfit,* p. 27 states that Pregenzer was a Moran backer. However, further newspaper articles make it clear that Pregenzer was allied with Druggan and Lake and that he was a Moran enemy, at least at the time the latter moved into Lake County.

132. *Chicago Daily News,* June 17, 1929, June 18, 1929.

133. *Chicago Tribune,* June 18, 1929.

134. Ibid., March 23, 1928.

135. *Chicago Daily News,* February 7, 1930.

136. *The Citizen-Advertiser,* February 8, 1932.

137. *Chicago Daily News,* January 26, 1928; *Chicago Tribune,* January 26, 1928.

138. *Chicago Tribune,* March 28, 1928.

139. In Chicago, the hoodlums were only able to intimidate politicians below the level of the mayor. The mayor had thousands of police officers under his command, could call on the Illinois National Guard and, if necessary, the US Army for assistance.

140. Lloyd Wendt and Herman Kogan, *Lords of the Levee* (Indianapolis: Bobbs-Merrill Company, 1943), pp. 344–45.

141. *Chicago Daily News,* April 25, 1930.

142. George Murray, *The Legacy of Al Capone* (New York: G. P. Putnam, 1975), p. 149.

143. *Chicago Tribune,* March 25, 1932.

144. Schoenberg, *Mr. Capone,* pp. 197, 220.

145. *Chicago Tribune,* December 27, 1928.

146. Ibid., November 28, 1928.

147. Ibid., April 30, 1929.

148. Ibid., February 16, 1929.

149. Ibid., January 5, 1929.

150. Moley, Sept. 20, 1931.

151. *Chicago Tribune,* December 11, 1923.

152. Edwin W. Sims, "Fighting Crime in Chicago: The Crime Commission," *Journal of the American Institute of Criminal Law and Criminology* 11 (May 1920): 21–28; George E. Simpson, "The CCC," *Journal of Criminal Law and Criminology* 26 (September 1935): 401–20.

153. *Chicago Tribune,* April 24, 1930, August 1, 1931.

154. Gerhardt Meyne of the CCC, in a letter to top law enforcement officials, cataloged the large number of men on the first list who had been arrested for or convicted of a crime during roughly the year following its publication. See Gerhardt F. Meyne to Judge John P. McGoorty et al., June 4, 1931. The Public Enemy lists, which appeared in the newspapers after 1931, were created by the CPD, rather than the CCC, and focused more heavily on common criminals.

155. *Chicago Tribune,* February 9, 1930. According to Tom Barnard (conversation with the author, November 13, 2013), the problems at the site were with the Hoisting Engineers' Union. At the time, this union was controlled by William Maloney and it worked closely with labor racketeer George "Red" Barker (*Chicago Tribune,* March 26, 1943). However, Barker was not yet a member of the Capone gang. Therefore, if the Secret Six targeted Al Capone, who was in a Pennsylvania prison in February 1930, above and beyond other Chicago racketeers, it correctly identified the worst gangland threat to Chicago—but paradoxically not the man who was responsible for the Meagher shooting.

156. Dennis E. Hoffman, *Business vs. Organized Crime: Chicago's Private War on Al Capone, 1929–1932* (Chicago: CCC, 1989), pp. 12–13.

157. Hoffman, *Business vs. Organized Crime*; Barnard, conversation with the author, November 13, 2013. Harrison Barnard names himself as a member of the Secret Six in his scrapbook, which is in the possession of his family. Hoffman, *Business vs. Organized Crime,* pp. 13–15, 24–25, working under the belief that there were six members in total, points to Randolph, Loesch, Gore, Insull, Paddock, and Rosenwald. Rosenwald was a major financial supporter of the group, which is consistent with his membership. *New York Times,* January 21, 1932. In fact, Insull was the largest contributor, followed by Rosenwald, to the CAC committee that oversaw and funded the Secret Six. See Harold Stewart to Nathan Levin, November 20, 1931.

158. Wainwright Evans, "Fighting a Crime Organization," *Nation's Business,* December 8, 1920, p. 17.

159. *Chicago Tribune,* October 31, 1930.

160. Hoffman, *Business vs. Organized Crime,* p. 17.

161. *Chicago Tribune,* January 22, 1933, April 16, 1933.

162. Wayne Johnson, conversation with the author, October 13, 2013. In the one such incident described by Randolph that can be identified, see Dennis E. Hoffman, *Scarface Al and the Crime Crusaders* (Carbondale, IL: Southern Illinois University Press, 2010), p. 144, four Chicago police officers and an undercover investigator, all of whom worked for the

Cook County State's Attorney's Office, were involved in a gun battle with robbers. *Chicago Tribune,* May 12, 14, 1930. In fact, Colonel Randolph was exaggerating when he called these five individuals "our men" since they were with the state's attorney's office.

163. Hoffman, *Scarface Al,* chap. 3.

164. The sources disagree on who led this deputation. Hoffman, *Scarface Al,* p. 51 names Loesch as the leader while Judge John Lyle (see *Chicago Tribune,* December 4, 1960) asserts that it was Colonel Robert McCormick of the *Chicago Tribune.* Elmer L. Irey and William J. Slocum, *The Tax Dodgers* (New York: Greenberg, 1948), p. 26, based on a statement by President Herbert Hoover, put Frank Knox at the head of the group. But this is most likely an error because Knox had no direct association with Chicago until he purchased the *Chicago Daily News* in 1931, and as late as 1930 he was still living in New Hampshire. Hoover and Irey may have confused McCormick with Knox, since both published Chicago newspapers not long after the meeting took place. Col. McCormick himself states that he first brought the problems to Hoover's attention. See Robert R. McCormick, *Memoirs: Thompson, Part II: Address by Colonel Robert R. McCormick* (Chicago: n. p., July 17, 1954).

165. Douglas Perry, *Eliot Ness: The Rise and Fall of an American Hero* (New York: Viking, 2014), pp. 51–52. Through diligent research, Scott Sroka, the grandson of Prohibition agent Joe Leeson of the Untouchables squad, obtained the personnel records of Ness's men, which pinpoint when the special detail was formed. Obviously, the October 1930 date conflicts with the claim that Ness was given overall command on September 28, 1929, and that this unit was created shortly thereafter. See Eliot Ness and Oscar Fraley, *The Untouchables* [New York: Julian Messner, Inc., 1957], pp. 19–25. There is, however, an element of truth in what Ness and Fraley wrote. The *Chicago Tribune,* September 21, 1929, reports that George E. Q. Johnson, Alexander Jamie, and others from Chicago met the previous day with authorities in the nation's capital to attack "the sources of the bootleggers' supply and get at the revenue which finances the organized gangs." This is exactly what the Untouchables unit was designed to do. Perhaps Ness was part of the group that met in Washington, DC, in September 1929, and then he received command of the unit when it was created in October 1930.

166. George E. Q. Johnson Jr., conversation with the author, 2001. Ness was connected to George E.Q. Johnson through his much older brother-in-law, Alexander Jamie.

167. Eliot Ness, *Civil Service Papers* (April 6, 1942); "Eliot Ness, Illinois,

Cook County, Birth Certificate," Illinois, https://familysearch.org/ark:/61903/1:1:QKDZ-S24W (accessed August 14, 2016).

168. *Chicago Tribune*, March 24, 1928.

169. Ibid., April 5, 1929.

170. Ibid., September 13, 1929.

171. *Chicago Daily News*, September 9, 1929.

172. Ibid., June 3, 1930, June 13, 1930.

173. *Chicago Tribune*, May 7, 1928.

174. *Chicago Daily News*, March 15, 1928; Robert Lombardo, "The Black Mafia: African-American Organized Crime in Chicago 1890–1965," *Crime, Law, and Social Change* 38 (July 2002): p. 48.

175. *Chicago Tribune*, April 5, 1928.

176. Ibid., September 29, 1928.

177. *Chicago Daily News*, December 29, 1928.

178. *Chicago Tribune*, May 7, 1928.

179. n. p., April 7, 1930.

180. Walter C. Reckless, *Vice in Chicago* (Chicago: University of Chicago Press, 1933), table 57.

181. *Chicago Daily News*, June 13, 1930.

182. Committee of Fifteen, *Annual Report-1930* (Chicago: Committee of Fifteen, 1931).

183. Juvenile Protective Association, *Road-House Survey*, University of Illinois at Chicago, Richard J. Daley Library, Department of Special Collections (July 25–August 31, 1929).

184. Ibid., p. 6.

185. *Chicago Tribune*, August 25, 1930.

186. Juvenile Protective Association, *Wheeling, Illinois, A-139*, University of Illinois at Chicago, Richard J. Daley Library, Department of Special Collections (August 24, 1929), p. 4.

187. Although Morton Grove is far from Saltis's district near the Union Stockyards, this is consistent with the broad Atlantic City peace agreement, which Saltis attended, and the resulting intergang cooperation. It is probably also related to the police shutdown of the New City district at the time, because Saltis would have had an excess capacity of beer and liquor that he could have sold elsewhere, in cooperation with other gangs.

188. Juvenile Protective Association, *Morton's* [Sic] *Grove Illinois Commercialized Vice*, University of Illinois at Chicago, Richard J. Daley Library, Department of Special Collections (May 11–26, 1929).

189. *Chicago Tribune*, November 11, 1930.

190. Ibid., June 4, 1928.

191. Owen P. White, "Looting the Loop" *Collier's* (May 12, 1928).

192. *Chicago Tribune*, May 9, 1930.

193. Ibid., February 15, 1930.

194. Ibid., December 28, 1929.

195. Ibid., April 21, 1930.

196. The closeness of the two gangs is evidenced by CPD chief of detectives John Stege referring to it as the "Capone-O'Donnell" group, and that Barker and White provided blood transfusions for Valley gangster and Capone ally George Druggan after the Fox Lake Massacre. *Chicago Tribune*, June 2, 1930; *Chicago Daily Times*, June 2, 1930.

197. *Chicago Tribune*, September 1, 1930.

198. Ibid., November 14, 1928, February 22, 1929.

199. Ibid., August 31, 1930.

200. Ibid., March 20, 1943.

201. Ibid., May 27, 1928.

202. Ibid., April 14, 1929.

203. Ibid., April 5, 1936. Several other union officials were killed during 1929 and 1930, but these incidents were most likely due to internal issues in these organizations as opposed to inroads by the bootleggers. Much of the violence in the business racketeering area was in the form of bombings, since the targets were often recalcitrant business owners whose property was vulnerable. For example, 60 percent of the bombings in Chicago during the first half of 1929 were related to business rackets. *Chicago Tribune*, July 16, 1929.

204. *Chicago Tribune*, October 10, 1963.

205. Roemer, *Accardo*, pp. 404–405.

206. Gus Russo, *The Outfit* (New York: Bloomsbury, 2001), p. 472.

207. David F. Musto, *The American Disease: Origins of Narcotic Control* (Oxford: Oxford University Press, 1999), chap. 1.

208. Ibid., p. 107.

209. Jill Jonnes, *Hep-Cats, Narcs, and Pipe Dreams* (Baltimore: Johns Hopkins University Press, 1996), pp. 25, 52; *Chicago Tribune*, June 21, 1915.

210. *Chicago Tribune*, March 12, 1915, December 6, 1918, December 7, 1918, and August 15, 1925.

211. W. A. Evans, *Chicago Tribune*, July 26, 1919, January 21, 1920.

212. *Chicago Tribune*, August 11, 1925. According to C. Alexander Hortis, *The Mob and the City* (Amherst, NY: Prometheus Books, 2014), p. 130, New York City was during this period "the center of the transatlantic

drug trade." This indicates that certain drugs from Europe entered the country in large quantities via that city.

213. Andrews, *X Marks the Spot*, p. 4.

214. *Chicago Daily Times*, February 17, 1931.

215. *Chicago Daily News*, April 25, 1930; New Republic Staff, "Al Capone Was Sent to Prison, But Still Beat the Courts," *New Republic*, July 1, 1931, https://newrepublic.com/article/116246/al-capone-1931-prison-conviction-tax-evasion (accessed August 5, 2016).

216. Martin Booth, *Opium* (New York: St. Martin's Press, 1996), pp. 197, 243.

217. George K. Turner, "The City of Chicago: A Study of Great Immoralities," *McClure's* (April 1907), p. 582.

218. *Chicago Tribune*, December 13, 1927. There is no evidence that the other bootlegging mobs in Chicago dealt in narcotics.

219. Nichols, "Report," Figure 10.

220. *Chicago Tribune*, November 23, 1929.

221. *Chicago American*, April 1, 1931; *Chicago Tribune*, April 2, 1931.

222. Booth, *Opium*, p. 244; Jonnes, *Hep-Cats*, pp. 76, 100.

223. *New York Times*, June 19, 1936; Musto, *American Disease*, p. 208; Jonnes, *Hep-Cats*, p. 73. Also, see Hortis, *Mob and the City*, chap. 5 for an extremely detailed investigation into the New York mob's involvement in narcotics.

CHAPTER 6: THE BEER WARS: 1930–1934

1. *Chicago Tribune*, June 4, 1930, November 9, 1931.

2. *Chicago Daily News*, June 3, 1930.

3. While this incident has never been completely explained, Del Bono's address on Halsted Street in the heart of Moran territory and a newspaper reference to him as a North Side gunman strongly suggest that he was with the Moran forces.

4. *Chicago Daily Times*, June 2, 1930.

5. *Chicago Daily News*, June 3, 1930; *Chicago Tribune*, June 2, 1930.

6. *Chicago Daily News*, June 2, 1930; *Chicago Tribune*, June 3, 1930.

7. *Chicago Daily News*, June 18, 1930.

8. *Chicago Herald and Examiner*, August 11, 1930. Given the timing of events, it is quite possible that the other ranking North Siders knew at the beginning of June about Zuta's scheme to murder Jake Lingle (see the

related discussion that follows), who was killed on June 9, 1930, and they left due to the expected repercussions from it. Ted Newberry would surely have communicated the plan to them if he himself was against it, and he and they were already dissatisfied.

9. See, for example, Rose Keefe, *The Man Who Got Away: The Bugs Moran Story* (Nashville: Cumberland House, 2005), p. 264.

10. *Chicago Tribune,* June 8, 1930.

11. *Chicago Daily Times,* June 3, 1930.

12. Keefe, *Man Who Got Away*, p. 264.

13. *Chicago Daily Times,* June 3, 1930.

14. *Chicago Tribune,* September 17, 1930; *Chicago Daily News,* October 21, 1930.

15. Chicago Crime Commission, "Re: Samuel McPherson Hunt," February 12, 1946; *Chicago Daily News,* June 3, 1930.

16. Russell, who was sixteen years older than Lingle, may have met him through Lingle's father-in-law, Matthew J. Sullivan, who was also a Chicago police officer. In fact, a William Russell—there were several on Chicago's police force—served at one time at the Lake Street station with Matthew Sullivan.

17. Elmer Williams, "Lingle and Lee Pick Russell" (speech, WCFL-AM radio, August 1930), Reverend Elmer Williams papers, Chicago History Museum.

18. Chicago Crime Commission, "Re: Martin F. Guilfoyle, aka 'Marty' Guilfoyle," October 10, 1946.

19. Robert J. Schoenberg, *Mr. Capone* (New York: William Morrow, 1992), pp. 274–77.

20. *Chicago Daily News,* August 2, 1930; *Chicago Herald and Examiner,* August 3, 1930.

21. *Chicago Daily News,* July 14, 1930.

22. Ibid., July 5, 1930.

23. Moran's acceptance of Zuta as the "master mind" in the North Side gang is essentially an admission that Moran was lacking in the strategy department. *Chicago Daily News,* August 2, 1930.

24. Two Aiello men, "Ash Can Pete" Inserra and Sam Siciliano, were killed on either side of Zuta's murder.

25. *Chicago Herald and Examiner,* August 11, 1930; *Chicago Tribune,* August 12, 1930; Chicago Crime Commission, "Re: Dominick Nuccio, alias Dominic Nuccio, Dominick Nutcchio, 'Libby' Nuccio, Hoodlum and Gambler," June 27, 1950.

26. *Chicago Tribune,* October 27, 1930.

27. Ibid., September 3, 1932.

28. Ibid., September 15, 1930.

29. *Chicago Tribune,* October 24, 1930.

30. *Chicago Daily News,* October 28, 1930.

31. n.p., October 24, 1930. A report discovered years later in the office of the chief investigator for the Cook County state's attorney states that Aiello's hideout was watched by Jack McGurn, Johnnie Moore (Claude Maddox), Tony Capezio, Rocco De Grazia, Lefty Louis (meaning Louis Campagna), George Neilsen, and Charley Ambergio. See *Chicago Tribune,* January 23, 1960. Ambergio is likely Circus gangster Lawrence Imburgio.

32. "Red" Carr was the joint owner of a saloon on Racine near Chicago Avenue, and in 1931 the Battaglia-Carr gang attacked a restaurant on N. Clark Street when it switched to Capone booze. *Chicago Tribune,* October 25, 1930; *Chicago Daily News,* January 2, 1931. These two facts clarify the area controlled by Battaglia and the Carr brothers.

33. As opposed to other claims, Sam Battaglia was never a member of the 42 Gang. See John J. Binder, *The Chicago Outfit* (Charleston: Arcadia Publishing, 2003), p. 83. Battaglia is, in fact, a common Italian surname, and there was at least one Battaglia (who was not a brother of "Teets" Battaglia) with the 42s, which is likely responsible for this confusion.

34. *Chicago Daily News,* June 19, 1931.

35. Keefe, *Man Who Got Away,* p. 292; *Chicago Tribune,* September 3, 1932.

36. James Doherty, "Letter to Mr. Lee" (private letter to the editor), *Chicago Tribune,* October 20, 1930.

37. n.p., May 18, 1931.

38. Matt Hoffman, an independent bootlegger in Wilmette who was selling high-quality beer in the northern suburbs, was killed on July 30, 1931. At least one newspaper blames the Capone gang for his death. However, Hoffman's relatives believe that the Touhys, who had previously threatened him in front of his wife Anna, were responsible. Richard L. Schneider, *Information on Matthew Hoffman/Roger Touhy* (1990).

39. Doherty, "Letter to Mr. Lee."

40. *Chicago Daily News,* October 31, 1931.

41. Little is heard from the south suburbs after 1929 because the Chicago Heights crowd had a tight hold on the area. Barring the killings of one or two minor transgressors, there were only three organized crime–related homicides in the vicinity during the rest of Prohibition: James

Strangis in January 1930; Blue Island racketeer Lorenzo Juliano in June 1930; and Carlo Piazza, a cousin of Phil Piazza, in September 1931. These were all likely due to internal problems in the Chicago Heights group.

42. Hal Andrews, "Gangsters Grip Chicago!" *Real Detective* 26 (September 1932): 90.

43. *Chicago Herald and Examiner*, February 7, 1924.

44. *Chicago Tribune*, November 20, 1925.

45. *Chicago American*, June 19, 1931; *Chicago Tribune*, April 9, 1932, July 20, 1934.

46. *Chicago American*, June 19, 1931; *Chicago Tribune*, April 30, 1932.

47. *Chicago Tribune*, September 3, 1932.

48. Ibid., April 14, 1931.

49. *Chicago American*, June 29, 1931; *Chicago Tribune*, April 22, 1931, June 30, 1931.

50. *Chicago Daily News*, May 13, 1931.

51. *Chicago Tribune*, June 30, 1931.

52. Ibid., June 26, 1931.

53. *Chicago American*, October 12, 1931.

54. *Chicago Daily News*, June 6, 1931.

55. *Chicago Tribune*, June 7, 1931.

56. *Chicago Daily News*, December 30, 1931.

57. This is essentially the map that appears in Andrews, "Gangsters Grip Chicago!" p. 28, after adjusting it to reflect the situation on January 1, 1932. Some minor corrections to Andrews's map have also been made based on more detailed information on the bootlegging gangs, their locations, and their members.

58. Elmer L. Irey and William J. Slocum, *The Tax Dodgers* (New York: Greenberg, 1948), chap. 2; John Kobler, *Capone* (New York: G. P. Putnam, 1971), pp. 277–78; Schoenberg, *Mr. Capone*, p. 298.

59. For further information on Eliot Ness and his career, see Paul W. Heimel, *Eliot Ness: The Real Story* (Coudersport, PA: Knox Books, 1997); John J. Binder, "Eliot Ness," in *The American Midwest: An Interpretive Encyclopedia*, ed. Richard Sisson, Christian Zacher, and Andrew Cayton (Bloomington, IN: Indiana University Press, 2006); Douglas Perry, *Eliot Ness: The Rise and Fall of an American Hero* (New York: Viking, 2014).

60. Heimel, *Eliot Ness*.

61. Ibid., p. 82.

62. Eliot Ness and Oscar Fraley, *The Untouchables* (New York; Julian Messner, Inc., 1957), pp. 218, 240.

63. Schoenberg, *Mr. Capone*, p. 298.

64. *Chicago Tribune*, April 3, 1932; *New York Times*, April 3, 1932; Chester Manly, *Chicago Tribune*, May 4, 1932.

65. Laurence Bergreen, *Capone* (New York: Simon and Schuster, 1994), p. 411.

66. *Chicago Tribune*, August 3, 1923.

67. Ibid., September 3, 1925.

68. Ibid., March 14, 1926.

69. Schoenberg, *Mr. Capone*, pp. 255–56.

70. Ibid., pp. 328–31.

71. *Chicago Daily News*, March 13, 1928.

72. *Washington Post*, December 26, 1931.

73. S.J. Duncan-Clark, *New York Times*, March 31, 1935.

74. Mars Eghigian Jr., *After Capone: The Life and World of Chicago Mob Boss Frank "The Enforcer" Nitti* (Nashville: Cumberland House, 2006), p. 212.

75. Nitti was apparently first mentioned in the press as the head man in December 1932, when the *Chicago Tribune* labels him as the "Capone gang chief." *Chicago Tribune*, December 20, 1932.

76. Chicago Crime Commission, "Re: Hawthorne Race Track (Greyhound Dog Races)," June 27, 1927; Chicago Crime Commission, "Known Chicago Gangsters for the Past 12 Years and Their Activities," May 25, 1931, p. 2.

77. *Chicago Tribune*, December 18, 1930, February 22, 1931, and June 15, 1931.

78. Andrews, "Gangsters Grip Chicago!" p. 88.

79. Murchie, *Chicago Tribune*, February 9, 1936.

80. *Chicago Daily News*, November 2, 1932; *Chicago Tribune*, November 3, 1932.

81. *Chicago Tribune*, June 15, 1931.

82. A list compiled by the CPD in early January 1933 names Murray Humphreys as Public Enemy number one. *New York Times*, January 11, 1933. Although Humphreys *may* have briefly served as a caretaker while Nitti was hospitalized, because he had broad business skills and Guzik, Volpe, and Barker were unavailable, he never held the top spot in the Capone gang on a longer-term basis.

83. Eghigian, *After Capone*, p. 273. In this interpretation of the events, Paul Ricca would have assumed the position of underboss after Rio's death in 1935.

84. Binder, *Chicago Outfit*, p. 55; Eghigian, *After Capone*, pp. 211–12.

85. *Chicago Daily News*, September 24, 1931.

86. *Chicago Tribune*, March 31, 1932, December 19, 1932.

87. Ibid., March 19, 1933.

88. Ibid., February 7, 1931, March 31, 1932.

89. In fact, the violence may have decreased in the early 1930s partly because Nitti was trying to keep the gang out of the public eye.

90. Various historians and authors, conversations with the author, 1995–2016.

91. Chicago Crime Commission, "Re: Slot Machines," August 6, 1951. I am grateful to Mars Eghigian for sharing his research materials with me on the Outfit's early years under Frank Nitti and discussing the subject with me in depth.

92. This is consistent with Matthew J. Luzi's conclusion that the Heights' guys continued to control everything in their former province after they joined with Capone, just as they had earlier. Matthew J. Luzi, conversation with the author, 2001. But their cut would have been somewhat different after the reorganization. For example, as opposed to sharing the profits from the gambling places in their area with Al Capone, they now would have given part of the profits to the gambling overseer. This change, if it was implemented in the 1930s as stated, seems to have worked quite well because there are no reports of important Capone gangsters being killed due to problems with it.

93. This synopsis of the Capone mob's leaders at the level below the underboss is based on the CCC's listing of the various division heads, which reflects a point in time no earlier than 1936 (based on when various individuals were in prison), and information from other sources about these activities in the early 1930s. See Chicago Crime Commission, "Re: Slot Machines."

94. *Chicago Tribune*, September 18, 1931.

95. Roger Biles, *Big City Boss in Depression and War* (DeKalb, IL: Northern Illinois University Press, 1984), p. 104; Mark H. Haller, "Policy Gambling, Entertainment, and the Emergence of Black Politics," *Journal of Social History* 24 (Summer 1991): 728.

96. *Chicago Tribune*, June 4, 1931.

97. Ibid., December 6, 1932.

98. Ibid., December 21, 1932.

99. Eghigian, *After Capone*, p. xv.

100. *Chicago Daily News*, October 30, 1934.

101. Binder, *Chicago Outfit*, p. 66.

102. State's Attorney Tom Courtney, who defeated John Swanson in 1932, broke with the Democratic machine in 1937 and, for a time, vigorously raided the gambling houses it sponsored.

103. *Chicago Tribune*, September 12, 1940, March 17, 1943.

104. *Chicago Daily News*, October 30, 1934.

105. Ibid.

106. Virgil W. Peterson, *Barbarians in Our Midst* (Boston: Atlantic-Little, Brown, 1952), pp. 176, 182.

107. Frederick J. Ashley, "Power of Aroused Citizens Bigger than Al Capone," *Chicago Commerce* (December 1931): 39–41.

108. *Chicago Tribune*, April 27, 1930, October 3, 1930, February 1, 1931, March 13, 1931, and December 25, 1932; *New York Herald Tribune*, December 2, 1932.

109. *Chicago Tribune*, September 1, 1932.

110. Ibid., November 6, 1932.

111. Ibid., March 17, 1933.

112. *Chicago Daily News*, June 19, 1931, June 24, 1931.

113. Ibid.

114. Ibid., September 24, 1931.

115. *Chicago Tribune*, April 15, 1932.

116. Ibid., May 22, 1933.

117. Ibid., August 10, 1931, August 24, 1931, and December 5, 1933.

118. Ibid., June 26, 1946.

119. *Chicago Defender*, September 26, 1931.

120. *Chicago Tribune*, September 20, 1931.

121. *Chicago Defender*, September 26, 1931.

122. *Chicago Tribune*, March 22, 1932; *Chicago Defender*, April 22, 1933.

123. Nathan Thompson, *Kings: The True Story of Chicago Policy Kings and Numbers Racketeers* (Chicago, IL: Bronzeville Press, 2003), p. 75; *Chicago Defender*, October 29, 1932.

124. Thompson, *Kings*, pp. 95, 98.

125. Ibid., pp. 70, 73.

126. *Chicago Defender*, December 12, 1931.

127. *Chicago Tribune*, September 6, 1930.

128. Ibid., June 28, 1931.

129. Juvenile Protective Association, *Commercialized Prostitution*, University of Illinois at Chicago, Richard J. Daley Library, Department of Special Collections (May 6–26, 1933).

130. Juvenile Protective Association, *Commercialized Prostitution*, University of Illinois at Chicago, Richard J. Daley Library, Department of Special Collections (July 1933).

131. Juvenile Protective Association, *Report H-59; 1839 S. Wabash Ave.*, University of Illinois at Chicago, Richard J. Daley Library, Department of Special Collections (May 18, 1933).

132. Juvenile Protective Association, *Commercialized Prostitution* (May 6–26, 1933), p. 6; Juvenile Protective Association, *Report F-3; Ropers*, University of Illinois at Chicago, Richard J. Daley Library, Department of Special Collections (May 26, 1933), p. 4.

133. Juvenile Protective Association, *Report D-34; Lexington Hotel*, University of Illinois at Chicago, Richard J. Daley Library, Department of Special Collections (May 24, 1933).

134. Juvenile Protective Association, *Commercialized Prostitution* (May 6–26, 1933), p. 16.

135. In taxi dance halls men paid ten cents a dance to sway with scantily clad young women, and according to several accounts more than dancing was available. Before his death in 1931, Mike "de Pike" Heitler ran this racket for the Capone gang.

136. Juvenile Protective Association, *Report A-5, Century - 315 S. Wabash*, University of Illinois at Chicago, Richard J. Daley Library, Department of Special Collections (July 18, 1933).

137. Juvenile Protective Association, *Commercialized Prostitution* (May 6–26, 1933), p. 13.

138. Eghigian, *After Capone*, p. 238.

139. *List of Employees of the Italian Village* (August 10, 1934). Gigante's name is spelled Giganti, and Rocco De Grazia also appears on the list.

140. *Chicago Daily News*, June 13, 1930; *Chicago Tribune*, December 5, 1940.

141. *Chicago Tribune*, March 9, 1931.

142. Ibid., November 25, 1931.

143. Ibid., July 22, 1932, October 11, 1932.

144. Ibid., May 2, 1933.

145. *Chicago American*, May 2, 1933.

146. *Chicago Tribune*, June 18, 1932.

147. Ibid., April 19, 1936.

148. Ibid., November 2, 1934.

149. Barbara W. Newell, *Chicago and the Labor Movement* (Urbana, IL; University of Illinois Press, 1961), chap. 5; *Chicago Tribune*, May 27, 1933; n.p., June 11, 1933.

150. Newell, *Chicago and the Labor Movement*, chap. 5.

151. *Chicago Tribune*, August 10, 1932.

152. Ibid., January 21, 1939.

153. According to another account (*Chicago Tribune*, March 20, 1934), Humphreys first met with Sumner in February or March 1932.

154. *Chicago Tribune*, March 20, 1934.

155. Ibid., August 10, 1932.

156. Ibid.

157. George Murray, *The Legacy of Al Capone* (New York: G. P. Putnam, 1975), p. 164; *Chicago Tribune*, May 12, June 28, 1933.

158. *Chicago Tribune*, July 9, 1939.

159. Joseph Ator, *Chicago Tribune*, March 29, 1936.

160. Wayne Thomis, *Chicago Tribune*, January 12, 1960.

161. *Chicago Tribune*, March 25, 1932, June 18, 1932.

162. Ibid., April 5, 1936.

163. Ibid., February 17, 1934.

164. Ibid., March 20, 1943.

165. Ibid., February 2, 1934.

166. Ibid., March 25, 1931; *Chicago Daily News*, June 30, 1931.

167. *Chicago Tribune*, September 21, 1932.

168. Walter Fitzmaurice, *Chicago Tribune*, May 14, 1933; *Chicago American*, May 2, 1933.

169. *Chicago Tribune*, October 2, 1931.

170. Ibid., August 11, 1932.

171. *Chicago Daily News*, November 6, 1931.

172. *Chicago Tribune*, September 20, 1936.

173. See, for example, Juvenile Protective Association, *Commercialized Prostitution* (July 1933), p. 9.

174. Blaise Picchi, *The Five Weeks of Giuseppe Zangara* (Chicago: Academy Chicago Publishers), pp. 28–29.

175. *Chicago Tribune*, October 28, 1933.

176. Ibid., March 30, 1932.

177. Ibid., April 9, 1932.

178. Ibid., March 31, 1932.

179. Based on the timing of the events, it is quite possible that Zwolinski was killed by Frank McErlane, who had a long-standing grudge against him. However, McErlane's purchase of Capone beer, which may also have been conditional on peace with the DMQ gang, and his general absence from the Beer Wars during 1932, weigh against this. If these two

murders were related, Kane and Zwolinski were most likely killed as the result of internal problems in the DMQ mob.

180. *Chicago Tribune,* October 9, 1932.

181. Ibid., November 28, 1930.

182. Ibid., February 2, 1931.

183. Ibid., March 26, 1933.

184. Ibid., June 19, 1933.

185. Melrose Park was the perfect forward base from which to attack the Touhy gang. The Circus Gang, if it had not already been absorbed by the Capones, was at this time no more than a subsidiary. For example, Hal Andrews, "Gangsters Grip Chicago!" *Real Detective* 26 (September 1932): p. 89 has Capezio and Maddox working directly under Capone in the fall of 1932 with the bootlegging in their former province controlled by Barney Clammage.

186. *Chicago Daily News,* June 20, 1932.

187. Ibid., December 16, 1932.

188. Ibid., June 20, 1932; *Chicago Tribune,* April 1, 1939. Murray Humphreys was heard by the FBI many years later, through a hidden microphone, discussing the Barker murder and who his companions were that night. FBI transcript, January 28, 1960. The conversation was conducted in a low whisper and the agent listening did not hear all of the details, so the transcript (which is also redacted in places) is not completely clear.

189. *Chicago Daily Times,* January 30, 1933. Based on this account, the Capone forces must have pushed John Horan out of his holdings—or he voluntarily stepped aside—following the ouster of Matt Kolb in the spring of 1931. After the gun battle with the Valley gangsters in Elk Grove in 1922, the Schultz-Horan gang never fired another shot during the Beer Wars.

190. *Chicago Tribune,* December 17, 1932.

191. *Chicago Daily News,* December 16, 1932; *Chicago Tribune,* December 18, 1932.

192. *Chicago Tribune,* December 18, 1932.

193. Ibid., February 3, 1933.

194. Ibid. In another unusual incident, a car full of West Side Capone gangsters, including Philip Mangano, the brother of "Dago" Lawrence, and the newly recruited Willie Bioff, fired at Chicago detectives with a machine gun. One officer was saved from serious harm when a bullet bounced off his badge. *Chicago Tribune,* May 10, 1932.

195. Ibid., April 30, 1933.

196. Ibid., July 2, 1933. The Touhys' last aggressive act against the Capone gang occurred on September 8, 1933, when they again tried to invade the Chicago Teamsters' offices on S. Ashland Avenue. This time the enemy was ready for them, and James Tribble was killed in a gun battle inside the building.

197. Ibid., February 23, 1934; James Doherty, *Chicago Tribune*, April 29, 1934.

198. *Chicago Tribune*, March 19, 1933, March 29, 1933, and April 1, 1933.

199. Schoenberg, *Mr. Capone*, p. 77. This term was common on the Western frontier, where cowboys would refer to the hands working together on a ranch as "our outfit," and also in the military. It most likely entered Chicago's gangster lexicon after World War I from the mouths of men who had served in France.

200. Lane, *Chicago Daily News*, June 23, 1943.

201. John Wolek was a long-time member of the Grand Avenue street crew, and Battaglia went on to become the operating boss of the Outfit in 1967.

202. Binder, *Chicago Outfit*, p. 119; Arthur J. Lurigio and John J. Binder, "The Chicago Outfit: Challenging the Myths about Organized Crime," *Journal of Contemporary Criminal Justice* 29 (May 2013): 199.

CHAPTER 7: THE FACE OF BATTLE: GANGLAND KILLINGS IN CHICAGO

1. Statement is attributed to Charles "Lucky" Luciano in John Kobler, *Capone* (New York: G. P. Putnam, 1971), p. 190.

2. The number of murders per year in Cook County is from the CCC for the years 1919 to 1929 and from various issues of the *Chicago Tribune* for the remaining years.

3. Colonel Ira Reeves, an official of the anti-Prohibition organization called the Crusaders, claimed that 304 gangsters were killed in bootleg wars in Chicago during a seven-year period, compared to an incomplete figure of somewhat more than five hundred for other American cities in total. *Chicago Tribune*, August 10, 1930. David R. Johnson, *American Law Enforcement: A History* (St. Louis: Forum Press, 1981), p. 145 reaches a similar conclusion about Chicago versus other cities.

4. Laurence Bergreen, *Capone* (New York: Simon and Schuster,

1994), pp. 128, 210; Douglas Perry, *Eliot Ness: The Rise and Fall of an American Hero* (New York: Viking, 2014), p. 46; various other writers and historians, conversations with the author, 2001–2016.

5. These results are originally reported in John J. Binder and Mars Eghigian, "Gangland Killings in Chicago, 1919–1933" (unpublished manuscript, 2008). John J. Binder and Mars Eghigian, "Gangland Killings in Chicago, 1919–1933," *Journal of Contemporary Criminal Justice* 29 (May 2013): 219–32 is a shorter version of that paper. Jeff Thurston provided us with inspiration and much useful information on gangland killings in Chicago during this era.

6. The CPD homicide reports are available at "Homicide in Chicago," Northwestern University School of Law, http://homicide.northwestern.edu/ (accessed in 2008).

7. *Chicago Tribune*, May 16, 1962.

8. Arthur V. Lashly, "Homicide (in Cook County)," *Illinois Crime Survey*, chap. XIII (Chicago: Illinois Association for Criminal Justice, 1929), pp. 610–11.

9. Chicago Crime Commission, "List of Murders Classed as Gangdom Murders by CCC, Based on Coroner's Verdicts, as Given by Mr. Pretzie," n.d.

10. The totals would also be downward biased if many bodies were never found, which would be the case if the victims were buried by their killers. However, gangland practice was the exact opposite. For example, a newspaper article refers to the discovery of Theodore Anton's buried body as the "first time . . . an earnest attempt was made to prevent the discovery of a victim's body" by gangland killers. *Chicago Tribune*, December 6, 1927. The disappearance and certain death of Moran gangster "Benny" Bennett in early 1930 is one of the very few recorded cases of a suspected Chicago area gangland killing during Prohibition in which the body was not found.

11. The classification of a killing or wounding as accidental (defined as unintentional) is usually less than clear cut and is based on the surrounding circumstances. Someone might have been an innocent bystander, but still been intentionally killed. For example, if gunmen planning to kill Smith saw him with Jones, they may intentionally have shot Jones also, although Jones was not originally a target, to eliminate him as a witness. That is, intent is defined at the moment the killings occurred.

12. Lashly, "Homicide (in Cook County)."

13. If nothing was found in the *Chicago Tribune*, the *Chicago Daily News* was examined in an attempt to obtain at least one newspaper article

for each murder. Data were also collected from newspaper articles in the files of John J. Binder and Mars Eghigian and in Jeff Thurston's files on gangland killings from 1931 to 1933. When articles from more than one newspaper were examined, the source ordering is the *Chicago Tribune*, *Chicago Daily News*, *Chicago American*, and lastly the *Chicago Times*. That is, if there is conflicting information in two newspapers, such as they disagree about why the victim was killed or whether he belonged to a major bootlegging gang, the higher-ordered source is used.

14. The *Chicago Daily News* was checked as well as the *Chicago Tribune* for each killing in 1933, unless all the required data were found in the *Tribune* article.

15. The CPD homicide records have virtually nothing to say about organized crime. This is not because the CCC killings occurred outside the city, but because the CPD reported only the barest factual details about each death.

16. The major exception to this rule is that all information about organized criminal occupations (vice, gambling, bootlegging, labor, or business racketeering) was taken down and used, regardless of the source. Ethnicity was treated similarly. While the newspapers and the CPD were quick to label victims as black or Chinese, they less frequently denoted them as Italian. If any source describes the victim as Italian or Chinese or Colored, or if the victim had an Italian surname, he was counted in that category.

17. Two killings erroneously listed in 1925 are changed to 1924.

18. See Frederic M. Thrasher, *The Gang* (Chicago: University of Chicago Press, 1937), pp. 208–11.

19. *Chicago Tribune*, March 11, 1921, February 10, 1924.

20. Russo, *The Outfit* (New York: Bloomsbury, 2001), pp. 31–32. He claims that two-thirds of all killings, not just gangland killings, were due to beer running (interpreted more broadly to mean bootlegging). There were 4,876 murders in Cook County from 1919 to 1933, and two-thirds of this figure is 3,251, which is easily ten times greater than the number of bootlegging killings on the CCC list.

21. Lashly, "Homicide (in Cook County)," p. 637.

22. Leigh B. Bienen and Bradley Rottinghaus, "Learning from the Past, Living in the Present: Understanding Homicide in Chicago, 1870–1930," *Journal of Criminal Law and Criminology* 92 (Spring/Summer 2002), p. 526.

23. Ibid., table 3.

24. For the killings with a known cause, the numbers in Chicago each year that were related to organized crime was determined. For the

killings in Chicago whose cause was unknown, the numbers that were due to organized crime was estimated based on the percentage with a known cause that were due to organized crime. The estimated number of killings due to organized crime is the sum of the two figures.

25. Four of the eight gangland victims found outside the county from 1931 to 1933 were members of major gangs. Two were Capone gangsters, one was in the Touhy mob, and one was a DMQ gangster. With twenty-four killings of major gang members on the CCC list during these three years (see table in Fig. 7.7), these four omitted cases represent an error rate of 17 percent.

26. Landesco, *Organized Crime in Chicago. Part III of The Illinois Crime Survey* (Chicago: Illinois Association for Criminal Justice, 1929), pp. 923.

27. See Bienen and Rottinghaus, "Understanding Homicide in Chicago," Table 3.

28. Binder and Eghigian, "Gangland Killings in Chicago," (2008), table 6.

29. If a gun was used, the weapon is coded as a pistol only if the sources explicitly state that a pistol was used or if it is obvious that the weapon was a handgun. If it appears that a pistol was used, but the details are not totally clear, the weapon is categorized as probably a pistol. In some cases the sources report that the victim was shot, but it is not clear which type of weapon was used. These cases are categorized as "gun (unknown)."

30. *Chicago American*, September 4, 1925; *Chicago Daily Journal*, September 4, 1925.

31. Herman N. Bundesen to Major Calvin Goddard, April 1, 1929.

32. In this instance McErlane fired the Thompson submachine gun one round at a time, as opposed to using it on full automatic. This is quite possible, even though this weapon is more commonly associated with large bursts of ammunition.

33. Robert J. Schoenberg, *Mr. Capone* (New York: William Morrow, 1992), p. 140; Thrasher, *The Gang*, p. 181.

34. Lashly, "Homicide (in Cook County)," p. 593.

35. Allsop, *The Bootleggers and Their Era* (Garden City, NY: Doubleday, 1961), p. 41; John J. Binder, *The Chicago Outfit* (Charleston: Arcadia Publishing, 2003), p. 37.

36. If the person was killed first and the body was then transported to a different location, this is not labeled as a one-way ride.

37. The first documented one-way ride in the Chicago area occurred in 1904. See Rose Keefe, "The Bate Auto Murder" (unpublished manuscript, 2008).

38. Lashly, "Homicide (in Cook County)."

39. The website of the National Safety Council (http://www.nsc.org/lrs/statinfo/odds.htm [accessed April 11, 2007]), based on forty-seven reported deaths due to lightning in 2003, calculated the probability as one in 6.188 million.

40. John J. Binder and Mars Eghigian, "Gangland Killings in Chicago, 1919–1933," (unpublished manuscript, 2008).

41. This statement was made by the narrator in Sarah Kass, Jonathan Gruber et al., "Al Capone and the Machine Gun Massacre," *Man, Moment, and Machine*, dir. Michael McInerney et al., aired November 7, 2006 (Bay Area, San Francisco, CA: History Channel).

42. Lashly, "Homicide (in Cook County)," p. 595.

43. John Drury, *Chicago in Seven Days* (New York: Robert M. McBride and Company, 1928), p. 79.

44. John H. Lyle, *Chicago Tribune*, December 11, 1960.

45. Binder, *Chicago Outfit*, p. 37.

46. Lashly, "Homicide (in Cook County)," p. 594; Citizen's Police Committee, *Chicago Police Problems* (Chicago: University of Chicago Press, 1931), p. 4.

47. See Virgil W. Peterson, *A Report on Chicago Crime for 1964* (Chicago: CCC, 1965), p. 43 and the CCC's list of gangland killings.

48. *Chicago Tribune*, January 27, 1925, November 3, 1926.

49. Much of this research appears in a double issue of the *Journal of Criminal Law and Criminology* (Spring/Summer 2002), which is largely devoted to articles using the CPD online database.

CHAPTER 8: CONCLUSION

1. Several of these points are made, with respect to the success of the Chicago Outfit in the years after 1933, by John J. Binder, *The Chicago Outfit* (Charleston: Arcadia Publishing, 2003), chap. 10.

2. In fact, if its only activity had been bootlegging, it is possible that the Capone gang would not have survived as a criminal entity beyond Prohibition.

3. Luzi, *The Boys in Chicago Heights* (Charleston: History Press, 2012), p. 23.

4. Binder, *Chicago Outfit*, p. 120.

APPENDIX: BLACK HAND MURDERS IN CHICAGO

1. Humbert Nelli, "Italians and Crime in Chicago: The Formative Years, 1890–1920," *American Journal of Sociology* 74 (January 1969), pp. 373–91; Robert Lombardo, "The Black Hand: Terror by Letter in Chicago," *Journal of Contemporary Criminal Justice* 18 (November 2002): p. 404.

2. Landesco, *Organized Crime in Chicago*, p. 947.

3. Ibid., p. 937.

4. *Chicago Tribune*, April 18, 1925.

5. *Chicago Tribune*, December 18, 1928.

6. John Landesco, "Prohibition and Crime," *Annals of the American Academy of Political and Social Science* 163 (September, 1932): 125, 127.

7. CPD, *Annual Report* (Chicago: CPD, various years).

8. The Citizens' Police Committee, *Chicago Police Problems*; Thrasher, *The Gang*, p. 204.

9. Landesco, *Organized Crime in Chicago*, p. 937.

10. *Chicago Tribune*, April 25, 1925.

11. Ibid., July 19, 1923.

12. Robert Lombardo, "Black Hand," pp. 395–96.

13. Landesco, "Prohibition and Crime," p. 125.

14. See, for example, James Doherty, *Chicago Tribune*, October 1, 1942. Only later did the Outfit itself extort money for "protection" from the business owners in these areas, a practice that continued well into the 1980s in Chicago, and in some parts of New York City still occurs today.

INDEX